National Center for Construction Education and Research

Instrumentation
Level One

Prentice
Hall

Upper Saddle River, New Jersey
Columbus, Ohio

National Center for Construction Education and Research

President: Dan Bennet
Vice President of Training Operations and Program Development: Don Whyte
Director of Curriculum Revision and Development: Daniele Dixon
Instrumentation Project Manager: Deborah Padgett
Production Manager: Debie Ness
Associate Editor: Rebecca Hassell
Copy Editors: Tara Cohen, Laura Parker
Desktop Publishers: Jessica Martin, Beverly Symes

The NCCER would like to acknowledge the contract service providers for this curricula: Topaz Publications, Liverpool, New York; Technical Communication Consultants, Inc., Seattle, WA; and Document Technology Resources, Manassas, VA.

This information is general in nature and intended for training purposes only. Actual performance of activities described in this manual requires compliance with all applicable operating, service, maintenance, and safety procedures under the direction of qualified personnel. References in this manual to patented or proprietary devices do not constitute a recommendation of their use.

11

ISBN 0-13-061602-8

Preface

This volume was developed by the National Center for Construction Education and Research (NCCER) in response to the training needs of the construction and maintenance industries. It is one of many in the NCCER's standardized craft training program. The program, covering more than 30 craft areas and including all major construction skills, was developed over a period of years by industry and education specialists. Sixteen of the largest construction and maintenance firms in the United States committed financial and human resources to the teams that wrote the curricula and planned the nationally accredited training process. These materials are industry-proven and consist of competency-based textbooks and instructor's guides.

The NCCER is a non-profit educational entity affiliated with the University of Florida and supported by the following industry and craft associations:

PARTNERING ASSOCIATIONS

- American Fire Sprinkler Association
- American Society for Training and Development
- American Welding Society
- Associated Builders and Contractors, Inc.
- Associated General Contractors of America
- Association for Career and Technical Education
- Carolinas AGC, Inc.
- Carolinas Electrical Contractors Association
- Citizens Democracy Corps
- Construction Industry Institute
- Construction Users Roundtable
- Design-Build Institute of America
- Merit Contractors Association of Canada
- Metal Building Manufacturers Association
- National Association of Minority Contractors
- National Association of State Supervisors for Trade and Industrial Education
- National Association of Women in Construction
- National Insulation Association
- National Ready Mixed Concrete Association
- National Utility Contractors Association
- National Vocational Technical Honor Society
- North American Crane Bureau
- Painting and Decorating Contractors of America
- Portland Cement Association
- SkillsUSA-VICA
- Steel Erectors Association of America
- Texas Gulf Coast Chapter ABC
- U.S. Army Corps of Engineers
- University of Florida
- Women Construction Owners and Executives, USA

Some of the features of the NCCER's standardized craft training program include:

- A proven record of success over many years of use by industry companies.
- National standardization providing portability of learned job skills and educational credits that will be of tremendous value to trainees.
- Recognition: upon successful completion of training with an accredited sponsor, trainees receive an industry-recognized certificate and transcript from the NCCER.
- Compliance with Apprenticeship, Training, Employer, and Labor Services (ATELS) requirements (formerly BAT) for related classroom training (CFR 29:29).
- Well-illustrated, up-to-date, and practical information.

Acknowledgments

This curriculum was revised as a result of the farsightedness and leadership of the following sponsors:

Austin Industrial
Cianbro Corporation
Fluor/F&PS

Fluor Global Services
Formosa Plastics Corporation
Lake Charles ABC

This curriculum would not exist were it not for the dedication and unselfish energy of those volunteers who served on the Authoring Team. A sincere thanks is extended to:

Tommy Arnold
Gordon Hobbs
Russ Michael
Glen Pratt

Jerry Reese
Jonathan Sacks
Doug Smith
Perry Thomason

A final note: This book is the result of a collaborative effort involving the production, editorial, and development staff at Prentice-Hall, Inc., and the National Center for Construction Education and Research. Thanks to all of the dedicated people involved in the many stages of this project.

Contents

Hand Tools for Instrumentation

COURSE MAP

This course map shows all of the modules in the first level of the Instrumentation curriculum. The suggested training order begins at the bottom and proceeds up. Skill levels increase as you advance on the course map. The local Training Program Sponsor may adjust the training order.

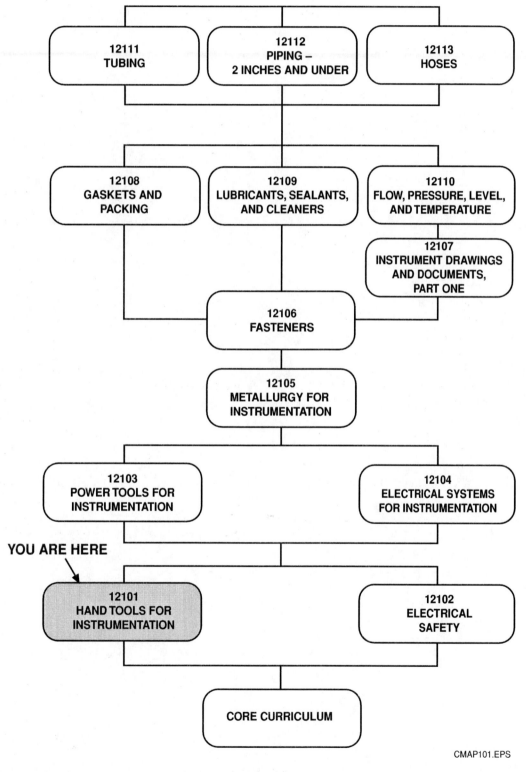

INSTRUMENTATION LEVEL ONE

12111
TUBING

12112
PIPING –
2 INCHES AND UNDER

12113
HOSES

12108
GASKETS AND
PACKING

12109
LUBRICANTS, SEALANTS,
AND CLEANERS

12110
FLOW, PRESSURE, LEVEL,
AND TEMPERATURE

12107
INSTRUMENT DRAWINGS
AND DOCUMENTS,
PART ONE

12106
FASTENERS

12105
METALLURGY FOR
INSTRUMENTATION

12103
POWER TOOLS FOR
INSTRUMENTATION

12104
ELECTRICAL SYSTEMS
FOR INSTRUMENTATION

YOU ARE HERE

12101
HAND TOOLS FOR
INSTRUMENTATION

12102
ELECTRICAL
SAFETY

CORE CURRICULUM

CMAP101.EPS

MODULE 12101 CONTENTS

Figures

Tables

Hand Tools for Instrumentation

OBJECTIVES

When you have completed this module, you will be able to do the following:

1. Identify hand tools used in instrumentation.
2. Select the proper hand tool for a job.
3. Inspect the condition of tools.
4. Properly maintain hand tools.
5. Use hand tools safely.
6. Assemble and safely operate oxyacetylene cutting equipment.

Prerequisites

Before you begin this module, it is recommended that you successfully complete the following: Core Curriculum.

Required Trainee Materials

1. Pencil and paper
2. Appropriate personal protective equipment

1.0.0 ◆ INTRODUCTION

Choosing the proper tools and knowing how to use them saves time and improves the quality of the work. This module describes many of the hand tools used in the instrumentation craft.

Some of the more common hand tools, such as hammers, wrenches, and screwdrivers, were covered in *Core Curriculum*.

The following common types of hand tools are presented in this module:

- **Taps**
- **Dies**
- Fish tape
- Vises
- Snips
- Knockouts
- Oxygen-acetylene system
- Screw and tap extractors
- Rivet guns
- Angle finder
- Wrap around
- Rodding-out tool

2.0.0 ◆ TAPS

Taps are used to cut new **female (internal) threads** or restore damaged internal threads in holes that have been drilled in metal or other materials. Bolts, screws, and studs can be screwed into the internal threads cut by the taps. A typical set of hand taps usually consists of three different types of taps: taper, plug, and bottoming, as shown in *Figure 1*.

Taps are made from high-quality tool steel, hardened and ground. On a tap, three or four grooves or **flutes** are usually cut lengthwise across the threads to form cutting edges. The flutes also provide clearance for chips and admit cutting fluid to lubricate the tap. The end of a tap's shank is square so that a tap wrench can be fitted over it and used to turn the tap into a hole. A range of sizes and pitches of taps is available for all recognized thread standards.

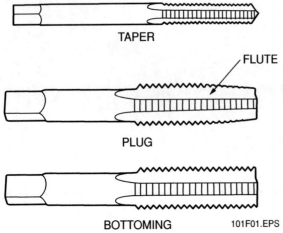

Figure 1 ◆ Tap set.

Taps may be sized in inches or metric units. For inch-sized taps, the major diameter, number of threads per inch, and type of thread are usually found stamped on the shank of the tap. For example: ⁹⁄₁₆ inch - 13 NC represents:

TAP SIZE (INCHES)

Major Diameter = ⁹⁄₁₆ inch

No. of Threads per Inch = 13

Type of Threads = National Coarse

Metric tap sizes are identified by the letter M followed by the nominal diameter of the thread in millimeters, and then the pitch in millimeters. For example: M 2.7 - 0.50 represents:

TAP SIZE (METRIC)

Metric Designation = M

Nominal Diameter of the
    Thread = 2.7 (millimeters)

Pitch of the Thread = 0.50 (millimeters)

After each use, clean the threads of the tap using a stiff wire brush, and lightly oil the threads. Store taps so that they do not contact each other or other tools. Prepare taps for long periods of nonuse by coating them with a rust-preventive compound. It is good practice to place taps in individual or threading boxes, and to store them in a dry place.

2.1.0 Taper Tap

The threaded end of a taper tap is usually tapered for a distance of 8 to 10 threads. It is used when tapping holes that go through the work and for starting the threads in a **blind hole** before using a bottoming tap.

2.2.0 Plug Tap

The threaded end of a plug tap is usually tapered for a distance of three or four threads. A plug tap is used for tapping through holes that go all the way through the work and for general tapping purposes. When a blind hole is being tapped, a plug tap may be used as an intermediate tap to thread the hole just prior to using a bottoming tap. A plug tap is often the only tap used to thread through a hole.

2.3.0 Bottoming Tap

The bottoming tap has full threads to the end of the tap with no taper, only a **chamfer** on the final thread. It is used for threading to the bottom of a blind hole.

2.4.0 Tap Wrenches

Taps are turned by tap wrenches. Two types of tap handle wrenches are shown in *Figure 2*. The tap wrench fits over the end of the tap providing a secure handle for turning the tap.

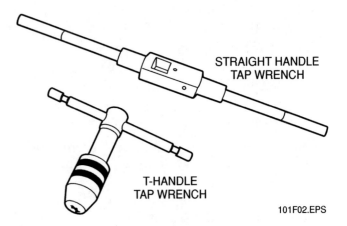

Figure 2 ◆ Tap handle wrenches.

2.5.0 Cutting Fluids

A cutting fluid must be used when tapping certain metals. Cutting fluids allow for better cutting action and finish. Cutting fluids also prolong tap life.

Recommended cutting fluids include soluble oil or lard oil for machine steel (hot and cold rolled), mineral lard oil or sulfur-based oil for tool steel (carbon and high-speed), and soluble oil for malleable iron.

When tapping brass, bronze, and cast iron, no cutting fluid is required. Brass or bronze cuttings do not stick to the tap, and cast iron cuttings combined with cutting fluid can damage the tap.

2.6.0 Procedure for Tapping a Hole

Tapping a hole cuts internal threads in the hole. Because taps are very hard and brittle, they are easily broken. Care should be used when tapping a hole to prevent breakage. When a tap breaks in a hole, it is very difficult to remove and may require that the work be scrapped.

Two primary reasons why taps break in the hole are unmatched hole-to-tap size, and too many threads being cut without backing the tap out to remove metal scraps.

When tapping a blind hole, sometimes all three taps are used in the following order: taper, plug, and bottoming. Be sure to remove all chips before using the bottoming tap. Make sure on a deep hole you do not fill the top with chips.

 WARNING!
Wear approved eye protection. In addition, wear hand protection when working with broken taps. Broken taps are razor-sharp.

Step 1   The hole to be tapped must be drilled to the correct size. The correct tap drill size is required so that the proper amount of material remains in the hole to make a good tap. *Table 1* gives the proper tap drill size for various tap sizes. Often the drill size is also marked on the tap. The drilled hole usually produces about 75 percent of the full thread.

Table 1 Tap, Thread, and Drill Chart

NC NATIONAL COARSE*			NF NATIONAL FINE*		
Tap Size	Threads per inch	Tap Drill Size	Tap Size	Threads per inch	Tap Drill Size
#5	40	#38	#5	44	#37
#6	32	#36	#6	40	#33
#8	32	#29	#8	36	#29
#10	24	#25	#10	32	#21
#12	24	#16	#12	28	#14
1/4	20	#7	1/4	28	#3
5/16	18	F	5/16	24	I
3/8	16	5/16	3/8	24	Q
7/16	14	U	7/16	20	25/64
1/2	13	27/64	1/2	20	29/64
9/16	12	31/64	9/16	18	33/64
5/8	11	17/32	5/8	18	37/64
3/4	10	21/32	3/4	16	11/16
7/8	9	49/64	7/8	14	13/16
1	8	7/8	1	14	15/16
1-1/8	7	63/64	1-1/8	12	1-3/64
1-1/4	7	1-7/64	1-1/4	12	1-11/64
1-3/8	6	1-7/32	1-3/8	12	1-19/64
1-1/2	6	1-11/32	1-1/2	12	1-27/64
1-3/4	5	1-9/16			
2	4-1/2	1-25/32			
NPT NATIONAL PIPE THREAD					
1/8	27	11/32	1	11-1/2	1-5/32
1/4	18	7/16	1-1/4	11-1/4	1-1/2
3/8	18	19/32	1-1/2	11-1/2	1-23/32
1/2	14	23/32	2	11-1/2	2-3/16
3/4	14	15/16	2-1/2	8	2-5/8

* The major diameter of an NC or NF number size tap or screw = (N × .013) + .060.
    Example: The major diameter of a #5 tap equals (5 × .013) + .060 = .125 diameter.
    Commercial Tap Drill Sizes (75% of thread depth) American National and Unified Form Thread

NOTE

Apply pressure to the drill as evenly as possible. If the hole is not round, it cannot be properly tapped.

Step 2 Select the correct size and type of tap. (See *Table 1*.) Use a high-speed stainless steel (HSS) tap for tapping stainless steel.

Step 3 Inspect the tap for cracks, broken or worn threads, or any other defects that might make it unsafe to use.

Step 4 Insert the square end of the tap into the tap wrench and tighten securely. Apply the proper cutting fluid to the tap.

Step 5 Insert the tap in the hole perpendicular to the work piece.

Step 6 Apply equal pressure on both handles of the tap wrench.

CAUTION

If even pressure is not applied, the tap will tend to lean to one side. It may break off in the hole and cause the threads to be deep on the pressure side.

Step 7 Turn the tap clockwise (for right-hand threads) for about two turns.

Step 8 Remove the tap wrench from the tap and check the tap for squareness by placing a square on the material. Check to see if the tap is aligned with the vertical part of the square. It is a good practice to check the tap for squareness at two positions, 90 degrees to each other.

Step 9 If the tap is not started squarely, remove it from the hole. Restart the tap by applying pressure in the opposite direction from which the tap leans.

CAUTION

Do not exert too much pressure on the tap, otherwise the tap might break.

Step 10 After the tap has been properly started, feed it into the hole by turning the tap wrench clockwise.

NOTE

At this point, pressure is no longer required. The tap will thread itself into the hole.

Step 11 After the tap has started to cut, turn the tap clockwise one-half turn. Then turn the tap counterclockwise about a one-quarter turn using a steady motion until you feel the chips break loose.

CAUTION

Failure to reverse direction to break chips may break the tap.

Step 12 Apply cutting fluid to the tap. Continue the process until the correct depth is achieved. On deep holes be sure to clean out the tap if it is full.

3.0.0 ◆ DIES

Dies are used to cut new **male (external) threads** or restore damaged external threads on rods, bolts, studs, etc. There are three types of dies commonly used in the instrumentation craft: solid, adjustable split, and adjustable screw plate. Illustrations of these dies are shown in *Figure 3*.

After each use, clean the die using a wire brush and then lightly oil the die. Store dies so that they do not contact each other or other tools. For long periods of nonuse, coat dies with a rust-preventive compound. Place in individual or threading boxes and store in a dry place.

3.1.0 Solid Dies

Solid dies are used for threading small rods and for recutting damaged threads. The die is provided with clearance holes that serve as outlets for chips. The solid die is not adjustable. Solid dies have flat sides, which allow them to be driven by a suitable wrench. Solid dies come in a variety of sizes for rethreading American Standard coarse and fine threads.

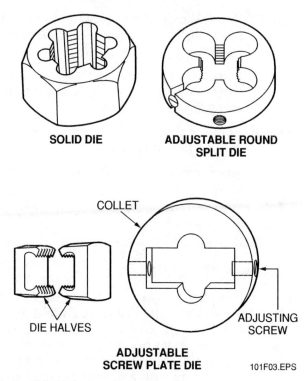

SOLID DIE   **ADJUSTABLE ROUND SPLIT DIE**

COLLET

DIE HALVES   ADJUSTING SCREW

ADJUSTABLE SCREW PLATE DIE

101F03.EPS

Figure 3 ◆ Threading dies.

3.2.0 Adjustable Split Dies

Adjustable split dies are also called *button dies* because of their shape. They can be used in either hand diestocks or machine holders. They can be adjusted a small amount by tightening or loosening the adjusting screw to cut different thread depths. The adjusting screw forces the sides of the die to move, setting the depth of the cut for the threads. Adjustable split dies come in a variety of sizes to cut American Standard coarse, fine, and special form threads.

3.3.0 Adjustable Screw Plate Dies

Adjustable screw plate bolt dies provide greater adjustment than the adjustable split die. The two die halves are held securely in a collet by means of a threaded plate. The die is adjusted by two adjusting screws that contact each die half. Adjustable screw plate dies come in a variety of sizes to cut American Standard coarse, fine, and special form threads. The upper side of each die half is stamped with the manufacturer's name and a serial number. The lower side is stamped

NOTE

Do not use die halves with different serial numbers.

with the same serial number. When assembling the die, verify that both serial numbers are facing down and that the serial numbers match.

The diestock is a holder in which the dies are placed for threading. *Figure 4* shows three different types of diestocks.

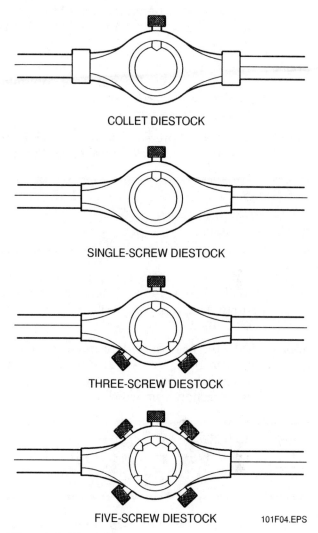

COLLET DIESTOCK

SINGLE-SCREW DIESTOCK

THREE-SCREW DIESTOCK

FIVE-SCREW DIESTOCK   101F04.EPS

Figure 4 ◆ Diestocks.

3.4.0 Procedure for Threading a Rod

Step 1   Fasten the work piece securely in a vise.

Step 2   Bevel (chamfer) the end of the work piece with a flat file or a grinder.

WARNING!

Wear approved eye protection and avoid sharp edges and sharp metal chips. When using a flat file, make sure the safety handle is installed on the tail of the file.

Step 3 Select the proper die and diestock for the work piece. Use HSS dies for threading stainless steel.

Step 4 Inspect the die for broken or worn threads, cracks, or any other defects that might make it unsafe to use.

Step 5 Lubricate the chamfered end of the work piece with a liberal amount of cutting lubricant.

Step 6 Insert the die into the diestock and tighten securely. Place the die squarely on the work piece with the tapered thread section facing down.

Step 7 Apply equal pressure on the diestock handles. Turn the die clockwise several turns.

NOTE
Apply cutting fluid frequently during the threading process.

Step 8 Make sure that the die has started squarely on the work piece. Check the die for squareness at two positions, 90 degrees to each other.

Step 9 If the die has not started squarely, remove the die from the work. Restart the die squarely by applying pressure in the opposite direction from which the die leans.

CAUTION
Exerting too much pressure on the die might break the die.

Step 10 Turn the die clockwise one turn, then reverse it approximately one-half turn to break the chips loose.

NOTE
If threading to a shoulder (*Figure 5*), continue with remaining steps.

Step 11 Stop cutting the thread about ⅛ inch from the shoulder.

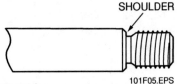
Figure 5 ◆ Shoulder.

Step 12 Remove the die and replace it in the diestock with the tapered thread section facing up.

Step 13 Start the die on the work piece and cut the thread until the die is about ¹⁄₁₆ inch away from the shoulder.

Step 14 Remove the die, clean the threads, and test the thread with a nut.

NOTE
Protect the finished threads by handling and storing properly.

4.0.0 ◆ FISH TAPE

A fish tape's primary purpose is to pull wire and cable through conduit. Fish tapes are made of tempered steel, stainless steel, and nonconductive materials specially designed for work in areas of energized circuits. Some of these nonconductive fish tapes are made with a fiberglass core and an outer nylon coating, providing strength and ease of pulling around corners.

Metal fish tapes, like the example shown in Figure 6, are typically made in coils of ⅛ inch to ⅜ inch wide and usually ¹⁄₆₄ inch to ³⁄₆₄ inch thick. The ¼ inch width fish tape is the most frequently used. Most metal fish tapes have a factory-bent hook on the end, while nonconductive fish tapes sometimes are made with a tape bar attached to the end. The purpose of the hook or tape bar is to provide a fastening point for the wires or cable. It helps the tape slide through conduit bends more easily, passing any wire or cable already in the conduit. The swivel head design of the tape bar helps to prevent binding during the pull. The reel is used to wind and store the tape.

After using a fish tape, wipe off any lubricant or dirt with a soft rag and store the tape in a dry place. Use spray rust preventive on tempered steel fish tapes.

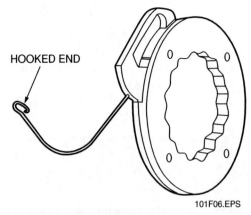
HOOKED END

Figure 6 ◆ Fish tape and reel.

4.1.0 Procedure for Using a Fish Tape

Step 1 Feed the tape bar through the conduit until it comes out the other end of the conduit or into a junction box. Do not use excessive force that will bend the tape. A bent tape is hard to push because of excessive drag.

Step 2 Attach the wire(s) or cable to the tape hook or tape bar. Cover it with sufficient electrical tape to contain the wire ends, but not an excessive amount that may cause binding while pulling.

Step 3 Pull the fish tape, along with the wire or cable, through the conduit by winding the fish tape onto its reel. Note that pulling wires is easier if another person guides the wires into the conduit at the same time the wires are being pulled.

5.0.0 ◆ VISES

Vises are primarily used to hold work pieces during specific jobs and are designed to meet the needs of the particular job to be done. Vises hold the work in a secure position so that a worker has both hands free for filing, drilling, bending, cutting, threading, or other jobs. Make sure the teeth on the vise jaws are in good condition.

Vises should be cleaned periodically with a wire brush and wiped with light oil. To avoid damage, do not strike vises with heavy objects.

Also, do not hold large work pieces in a small vise. This can spring the jaws and damage the vise. The screws and slides of vises should be oiled frequently.

There are three types of vises commonly used for instrumentation work: combination bench and pipe vise, yoke pipe vise, and a chain pipe vise.

5.1.0 Combination Bench and Pipe Vise

A combination bench and pipe vise (*Figure 7*), equipped with secondary pipe jaws, can be used to hold pipe or tubing. The secondary jaws can be fitted with soft jaws, strips of lead, copper, or other material, so they can be used to hold coated pipes or pipes made of softer materials, such as copper.

When the vise is not in use, close the jaws, leaving a small gap between the jaws, and keep the handle in a vertical position.

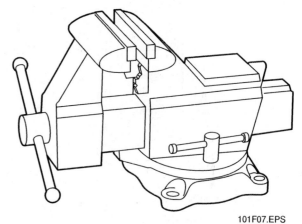

101F07.EPS

Figure 7 ◆ Combination bench and pipe vise.

5.1.1 Procedure for Using a Combination Bench and Pipe Vise

Step 1 Inspect the vise for any defects that might make it unsafe to use.

Step 2 Turn the handle counterclockwise to open the jaws.

Step 3 Place the work piece between the jaws.

Step 4 Tighten the jaws by turning the handle clockwise until the work piece is held between the jaws in a secure position so that the material does not slip.

5.2.0 Yoke Pipe Vise

A yoke pipe vise has an inverted U-shaped frame which is hinged to a base as shown in *Figure 8*. The base of the vise is bolted to a workbench or table. The base has a V-shaped seat that is designed to hold pipe and to prevent it from rolling.

Another kind of yoke pipe vise is the post yoke vise that is secured to a post at the job site.

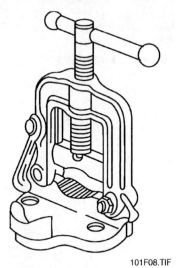

101F08.TIF

Figure 8 ◆ Yoke pipe vise.

5.2.1 Procedure for Using a Yoke Pipe Vise

WARNING!
Make sure the vise is securely fastened to the workbench or table to prevent the work piece and vise from falling. Always wear approved eye protection.

Step 1   Inspect the vise for any defects that might make it unsafe to use.

Step 2   Lift the hold-down hook and swing the frame open.

Step 3   Place the pipe on the lower jaw.

Step 4   Close the frame and latch the hold-down hook to the side of the frame.

NOTE
If it does not latch, open the jaw until the hook falls in place.

Step 5   Tighten the pipe in the jaws by turning the handle clockwise until the pipe is held in a secure position so that it does not slip.

5.3.0 Chain Pipe Vise

The chain pipe vise as shown in *Figure 9* has no jaws. It has a V-shaped, serrated seat where the pipe is placed. The pipe is held by the **serrated** seat while the upper portion is held by a steel chain. In the field, yoke and chain pipe vises are often mounted on tripods.

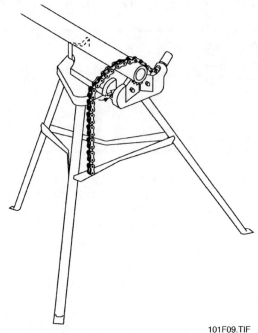

101F09.TIF

Figure 9 ◆ Chain pipe vise.

5.3.1 Procedure for Using a Chain Pipe Vise

WARNING!
Always wear approved eye protection. On collapsible models of chain vises, make sure all legs are fully extended to prevent the stand from tipping over.

Step 1   Inspect the vise for any defects that might make it unsafe to use.

Step 2   Mount the chain pipe vise on a secure object like a post, bench, or tripod.

Step 3   Lift the loose end of the chain off the left side of the vise frame.

Step 4   Place the pipe on the serrated seat.

Step 5   Pull the chain over the pipe and insert one of the links into the notches in the frame.

Step 6   Turn the handle to pull the chain tight against the serrated jaws until the pipe does not slip.

6.0.0 ◆ SNIPS

Metal cutting snips operate like scissors to cut sheet metal and other types of thin metal. They are made in a variety of types, each designed to do a specific job. It is important to select the correct type of snips for the job.

There are right-hand and left-hand snips. As sheet metal is being cut with right-hand snips, the metal on the left-hand side of the snips curls upward and the metal on the right side curls downward, permitting the snips to progress through the cut. When using left-hand snips, the metal curls the opposite way.

After using snips, apply a thin coat of machine oil to the entire length of the blade and work the oil into the fulcrum of the snips.

Two of the most common types of snips used in the instrumentation craft are straight pattern snips and aviation pattern snips.

6.1.0 Straight Pattern Snips

Straight pattern snips are used for cutting sheet metals along straight lines. They are available in several sizes and types depending on the length of desired cut. A pair of straight pattern snips is shown in *Figure 10*.

Compound-lever bench shears (*Figure 10*) are used to cut straight lines in heavy-gauge metals. The compound-lever shear can handle metals up to 12-gauge thickness. The hardened alloy steel blades of most compound-lever bench shears are replaceable.

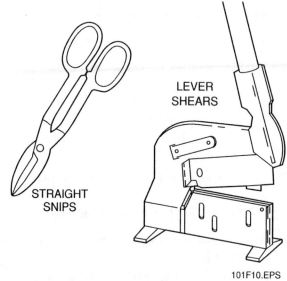

Figure 10 ◆ Straight pattern snips.

6.2.0 Aviation Snips

Aviation snips are used to cut straight and circular patterns in sheet metals. These snips are useful for cutting small size work in close areas. Standards have been established for color coding the handles (grips) of aviation pattern snips, indicating the direction of cut: red grips cut left, green grips cut right, and yellow grips cut straight. Three types of aviation pattern snips are shown in *Figure 11*.

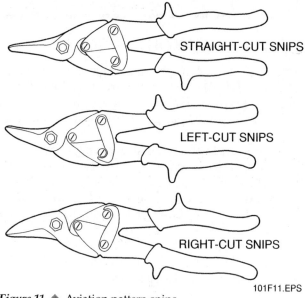

Figure 11 ◆ Aviation pattern snips.

6.3.0 Procedure for Using Snips

WARNING!
Follow all safety precautions. Always be careful when cutting metal since the cut edges are very sharp.

Step 1 Select the proper snips for the job.

Step 2 Inspect the blades for correct adjustment, blade sharpness, or any defects that might make them unsafe to use.

Step 3 Place the top blade of the snips slightly to the outside of the cutting line toward the waste portion.

Step 4 Position the blades perpendicular to the surface of the work at the start, and keep them square throughout the job.

WARNING!
Keep your hands away from the pinch points.

Step 5 Cut the material by exerting pressure on the handles of the snips.

NOTE
While cutting, do not close the snips completely. Open them when the blade tips are about ¼ inch from closing and then push them forward. If the blades are allowed to come together at the end of each cut, the metal will tear.

7.0.0 ◆ KNOCKOUT PUNCHES

Knockout punches are used to enlarge knockouts and punch holes for conduit in metal boxes, cabinets, and panels. Hand knockout punches can be used on up to 10-gauge stainless steel and mild steel.

A knockout punch consists of three parts: a die, punch, and drive screw, as shown in *Figure 12*. On a conduit knockout punch, the size of conduit is stamped on the die. The size of conduit is the inside diameter. The actual hole made by the knockout punch will be larger than the conduit size indicated.

A knockout punch can be operated with a wrench, **ratchet**, or hydraulics.

NOTE
Be aware that there are other types of knockout punches. Be sure to use the proper type of knockout punch for the job.

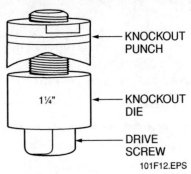

Figure 12 ◆ Knockout punch.

7.1.0 Procedure for Using a Knockout Punch

WARNING!
Holes made using knockout punches have sharp edges. Use approved eye and hand protection when performing these tasks.

De-energize and lockout/tagout all live circuits before reaching into, drilling, or punching out electrical enclosures. Hydraulic-operated pumps commonly used with knockout punch sets generate extremely high pressures. Exercise caution when using a hydraulic-operated pump.

Step 1 Select the proper size and type of knockout punch for the job to be performed.

Step 2 Inspect the knockout punch for nicks, cracks, or any defects that may make it unsafe to use.

Step 3 Inspect the ratchet handle, driver body, leverage handle, die, punch, and adapter screw for defects that might make any of them unsafe to use.

Step 4 Drill a hole in the work piece large enough for the drive screw to go through.

NOTE
If the drive screw binds in the hole that is drilled to accommodate it, the hole should be enlarged before beginning the task. Otherwise, the metal slug will be difficult to remove from the punch set once the knockout task is completed.

INSTRUMENTATION LEVEL ONE — TRAINEE MODULE 12101

Step 5 Insert the drive screw through the knock-out die.

Step 6 Insert the drive screw with knockout die into the hole. Be sure that the cutting edge is facing in the direction of the material to be cut.

Step 7 Screw the knockout punch onto the drive screw until it is hand-tight.

NOTE

Center the hole to be punched.

Step 8 Turn the drive screw with a wrench or ratchet handle. This draws the knockout punch through the metal until a hole is cut.

Step 9 Remove the knockout punch and disassemble it to remove the slug after each use. Clean and rustproof the knockout punch.

8.0.0 ◆ OXYACETYLENE SYSTEM

When cutting or burning with an oxyacetylene (oxygen-acetylene) system, it is important that the equipment be set up properly. An oxyacetylene system consists of two **cylinders** (oxygen and acetylene), two regulators, hoses, and a cutting torch (*Figure 13*).

Do not handle acetylene and oxygen cylinders with oily hands or gloves. Keep grease away from the cylinders and do not use oil or grease on cylinder attachments or valves. The mixture of oil and oxygen will cause an explosion.

WARNING!

An oxyacetylene system is extremely dangerous. The gases in the cylinders are under pressure and must be handled properly. The cylinders must be secured at all times. The oxygen-acetylene system may be placed in an approved cart for transportation to the job site.

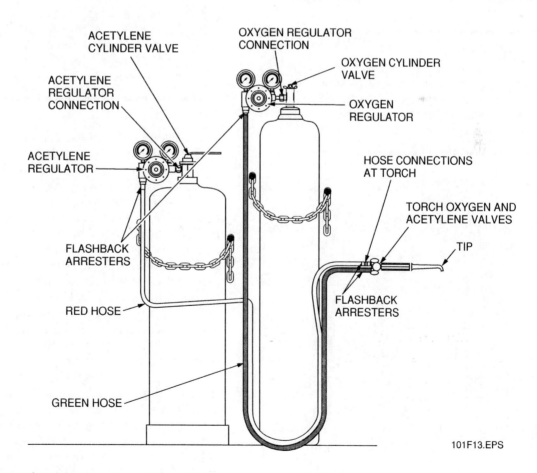

101F13.EPS

Figure 13 ◆ Oxyacetylene system.

8.1.0 Oxygen and Acetylene Gas Cylinders

Oxygen and acetylene gas cylinders come in several different sizes. The pressurized gases in these cylinders are dangerous and must be handled properly. The gas cylinders are equipped with valves to start and stop the flow of gas from the cylinders.

WARNING!

Be sure all parts of the system are clean and free of foreign materials. Do not contaminate any parts with Teflon® or petroleum-based products because they can cause spontaneous combustion.

Oxygen cylinder valves are fitted with right-hand threads, while acetylene cylinder valves are fitted with left-hand threads. The different valves help prevent accidental mixing of oxygen and acetylene equipment. The valves are protected by removable metal caps (*Figure 14*) when the cylinder is not hooked up for use. The protective valve cap is one of the most important pieces of safety equipment associated with oxyacetylene equipment.

WARNING!

Do not store or transport cylinders without the caps installed. Dropping a cylinder without the cap installed may result in breaking the valve off the cylinder, allowing the escaping gas to propel the cylinder like a missile.

101F14.EPS

Figure 14 ◆ Removable protective metal valve cap.

A properly fitting gang wrench, such as the one shown in *Figure 15*, should be used to tighten connections when assembling the oxygen-acetylene cutting system.

The oxygen contained in the oxygen cylinder is a colorless, tasteless, odorless gas that is slightly heavier than air. It is nonflammable, but will support combustion with other elements. When full, the cylinder is charged to approximately 2,200 **pounds per square inch (psi)**.

The acetylene contained in the acetylene cylinder is a colorless gas, with an unpleasant odor that is easily detected when the gas is exposed to air. When full, the cylinder is charged to approximately 250 psi.

101F15.EPS

Figure 15 ◆ Gang wrench.

WARNING!

Acetylene is an unstable gas and may explode at pressures over 15 psi. Accumulations of acetylene in a range of 3 percent to 90 percent in air or oxygen create an explosive condition. Do not allow gas to escape or accumulate.

Acetylene is dissolved in a liquid called acetone and placed in a cylinder filled with a porous material. This porous filler material absorbs the acetone and acetylene, keeping it stable and reducing the danger of an explosion. Because of the liquid acetone inside the cylinder, acetylene cylinders must always be used in an upright position. If the cylinder is tipped over, stand the cylinder upright and wait at least 30 minutes before using it. If liquid acetone is withdrawn from a cylinder, it will gum up the safety check valves and regulators.

During use, transportation, and storage, oxygen and acetylene cylinders must be secured with a stout cable or chain in the upright position to prevent them from falling and injuring people or damaging equipment. When stored at the job site, the cylinders must be stored separately with at least 20 feet between them, or with a 5-foot high, ½-hour minimum fire wall separating them. Store empty cylinders away from partially full or full cylinders and make sure that they are properly marked to clearly show that they are empty.

8.2.0 Oxygen and Acetylene Regulators

Oxygen and acetylene regulators, as shown in *Figure 16*, are attached to their respective cylinder valves. These regulators control the amount of oxygen and acetylene that flows through the hoses to the torch. Each regulator has two gauges. One gauge indicates the pressure inside the cylinder, while the other gauge indicates the working gas pressure going to the torch. The regulator adjusting screw controls the gas pressure. Turned clockwise, it increases the flow of gas. Turned counterclockwise, it reduces or stops the flow of gas.

Oxygen regulators are different than fuel gas regulators. Oxygen regulators are often painted green and always have right-hand threads on all connections. The oxygen regulator's high-pressure gauge generally reads up to 3,000 psig and includes a second scale which shows the amount of oxygen in the cylinder in terms of cubic feet. The low-pressure or working-pressure gauge may read to 100 psig or higher.

Fuel gas regulators are often painted red and always have left-hand threads on all the connections. As a reminder that the regulator has left-hand threads, a V-notch is cut around the nut. The fuel gas regulator's high-pressure gauge usually reads up to 400 psig. The low-pressure or working-pressure gauge may read up to 40 psig, but is always red-lined at 15 psig as a reminder that acetylene pressure should not be increased over 15 psig.

It should be pointed out that there are two types of regulators: single-stage and two-stage. Single-stage regulators reduce the pressure in one step. As gas is drawn from the cylinder, the internal pressure of the cylinder decreases. A single-stage regulator is unable to compensate for this decrease in internal cylinder pressure. Therefore, it is necessary to adjust the output pressure periodically as the gas in the cylinder is consumed.

The two-stage regulator reduces pressure in two steps. It first reduces the input pressure from the cylinder to a predetermined intermediate pressure. The intermediate pressure is then adjusted by the pressure adjusting screw. With this type of regulator, the delivery pressure to the torch remains constant and no readjustment is necessary as the gas in the cylinder is consumed.

> **WARNING!**
>
> Regulators must be kept clean and free of all contaminants. Do not apply any type of lubricant or cleaning solution to regulators.

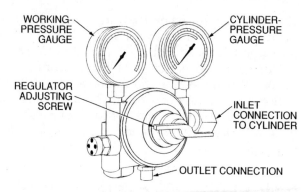

OXYGEN REGULATOR

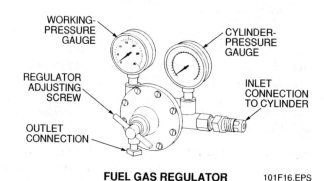

FUEL GAS REGULATOR

101F16.EPS

Figure 16 ◆ Gas regulators.

To prevent damage to regulators, always follow these guidelines:

- Never submit regulators to jarring or shaking, as this can damage the equipment beyond repair.
- Always check that the adjusting screw is released before the cylinder valve is turned on and released when the welding has been completed.
- Always open the cylinder valves slowly.
- Never use oil to lubricate a regulator, as this can result in an explosion.
- Never use fuel gas regulators on oxygen cylinders, or oxygen regulators on fuel gas cylinders.
- Never work with a defective regulator. If it is not working properly, shut off the gas supply and have the regulator repaired by someone who is qualified to work on it.
- Never use pliers or channel locks to install or remove regulators.

8.3.0 Flashback Arrestors and Check Valves

Flashback arrestors are safety devices that stop fire. They prevent flashbacks from reaching the regulator. They have a flame-retarding filter that will allow heat, but not flames, to pass through. Flash arrestors often contain a check valve. Check valves allow gas to flow in one direction only.

Check valves consist of a ball and spring that open inside a cylinder to allow gas to move in one direction but close if the gas attempts to flow in the opposite direction. Flash arrestors can be attached to the torch handle connections or to the outlet of the regulator, or both. They have arrows on them to indicate flow direction. When installing flash arrestors/check valves, be sure the arrow matches the gas flow direction.

8.4.0 Oxygen and Acetylene Hoses

The hoses going from the regulators to the torch are color coded. Green is normally used for oxygen and red for acetylene. The oxygen hose fittings have right-hand threads, and the acetylene hose fittings have left-hand threads, to match the regulator connections. Proper care and maintenance of the hose is important for maintaining a safe, efficient work area. Remember the following guidelines for hoses:

- Never use pipefitting compounds or lubricants around hose connections. These compounds often contain oil or grease, which ignite and burn or explode around oxygen.
- Protect the hose from molten **slag** or sparks, which will burn the exterior. Although some hoses are flame retardant, they will burn.
- Remove the hoses from under the metal being cut. If the metal falls on the hose, it will cut it.
- Frequently inspect and replace hoses that show signs of cuts, burns, worn areas, cracks, or damaged fittings.

8.5.0 Cutting Torch

The cutting torch, shown in *Figure 17*, mixes the oxygen and acetylene in the proper proportion and controls the amount of the mixture at the cutting tip. The cutting torch has two needle valves, one for adjusting the flow of oxygen and one for adjusting the flow of acetylene. Increased oxygen for cutting is injected into the cutting tip flame by the cutting oxygen lever.

8.6.0 Cutting Tips

Cutting torch tips, or nozzles, fit into the cutting torch and are secured with a tip wrench. There are one- and two-piece cutting tips. One-piece cutting tips are made from a solid piece of copper. Two-piece tips have a separate external sleeve and internal section. One-piece torch tips are always used with acetylene cutting because of the high temperatures involved. As shown in *Figure 18*, the acetylene cutting tip has a single hole in the center for the delivery of cutting oxygen holes, and it can have four, six, or eight smaller preheat holes. These are used to provide a flame to preheat the metal to the correct temperature for cutting.

Using the correct cutting tip for the thickness of metal being cut is essential to achieving quality cuts. The cutting torch tip used depends on the base metal thickness and the type of fuel gas being used. Most manufacturers supply charts showing the correct torch tips and gas pressures to be used for cutting metals of various thickness. *Table 2* shows an example of a typical cutting tip chart that lists recommended tip sizes and gas pressures for use with acetylene fuel gas.

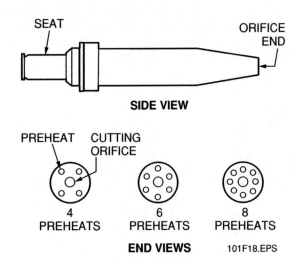

Figure 18 ◆ Acetylene cutting torch tips.

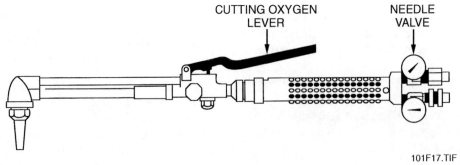

Figure 17 ◆ Cutting torch.

Table 2 Example of a Typical Cutting Tip Chart

Metal Thickness	Tip Size	Cutting Oxygen Pressure (psig)	Preheat Oxygen (psig)	Acetylene Pressure (psig)	Speed I.P.M.	Kerf Width
1/8"	000	20/25	3/5	3/5	20/30	.04
1/4"	00	20/25	3/5	3/5	20/28	.05
3/8"	0	25/30	3/5	3/5	18/26	.06
1/2"	0	30/35	3/6	3/5	16/22	.06
3/4"	1	35/40	4/7	3/5	15/20	.07
1"	2	35/40	4/8	3/6	13/18	.09
2"	3	40/45	5/10	4/8	10/12	.11
3"	4	40/50	5/10	5/11	8/10	.12
4"	5	45/55	6/12	6/13	6/9	.15
6"	6	45/55	6/15	8/14	4/7	.15
10"	7	45/55	6/20	10/15	3/5	.34
12"	8	45/55	7/25	10/15	3/4	.41

8.7.0 Procedure for Assembling an Oxyacetylene System

Before beginning a cutting operation with an oxygen-acetylene cutting torch, the equipment has to be assembled into a cutting system, as shown earlier in this module.

WARNING!

There are many hazards associated with using an oxyacetylene system, including high pressures, high heat, and explosion potential. You should not attempt to use this system unless you have been properly trained to do so.

Step 1 Properly secure the oxygen and acetylene cylinders to a cylinder cart, a wall, or any structure that prevents them from falling.

Step 2 Remove the metal caps from the cylinders and place them out of the way.

WARNING!

Do not stand in front of the valve opening when **cracking the valve** to avoid injury from dirt that may be lodged in the valve.

Step 3 Slowly crack open and immediately close each cylinder valve for a brief moment to clear any dirt that may be in the valve opening.

Step 4 Inspect the cylinder valve threads for damage or dirt. Wipe away any dirt with a clean, dry cloth.

Step 5 Inspect all equipment for obvious signs of damage.

Step 6 Turn the adjusting screw on the oxygen regulator counterclockwise until it is loose, then attach the oxygen regulator to the oxygen cylinder valve and tighten the fitting with a wrench. Do not overtighten.

Step 7 Turn the adjusting screw on the acetylene regulator counterclockwise until it is loose, then attach the acetylene regulator to the acetylene cylinder valve and tighten the fitting with a wrench. Do not overtighten.

Step 8 Install a flashback arrestor to the hose connection on the oxygen regulator, then attach the green hose to the arrestor on the oxygen regulator and tighten the fitting with a wrench. Do not overtighten.

Step 9 Install a flashback arrestor to the hose connection on the acetylene regulator, then attach the red hose to the arrestor on the acetylene regulator and tighten the fitting with a wrench. Do not overtighten.

WARNING!

Do not stand directly in front of or behind the oxygen or acetylene regulators when opening the cylinder valves because the pressure may blow the regulator apart, causing personal injury.

Step 10 Purge (clean) the oxygen hose as follows:

- Slowly open the oxygen cylinder valve until a small amount of pressure is registered on the oxygen high-pressure gauge; then slowly open the valve completely, allowing the pressure in the gauge to rise gradually.

- Turn the oxygen regulator adjusting screw clockwise until a small amount of pressure shows on the oxygen working-pressure gauge. Allow a small amount of pressure to build up so that it purges the oxygen hose, cleaning it.

- Turn the oxygen regulator adjusting screw counterclockwise until it is loose. This will shut off the regulator output.

Step 11 Purge (clean) the acetylene hose as follows:

- Slowly open the acetylene cylinder valve until a small amount of pressure is registered on the acetylene high-pressure gauge; then slowly open the valve about one-half turn.

- Turn the acetylene regulator adjusting screw clockwise until a small amount of pressure shows on the acetylene working-pressure gauge. Allow a small amount of pressure to build up so that it purges the acetylene hose, cleaning it.

- Turn the acetylene regulator adjusting screw counterclockwise until it is loose. This will shut off the regulator output.

Step 12 Attach flashback arrestors on the cutting torch and tighten with a wrench. Do not overtighten. Close the torch oxygen and acetylene valves.

Step 13 Attach the oxygen and acetylene hoses to the proper fitting on the cutting torch and tighten with a wrench. Do not overtighten.

Step 14 Select the proper size cutting tip for the thickness of metal to be cut and install the tip on the torch.

NOTE

Some manufacturers recommend tightening the tip nut with a wrench. Others recommend tightening the nut by hand. Check the tip manual to see if the manufacturer recommends that the nut be tightened manually or with a wrench.

Step 15 Adjust the oxyacetylene system working pressures as follows:

- Slowly turn the oxygen regulator adjusting screw clockwise until the working pressure on the gauge is set as recommended by the manufacturer for the cutting tip to be used.

WARNING!

Never adjust the acetylene regulator higher than 15 psig because acetylene becomes unstable and volatile at this pressure.

- Slowly turn the acetylene regulator adjusting screw clockwise until the working pressure is set as recommended by the manufacturer for the cutting tip to be used.

WARNING!

Oxyacetylene equipment must be tested for leaks immediately after it is set up. Leaks could cause a fire or explosion if undetected. To test for leaks, brush an approved, commercially prepared leak-testing formula or a solution of detergent and water at all threaded connections and valve stems. If bubbles form, a leak is present.

If using a detergent and water solution to test for leaks, use only a nonoil-based detergent. This is because in the presence of oxygen, any oil in the detergent can cause fires or explosions.

Step 16 Check the oxyacetylene equipment for leaks at the following points:

- Oxygen cylinder valve
- Acetylene gas cylinder valve
- Oxygen regulator inlet connection
- Acetylene regulator inlet connection
- Hose and flashback arrestor connections at the regulators and torch

If there is a leak at the fuel gas cylinder valve stem, attempt to stop it by tightening the packing gland. If this does not stop the leak, mark and remove the cylinder and notify the supplier. For other leaks, tighten the connections slightly with a wrench. If this does not stop the leak, turn off the gas pressure, open all connections, and inspect the screw threads.

CAUTION

Be careful not to overtighten connections. The brass connections used will strip or deform if overtightened. Repair or replace equipment that does not seal properly.

Step 17 Coil up the hose and secure the torch to prevent damage while preparing further for cutting metal as outlined in the next section. If the oxyacetylene equipment is not going to be used for cutting in the immediate future, shut down the system as outlined later in this module.

8.8.0 Preparing Metal for Cutting

Instrumentation personnel commonly cut pipe and metal plates used for mounting instruments at a job site. Before metal can be cut, the equipment must be set up and the metal prepared. One important step is to properly layout the cut by marking it with soapstone or punch marks. The few minutes this takes will result in a quality job reflecting craftsmanship and pride in your work. Follow these steps to prepare to make a cut:

Step 1 Prepare the metal to be cut by cleaning any rust, scale, or other foreign matter from the surface.

Step 2 If possible, position the work so you will be comfortable when cutting.

Step 3 Mark the lines to be cut with soapstone or a punch.

Step 4 Light the torch and adjust the flame for cutting as outlined in the next section.

8.9.0 Lighting an Oxyacetylene Torch and Adjusting the Flame

To be able to safely use a cutting torch, the operator must understand the flame, be able to adjust it, and react to unsafe conditions. The following sections describe the oxyacetylene flame and how to control it safely.

8.9.1 Oxyacetylene Torch Flames

There are three types of flames (*Figure 19*):

- Neutral
- Carburizing
- Oxidizing

A neutral flame burns proper proportions of oxygen and fuel gas. The inner cone is light blue in color, surrounded by a darker blue outer flame envelope that results when the oxygen in the air combines with the superheated gases from the inner cone. A neutral flame is used for all but special cutting applications.

A carburizing flame has a white feather shape created by an excess of acetylene. The length of the feather depends on the amount of excess acetylene present in the flame. The outer flame envelope is longer than that of the neutral flame, and it is much brighter in color. The excess acetylene in the carburizing flame produces large amounts of carbon. The carbon will combine with red-hot or molten metal, making the metal hard and brittle. The carburizing flame is cooler than a neutral flame and is never used for cutting. It is used for some special heating applications.

An oxidizing flame has an excess of oxygen. Its inner cone is shorter, much bluer in color, and more pointed than a neutral flame. The outer flame envelope is very short and often fans out at the ends. An oxidizing flame is the hottest flame. The excess oxygen in the flame can combine with many metals, forming a hard, brittle, low-strength oxide.

8.9.2 Torch Flame Backfire and Flashbacks

Sometimes a torch flame goes out with a loud pop or snap. When this happens, a backfire has occurred. Backfires are usually caused when the tip or nozzle touches the work surface or when a bit of hot slag briefly interrupts the flame. When a backfire occurs, you can relight the torch immediately. Sometimes the torch even relights itself. If a backfire recurs without the tip making contact with the base metal, shut off the torch and find the cause.

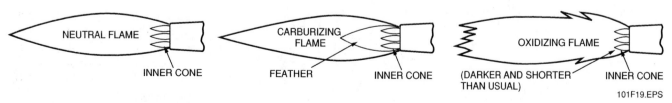

Figure 19 ◆ Oxyacetylene torch flames.

Some possible causes of backfire are:

- Improper operating pressures
- A loose torch tip
- Dirt in the torch tip seat or a bad seat

When the flame goes out and burns back inside the torch with a hissing or whistling sound, a flashback is occurring. Immediately shut off the torch because a flame is burning inside the torch. If the flame is not extinguished quickly, the end of the torch will melt off. The flashback will stop as soon as the oxygen valve is closed. Therefore, quick action is crucial. Flashbacks can cause fires and explosions within the cutting rig and therefore are very dangerous. Flashbacks can be caused by:

- Equipment failure
- Overheated torch tip
- Slag or spatter hitting and sticking to the torch tip

After a flashback has occurred, wait until the torch has cooled before relighting it. Before you relight it, blow oxygen through the torch for several seconds to remove soot that may have built up in the torch during the flashback. If you hear the hissing or whistling, or if the flame does not appear normal, shut off the torch immediately and have the torch serviced by qualified personnel.

8.9.3 Lighting the Torch and Adjusting the Flame

After the cutting equipment has been properly set up, the torch can be lit and the flame adjusted for cutting. When lighting a torch and cutting metals, appropriate personal protective equipment (*Figure 20*) must always be worn to prevent injury.

Follow these steps to light the torch:

Step 1 If not done earlier, choose the appropriate cutting torch tip according to the base metal thickness you will be cutting and fuel gas you are using. Refer to manufacturer's charts. You may have to readjust the oxygen and acetylene pressure depending on the tip selected.

Step 2 If not done earlier, adjust the oxygen and acetylene cylinder valves and regulator adjusting screws to obtain the proper working pressures.

Step 3 Open the torch acetylene valve about one-quarter turn.

Step 4 While holding the friction lighter near the front of the torch tip, strike a spark to ignite a torch flame.

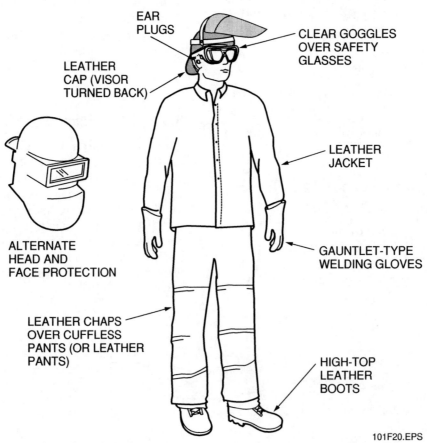

EAR PLUGS

CLEAR GOGGLES OVER SAFETY GLASSES

LEATHER CAP (VISOR TURNED BACK)

LEATHER JACKET

ALTERNATE HEAD AND FACE PROTECTION

LEATHER CHAPS OVER CUFFLESS PANTS (OR LEATHER PANTS)

GAUNTLET-TYPE WELDING GLOVES

HIGH-TOP LEATHER BOOTS

101F20.EPS

Figure 20 ◆ Wear appropriate personal protective equipment.

101F21.EPS

Figure 21 ◆ Friction lighter.

Step 5   When the torch is lit, adjust the torch acetylene valve to increase the flow of acetylene gas until the flame stops smoking.

Step 8   Slowly open the torch oxygen valve and adjust the flow of oxygen to obtain a neutral torch flame.

Step 9   Press the cutting oxygen lever all the way down and observe the flame. As shown in *Figure 22*, it should have a long, high-pressure oxygen center cutting jet up to 8 inches long extending from the cutting oxygen hole.

NOTE

If the torch flame is not correct, check that the working pressures are as recommended on the manufacturer's chart and clean the cutting tip. If this does not clear up the problem, change the cutting tip.

Step 10   If the oxyacetylene equipment is not going to be used for cutting in the immediate future, close the torch acetylene valve quickly to extinguish the flame, then close the torch oxygen valve. Following this, shut down the equipment.

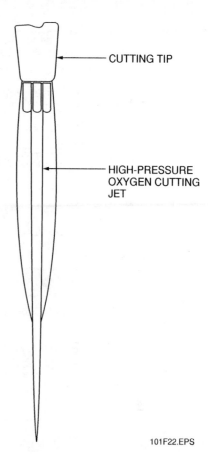

CUTTING TIP

HIGH-PRESSURE OXYGEN CUTTING JET

101F22.EPS

Figure 22 ◆ Proper torch cutting flame.

8.10.0 Cutting Metals With Oxyacetylene Equipment

As explained earlier, instrumentation personnel commonly cut pipe and steel plates used for mounting instruments at a job site. Before metal can be cut, the equipment must be set up and the metal prepared. The following sections explain how to recognize good and bad cuts and how to make a straight-line cut on steel.

8.10.1 Recognizing Good and Bad Cuts

Before attempting to make a cut, you must be able to recognize good and bad cuts (*Figure 23*) and know what causes bad cuts. A good **kerf**, or cut edge, has several characteristics:

• A good cut has a square top edge that is sharp and straight, not ragged. The bottom edge can have some slag adhering to it, but not an excessive amount. What slag there is should be easily removed with a chipping hammer. The **drag lines** should be nearly vertical and not very pronounced.

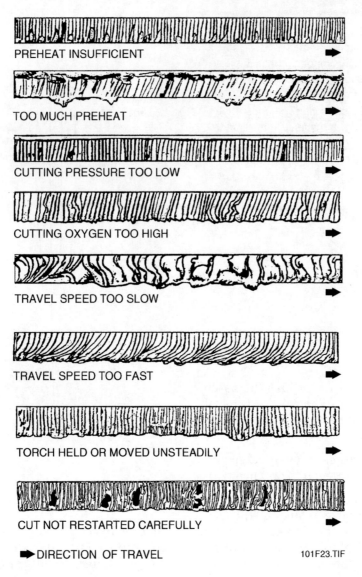

PREHEAT INSUFFICIENT

TOO MUCH PREHEAT

CUTTING PRESSURE TOO LOW

CUTTING OXYGEN TOO HIGH

TRAVEL SPEED TOO SLOW

TRAVEL SPEED TOO FAST

TORCH HELD OR MOVED UNSTEADILY

CUT NOT RESTARTED CAREFULLY

➡ DIRECTION OF TRAVEL   101F23.TIF

Figure 23 ◆ Examples of cuts.

- When preheat is insufficient, bad gouging results at the bottom of the cut because of too slow travel speed.
- Too much preheat will result in the top surface melting over the cut, an irregular cut edge, and an excessive amount of slag.
- When the cutting oxygen pressure is too low, the top edge will melt over because of the resulting slow cutting speed.
- Using cutting oxygen pressure that is too high will cause the operator to lose control of the cut, resulting in an uneven kerf.
- A travel speed that is too slow results in bad gouging at the bottom of the cut and irregular drag lines.
- When the travel speed is too fast, there will be gouging at the bottom of the cut, a pronounced break in the drag line, and an irregular kerf.

- A torch that is held or moved unsteadily across the metal being cut can result in a wavy and irregular kerf.
- When a cut is lost and then not restarted carefully, bad gouges at the point where the cut is restarted will result.

8.10.2 Cutting Steel

Cutting steel and other metals with an oxyacetylene cutting torch requires extensive practice in order to gain experience and expertise in the task. Many kinds of cutting tasks can be done using oxyacetylene equipment. Since instrumentation personnel are often required to cut thicker pieces of steel (steel over $\frac{3}{16}$ inch thick), a procedure for doing so is outlined here. The steps to cut thick steel are shown in *Figure 24*.

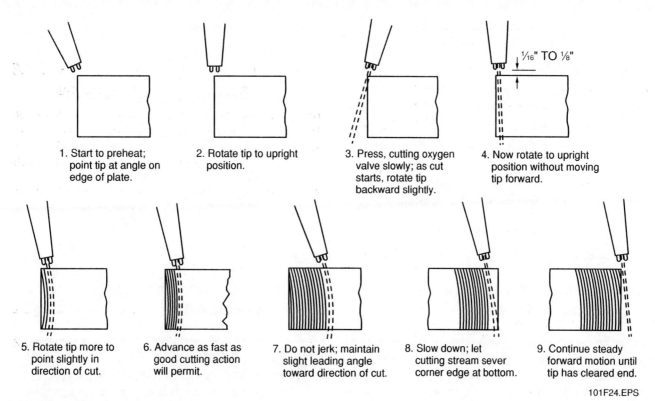

1. Start to preheat; point tip at angle on edge of plate.

2. Rotate tip to upright position.

3. Press, cutting oxygen valve slowly; as cut starts, rotate tip backward slightly.

4. Now rotate to upright position without moving tip forward.

1/16" TO 1/8"

5. Rotate tip more to point slightly in direction of cut.

6. Advance as fast as good cutting action will permit.

7. Do not jerk; maintain slight leading angle toward direction of cut.

8. Slow down; let cutting stream sever corner edge at bottom.

9. Continue steady forward motion until tip has cleared end.

101F24.EPS

Figure 24 ◆ Cutting thick steel.

After the cut has been made, close the torch acetylene valve quickly to extinguish the flame, then close the torch oxygen valve. If no further cutting is to be done, shut down the equipment.

8.11.0 Shutting Down the Oxyacetylene Equipment

When a cutting job is completed and the oxyacetylene equipment is no longer needed, it must be shut down. Follow these steps to shut down the oxyacetylene equipment:

Step 1   Close the acetylene cylinder valve.

Step 2   Close the oxygen cylinder valve.

Step 3   Open the torch acetylene valve to allow the trapped gas to escape. Do not proceed until all pressure is released and the acetylene working pressure gauge reads 0 psig.

Step 4   Turn the acetylene regulator adjusting screw counterclockwise until it is loose.

Step 5   Close the torch acetylene valve.

Step 6   Open the torch oxygen valve to allow the trapped gas to escape. Do not proceed until all pressure is released and the oxygen working pressure gauge reads 0 psig.

Step 7   Turn the oxygen regulator adjusting screw counterclockwise until it is loose.

Step 8   Close the torch oxygen valve.

Step 9   Coil up the hose and secure the torch to prevent damage.

9.0.0 ◆ EXTRACTORS

Screw and tap extractors are used to remove broken screws and taps without damaging the surrounding material or the threaded hole. Most screw and tap extractor sets include twist drills, straight flute extractors, spiral tapered extractors, and tap extractors as shown on *Figure 25*.

9.1.0 Straight Flute Extractors

Straight flute extractors have flutes from end to end with a turn nut in the center for turning the extractor with a wrench. These extractors are commonly used to remove broken screws from ¼ inch to ½ inch outside diameter.

9.2.0 Spiral Tapered Extractors

Spiral tapered extractors have thread-like flutes that are cut in a spiral. They have a square head on the end for turning the extractor with a wrench. These extractors are commonly used to remove broken screws from 3/16 inch to 2⅛ inch outside diameter.

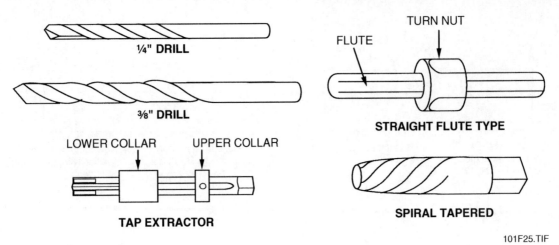

Figure 25 ◆ Screw and tap extractors.

9.3.0 Procedure for Removing a Broken Screw

> **WARNING!**
>
> Broken screws have sharp edges. Exercise caution when working to remove broken screws. Always wear approved eye protection and hand protection as required.

Step 1 Select the proper size drill bit and screw extractor for the job.

Step 2 Inspect the drill bit and screw extractor for any broken flutes or edges, or any other defects that might make them unsafe for use.

Step 3 Center punch the broken screw as close to the center as possible.

Step 4 Using a drill bit considerably smaller than the distance between opposite flutes on the extractor, carefully drill a hole through the broken screw.

Step 5 Insert the screw extractor into the hole.

Step 6 Turn the extractor counterclockwise to remove the broken screw from the hole.

9.4.0 Tap Extractors

Tap extractors are similar to the screw extractors, except that they have four fingers that slip into the flutes of a broken tap. Tap extractors have an adjustable collar to support the fingers close to the broken tap. A wrench is fitted onto the extractor and turned counterclockwise to remove a right-hand tap. Tap extractors are made for different sizes of taps.

9.5.0 Procedure for Removing a Broken Tap

> **WARNING!**
>
> Broken taps cannot be drilled out because taps are harder than drill bits, and broken taps have very sharp edges. Exercise caution when working to remove broken taps. Always wear approved eye protection and hand protection as required.

Step 1 Select the proper tap extractor for the tap to be removed.

Step 2 Inspect the tap extractor for any broken flutes or any other defects that might make it unsafe for use.

Step 3 Slide the upper collar to which the fingers are attached down the flutes so that the fingers project well below the end of the extractor's body.

Step 4 Slide the extractor's fingers into the flutes of the broken tap, making sure they go down into the hole as far as possible.

Step 5 Slide the extractor's body down until it rests on top of the broken tap.

> **NOTE**
>
> This must be done to give maximum support to the fingers.

Step 6 Slide the extractor's lower collar down until it rests on top of the work.

Step 7 Apply a wrench to the square section on the top of the tap extractor's body.

Step 8 Turn the wrench gently in a counter-clockwise direction to remove the broken tap. It may be necessary to turn the extractor back and forth to free the tap sufficiently to back it out.

10.0.0 ◆ RIVET GUN

A rivet gun (*Figure 26*) is used to install blind rivets through drilled or punched holes. With the mandrel and nosepiece of appropriate size, hand-operated rivet guns can be used with various sizes of aluminum and steel rivets.

10.1.0 Procedure for Using a Rivet Gun

 WARNING!
Know what you are riveting. Exercise extreme caution when installing rivets on or near energized circuit enclosures.

Step 1 Select the correct length and diameter of blind rivet to be used.

Step 2 Select the appropriate drill bit for the size of rivet being used.

Step 3 Drill a hole through both parts being connected.

Step 4 Inspect the rivet gun for any defects that might make it unsafe for use.

Step 5 Place the rivet mandrel into the proper size setting tool.

 WARNING!
Wear approved eye and face protection when riveting. Keep hands free from pinching points on rivet gun.

Step 6 Insert the rivet end into the predrilled hole.

Step 7 Squeezing the handle of the rivet gun causes the jaws in the setting tool to grip the mandrel. The mandrel is pulled up, expanding the rivet until it breaks at the shear point.

11.0.0 ◆ ANGLE FINDER

Angle finders are used to determine angles for many applications, such as when bending pipe or conduit (*Figure 27*). Typically, they indicate angles from 0 degrees to 90 degrees in any quadrant with an accuracy of one-half of 1 degree. Some have charts that can be used to convert angles in degrees to pitch per inch or pitch per foot. Some models are made with a magnetic base and V-grooved sides for use on round surfaces. Some are combined with plumb and level vials.

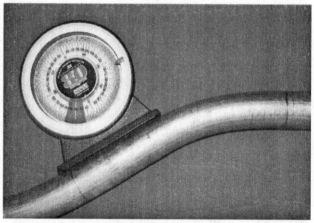

101F27.EPS

Figure 27 ◆ Angle finder used to determine angle of pipe bend.

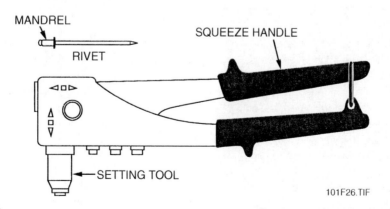

101F26.TIF

Figure 26 ◆ Rivet gun.

12.0.0 ◆ WRAP AROUND

A wrap around (*Figure 28*) is used to mark a straight line completely around a round piece of material, like a pipe, in order to make a straight cut. Typically, a strip of leather or other flexible material is used as a wrap around.

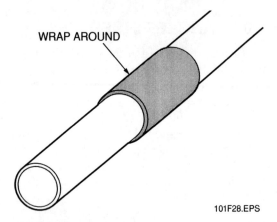

WRAP AROUND

101F28.EPS

Figure 28 ◆ Wrap around.

13.0.0 ◆ RODDING-OUT TOOL

Rodding-out tools are used to clean lines of any solid debris that may accumulate in piping or tubing legs, especially in blow-down lines.

Figure 29 shows an example of a rodding-out tool. Rods and accessories, such as augers or brushes used to clear the line, must be sized according to the line to be cleared.

The purpose of blow-down lines is to allow a pressurized cleanout of the line by using the air or process pressure in the line to clear debris. However, in certain conditions this pressure may not be sufficient to clear out hardened solids, and a rodding-out tool must be used.

Most blow-down lines are equipped with a straight-through passage valve, such as a ball valve at the end that vents to the atmosphere. It is through this valve opening that the rodding-out tool is normally inserted to clear the line of debris.

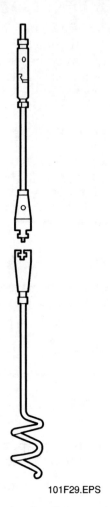

101F29.EPS

Figure 29 ◆ Rodding-out tool and accessories.

SUMMARY

In this module, we have covered many of the basic hand tools that are used in the instrumentation craft. Additional hand tools are covered in other modules. Whatever job you do, select the proper tool, inspect it, maintain it, and use it safely. Proper use and care of hand tools makes the job easier to perform, extends the life of the tool, and provides for a quality product.

WARNING!

You must know what the content and potential pressure are in the line. A restriction may cause high pressures to be present but not apparent when the blow-down valve is opened. Wear approved personal protective equipment based on pressures and line content and never allow the blow-down vent opening to be positioned anywhere near your face or body. Only use rodding-out tools after all other normal procedures for clearing the line have been exhausted.

REVIEW QUESTIONS

1. One of the purposes of flutes on a tap is to _____.
   a. provide clearance for chips
   b. compensate for an undersized hole
   c. allow tapping without a lubricant
   d. make the tap lighter in weight

2. A(n) _____ is used for threading small rods and for recutting damaged threads.
   a. adjustable split die
   b. adjustable screw plate die
   c. solid die
   d. thread chaser

3. The type of die that you should use to thread stainless steel is _____.
   a. carbon steel
   b. aluminum
   c. HSS
   d. copper

4. A fiberglass core fish tape is used to _____.
   a. rod out blow down lines
   b. mark lines around material round in shape
   c. pull wires in areas of energized circuits
   d. measure conduit runs

5. When storing snips the cutting jaws should be _____.
   a. secured in the open position
   b. secured in the closed position
   c. removed
   d. unsecured in the open position

6. The blades of most _____ are replaceable.
   a. aviation pattern snips
   b. tin snips
   c. compound lever bench shears
   d. straight pattern snips

7. Aviation pattern snips with red grips are made to cut _____.
   a. left
   b. right
   c. straight
   d. circular

8. The size shown on a conduit knockout punch is normally the _____.
   a. outside diameter of the conduit
   b. thickness of the metal the knockout will go through
   c. inside diameter of the conduit
   d. size wrench used to turn the drive screw

9. Acetylene cylinder valves are fitted with _____.
   a. left-hand threads
   b. snap-on fittings
   c. right-hand threads
   d. ferrule fittings

10. Acetylene can explode at a pressure _____ psi.
    a. between 5 and 10
    b. between 10 and 15
    c. under 15
    d. over 15

11. On an oxygen-acetylene rig, the acetylene hose is _____.
    a. green
    b. red
    c. yellow
    d. blue

12. The component of an oxyacetylene system that mixes the gases in proper proportions is a (an) _____.
    a. acetylene regulator
    b. cutting torch
    c. hose assembly
    d. oxygen regulator

13. The multiple holes around the large hole in a cutting tip are used to provide _____.
    a. cutting oxygen for the cutting operation
    b. a flame that preheats the metal to the correct temperature for cutting
    c. acetylene for the cutting operation
    d. oxygen to remove any slag buildup

14. All of the following are types of extractor tools *except* _____.
    a. straight flute
    b. spiral tapered
    c. tap
    d. rodding out

15. A (an) _____ can be used to draw a straight line around a pipe.
    a. angle finder
    b. fish tape
    c. wrap around
    d. hacksaw

Trade Terms Introduced in This Module

Blind hole: A hole that does not go all the way through the work.

Chamfer: An angle cut (or ground) on only the edge or end of a piece of material.

Cracking a valve: A momentary opening of a valve to blow out any dust or dirt that may have collected in the valve.

Cylinder: A metal container used to hold and store pressurized gases.

Die: A tool used to make male threads on the outside of a pipe or bolt.

Drag lines: The lines on a kerf that result from the travel of the cutting oxygen stream into, through, and out of the metal.

Female (internal) threads: Threads on the inside of a pipe or nut.

Flute: Parallel grooves running lengthwise along the tap and assisting in cutting threads.

Kerf: The width of a cut produced by a cutting operation such as that made with oxyacetylene equipment.

Male (external) threads: Threads on the outside of a pipe or bolt.

Pounds per square inch (PSI): Normally used to indicate the pressure at which gases are stored and used.

Ratchet: A device that allows a tool to rotate in one direction at a time.

Serrated: Having a saw-tooth edge.

Slag: The material that forms on the underside of an oxyfuel gas or arc cut.

Tap: A tool used to make female threads on the inside of a pipe or nut.

Additional Resources

This module is intended to present thorough resources for task training. The following reference works are suggested for further study. These are optional materials for continued education rather than for task training.

Modern Welding, 1996. Andrew Daniel Althouse, Carl H. Turnquist, William A. Bowditch. Tinley Park, IL: The Goodheart-Willcox Company, Inc.

Figure Credits

Thomas Burke	101F14
Gerald Shannon	101F15
Victor Equipment Company, Division of Thermadyne Industries, Inc.	101F24
Veronica Westfall	101F27

The NCCER makes every effort to keep these textbooks up-to-date and free of technical errors. We appreciate your help in this process. If you have an idea for improving this textbook, or if you find an error, a typographical mistake, or an inaccuracy in the NCCER's Craft Training textbooks, please write us, using this form or a photocopy. Be sure to include the exact module number, page number, a detailed description, and the correction, if applicable. Your input will be brought to the attention of the Technical Review Committee. Thank you for your assistance.

Instructors – If you found that additional materials were necessary in order to teach this module effectively, please let us know so that we may include them in the Equipment and Materials list in the Instructor's Guide.

Write: Curriculum Revision and Development Department
National Center for Construction Education and Research
P.O. Box 141104, Gainesville, FL 32614-1104

Fax: 352-334-0932

E-mail: curriculum@nccer.org

Craft _____ Module Name _____

Copyright Date _____ Module Number _____ Page Number(s) _____

Description _____

_____

_____

_____

(Optional) Correction _____

_____

_____

(Optional) Your Name and Address _____

_____

_____

Electrical Safety

COURSE MAP

This course map shows all of the task modules in the first level of the Instrumentation curriculum. The suggested training order begins at the bottom and proceeds up. Skill levels increase as you advance on the course map. The local Training Program Sponsor may adjust the training order.

INSTRUMENTATION LEVEL ONE

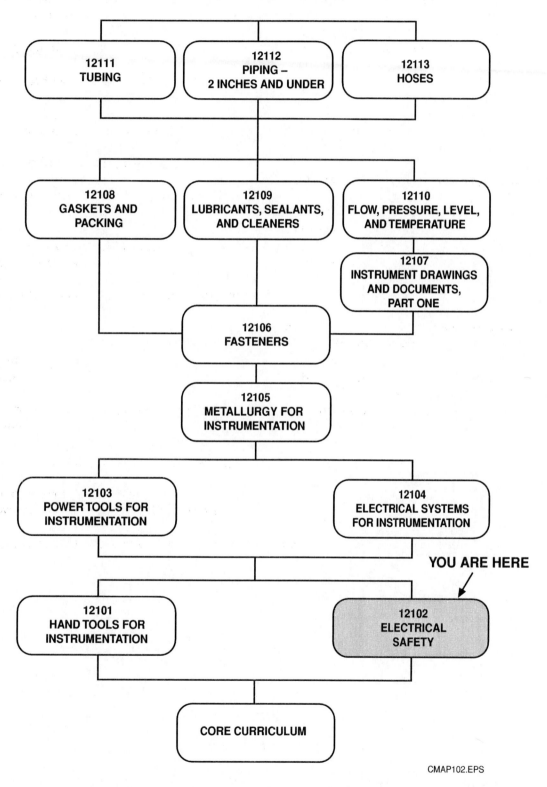

CMAP102.EPS

MODULE 12102 CONTENTS

Figures

Tables

Electrical Safety

Objectives

When you complete this module, you will be able to do the following:

1. Demonstrate safe working procedures in a construction environment.
2. Explain the purpose of OSHA and how it promotes safety on the job.
3. Identify electrical hazards and how to avoid or minimize them in the workplace.
4. Explain safety issues concerning lockout/tagout procedures, personal protection using assured grounding and isolation programs, confined space entry, respiratory protection, and fall protection systems.

Prerequisites

Before you begin this module, it is recommended that you successfully complete the following modules: Core Curriculum, Instrumentation Level One, Module 12101.

Required Trainee Materials

1. Pencil and paper
2. Copy of the latest edition of the *National Electrical Code*
3. *OSHA Electrical Safety Guidelines* (pocket guide)
4. Appropriate personal protective equipment

1.0.0 ◆ INTRODUCTION

You will be exposed to many potentially hazardous conditions on the job site. No training manual, set of rules and regulations, or listing of hazards can make working conditions completely safe. However, it is possible to work a full career without serious accident or injury. To reach this goal, you need to be aware of potential hazards and stay constantly alert to these hazards. You must take the proper precautions and practice the basic rules of safety. You must be safety-conscious at all times. Safety should become a habit. Keeping a safe attitude on the job will go a long way in reducing the number and severity of accidents. Remember that your safety is up to you.

As an apprentice, you need to be especially careful. You should only work under the direction of experienced personnel who are familiar with the various job site hazards and the means of avoiding them.

The most life-threatening hazards on a construction site are:

- Falls when you are working in high places
- Electrocution caused by coming into contact with live electrical circuits
- The possibility of being crushed by falling materials or equipment
- The possibility of being struck by flying objects or moving equipment/vehicles such as trucks, forklifts, and construction equipment

Note: The designations "National Electrical Code," "NE Code," and "NEC," where used in this document, refer to the *National Electrical Code*®, which is a registered trademark of the National Fire Protection Association, Quincy, MA. *All National Electrical Code (NEC) references in this module refer to the 1999 edition of the NEC.*

Other hazards include cuts, burns, back sprains, and getting chemicals or objects in your eyes. Most injuries, both those that are life-threatening and those that are less severe, are preventable if the proper precautions are taken.

2.0.0 ◆ ELECTRICAL SHOCK

Electricity can be described as a potential that results in the movement of electrons in a conductor. This movement of electrons is called *electrical current*. Some substances, such as silver, copper, steel, and aluminum, are excellent conductors. The human body is also a conductor. The conductivity of the human body greatly increases when the skin is wet or moistened with perspiration.

Electrical current flows along the path of least resistance to return to its source. The source return point is called the *neutral* or *ground* of a circuit. If the human body contacts an electrically energized point and is also in contact with the ground or another point in the circuit, the human body becomes a path for the current to return to its source. *Table 1* shows the effects of current passing through the human body. One mA is one milliamp, or one one-thousandth of an ampere.

A primary cause of death from electrical shock is when the heart's rhythm is overcome by an electrical current. Normally, the heart's operation uses a very low-level electrical signal to cause the heart to contract and pump blood. When an abnormal electrical signal, such as current from an electrical shock, reaches the heart, the low-level heartbeat signals are overcome. The heart begins twitching in

an irregular manner and goes out of rhythm with the pulse. This twitching is called **fibrillation.** Unless the normal heartbeat rhythm is restored using special defibrillation equipment (paddles), the individual will die. No known case of heart fibrillation has ever been corrected without the use of defibrillation equipment by a qualified medical practitioner. Other effects of electrical shock may include immediate heart stoppage and burns. In addition, the body's reaction to the shock can cause a fall or other accident. Delayed internal problems can also result.

2.1.0 The Effect of Current

The amount of current measured in amperes that passes through a body determines the outcome of an electrical shock. The higher the voltage, the greater the chance for a fatal shock. In a one-year study in California, the following results were observed by the State Division of Industry Safety:

• Thirty percent of all electrical accidents were caused by contact with conductors. Of these accidents, 66 percent involved low-voltage conductors (those carrying 600 volts [V] or less).

NOTE

Electric shocks or burns are a major cause of accidents in our industry. According to the Bureau of Labor Statistics, electrical shock is the leading cause of death in the electrical industry.

• Portable, electrically operated hand tools made up the second largest number of injuries (15 percent). Almost 70 percent of these injuries happened when the frame or case of the tool became energized. These injuries could have been prevented by following proper safety practices, using grounded or double-insulated tools, and using **ground fault circuit interrupter (GFCI)** protection.

In one ten-year study, investigators found 9,765 electrical injuries that occurred in accidents. Over 18 percent of these injuries involved contact with voltage levels of over 600 volts. A little more than 13 percent of these high-voltage injuries resulted in death.

These high-voltage totals included limited-amperage contacts, which are often found on electronic equipment. When tools or equipment touch high-voltage overhead lines, the chance that a resulting injury will be fatal climbs to 28 percent. Of the low-voltage injuries, 1.4 percent were fatal.

Table 1 Current Level Effects on the Human Body

Current Value	Typical Effects
Less than 1mA	No sensation.
1 to 20mA	Sensation of shock, possibly painful. May lose some muscular control between 10 and 20mA.
20 to 50mA	Painful shock, severe muscular contractions, breathing difficulties.
50 to 200mA	Same symptoms as above, only more severe, up to 100mA. Between 100 and 200mA, ventricular fibrillation may occur. Typically results in almost immediate death unless special medical equipment and treatment are available.
Over 200mA	Severe burns and muscular contractions. The chest muscles contract and stop the heart for the duration of the shock.

These statistics have been included to help you gain respect for the environment where you work and to stress how important safe working habits really are.

2.1.1 Body Resistance

Electricity travels in closed circuits, and its normal route is through a conductor. Shock occurs when the body becomes part of the electric circuit (*Figure 1*). The current must enter the body at one point and leave at another. Shock normally occurs in one of three ways: the person must come in contact with both wires of the electric circuit; one wire of the electric circuit and the ground; or a metallic part that has become hot by being in contact with an energized wire while the person is also in contact with the ground.

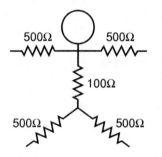

- HAND TO HAND 1000Ω
- 120 VOLT
- FORMULA: I = E/R
- 120/1000 = 0.120 AMPS OR 120 MILLIAMPS

102F01.EPS

Figure 1 ◆ Body resistance.

To fully understand the harm done by electrical shock, we need to understand something about the physiology of certain body parts: the skin, the heart, and muscles.

- Skin covers the body and is made up of three layers. The most important layer, as far as electric shock is concerned, is the outer layer of dead cells referred to as the *horny layer*. This layer is composed mostly of a protein called *keratin*, and it is the keratin that provides the largest percentage of the body's electrical resistance. When it is dry, the outer layer of skin may have a resistance of several thousand ohms, but

when it is moist, there is a radical drop in resistance, as is also the case if there is a cut or abrasion that pierces the horny layer. The amount of resistance provided by the skin will vary widely from individual to individual. A worker with a thick horny layer will have a much higher resistance than a child. The resistance will also vary widely at different parts of the body. For instance, the worker with high-resistance hands may have low-resistance skin on the back of his calf. The skin, like any insulator, has a breakdown voltage at which it ceases to act as a resistor and is simply punctured, leaving only the lower-resistance body tissue to impede the flow of current in the body. The breakdown voltage will vary with the individual, but is in the area of 600V. Since most industrial power distribution systems operate at 480V or higher, technicians working at these levels need to have special awareness of the shock potential.

- The heart is the pump that sends life-sustaining blood to all parts of the body. The blood flow is caused by the contractions of the heart muscle, which is controlled by electrical impulses. The electrical impulses are delivered by an intricate system of nerve tissue with built-in timing mechanisms, which make the chambers of the heart contract at exactly the right time. An outside electric current of as little as 75 milliamperes can upset the rhythmic, coordinated beating of the heart by disturbing the nerve impulses. When this happens, the heart is said to be in *fibrillation*, and the pumping action stops. Death will occur quickly if the normal beat is not restored. Remarkable as it may seem, what is needed to defibrillate the heart is a shock of an even higher intensity.

- The other muscles of the body are also controlled by electrical impulses delivered by nerves. Electric shock can cause loss of muscular control, resulting in the inability to let go of an electrical conductor. Electric shock can also cause injuries of an indirect nature in which involuntary muscle reaction from the electric shock can cause bruises, fractures, and even deaths resulting from collisions or falls.

Severity of shock—The severity of shock received when a person becomes a part of an electric circuit is affected by three primary factors: the amount of current flowing through the body (measured in amperes), the path of the current through the body, and the length of time the body is in the circuit. Other factors that may affect the severity of the shock are the frequency of the current, the phase of the heart cycle when shock occurs, and the general health of the person prior to the shock. Effects can range from a barely perceptible tingle to immediate cardiac arrest. Although there are no absolute limits, or even known values that show the exact injury at any given amperage range, *Table 1* lists the general effects of electric current on the body for different current levels. As this table illustrates, a difference of only 100 milliamperes exists between a current that is barely perceptible and one that can kill.

A severe shock can cause considerably more damage to the body than is visible. For example, a person may suffer internal hemorrhages and destruction of tissues, nerves, and muscle. In addition, shock is often only the beginning in a chain of events. The final injury may well be from a fall, cuts, burns, or broken bones.

2.1.2 Burns

The most common shock-related injury is a burn. Burns suffered in electrical accidents may be of three types: electrical burns, arc burns, and thermal contact burns.

- Electrical burns are the result of electric current flowing through the tissues or bones. Tissue damage is caused by the heat generated by the current flow through the body. An electrical burn is one of the most serious injuries you can receive, and should be given immediate attention. Since the most severe burning is likely to be internal, what may appear at first to be a small surface wound could, in fact, be an indication of severe internal burns.

- Arc burns make up a substantial portion of the injuries from electrical malfunctions. The electric arc between metals can be up to 35,000°F, which is about four times hotter than the surface of the sun. Workers several feet from the source of the arc can receive severe or fatal burns. Since most electrical safety guidelines recommend safe working distances based on shock considerations, workers can be following these guidelines and still be at risk from arc. Electric arcs can occur due to poor electrical contact or failed insulation. Electrical arcing is caused by the passage of substantial amounts of current through the vaporized terminal material (usually metal or carbon).

CAUTION

Since the heat of the arc is dependent on the short circuit current available at the arcing point, arcs generated on 480V systems can be just as dangerous as those generated at 13,000V.

- The third type of burn is a thermal contact burn. It is caused by contact with objects thrown during the blast associated with an electric arc. This blast comes from the pressure developed by the near-instantaneous heating of the air surrounding the arc, and from the expansion of the metal as it is vaporized. (Copper expands by a factor in excess of 65,000 times in boiling.) These pressures can be great enough to hurl people, switchgear, and cabinets considerable distances. Another hazard associated with the blast is the hurling of molten metal droplets, which can also cause thermal contact burns and associated damage. A possible beneficial side effect of the blast is that it could hurl a nearby person away from the arc, thereby reducing the effect of arc burns.

3.0.0 ◆ REDUCING YOUR RISK

There are many things that can be done to greatly reduce the chance of receiving an electrical shock. Always comply with your company's safety policy and all applicable rules and regulations, including job site rules. In addition, the Occupational Safety and Health Administration (OSHA) publishes the *Code of Federal Regulations (CFR)*. CFR Part 1910 covers the OSHA standards for general industry and CFR Part 1926 covers the OSHA standards for the construction industry.

Do not approach any electrical conductors closer than indicated in *Table 2* unless you are sure they are de-energized and your company has designated you as a qualified individual. Also, the values given in the table are *minimum* safe clearance distances; if you already have standard distances established, these are provided only as supplemental information. These distances are listed in CFR 1910.333/1926.416.

Table 2 Approach Distances for Qualified Employees—
Alternating Current

Voltage Range (Phase-to-Phase)	Minimum Approach Distance
300V and less	Avoid contact
Over 300V, not over 750V	1 ft. 0 in. (30.5 cm)
Over 750V, not over 2kV	1 ft. 6 in. (46 cm)
Over 2kV, not over 15kV	2 ft. 0 in. (61 cm)
Over 15kV, not over 37kV	3 ft. 0 in. (91 cm)
Over 37kV, not over 87.5kV	3 ft. 6 in. (107 cm)
Over 87.5kV, not over 121kV	4 ft. 0 in. (122 cm)
Over 121kV, not over 140kV	4 ft. 6 in. (137 cm)

3.1.0 Protective Equipment

You should also become familiar with common personal protective equipment. In particular, know the voltage rating of each piece of equipment. Rubber gloves are used to prevent the skin from coming into contact with energized circuits. A separate leather cover protects the rubber glove from punctures and other damage (see *Figure 2*). OSHA addresses the use of protective equipment, apparel, and tools in CFR 1910.335(a). This article is divided into two sections: *Personal Protective Equipment* and *General Protective Equipment and Tools*.

102F02.EPS

Figure 2 ◆ Rubber gloves and leather protectors.

The first section, *Personal Protective Equipment,* includes the following requirements:

- Employees working in areas where there are potential electrical hazards shall be provided with, and shall use, electrical protective equipment that is appropriate for the specific parts of the body to be protected and for the work to be performed.
- Protective equipment shall be maintained in a safe, reliable condition and shall be periodically inspected or tested, as required by CFR 1910.137/1926.95.
- If the insulating capability of protective equipment may be subject to damage during use, the insulating material shall be protected.
- Employees shall wear nonconductive head protection wherever there is a danger of head injury from electric shock or burns due to contact with exposed energized parts.
- Employees shall wear protective equipment for the eyes and face wherever there is danger of injury to the eyes or face from electric arcs or flashes, or from flying objects resulting from an electrical explosion.

The second section, *General Protective Equipment and Tools,* includes the following requirements:

- When working near exposed energized conductors or circuit parts, each employee shall use insulated tools or handling equipment if the tools or handling equipment might make contact with such conductors or parts. If the insulating capability of insulated tools or handling equipment is subject to damage, the insulating material shall be protected.
- Fuse handling equipment, insulated for the circuit voltage, shall be used to remove or install fuses when the fuse terminals are energized.
- Ropes and handlines used near exposed energized parts shall be nonconductive.
- Protective shields, protective barriers, or insulating materials shall be used to protect each employee from shock, burns, or other electrically related injuries while that employee is working near exposed energized parts that might be accidentally contacted or where dangerous electric heating or arcing might occur. When normally enclosed live parts are exposed for maintenance or repair, they shall be guarded to protect unqualified persons from contact with the live parts.

The types of electrical safety equipment, protective apparel, and protective tools available for use are quite varied. We will discuss the most common types of safety equipment. These include:

- Rubber protective equipment, including gloves and blankets
- Protective apparel
- Personal clothing
- Hot sticks
- Fuse pullers
- Shorting probes
- Eye and face protection

3.1.1 1910.335(a)(1)/1926.951(a) Rubber Protective Equipment

At some point during the performance of their duties, all electrical workers will be exposed to energized circuits or equipment. Two of the most important articles of protection for electrical workers are insulated rubber gloves and rubber blankets, which must be matched to the voltage rating for the circuit or equipment. Rubber protective equipment is designed for the protection of the user. If it fails during use, a serious injury could occur.

Rubber protective equipment is available in two types. Type 1 designates rubber protective equipment that is manufactured of natural or synthetic rubber that is properly vulcanized, and Type 2 designates equipment that is ozone resistant, made from any elastomer or combination of elastomeric compounds. Ozone is a form of oxygen that is produced from electricity and is present in the air surrounding a conductor under high voltages. Normally, ozone is found at voltages of 10kV and higher, such as those found in electric utility transmission and distribution systems. Type 1 protective equipment can be damaged by *corona cutting*, which is the cutting action of ozone on natural rubber when it is under mechanical stress. Type 1 rubber protective equipment can also be damaged by ultraviolet rays. However, it is very important that the rubber protective equipment in use today be made of natural rubber or Type 1 equipment. Type 2 rubber protective equipment is very stiff and is not as easily worn as Type 1 equipment.

Various classes—The American National Standards Institute (ANSI) and the American Society for Testing of Materials (ASTM) have designated a specific classification system for rubber protective equipment. The voltage ratings are as follows:

- Class 0   1,000V
- Class 1   7,500V
- Class 2   17,500V
- Class 3   26,500V
- Class 4   36,000V

Inspection of protective equipment—Before rubber protective equipment can be worn by personnel in the field, all equipment must have a current test date stenciled on the equipment, and it must be inspected by the user. Insulating gloves must be tested each day by the user before they can be used. They must also be tested during the day if their insulating value is ever in question. Because rubber protective equipment is going to be used for personal protection and serious injury could result from its misuse or failure, it is important that an adequate safety factor be provided between the voltage on which it is to be used and the voltage at which it was tested.

All rubber protective equipment must be marked with the appropriate voltage rating and last inspection date. The markings that are required to be on rubber protective equipment must be applied in a manner that will not interfere with the protection that is provided by the equipment.

WARNING!
Never work on anything energized without direct instruction from your employer!

Gloves—Both high- and low-voltage rubber gloves are of the gauntlet type and are available in various sizes. To get the best possible protection and service life, here are a few general rules that apply whenever they are used in electrical work:

- Always wear leather protectors over your gloves. Any direct contact with sharp or pointed objects may cut, snag, or puncture the gloves and take away the protection you are depending on. Leather protectors are required by the National Fire Protection Association's Standard 70-E if the insulating capabilities of the gloves are subject to damage. (The standards of the National Fire Protection Association [NFPA] are incorporated into the OSHA standards.)

- Always wear rubber gloves right side out (serial number and size to the outside). Turning gloves inside out places a stress on the preformed rubber.

- Always keep the gauntlets up. Rolling them down sacrifices a valuable area of protection.

- Always inspect and field check gloves before using them. Always check the inside for any debris. The inspection of gloves is covered in more detail later in this section.

- Use light amounts of talcum powder or cotton liners with the rubber gloves. This gives the user more comfort, and it also helps to absorb some of the perspiration that can damage the gloves over years of use.

- Wash the rubber gloves in lukewarm, clean, fresh water after each use. Dry the gloves inside and out prior to returning to storage. Never use any type of cleaning solution on the gloves.

- Once the gloves have been properly cleaned, inspected, and tested, they must be properly stored. They should be stored in a cool, dry, dark place that is free from ozone, chemicals, oils, solvents, or other materials that could damage the gloves. Such storage should not be in the vicinity of hot pipes or direct sunlight. Both gloves and sleeves should be stored in their natural shape and kept in a bag or box inside their protectors. They should be stored undistorted, right side out, and unfolded.

- Gloves can be damaged by many different chemicals, especially petroleum-based products such as oils, gasoline, hydraulic fluid inhibitors, hand creams, pastes, and salves. If contact is made with these or other petroleum-based products, the contaminant should be wiped off immediately. If any signs of physical damage or chemical deterioration are found (e.g., swelling, softness, hardening, stickiness, ozone deterioration, or sun checking), the protective equipment must not be used.

- Never wear watches or rings while wearing rubber gloves; this can cause damage from the inside out and defeats the purpose of using rubber gloves. Never wear anything conductive.
- Rubber gloves must be tested every six months by a certified testing laboratory. Always check the inspection date before using gloves.
- Use rubber gloves only for their intended purpose, not for handling chemicals or other work. This also applies to the leather protectors.

Before rubber gloves are used, a visual inspection and an air test should be made. This should be done prior to use and as many times during the day as you feel necessary. To perform a visual inspection, stretch a small area of the glove, checking to see that no defects exist, such as:

- Embedded foreign material
- Deep scratches
- Pinholes or punctures
- Snags or cuts

Gloves and sleeves can be inspected by rolling the outside and inside of the protective equipment between the hands. This can be done by squeezing together the inside of the gloves or sleeves to bend the outside area and create enough stress to the inside surface to expose any cracks, cuts, or other defects. When the entire surface has been checked in this manner, the equipment is then turned inside out, and the procedure is repeated. It is very important not to leave the rubber protective equipment inside out.

Remember, any damage at all reduces the insulating ability of the rubber glove. Look for signs of deterioration from age, such as hardening and slight cracking. Also, if the glove has been exposed to petroleum products, it should be considered suspect because deterioration can be caused by such exposure. Gloves that are found to be defective must be turned in for disposal. Never leave a damaged glove lying around; someone may think it is a good glove and not perform an inspection prior to using it.

After visually inspecting the glove, other defects may be observed by applying the air test.

Step 1   Stretch the glove and look for any defects, as shown in *Figure 3*.

Step 2   Twirl the glove around quickly or roll it down from the glove gauntlet to trap air inside, as shown in *Figure 4*.

Step 3   Trap the air by squeezing the gauntlet with one hand. Use the other hand to squeeze the palm, fingers, and thumb to check for weaknesses and defects. See *Figures 5* and *6*.

Step 4   Hold the glove up to your ear to try to detect any escaping air.

Step 5   If the glove does not pass this inspection, it must be turned in for disposal.

 CAUTION
Never use compressed gas for the air test as this can damage the glove.

102F03.EPS

Figure 3 ◆ Inspection.

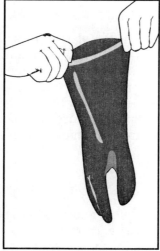

102F04.EPS

Figure 4 ◆ Trapping air.

102F05.EPS

Figure 5 ◆ Inflated glove.

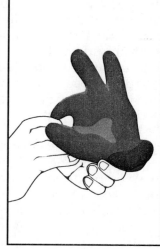

102F06.EPS

Figure 6 ◆ Inspecting glove.

Insulating blankets—An insulating blanket is a versatile cover-up device best suited for the protection of maintenance technicians against accidental contact with energized electrical equipment.

These blankets are designed and manufactured to provide insulating quality and flexibility for use in covering. Insulating blankets are designed only for covering equipment and should not be used on the floor. (Special rubber mats are available for floor use.) Use caution when installing on sharp edges or covering pointed objects.

Blankets must be inspected yearly and should be checked before each use. To check rubber blankets, place the blanket on a flat surface and roll the blanket from one corner to the opposite corner. If there are any irregularities in the rubber, this method will expose them. After the blanket has been rolled from each corner, it should then be turned over and the procedure repeated.

Insulating blankets are cleaned in the same manner as rubber gloves. Once the protective equipment has been properly cleaned, inspected, and tested, it must be properly stored. It should be stored in a cool, dry, dark place that is free from ozone, chemicals, oils, solvents, or other materials that could damage the equipment. Such storage should not be in the vicinity of hot pipes or direct sunlight. Blankets may be stored rolled in containers that are designed for this use; the inside diameter of the roll should be at least two inches.

3.1.2 Protective Apparel

Besides rubber gloves, there are other types of special application protective apparel, such as fire suits, face shields, and rubber sleeves.

Manufacturing plants should have other types of special application protective equipment available for use, such as high-voltage sleeves, high-voltage boots, nonconductive protective helmets, nonconductive eyewear and face protection, and switchboard blankets.

All equipment should be inspected before use and during use, as necessary. The equipment used and the extent of the precautions taken depend on each individual situation; however, it is better to be overprotected than underprotected when you are trying to prevent electrocution.

When working with high voltages, flash suits may be required in some applications. Some plants require them to be worn for all switching and rack-in or rack-out operations.

Face shields should also be worn during all switching operations where arcs are a possibility. The thin plastic type of face shield should be avoided because it will melt when exposed to the extremely high temperatures of an electrical arc.

Rubber sleeves are another type of protective apparel that should be worn during switching operations and breaker racking. Sleeves must be inspected yearly.

3.1.3 Personal Clothing

Any individual who will perform work in an electrical environment or in plant substations should dress accordingly. Avoid wearing synthetic-fiber clothing; these types of materials will melt when exposed to high temperatures and will actually increase the severity of a burn. Wear cotton clothing, fiberglass-toe boots or shoes, and hard hats. Use hearing protection where needed.

3.1.4 Hot Sticks

Hot sticks are insulated tools designed for the manual operation of disconnecting switches, fuse removal and insertion, and the application and removal of temporary grounds.

A hot stick is made up of two parts, the head or *hood* and the insulating rod. The head can be made of metal or hardened plastic, while the insulating section may be wood, plastic, laminated wood, or other effective insulating materials. There are also telescoping sticks available.

Most plants have hot sticks available for different purposes. Select a stick of the correct type and size for the application.

Storage of hot sticks is important. They should be hung up vertically on a wall to prevent any damage. They should also be stored away from direct sunlight and prevented from being exposed to petroleum products. The preferred method of storage is to place the stick in a long section of capped pipe.

3.1.5 Fuse Pullers

Use the plastic or fiberglass style of fuse puller for removing and installing low-voltage cartridge fuses. All fuse pulling and replacement operations must be done using fuse pullers.

The best type of fuse puller is one that has a spread guard installed. This prevents the puller from opening if resistance is met when installing fuses.

3.1.6 Shorting Probes

Before working on de-energized circuits that have capacitors installed, you must discharge the capacitors using a safety shorting probe. When using a shorting probe, first connect the test clip to a good ground to make contact. If necessary, scrape the paint from the metal surface. Then, hold the shorting probe by the handle and touch the probe end of the shorting rod to the points to be shorted. The probe end can be hooked over the part or terminal to provide a constant connection to ground. Never touch any metal part of the shorting probe while grounding circuits or components. Whenever possible, especially when working on or near any de-energized high-voltage circuits, shorting probes should be connected and then left attached to the de-energized portion of any circuit for the duration of the work. This action serves as an extra safety precaution against any accidental application of voltage to the circuit.

3.1.7   *Eye and Face Protection*

NFPA 70-E requires that protective equipment for the eyes and face shall be used whenever there is danger of injury to the eyes or face from electrical arcs or flashes, or from flying or falling objects resulting from an electrical explosion.

3.2.0 Verify That Circuits Are De-energized

You should always assume that all the circuits are energized until you have verified that the circuit is de-energized. Follow these steps to verify that a circuit is de-energized:

Step 1   Ensure that the circuit is properly tagged and locked out (OSHA 1910.333/1926.417).

Step 2   Verify the test instrument operation on a known source.

Step 3   Using the test instrument, check the circuit to be de-energized. The voltage should be zero.

Step 4   Verify the test instrument operation, once again on a known power source.

3.3.0 Other Precautions

There are several other precautions you can take to help make your job safer. For example:

- Always remove all jewelry (e.g., rings, watches, bracelets, and necklaces) before working on electrical equipment. Most jewelry is made of conductive material and wearing it can result in a shock, as well as other injuries if the jewelry gets caught in moving components.
- When working on energized equipment, it is safer to work in pairs. In doing so, if one of the workers experiences a harmful electrical shock, the other worker can quickly de-energize the circuit and call for help.

- Plan each job before you begin it. Make sure you understand exactly what it is you are going to do. If you are not sure, ask your supervisor.
- You will need to look over the appropriate prints and drawings to locate isolation devices and potential hazards. Never defeat safety interlocks. Remember to plan your escape route before starting work. Know where the nearest phone is and the emergency number to dial for assistance.
- If you realize that the work will go beyond the scope of what was planned, stop and get instructions from your supervisor before continuing. Do not attempt to plan as you go.
- It is critical that you stay alert. Work places are dynamic, and situations relative to safety are always changing. If you leave the work area to pick up material, take a break, or have lunch, reevaluate your surroundings when you return. Remember, plan ahead.

4.0.0 ◆ OSHA

The purpose of the Occupational Safety and Health Administration (OSHA) is "to assure safe and healthful working conditions for working men and women." OSHA is authorized to enforce standards and assist and encourage the states in their efforts to ensure safe and healthful working conditions. OSHA assists states by providing for research, information, education, and training in the field of occupational safety and health.

The law that established OSHA specifies the duties of both the employer and employee with respect to safety. Some of the key requirements are outlined here. This list does not include everything, nor does it override the procedures called for by your employer.

- Employers shall provide a place of employment free from recognized hazards likely to cause death or serious injury.
- Employers shall comply with the standards of the act.
- Employers shall be subject to fines and other penalties for violation of those standards.

 WARNING!
OSHA states that employees have a duty to follow the safety rules laid down by the employer. Additionally, some states can reduce the amount of benefits paid to an injured employee if that employee was not following known, established safety rules. Your company may also terminate you if you violate an established safety rule.

4.1.0 Safety Standards

The OSHA standards are split into several sections. As discussed earlier, the two that affect you the most are CFR 1926, construction specific, and CFR 1910, which is the standard for general industry. Either or both may apply depending on where you are working and what you are doing. If a job site condition is covered in the 1926 book, then that standard takes precedent. However, if a more stringent requirement is listed in the 1910 standard, it should also be met. An excellent example is the current difference in the two standards on confined spaces; if someone gets hurt or killed, the decision to use the less stringent 1926 standard could be called into question. OSHA's *General Duty Clause* states that an employer should have known all recognized hazards and removed the hazard or protected the employee.

To protect workers from the occupational injuries and fatalities caused by electrical hazards, OSHA has issued a set of design safety standards for electrical utilization systems. These standards are 1926.400–449 and 1910.302–308. OSHA also recognizes the *National Electrical Code (NEC)* for certain installations.

NOTE

OSHA does *not* recognize the current edition of the NEC; it generally takes several years for that to occur.

The CFR 1910 standard must be followed whenever the construction standard CFR 1926 does not address an issue that is covered by CFR 1910, or for a pre-existing installation. If the CFR 1910 standard is more stringent than CFR 1926, then the more stringent standard should be followed. OSHA does not update their standards in a timely manner, and as such, there are often differences in similar sections of the two standards. Safety should always be first, and the more protective work rules should always be chosen.

4.1.1 1910.302–308/1926.402–408 Design Safety Standards for Electrical Systems

This section contains design safety regulations for all the electrical equipment and installations used to provide power and light to employee workplaces. The articles listed are outlined in the following sections.

4.1.2 1910.302/1926.402 Electric Utilization Systems

This article identifies the scope of the standard. Listings are included to show which electrical installations and equipment are covered under the standard, and which installations and equipment are not covered under the standard. Furthermore, certain sections of the standard apply only to utilization equipment installed after March 15, 1972, and some apply only to equipment installed after April 16, 1981. Article 1910.302 (1926.402) addresses these oddities and provides guidance to clarify them.

4.1.3 1910.303/1926.403 General Requirements

This article covers topics that mostly concern equipment installation clearances, identification, and examination. Some of the major subjects addressed in this article are:

- Equipment installation examinations
- Splicing
- Marking
- Identification of disconnecting means
- Workspace around electrical equipment

4.1.4 1910.304/1926.404 Wiring Design and Protection

This article covers the application, identification, and protection requirements of grounding conductors, outside conductors, service conductors, and equipment enclosures. Some of the major topics discussed are:

- Grounded conductors
- Outside conductors
- Service conductors
- Overcurrent protection
- System grounding requirements

4.1.5 1910.305/1926.405 Wiring Methods, Components, and Equipment for General Use

In general, this article addresses the wiring method requirements of raceways, cable trays, pull and junction boxes, switches, and switchboards; the application requirements of temporary wiring installations; the equipment and conductor requirements for general wiring; and the protection requirements of motors, transformers, capacitors, and storage batteries.

Some of the major topics are:

- Wiring methods
- Cabinets, boxes, and fittings
- Switches
- Switchboards and panelboards
- Enclosures for damp or wet locations
- Conductors for general wiring
- Flexible cords and cables
- Portable cables
- Equipment for general use

4.1.6 1910.306/1926.406
Specific Purpose Equipment and Installations

This article addresses the requirements of special equipment and installations not covered in other articles. Some of the major types of equipment and installations found in this article are:

- Electric signs and outline lighting
- Cranes and hoists
- Elevators, dumbwaiters, escalators, and moving walks
- Electric welders
- Data processing systems
- X-ray equipment
- Induction and dielectric heating equipment
- Electrolytic cells
- Electrically driven or controlled irrigation machines
- Swimming pools, fountains, and similar installations

4.1.7 1910.307/1926.407
Hazardous (Classified) Locations

This article covers the requirements for electric equipment and wiring in locations that are classified because they contain: (1) flammable vapors, liquids, and/or gases, or combustible dust or fibers; and (2) the likelihood that a flammable or combustible concentration or quantity is present. Some of the major topics covered in this article are:

- Scope
- Electrical installations in hazardous locations
- Conduit
- Equipment in Division 2 locations

4.1.8 1910.308/1926.408 Special Systems

This article covers the wiring methods, grounding, protection, identification, and other general requirements of special systems not covered in other articles.

Some of the major subtopics found in this article are:

- Systems over 600 volts nominal
- Emergency power systems
- Class 1, 2, and 3 remote control, signaling, and power-limited circuits
- Fire-protective signaling systems
- Communications systems

4.1.9 1910.331/1926.416 Scope

This article serves as an overview of the following articles and also provides a summary of the installations that this standard allows qualified and unqualified persons to work on or near, as well as the installations that this standard does *not* cover.

4.1.10 1910.332 Training

The training requirements contained in this article apply to employees who face a risk of electric shock. Some of the topics that appear in this article are:

- Content of training
- Additional requirements for unqualified persons
- Additional requirements for qualified persons
- Type of training

4.1.11 1910.333/1926.416–417
Selection and Use of Work Practices

This article covers the implementation of safety-related work practices necessary to prevent electrical shock and other related injuries to the employee. Some of the major topics addressed in this article are listed here:

- General
- Working on or near exposed de-energized parts
- Working on or near exposed energized parts

4.1.12 1910.334/1926.431
Use of Equipment

This article was added to reinforce the regulations pertaining to portable electrical equipment, test equipment, and load break switches. Major topics include:

- Portable electric equipment
- Electric power and lighting circuits
- Test instruments and equipment

4.1.13 1910.335/1926.416
Safeguards for Personnel Protection

This article covers the personnel protection requirements for employees in the vicinity of electrical hazards. It addresses regulations that protect personnel working on equipment as well as personnel working nearby. Some of the major topics are:

- Use of protective equipment
- Alerting techniques

Now that background topics have been covered and an overview of the OSHA electrical safety standards has been provided, it is time to move on to topics related directly to safety. As we discuss these topics, we will continually refer to the OSHA standards to identify the requirements that govern them.

OSHA 1926 Subpart K also addresses electrical safety requirements that are necessary for the practical safeguarding of employees involved in construction work.

4.2.0 Safety Philosophy and General Safety Precautions

The most important piece of safety equipment required when performing work in an electrical environment is common sense. All areas of electrical safety precautions and practices draw upon common sense and attention to detail. One of the most dangerous conditions in an electrical work area is a poor attitude toward safety.

 WARNING!
Only qualified individuals may work on electrical equipment. Your employer will determine who is qualified. Remember, your employer's safety rules must always be followed.

As stated in CFR 1910.333(a)/1926.403, safety-related work practices shall be employed to prevent electric shock or other injuries resulting from either direct or indirect electrical contact when work is performed near or on equipment or circuits that are or may be energized. The specific safety-related work practices shall be consistent with the nature and extent of the associated electrical hazards. The following are considered some of the basic and necessary attitudes and electrical safety precautions that lay the groundwork for a proper safety program. Before going on any electrical work assignment, these safety precautions should be reviewed and adhered to.

- *All work on electrical equipment should be done with circuits de-energized and cleared or grounded*—It is obvious that working on energized equipment is much more dangerous than working on equipment that is de-energized. Work on energized electrical equipment should be avoided if at all possible. CFR 1910.333(a)(1)/1926.403 states that live parts to which an employee may be exposed shall be de-energized before the employee works on or near them, unless the employer can demonstrate that de-energizing introduces additional or increased hazards or is not possible because of equipment design or operational limitations. Live parts that operate at less than 50 volts to ground need not be de-energized if there will be no increased exposure to electrical burns or to explosion due to electric arcs.

- *All conductors, buses, and connections should be considered energized until proven otherwise*—As stated in 1910.333(b)(1)/1926.417, conductors and parts of electrical equipment that have not been locked out or tagged out in accordance with this section should be considered energized. Routine operation of the circuit breakers and disconnect switches contained in a power distribution system can be hazardous if not approached in the right manner. Several basic precautions that can be observed in switchgear operations are:

  - Wear proper clothing made of 100 percent cotton or fire-resistant fabric.
  - Eye, face, and head protection should be worn. Turn your head away whenever closing devices.
  - Whenever operating circuit breakers in low-voltage or medium-voltage systems, always stand off to the side of the unit.
  - Always try to operate disconnect switches and circuit breakers under a no-load condition.
  - Never intentionally force an interlock on a system or circuit breaker.
  - Always verify what you are closing a device into; you could violate a lockout or close into a hard fault.

Often, a circuit breaker or disconnect switch is used for providing lockout on an electrical system. To ensure that a lockout is not violated, perform the following procedures when using the device as a lockout point:

- Breakers must always be locked out and tagged as discussed previously whenever you are working on a circuit that is tied to an energized breaker. Breakers capable of being opened and racked out to the disconnected position should have this done. Afterward, approved safety locks must be installed. The breaker may be removed from its cubicle completely to prevent unexpected mishaps. Always follow the standard rack-out and removal procedures that were supplied with the switchgear. Once removed, a sign must be hung on the breaker identifying its use as a lockout point, and approved safety locks must be installed when the breaker is used for isolation. In addition, the closing springs should be discharged.

- Some of the circuit breakers used are equipped with keyed interlocks for protection during operation. These locks are generally called *kirklocks* and are relied upon to ensure proper sequence of operation only. These are not to be used for the purpose of locking out a circuit or system. Where disconnects are installed for use in isolation, they should never be opened under load. When opening a disconnect manually, it should be done quickly with a positive force. Again, lockouts should be used when the disconnects are open.

- Whenever performing switching or fuse replacements, always use the protective equipment necessary to ensure personnel safety. *Never* make the assumption that because things have gone fine the last 999 times, they will not go wrong this time. Always prepare yourself for the worst case accident when performing switching.

- Whenever re-energizing circuits following maintenance or removal of a faulted component, extreme care should be used. Always verify that the equipment is in a condition to be re-energized safely. All connections should be insulated and all covers should be installed. Have all personnel stand clear of the area for the initial re-energization. *Never* assume everything is in perfect condition. Verify the conditions.

The following procedure is provided as a guideline for ensuring that equipment and systems will not be damaged by reclosing low-voltage circuit breakers into faults. If a low-voltage circuit breaker has opened for no apparent reason, perform the following:

Step 1 Verify that the equipment being supplied is not physically damaged and shows no obvious signs of overheating or fire.

Step 2 Make all appropriate tests to locate any faults.

Step 3 Reclose the feeder breaker. Stand off to the side when closing the breaker.

Step 4 If the circuit breaker trips again, do not attempt to reclose the breaker. In a plant environment, Electrical Engineering should be notified, and the cause of the trip should be isolated and repaired.

The same general procedure should be followed for fuse replacement, with the exception of transformer fuses. If a transformer fuse blows, the transformer and feeder cabling should be inspected and tested before reenergizing. A blown fuse to a transformer is very significant because it normally indicates an internal fault. Transformer failures are catastrophic in nature and can be extremely dangerous. If applicable, contact the in-plant Electrical Engineering Department prior to commencing any effort to reenergize a transformer.

Power must always be removed from a circuit when removing and installing fuses. The air break disconnects (or quick disconnects) provided on the upstream side of a large transformer must be opened prior to removing the transformer's fuses. Otherwise, severe arcing will occur as the fuse is removed. This arcing can result in personnel injury and equipment damage.

To replace fuses servicing circuits below 600 volts:

- Secure power to fuses or ensure all downstream loads have been disconnected.
- Always use a positive force to remove and install fuses.

When replacing fuses servicing systems above 600 volts:

- Open and lock out the disconnect switches.
- Unlock the fuse compartment.
- Verify that the fuses are de-energized.
- Attach the fuse removal hot stick to the fuse and remove it.

4.3.0 Electrical Regulations

OSHA has certain regulations that apply to job site electrical safety. These regulations include:

- All electrical work shall be in compliance with the latest NEC and OSHA standards.

NOTE

OSHA may not recognize the current edition of the NEC, which can sometimes cause problems; however, OSHA typically will *not* cite for any differences.

- The noncurrent-carrying metal parts of fixed, portable, and plug-connected equipment shall be grounded. It is best to choose **grounded tools.** However, portable tools and appliances protected by an approved system of double insulation need not be grounded. *Figure 7* shows an example of a **double-insulated/ ungrounded tool.**

- Extension cords shall be the three-wire type, shall be protected from damage, and shall not be fastened with staples or hung in a manner that could cause damage to the outer jacket or insulation. Never run an extension cord through a doorway or window that can pinch the cord. Also, never allow vehicles or equipment to drive over cords.

- Exposed lamps in temporary lights shall be guarded to prevent accidental contact, except where lamps are deeply recessed in the reflector. Temporary lights shall not be suspended, except in accordance with their listed labeling.

- Receptacles for attachment plugs shall be of an approved type and properly installed. Installation of the receptacle will be in accordance with the listing and labeling for each receptacle and shall be GFCI-protected if the setting is a temporarily wired construction site. If permanent receptacles are used with extension cords, then you must use GFCI protection.

- Each disconnecting means for motors and appliances and each service feeder or branch circuit at the point where it originates shall be legibly marked to indicate its purpose and voltage.

- Flexible cords shall be used in continuous lengths (no splices) and shall be of a type listed in *NEC Table 400-4.*

- Personnel safety ground fault protection for temporary construction is required. There are two methods for accomplishing this: an assured grounding program (this method is still used but should be used in conjunction with a GFCI program) or ground fault protection receptacles or breakers. Each employer will set the standard and method to be used. *Figure 8* shows a typical ground-fault circuit interrupter.

4.3.1 OSHA Lockout/Tagout Rule

OSHA released the 29 CFR 1926 lockout/tagout rule in December 1991. This rule covers the specific procedure to be followed for the "servicing and maintenance of machines and equipment in which the unexpected energization or startup of the machines or equipment, or releases of stored energy, could cause injury to employees. This standard establishes minimum performance requirements for the control of such hazardous energy."

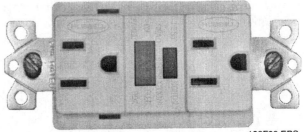

102F09.EPS

Figure 8 ◆ Typical GFCI.

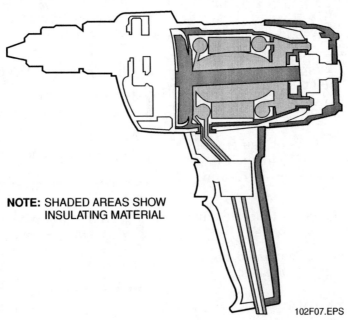

NOTE: SHADED AREAS SHOW INSULATING MATERIAL

102F07.EPS

Figure 7 ◆ Double-insulated electric drill.

The purpose of the OSHA procedure is to ensure that equipment is isolated from all potentially hazardous energy (e.g., electrical, mechanical, hydraulic, chemical, or thermal), and tagged and locked out before employees perform any servicing or maintenance activities in which the unexpected energization, startup, or release of stored energy could cause injury. All employees shall be instructed in the lockout/tagout procedure.

CAUTION

Although 99 percent of your work may be electrical, be aware that you may also need to lock out mechanical equipment.

The following is an example of a lockout/tagout procedure. Make sure to use the procedure that is specific to your employer or job site.

WARNING!

This procedure is provided for your information only. The OSHA procedure provides only the minimum requirements for lockouts/tagouts. Consult the lockout/tagout procedure for your company and the plant or job site at which you are working. Remember that your life could depend on the lockout/tagout procedure. It is critical that you use the correct procedure for your site.

I.   *Introduction*

A. This lockout/tagout procedure has been established for the protection of personnel from potential exposure to hazardous energy sources during construction, installation, service, and maintenance of electrical energy systems.

B. This procedure applies to and must be followed by all personnel who may be potentially exposed to the unexpected startup or release of hazardous energy (e.g., electrical, mechanical, pneumatic, hydraulic, chemical, or thermal).

Exception: This procedure does not apply to process and/or utility equipment or systems with cord and plug power supply systems when the cord and plug are the only source of hazardous energy, are removed from the source, and remain under the exclusive control of the authorized employee.

Exception: This procedure does not apply to troubleshooting (diagnostic) procedures and installation of electrical equipment and systems when the energy source cannot be de-energized because continuity of service is essential or shutdown of the system is impractical. Additional personal protective equipment for such work is required and the safe work practices identified for this work must be followed.

II. *Definitions*

• Affected employee—Any person working on or near equipment or machinery when maintenance or installation tasks are being performed by others during lockout/tagout conditions.

• Appointed authorized employee—Any person appointed by the job site supervisor to coordinate and maintain the security of a group lockout/tagout condition.

• Authorized employee—Any person authorized by the job site supervisor to use lockout/tagout procedures while working on electrical equipment.

• Authorized supervisor—The assigned job site supervisor who is in charge of coordination or procedures and maintenance of security of all lockout/tagout operations at the job site.

• Energy isolation device—An approved electrical disconnect switch capable of accepting approved lockout/tagout hardware for the purpose of isolating and securing a hazardous electrical source in an open or safe position.

• Lockout/tagout hardware—A combination of padlocks, danger tags, and other devices designed to attach to and secure electrical isolation devices.

III. *Training*

A. Each authorized supervisor, authorized employee, and appointed authorized employee shall receive initial and as-needed user-level training in lockout/tagout procedures.

B. Training is to include recognition of hazardous energy sources, the type and magnitude of energy sources in the workplace, and the procedures for energy isolation and control.

C. Retraining will be conducted on an as-needed basis whenever lockout/tagout procedures are changed or there is evidence that procedures are not being followed properly.

IV. *Protective Equipment and Hardware*

A. Lockout/tagout devices shall be used exclusively for controlling hazardous electrical energy sources.

B. All padlocks must be numbered and assigned to one employee only.

C. No duplicate or master keys will be made available to anyone except the site supervisor.

D. A current list with the lock number and authorized employee's name must be maintained by the site supervisor.

E. Danger tags must be of the standard white, red, and black DANGER—DO NOT OPERATE design and shall include the authorized employee's name, the date, and the appropriate network company (use permanent markers).

F. Danger tags must be used in conjunction with padlocks, as shown in *Figure 9*.

V. *Procedures*

A. Preparation for lockout/tagout:

1. Check the procedures to ensure that no changes have been made since you last used a lockout/ tagout.

2. Identify all authorized and affected employees involved with the pending lockout/tagout.

B. Sequence for lockout/tagout:

1. Notify all authorized and affected personnel that a lockout/tagout is to be used and explain the reason why.

2. Shut down the equipment or system using the normal OFF or STOP procedures.

3. Lock out energy sources and test disconnects to be sure they cannot be moved to the ON position and open the control cutout switch. If there is no cutout switch, block the magnet in the switch open position before working on electrically operated equipment/apparatus such as motors, relays, etc. Remove the control wire.

4. Lock and tag the required switches in the open position. Each authorized employee must affix a separate lock and tag. An example is shown in *Figure 10*.

5. Dissipate any stored energy by attaching the equipment or system to ground.

6. Verify that the test equipment is functional via a known power source.

7. Confirm that all switches are in the open position and use test equipment to verify that all parts are de-energized.

8. If it is necessary to temporarily leave the area, upon returning, retest to ensure that the equipment or system is still de-energized.

Figure 9 ◆ Lockout/tagout device.

Figure 10 ◆ Multiple lockout/tagout device.

C. Restoration of energy:
  1. Confirm that all personnel and tools, including shorting probes, are accounted for and removed from the equipment or system.
  2. Completely reassemble and secure the equipment or system.
  3. Replace and/or reactivate all safety controls.
  4. Remove locks and tags from isolation switches. Authorized employees must remove their own locks and tags.
  5. Notify all affected personnel that the lockout/tagout has ended and the equipment or system is energized.
  6. Operate or close isolation switches to restore energy.

VI. *Emergency Removal Authorization*
  A. In the event a lockout/tagout device is left secured, and the authorized employee is absent, or the key is lost, the authorized supervisor can remove the lockout/tagout device.
  B. The authorized employee must be informed that the lockout/tagout device has been removed.
  C. Written verification of the action taken, including informing the authorized employee of the removal, must be recorded in the job journal.

4.4.0 Other OSHA Regulations

There are other OSHA regulations that you need to be aware of on the job site. For example:

- OSHA requires the posting of hard hat areas. Be alert to those areas and always wear your hard hat properly, with the bill in front. Hard hats should be worn whenever overhead hazards exist, or there is the risk of exposure to electric shock or burns.
- You should wear safety shoes on all job sites. Keep them in good condition.
- Do not wear clothing with exposed metal zippers, buttons, or other metal fasteners. Avoid wearing loose-fitting or torn clothing.
- Protect your eyes. Your eyesight is threatened by many activities on the job site. Always wear safety glasses with full side shields. In addition, the job may also require protective equipment such as face shields or goggles.

4.4.1 *Testing for Voltage*

OSHA also requires that you inspect or test existing conditions before beginning work on electrical equipment or lines. Usually, you will use a voltmeter/sensor or voltage tester to do this. You should assume that all electrical equipment and lines are energized until you have determined that they are not. Do not proceed to work on or near energized parts until the operating voltage is determined.

After the electrical equipment to be worked on has been locked and tagged out, the equipment must be verified as de-energized before work can proceed. This section sets the requirements that must be met before any circuits or equipment can be considered de-energized. First, and most importantly, only qualified persons may verify that a circuit or piece of equipment is de-energized. Before approaching the equipment to be worked on, the qualified person shall operate the equipment's normal operating controls to check that the proper energy sources have been disconnected.

Upon opening a control enclosure, the qualified person shall note the presence of any components that may store electrical energy. Initially, these components should be avoided.

To verify that the lockout was adequate and the equipment is indeed de-energized, a qualified person must use appropriate test equipment to check for power, paying particular attention to induced voltages and unrelated feedback voltage.

Ensure that your testing equipment is working properly by performing the *live-dead-live* check before each use. To perform this test, first check your voltmeter on a known live voltage source. This known source must be in the same range as the electrical equipment you will be working on. Next, without changing scales on your voltmeter, check for the presence of power in the equipment you have locked out. Finally, to ensure that your voltmeter did not malfunction, check it again on the known live source. Performing this test will assure you that your voltage testing equipment is reliable.

In accordance with OSHA section 1910.333(b)(2)(iv)/1926.417(d)(4)(ii), if the circuit to be tested normally operates at more than 600 volts, the live-dead-live check must be performed.

Once it has been verified that power is not present, stored electrical energy that might endanger personnel must be released. A qualified person must use the proper devices to release the stored energy, such as using a shorting probe to discharge a capacitor.

5.0.0 ◆ LADDERS AND SCAFFOLDS

Ladders and scaffolds account for about half of the injuries from workplace electrocutions. The involuntary recoil that can occur when a person is shocked can cause the person to be thrown from a ladder or high place.

5.1.0 Ladders

Many job site accidents involve the misuse of ladders. Make sure to follow these general rules every time you use any ladder. Following these rules can prevent serious injury or even death.

- Before using any ladder, inspect it. Look for loose or missing rungs, cleats, bolts, or screws, and check for cracked, broken, or badly worn rungs, cleats, or side rails.
- If you find a ladder in poor condition, do not use it. Report it and tag it for repair or disposal.
- Never modify a ladder by cutting it or weakening its parts.
- Do not set up ladders where they may be run into by others, such as in doorways or walkways. If it is absolutely necessary to set up a ladder in such a location, protect the ladder with barriers.
- Do not increase a ladder's reach by standing it on boxes, barrels, or anything other than a flat surface.
- Check your shoes for grease, oil, or mud before climbing a ladder. These materials could make you slip.
- Always face the ladder and hold on with both hands when climbing up or down.
- Never lean out from the ladder. Keep your belt buckle centered between the rails. If something is out of reach, get down and move the ladder.

> **WARNING!**
> When performing electrical work, always use ladders made of nonconductive material.

5.1.1 Straight and Extension Ladders

There are some specific rules to follow when working with straight and extension ladders:

- Always place a straight ladder at the proper angle. The distance from the ladder feet to the base of the wall or support should be about one-fourth the working height of the ladder (see *Figure 11*).

- Secure straight ladders to prevent slipping. Use ladder shoes or hooks at the top and bottom. Another method is to secure a board to the floor against the ladder feet. For brief jobs, someone can hold the straight ladder.
- Side rails should extend above the top support point by at least 36 inches (see *Figure 11*).

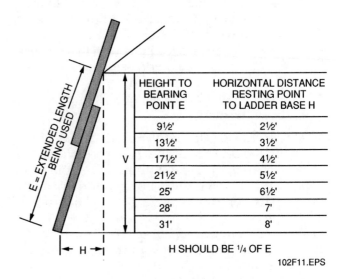

HEIGHT TO BEARING POINT E	HORIZONTAL DISTANCE RESTING POINT TO LADDER BASE H
9½'	2½'
13½'	3½'
17½'	4½'
21½'	5½'
25'	6½'
28'	7'
31'	8'

H SHOULD BE ¼ OF E

102F11.EPS

Figure 11 ◆ Straight ladder positioning.

- It takes two people to safely extend and raise an extension ladder. Extend the ladder only after it has been raised to an upright position.
- Never carry an extended ladder.
- Never use two ladders spliced together.
- Ladders should not be painted because paint can hide defects.

5.1.2 Step Ladders

There are also a few specific rules to use with a step ladder:

- Always open the step ladder all the way and lock the spreaders to avoid collapsing the ladder accidentally.
- Use a step ladder that is high enough for the job so that you do not have to reach. Get someone to hold the ladder if it is more than 10 feet high.
- Never use a step ladder as a straight ladder.
- Never stand on or straddle the top two rungs of a step ladder.
- Ladders are not shelves.

WARNING!
Do not leave tools or materials on a step ladder.

Sometimes you will need to move or remove protective equipment, guards, or guardrails to complete a task using a ladder. Remember, always replace what you moved or removed before leaving the area.

5.2.0 Scaffolds

Working on scaffolds also involves being safe and alert to hazards. In general, keep scaffold platforms clear of unnecessary material or scrap. These can become deadly tripping hazards or falling objects. Carefully inspect each part of the scaffold as it is erected. Your life may depend on it! Makeshift scaffolds have caused many injuries and deaths on job sites. Use only scaffolding and planking materials designed and marked for their specific use. When working on a scaffold, follow the established specific requirements set by OSHA for the use of fall protection. When appropriate, wear an approved harness with a lanyard properly anchored to the structure.

NOTE
The following requirements represent a compilation of the more stringent requirements of both CFR 1910 and CFR 1926.

The following are some of the basic OSHA rules for working safely on scaffolds:

- Scaffolds must be erected on sound, rigid footing that can carry the maximum intended load.
- Guardrails and toe boards must be installed on the open sides and ends of platforms that are higher than six feet above the ground or floor.
- There must be a screen of ½-inch maximum openings between the toe board and the midrail where persons are required to work or pass under the scaffold.
- Scaffold planks must extend over their end supports not less than six inches nor more than 12 inches and must be properly blocked.
- If the scaffold does not have built-in ladders that meet the standard, then it must have an attached ladder access.

- All employees must be trained to erect, dismantle, and use scaffold(s).
- Unless it is impossible, fall protection must be worn while building or dismantling all scaffolding.
- Work platforms must be completely decked for use by employees.
- Your hard hat is the first line of protection from falling objects. Your hard hat, however, cannot protect your shoulders, arms, back, or feet from the danger of falling objects. The person working below depends on those working above. When you are working above the ground, be careful so that material, including your tools, cannot fall from your work site. Use trash containers or other similar means to keep debris from falling and never throw or sweep material from above.

6.0.0 ◆ LIFTS, HOISTS, AND CRANES

On the job, you may be working in the operating area of lifts, hoists, or cranes. The following safety rules are for those who are working in the area with overhead equipment but are not directly involved in its operation.

- Stay alert and pay attention to the warning signals from operators.
- Never stand or walk under a load, regardless of whether it is moving or stationary.
- Always warn others of moving or approaching overhead loads.
- Never attempt to distract signal persons or operators of overhead equipment.
- Obey warning signs.
- Do not use equipment that you are not qualified to operate.

7.0.0 ◆ LIFTING

Back injuries cause many lost working hours every year. That is in addition to the misery felt by the person with the hurt back! Learn how to lift properly and size up the load. To lift, first stand close to the load. Then, squat down and keep your back straight. Get a firm grip on the load and keep the load close to your body. Lift by straightening your legs. Make sure that you lift with your legs and not your back. Do not be afraid to ask for help if you feel the load is too heavy. See *Figure 12* for an example of proper lifting.

Figure 12 ◆ Proper lifting.

102F12.EPS

8.0.0 ◆ BASIC TOOL SAFETY

When using any tools for the first time, read the operator's manual to learn the recommended safety precautions. If you are not certain about the operation of any tool, ask the advice of a more experienced worker. Before using a tool, you should know its function and how it works.

Always use the right tool for the job. Incorrectly using tools is one of the leading causes of job site injury. Using a hammer as a pry bar or a screwdriver as a chisel can cause damage to the tool and injure you in the process.

9.0.0 ◆ CONFINED SPACE ENTRY PROCEDURES

Occasionally, you may be required to do your work in a manhole or vault. If this is the case, there are some special safety considerations that you need to be aware of. For details on the subject of working in manholes and vaults, refer to 1910.146/1926.21(a)(6)(i) and (ii) and the *National Electrical Safety Code*. The general precautions are listed in the following paragraphs.

9.1.0 General Guidelines

A confined space includes (but is not limited to) any of the following: a manhole, boiler, tank, trench (four feet or deeper), tunnel, hopper, bin, sewer, vat, pipeline, vault, pit, air duct, or vessel. A confined space is identified as follows:

- It has limited entry and exit.
- It is not intended for continued human occupancy.
- It has poor ventilation.
- It has the potential for entrapment/engulfment.
- It has the potential for accumulating a dangerous atmosphere.
- Entry into a confined space occurs when any part of the body crosses the plane of entry. No employee shall enter a confined space unless the employee has been trained in confined space entry procedures.
- All hazards must be eliminated or controlled before a confined space entry is made.
- All appropriate personal protective equipment shall be worn at all times during confined space entry and work. The minimum required equipment includes a hard hat, safety glasses, full body harness, and life line.
- Ladders used for entry must be secured.
- A rescue retrieval system must be in use when entering confined spaces and while working in permit-required confined spaces (discussed later). Each employee must be capable of being rescued by the retrieval system.
- Only no-entry rescues will be performed by company personnel. Entry rescues will be performed by trained rescue personnel identified on the entry permit.
- The area outside the confined space must be properly barricaded, and appropriate warning signs must be posted.
- Entry permits can be issued and signed by job site supervisors only. Permits must be kept at the confined space while work is being conducted. At the end of the shift, the entry permits must be made part of the job journal and retained for one year.

9.2.0 Confined Space Hazard Review

Before determining the proper procedure for confined space entry, a hazard review shall be performed. The hazard review shall include, but not be limited to, the following conditions:

- The past and current uses of the confined space
- The physical characteristics of the space including size, shape, air circulation, etc.

- Proximity of the space to other hazards
- Existing or potential hazards in the confined space, such as:
  - Atmospheric conditions (oxygen levels, flammable/explosive levels, and/or toxic levels)
  - Presence/potential for liquids
  - Presence/potential for particulates
- Potential for mechanical/electrical hazards in the confined space (including work to be done)

Once the hazard review is completed, the supervisor, in consultation with the project managers and/or safety manager, shall classify the confined space as one of the following:

- A nonpermit confined space
- A permit-required confined space controlled by ventilation
- A permit-required confined space

Once the confined space has been properly classified, the appropriate entry and work procedures must be followed.

9.3.0 Entry and Work Procedures

Nonpermit spaces—A hazard review checklist must be completed before a confined space is designated as a *nonpermit space*. The checklist must be made part of the job journal, and a copy of the checklist must be sent to the safety office. A nonpermit confined space must meet the following criteria:

- There is no actual or potential atmospheric hazard.

> **NOTE**
> Using ventilation to clear the atmosphere does not meet this criterion

- There are no actual or potential physical, electrical, or mechanical hazards capable of causing harm or death.

Documentation using the hazards checklist and entry permit forms, and verifying that the confined space is hazard-free, must be made available to employees and maintained at the confined space while work is conducted. If it is necessary to enter the space to verify that it is hazard-free or to eliminate hazards, entry must be made under the requirements of a permit-required space.

An employee may enter the confined space using the minimum fall protection of harness and anchored life line. Once in the space, the employee may disconnect the life line and reconnect it before exiting.

If the work being done creates a hazard, the space must be reclassified as a permit-required space. If any other atmospheric, physical, electrical, or mechanical hazards arise, the space is to be evacuated immediately and reclassified as a permit-required entry space.

Permit-required spaces controlled by ventilation—A hazard review checklist must be completed before a confined space is designated as a *permit-required space controlled by ventilation*. The checklist must be made part of the job journal, and a copy of the checklist must be sent to the safety office. A permit-required confined space controlled by ventilation must meet the following criteria:

- The only hazard in the confined space is an actual/potential atmospheric hazard.
- Continuous forced-air ventilation maintains a safe atmosphere (i.e., within the limits designated on the entry permit).
- Inspection and monitoring data are documented.
- No other physical, electrical, or mechanical hazard exists.

An entry permit must be issued and signed by the job site supervisor and be kept at the confined space while work is being conducted.

Atmospheric testing must be conducted before entry into the confined space and in the following order:

- Oxygen content
- Flammable gases and vapors
- Toxic contaminants

Unacceptable atmospheric conditions must be eliminated with forced air ventilation. If continuous forced air ventilation is required to maintain an acceptable atmosphere, employees may not enter until forced air ventilation has eliminated any hazardous atmosphere. Periodic atmospheric testing must be conducted during the work shift to ensure that the atmosphere remains clear. Periodic monitoring must be documented on the entry permit. If atmospheric conditions change, employees must exit the confined space immediately, and atmospheric conditions must be re-evaluated. Continuous communication must be maintained with the employees working in the confined space.

If hot work is to be performed, a hot work permit is required, and the hazard analysis must document that the hot work does not create additional hazards that are not controlled by ventila-

tion only. Hot work is defined as any work that produces arcs, sparks, flames, heat, or other sources of ignition.

A rescue plan using trained rescue personnel must be in place prior to the start of work in the confined space. All employees should be aware of the rescue plan and how to activate it.

Permit-required confined spaces—A hazard review checklist must be completed before a confined space is designated as a *permit-required confined space*. The checklist must be made part of the job journal, and a copy must be sent to the safety office. A permit-required space meets the following criteria:

- There are actual/potential hazards, other than a hazardous atmosphere.
- Ventilation alone does not eliminate atmospheric hazards.
- Conditions in and around the confined space must be continually monitored.

An entry permit must be issued and signed by the job site supervisor. The permit is to be kept at the confined space while work is being performed in the space.

Atmospheric testing must be conducted before entry into the confined space and in the following order:

- Oxygen content
- Flammable gases and contaminants
- Toxic contaminants

Unacceptable atmospheric conditions must be eliminated/controlled prior to employee entry. Methods of elimination may include isolation, purging, flushing, or ventilating. Continuous atmospheric monitoring must be conducted while employees are in the confined space. Triggering of a monitoring alarm means employees should evacuate the confined space immediately. Any other physical hazards must be eliminated or controlled by engineering and work practice controls before entry. Additional personal protective equipment should be used as a follow-up to the above methods. An attendant, whose job it is to monitor conditions in and around the confined space and to maintain contact with the employees in the space, must be stationed outside the confined space for the duration of entry operations.

If hot work is to be performed, a hot work permit is required, and the hazard analysis must document the additional hazards and precautions to be considered.

A rescue plan using trained rescue personnel must be in place before confined space entry. The attendant should be aware of the rescue plan and have the means to activate it.

10.0.0 ◆ FIRST AID

You should be prepared in case an accident does occur on the job site or anywhere else. First aid training that includes certification classes in CPR and artificial respiration could be the best insurance you and your fellow workers ever receive. Make sure that you know where first aid is available at your job site. Also, make sure you know the accident reporting procedure. Each job site should also have a first aid manual or booklet giving easy-to-find emergency treatment procedures for various types of injuries. Emergency first aid telephone numbers should be readily available to everyone on the job site. Refer to CFR 1910.151/1926.23 and 1926.50 for specific requirements.

11.0.0 ◆ SOLVENTS AND TOXIC VAPORS

Many solvents give off vapors that are toxic enough to make people temporarily ill or even cause permanent injury. Many solvents are skin and eye irritants. Solvents can also be systemic poisons when they are swallowed or absorbed through the skin.

Solvents in spray or aerosol form are dangerous in another way. Small aerosol particles or solvent vapors mix with air to form a combustible mixture with oxygen. The slightest spark could cause an explosion in a confined area because the mix is perfect for fast ignition. There are procedures and methods for using, storing, and disposing of most solvents and chemicals. These procedures are normally found in the Material Safety Data Sheets (MSDSs) available at your facility.

An MSDS is required for all materials that could be hazardous to personnel or equipment. These sheets contain information on the material,

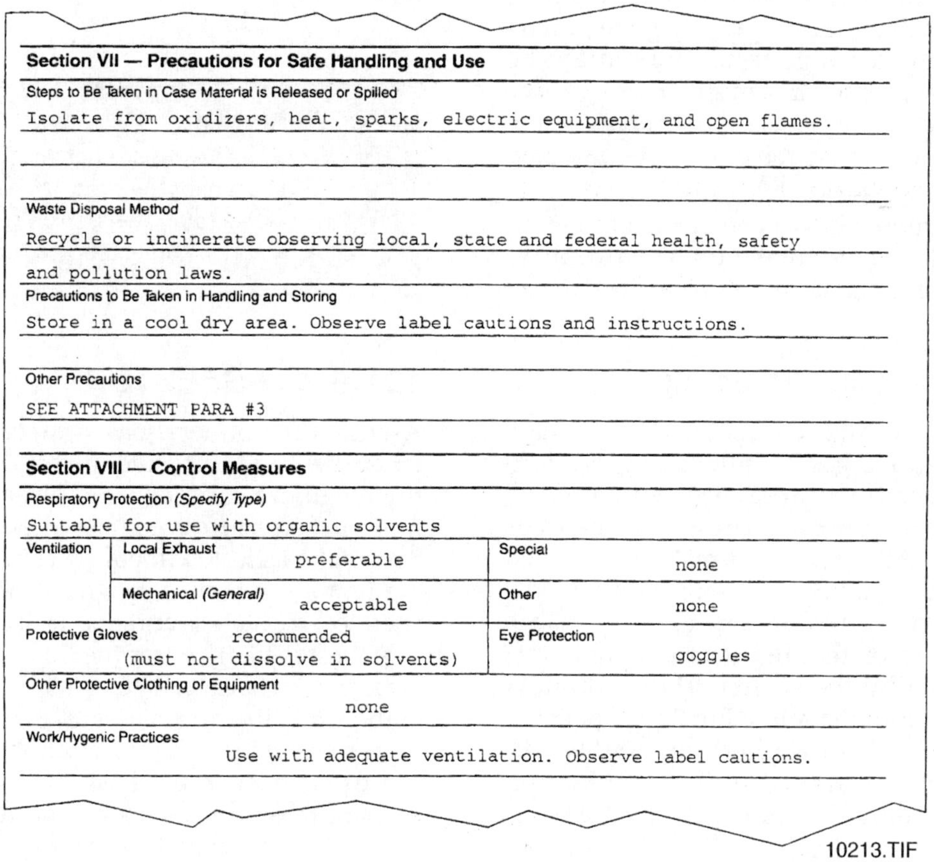

Section VII — Precautions for Safe Handling and Use

Steps to Be Taken in Case Material is Released or Spilled
Isolate from oxidizers, heat, sparks, electric equipment, and open flames.

Waste Disposal Method
Recycle or incinerate observing local, state and federal health, safety and pollution laws.

Precautions to Be Taken in Handling and Storing
Store in a cool dry area. Observe label cautions and instructions.

Other Precautions
SEE ATTACHMENT PARA #3

Section VIII — Control Measures

Respiratory Protection (Specify Type)
Suitable for use with organic solvents

| Ventilation | Local Exhaust | preferable | Special | none |
| | Mechanical (General) | acceptable | Other | none |

| Protective Gloves | recommended (must not dissolve in solvents) | Eye Protection | goggles |

Other Protective Clothing or Equipment
none

Work/Hygenic Practices
Use with adequate ventilation. Observe label cautions.

10213.TIF

Figure 13 ◆ Portion of an MSDS.

such as the manufacturer and chemical makeup. As much information as possible is kept on the hazardous material to prevent a dangerous situation; or, in the event of a dangerous situation, the information is used to rectify the problem in as safe a manner as possible. See *Figure 13* for an example of procedures you may find on the job.

11.1.0 Precautions When Using Solvents

It is always best to use a nonflammable, nontoxic solvent whenever possible. However, any time solvents are used, it is essential that your work area be adequately ventilated and that you wear the appropriate personal protective equipment:

- A chemical face shield with chemical goggles should be used to protect the eyes and skin from sprays and splashes.
- A chemical apron should be worn to protect your body from sprays and splashes. Remember that some solvents are acid-based. If they come into contact with your clothes, solvents can eat through your clothes to your skin.
- A paper filter mask does not stop vapors; it is used only for nuisance dust. In situations where a paper mask does not supply adequate protection, chemical cartridge respirators might be needed. These respirators can stop many vapors if the correct cartridge is selected. In areas where ventilation is a serious problem, a self-contained breathing apparatus (SCBA) must be used.
- Make sure that you have been given a full medical evaluation and that you are properly trained in using respirators at your site.

11.2.0 Respiratory Protection

Protection against high concentrations of dust, mist, fumes, vapors, gases, and/or oxygen deficiency is provided by appropriate respirators.

Appropriate respiratory protective devices should be used for the hazardous material involved and the extent and nature of the work performed.

An air-purifying respirator is, as its name implies, a respirator that removes contaminants from air inhaled by the wearer. The respirators may be divided into the following types: particulate-removing (mechanical filter), gas- and vapor-removing (chemical filter), and a combination of particulate-removing and gas- and vapor-removing.

Particulate-removing respirators are designed to protect the wearer against the inhalation of particulate matter in the ambient atmosphere. They

may be designed to protect against a single type of particulate, such as pneumoconiosis-producing and nuisance dust, toxic dust, metal fumes or mist, or against various combinations of these types.

Gas- and vapor-removing respirators are designed to protect the wearer against the inhalation of gases or vapors in the ambient atmosphere. They are designated as gas masks, chemical cartridge respirators (nonemergency gas respirators), and self-rescue respirators. They may be designed to protect against a single gas such as chlorine; a single type of gas, such as acid gases; or a combination of types of gases, such as acid gases and organic vapors.

If you are required to use a respiratory protective device, you must be evaluated by a physician to ensure that you are physically fit to use a respirator. You must then be fitted and thoroughly instructed in the respirator's use.

Any employee whose job entails having to wear a respirator must keep his face free of facial hair in the seal area.

Respiratory protective equipment must be inspected regularly and maintained in good condition. Respiratory equipment must be properly cleaned on a regular basis and stored in a sanitary, dustproof container.

WARNING!
Do not use any respirator unless you have been fitted for it and thoroughly understand its use. As with all safety rules, follow your employer's respiratory program and policies.

12.0.0 ◆ ASBESTOS

Asbestos is a mineral-based material that is resistant to heat and corrosive chemicals. Depending on the chemical composition, asbestos fibers may range in texture from coarse to silky. The properties that make asbestos fibers so valuable to industry are its high tensile strength, flexibility, heat and chemical resistance, and good frictional properties.

Asbestos fibers enter the body by inhalation of airborne particles or by ingestion and can become embedded in the tissues of the respiratory or digestive systems. Years of exposure to asbestos can cause numerous disabling or fatal diseases. Among these diseases are asbestosis, an emphysema-like condition; lung cancer; mesothelioma, a cancerous tumor that spreads rapidly in the cells of membranes covering the lungs and body organs; and gastrointestinal cancer.

12.1.0 Monitoring

Employers who have a workplace or work operation covered by OSHA 3096 (*Asbestos Standard for the Construction Industry*) must perform initial monitoring to determine the airborne concentrations of asbestos to which employees may be exposed. If employers can demonstrate that employee exposures are below the action level and/or excursion limit by means of objective or historical data, initial monitoring is not required. If initial monitoring indicates that employee exposures are below the action level and/or excursion limit, then periodic monitoring is not required. Within regulated areas, the employer must conduct daily monitoring unless all workers are equipped with supplied-air respirators operated in the positive-pressure mode. If daily monitoring by statistically reliable measurements indicates that employee exposures are below the action level and/or excursion limit, then no further monitoring is required for those employees whose exposures are represented by such monitoring. Employees must be given the chance to observe monitoring, and affected employees must be notified as soon as possible following the employer's receipt of the results.

12.2.0 Regulated Areas

The employer must establish a regulated area where airborne concentrations of asbestos exceed or can reasonably be expected to exceed the locally determined exposure limit, or when certain types of construction work are performed, such as cutting asbestos-cement sheets and removing asbestos-containing floor tiles. Only authorized personnel may enter regulated areas. All persons entering a regulated area must be supplied with an appropriate respirator. No smoking, eating, drinking, or applying cosmetics is permitted in regulated areas. Warning signs must be displayed at each regulated area and must be posted at all approaches to regulated areas. These signs must bear the following information:

> ### DANGER
> ASBESTOS
> CANCER AND LUNG DISEASE HAZARD
> AUTHORIZED PERSONNEL ONLY
> RESPIRATORS AND PROTECTIVE CLOTHING
> ARE REQUIRED IN THIS AREA

Where feasible, the employer shall establish negative-pressure enclosures before commencing asbestos removal, demolition, and renovation operations. The setup and monitoring requirements for negative-pressure enclosures are as follows:

- A competent person shall be designated to set up the enclosure and ensure its integrity and supervise employee activity within the enclosure.
- Exemptions are given for small-scale, short-duration maintenance or renovation operations.
- The employer shall conduct daily monitoring of the exposure of each employee who is assigned to work within a regulated area. Short-term monitoring is required whenever asbestos concentrations will not be uniform throughout the workday and where high concentrations of asbestos may reasonably be expected to be released or created in excess of the local limit.

In addition, warning labels must be affixed on all asbestos products and to all containers of asbestos products, including waste containers, that may be in the workplace. The label must include the following information:

> ### DANGER
> CONTAINS ASBESTOS FIBERS
> AVOID CREATING DUST
> CANCER AND LUNG DISEASE HAZARD

12.3.0 Methods of Compliance

To the extent feasible, engineering and work practice controls must be used to reduce employee exposure to within the permissible exposure limit (PEL). The employer must use one or more of the following control methods to achieve compliance:

- Local exhaust ventilation equipped with high-efficiency particulate air (HEPA) filter dust collection systems
- General ventilation systems
- Vacuum cleaners equipped with HEPA filters
- Enclosure or isolation of asbestos dust-producing processes
- Use of wet methods, wetting agents, or removal encapsulants during asbestos handling, mixing, removal, cutting, application, and cleanup
- Prompt disposal of asbestos-containing wastes in leak-tight containers

Prohibited work practices include the following:

- The use of high-speed abrasive disc saws that are not equipped with appropriate engineering controls
- The use of compressed air to remove asbestos-containing materials, unless the compressed air is used in conjunction with an enclosed ventilation system

Where engineering and work practice controls have been instituted but are insufficient to reduce employee exposure to a level that is at or below the PEL, respiratory protection must be used to supplement these controls.

13.0.0 ◆ BATTERIES

Working around wet cell batteries can be dangerous if the proper precautions are not taken. Batteries often give off hydrogen gas as a by-product. When hydrogen mixes with air, the mixture can be explosive in the proper concentration. For this reason, smoking is strictly prohibited in battery rooms, and only insulated tools should be used. Proper ventilation also reduces the chance of explosion in battery areas. Follow your company's procedures for working near batteries. Also, ensure that your company's procedures are followed for lifting heavy batteries.

13.1.0 Acids

Batteries also contain acid, which will eat away human skin and many other materials. Personal protective equipment for battery work typically includes chemical aprons, sleeves, gloves, face shields, and goggles to prevent acid from contacting skin and eyes. Follow your site procedures for dealing with spills of these materials. Also, know the location of first aid when working with these chemicals.

CAUTION

If you come in contact with battery acid, report it immediately to your supervisor.

13.2.0 Wash Stations

Because of the chance that battery acid may contact someone's eyes or skin, wash stations are located near battery rooms. Do not connect or disconnect batteries without proper supervision. Everyone who works in the area should know where the nearest wash station is and how to use it. Battery acid should be flushed from the skin and eyes with large amounts of water or with a neutralizing solution.

14.0.0 ◆ PCBs

Polychlorinated biphenyls (PCBs) are chemicals that were marketed under various trade names as a liquid insulator/cooler in older transformers. In addition to being used in older transformers, PCBs are also found in some large capacitors and in the small ballast transformers used in street lighting and ordinary fluorescent light fixtures. Disposal of these materials is regulated by the EPA and must be done through a regulated disposal company; use extreme caution and follow your facility procedures.

WARNING!

Do not come into contact with PCBs. They present a variety of serious health risks, including lung damage and cancer.

15.0.0 ◆ FALL PROTECTION

Fall protection is extremely important on the job site. The following sections cover many of the relevant fall protection procedures and systems you will use.

15.1.0 Fall Protection Procedures

Fall protection must be used when employees are on a walking or working surface that is six feet or more above a lower level and has an unprotected edge or side. The areas covered include, but are not limited to:

- Finished and unfinished floors or mezzanines
- Temporary or permanent walkways/ramps
- Finished or unfinished roof areas
- Elevator shafts and hoist-ways
- Floor, roof, or walkway holes
- Working six feet or more above dangerous equipment

Exception: If the dangerous equipment is unguarded, fall protection must be used at all heights regardless of the fall distance.

Fall protection is not required during inspection, investigation, or assessment of job site conditions before or after construction work.

These fall protection guidelines do not apply to the following areas. Fall protection for these areas is located in the subparts cited in parentheses.

- Cranes and derricks (1926 subpart N/1910 subpart N)
- Scaffolding (1926 subpart L/1910 subpart D)
- Electrical power transmission and distribution (1926 subpart V/1910 subpart R)
- Stairways and ladders (1926 subpart X/1910 subpart D)
- Excavations (1926 subpart P)

Fall protection must be selected in order of preference as listed below. Selection of a lower-level system, such as safety nets, must be based only on feasibility of protection. The list includes, but is not limited to, the following:

- Guardrail systems and hole covers
- Personal fall arrest systems
- Safety nets

These fall protection procedures are designed to warn, isolate, restrict, or protect workers from a potential fall hazard.

15.2.0 Types of Fall Protection Systems

The type of system selected shall depend on the fall hazards associated with the work to be performed. First, a hazard analysis shall be conducted by the job site supervisor prior to the start of work. Based on the hazard analysis, the job site supervisor and project manager, in consultation with the safety manager, will select the appropriate fall protection system. All employees will be instructed in the use of the fall protection system before starting work.

Summary

Safety must be your concern at all times so that you do not become either the victim of an accident or the cause of one. Safety requirements and safe work practices are provided by OSHA and your employer. It is essential that you adhere to all safety requirements and follow your employer's safe work practices and procedures. Also, you must be able to identify the potential safety hazards of your job site. The consequences of unsafe job site conduct can often be expensive, painful, or even deadly. Report any unsafe act or condition immediately to your supervisor. You should also report all work-related accidents, injuries, and illnesses to your supervisor immediately. Remember, proper construction techniques, common sense, and a good safety attitude will help to prevent accidents, injuries, and fatalities.

Review Questions

1. The most life-threatening hazards on a construction site include all of the following *except* _____.
   a. falls
   b. electrocution
   c. being crushed or struck by falling or flying objects
   d. chemical exposure

2. If a person's heart begins to fibrillate due to an electrical shock, the solution is to _____.
   a. leave the person alone until the fibrillation stops
   b. administer heart massage
   c. use the Heimlich maneuver
   d. have a qualified person use emergency defibrillation equipment

3. The majority of injuries due to electrical shock are caused by _____.
   a. electrically operated hand tools
   b. contact with low-voltage conductors
   c. contact with high-voltage conductors
   d. lightning

4. Class 0 rubber gloves are used when working with voltages less than _____.
   a. 1,000 volts
   b. 7,500 volts
   c. 17,500 volts
   d. 26,500 volts

5. An important use of a hot stick is to _____.
   a. keep cattle moving
   b. keep your hands warm
   c. replace fuses
   d. test circuits to see if they are live

6. The following statement correctly describes a double-insulated power tool.
   a. There is twice as much insulation on the power cord.
   b. It can safely be used in place of a grounded tool.
   c. It is made entirely of plastic or other non-conducting material.
   d. The entire tool is covered in rubber.

7. The following applies in a lockout/tagout procedure.
   a. Only the supervisor can install lockout/tagout devices.
   b. If several employees are involved, the lockout/tagout equipment is applied only by the first employee to arrive at the disconnect.
   c. Lockout/tagout devices applied by one employee can be removed by another employee as long as it can be verified that the first employee has left for the day.
   d. Lockout/tagout devices are installed by every authorized employee involved in the work.

8. The proper distance from the feet of a straight ladder to the wall is _____.
   a. one-fourth the working height of the ladder
   b. one-half the height of the ladder
   c. three feet
   d. one-fourth of the square root of the height of the ladder

9. The minimum and maximum distances (in inches) that a scaffold plank can extend beyond its end support are _____.
   a. 4, 8
   b. 6, 10
   c. 6, 12
   d. 8, 12

10. The following condition applies to a permit-required confined space, but not to a permit-required space controlled by ventilation.
    a. A hazard review checklist must be completed.
    b. An attendant, whose job is to monitor the space, must be stationed outside the space.
    c. Unacceptable atmospheric conditions must be eliminated.
    d. Atmospheric testing must be conducted.

Trade Terms Introduced in This Module

Double-insulated/ungrounded tool: An electrical tool that is constructed so that the case is insulated from electrical energy. The case is made of a nonconductive material.

Fibrillation: Very rapid irregular contractions of the muscle fibers of the heart that result in the heartbeat and pulse going out of rhythm with each other.

Grounded tool: An electrical tool with a three-prong plug at the end of its power cord or some other means to ensure that stray current travels to ground without passing through the body of the user. The ground plug is bonded to the conductive frame of the tool.

Ground fault circuit interrupter (GFCI): A protective device that functions to de-energize a circuit or portion thereof within an established period of time when a current to ground exceeds some predetermined value that is less than that required to operate the overcurrent protective device of the supply circuit.

Polychlorinated biphenyls (PCBs): Toxic chemicals that may be contained in liquids used to cool certain types of large transformers and capacitors.

Additional Resources

This module is intended to present thorough resources for task training. The following reference works are suggested for further study. These are optional materials for continued education rather than for task training.

*29 CFR Parts 1900-1910, Standards for General Industry.*Occupational Safety and Health Administration, U.S. Department of Labor.

29 CFR Parts 1926, Standards for the Construction Industry. Occupational Safety and Health Administration, U.S. Department of Labor.

National Electrical Code Handbook. Quincey, MA: National Fire Protection Association.

National Electrical Safety Code. Quincey, MA: National Fire Protection Association.

Figure Credits

Veronica Westfall   102F02, 102F08, 102F09

NCCER CRAFT TRAINING USER UPDATES

The NCCER makes every effort to keep these textbooks up-to-date and free of technical errors. We appreciate your help in this process. If you have an idea for improving this textbook, or if you find an error, a typographical mistake, or an inaccuracy in the NCCER's Craft Training textbooks, please write us, using this form or a photocopy. Be sure to include the exact module number, page number, a detailed description, and the correction, if applicable. Your input will be brought to the attention of the Technical Review Committee. Thank you for your assistance.

Instructors – If you found that additional materials were necessary in order to teach this module effectively, please let us know so that we may include them in the Equipment and Materials list in the Instructor's Guide.

Write: Curriculum Revision and Development Department
National Center for Construction Education and Research
P.O. Box 141104, Gainesville, FL 32614-1104

Fax: 352-334-0932

E-mail: curriculum@nccer.org

Craft _____ Module Name _____

Copyright Date _____ Module Number _____ Page Number(s) _____

Description _____

_____

_____

_____

(Optional) Correction _____

_____

_____

(Optional) Your Name and Address _____

_____

_____

Power Tools for Instrumentation

COURSE MAP

This course map shows all of the modules in the first level of the Instrumentation curriculum. The suggested training order begins at the bottom and proceeds up. Skill levels increase as you advance on the course map. The local Training Program Sponsor may adjust the training order.

INSTRUMENTATION LEVEL ONE

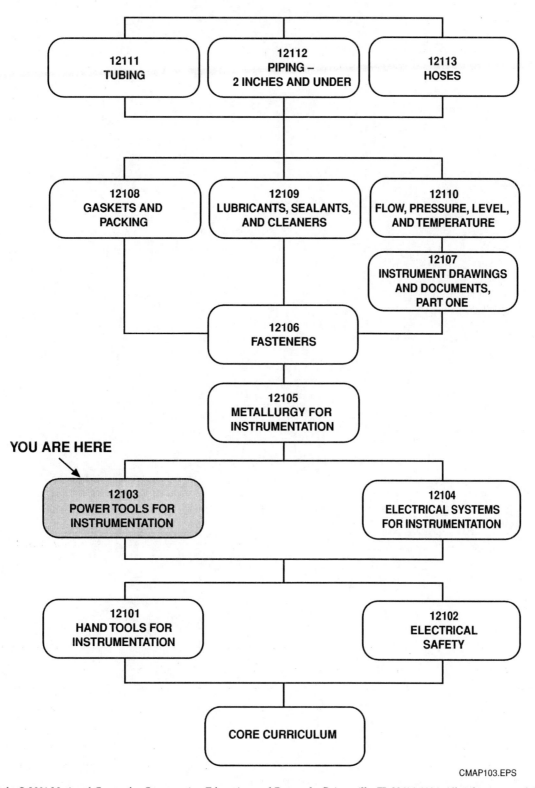

CMAP103.EPS

Figures

Tables

Power Tools for Instrumentation

Objectives

When you have completed this module, you will be able to do the following:

1. Identify power tools used in instrumentation.
2. Select the proper power tool for a job.
3. Inspect the condition of the power tool.
4. Properly maintain power tools.
5. Use power tools safely.

Prerequisites

Before you begin this module, it is recommended that you successfully complete the following modules: Core Curriculum; Instrumentation Level One, Modules 12101 and 12102.

Required Trainee Materials

1. Pencil and paper
2. Appropriate personal protective equipment

1.0.0 ◆ INTRODUCTION

The instrumentation craftsperson must use the correct tools to do the work quickly, accurately, and safely. Choosing the proper tools and knowing how to use them saves time and improves the quality of the work.

This module presents some of the common types of the following power tools:

- Electric and pneumatic power hammers and drills
- Electric soldering guns and irons
- Hydraulic knockout punches
- Electric threading machines
- Powder-actuated tools

Power tools, such as drills, saws, and grinders, are covered more extensively in later modules.

2.0.0 ◆ ELECTRIC AND PNEUMATIC POWER HAMMERS AND DRILLS

Anchor bolts are commonly used to secure equipment to the floor, wall, or ceiling. The holes for these anchors are bored in concrete or brick. Electric and pneumatic hammers and drills are often used to bore holes for anchor bolts and other fastening devices.

A variety of drill bits, chisels, and other types of tools can be attached to electric and pneumatic hammers and drills. Each of these attachments is designed to perform a specific job. While it takes a little practice to properly handle and use power hammers and drills, they are very useful and effective tools for many instrumentation jobs.

2.1.0 Safety Precautions

The following safety precautions should be followed when working with electric and pneumatic power hammers and drills.

- Never remove the third prong from the electric plug of any power tool. In order to protect yourself from any dangers associated with electrical shock caused by power tools, you should use **double-insulated tools** and only plug power tools into GFCI-protected circuits or receptacles.
- Closely inspect the plug and power cord of electrical tools to make sure they are not damaged.
- Always unplug an electrical tool when servicing to protect against an electric shock and accidental operation.

- Do not use the power cord to carry an electrical tool or to pull the plug out of the outlet. This can damage the cord and plug, and could cause the tool to become an electrical hazard.
- Do not operate an electrical tool while standing in a wet or damp area without ground fault protection.
- Do not operate an electrical tool in areas containing gasoline, naphtha, or other flammable gases. A small spark from the tool's motor can set off these explosive gases and cause serious injury.
- Wear an approved breathing apparatus to avoid breathing the fine dust and powders created during the use of power tools.
- Always wear earplugs when using power tools to help mask the noise caused by the tools and the bit rotating or pounding against the work.
- Keep the work area clean so loose debris does not catch in the moving parts of the power tools.
- Always wear proper eye protection, and keep the lenses clean.
- Remove the chuck key from the chuck before using a power hammer or drill. Do not use a screwdriver in place of a chuck key.
- Keep your finger off the throttle or switch when the electrical power tool is connected to the power supply. Don't touch the throttle or switch until you are ready to work.
- Never wear loose clothing while operating a power tool. Clothing can get caught in the rotating bit, causing you to lose control of the tool.
- When working with power tools, be absolutely certain that all fittings are securely tightened and drill bits, chisels, or other removable parts are locked in place.
- Keep hoses and fittings on pneumatic tools in good condition.
- Always inspect bits carefully before using. Surface cracks or chips may indicate a defective bit that could fail under load.
- Keep drill bits sharp and properly stored when not in use.

2.2.0 Electric Hammers

There are two basic types of portable electric hammers: the **percussion** hammer and the **rotary** hammer. Electric percussion hammers deliver sharp, rapid blows that are measured in **blows per minute (bpm)**, often called the *hammering rate*. Electric percussion hammers come in a wide range of bpm capabilities to perform different jobs.

The rotary hammer, in addition to delivering hammering blows, provides a rotating action. Rotary hammers come in a variety of types with a wide range of capacities in blows per minute and **revolutions per minute (rpm)**.

To ensure proper performance under load, the motor and other parts of an electric hammer should be lubricated in accordance with the manufacturer's recommendations. Vibration during operation of an electric hammer may cause screws to loosen, so they need to be checked periodically to make sure that they are tight and properly installed. It is also important to keep the vents of an electric hammer open and free from obstruction to avoid overheating the motor. If these vent holes become clogged with dust and dirt, carefully blow them out with an air gun.

2.2.1 Electric Percussion Hammers

The electric percussion hammer pounds the bit into the work through a direct spring action that transmits a hammer blow to the bit. An electric percussion hammer is shown in *Figure 1*.

A percussion hammer is used primarily to drill holes in concrete and masonry for installation of conduit, pipe, and anchors. It can also be used to chip, channel, and chisel brickwork, and for demolition work.

A star drill bit is usually used with the percussion hammer, but percussion carbide-tipped bits are also available. Since a percussion hammer does not rotate, a special extension handle is often attached to the hammer. The extension handle allows the operator to rotate the bit by hand during the hammering process. The extension handle and chuck are a complete assembly which is inserted into the hammer and locked in place.

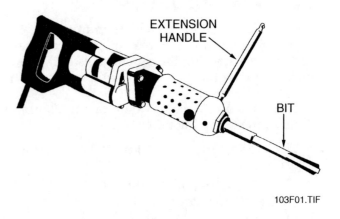

103F01.TIF

Figure 1 ◆ Electric percussion hammer.

2.2.2 Electric Rotary Hammers

The electric rotary hammer (*Figure 2*) can be used for hammering, drilling, or for hammering and drilling at the same time.

An electric rotary hammer is used primarily for drilling holes in concrete or masonry. On some models of electric rotary hammers, an adapter is fitted into the nose of the hammer when hammering action only is needed. The adapter keeps the bit from rotating. Many rotary hammers can also be set to operate without the hammering action to drill metal or wood. When used for drilling only, a chuck adapter is inserted into the nose, and a drill chuck is mounted on the adapter.

When drilling holes in concrete or masonry, a carbide-tipped bit is normally used with a rotary hammer. An adjustable depth gauge rod is mounted on the side of the housing. The depth gauge is used to set the required depth for the hole to be drilled.

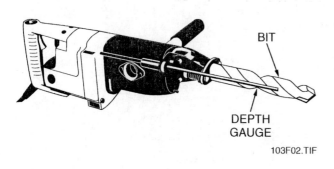

Figure 2 ◆ Electric rotary hammer.

2.3.0 Pneumatic Hammers and Rotary Drills

There are two basic types of portable pneumatic hammers and drills: the pneumatic rotary drill and the pneumatic hammer. Pneumatic rotary drills are available in a variety of rpm speeds, with higher speeds used for drilling light metals and materials and lower speeds for heavy work. Pneumatic rotary drills provide only rotary action, no hammering motion. Pneumatic hammers deliver sharp, rapid hammering blows to the work, and may also include a rotating motion.

Most portable pneumatic drills and hammers are designed to operate at 90 psi air **pressure**. Air hoses and fittings should be of the type and size recommended by the manufacturer. Hoses and fittings should be checked frequently for damage and leaks. Leaking hoses or fittings reduce the air supply pressure, which hampers the operating efficiency of the drill or hammer.

Pneumatic drills and hammers require a mist of **pneumatic oil** in the air supply to lubricate them. A typical air supply system contains a filter, a regulator, and a lubricator, as shown in *Figure 3*. After the air is filtered and the pressure is set by the regulator, pneumatic oil is added to the air as it leaves the lubricator and goes to the pneumatic tool.

After using a pneumatic drill or hammer, disconnect the air supply, clean the housing, and always make sure that the air line connections are free of dirt. Coil the hoses carefully with no kinks or bends, and properly store the hoses by hanging them on a hook. Replace any fittings that have damaged or stripped threads. Occasionally, oil the throttle mechanism to keep it operating smoothly.

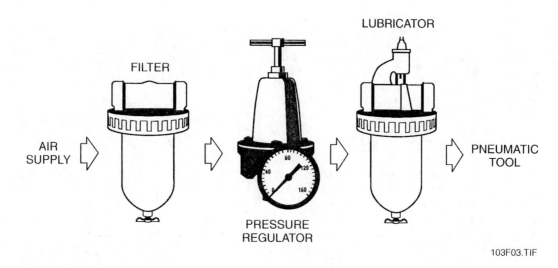

Figure 3 ◆ Pneumatic tool lubrication components.

2.3.1 Pneumatic Rotary Drills

Pneumatic rotary drills are made in four basic types: pistol-grip, in-line, heavy-duty, and right-angle, as shown in *Figure 4*.

The pistol-grip design is considered a light-duty drill. Pistol-grip drills normally accept bits up to ½ inch in diameter. An in-line drill is typically used for medium- to heavy-duty drilling. The heavy-duty drill typically holds 3 inch and larger bits for big jobs. When vertical clearance is tight, a right-angle drill is often used to help reach the work.

A rotary air motor turns the bit in a pneumatic rotary drill. The drill may be constant speed, dual speed, or variable speed. The variable speed motors in pneumatic drills typically operate in a range from 0 to 20,000 rpm. The variable speed motor allows the bit to be started slowly into the work with increasing speed applied as the bit progresses through the material.

The size of a pneumatic drill is usually designated by the largest diameter bit the drill will accept. Bit sizes normally range from ¼ inch to 3 inches, with some larger bits also available for big jobs. Suggested speeds for different sizes of high-speed steel drill bits for pneumatic drills are shown in *Table 1*.

By using the chart, the required rpm speed can be found for a specific size of drill bit being used to drill in a particular type of material. For example, a ⅛ inch high-speed steel drill bit for drilling in wood requires a drilling speed between 9,167 and 12,222 rpm. The range of speeds suggested on the chart is necessary because of varying characteristics of the materials, different material thicknesses, and the required accuracy of the job. When

selecting a pneumatic drill, all of these factors must be taken into consideration. Another important factor is the required air pressure. Make sure that the air supply pressure meets the requirements recommended by the manufacturer. The drill will not operate properly if the air supply pressure is not correct.

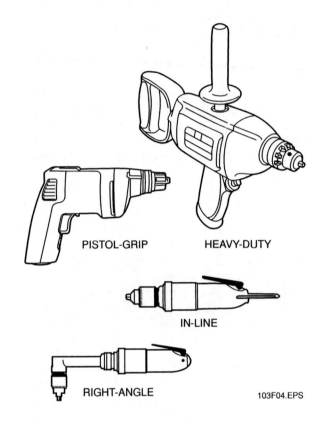

PISTOL-GRIP   HEAVY-DUTY

IN-LINE

RIGHT-ANGLE   103F04.EPS

Figure 4 ◆ Pneumatic drills.

Table 1 Suggested RPM Speeds for High-Speed Drills

Revolutions Per Minute (RPM)											
Drill Dia.	**Stainless Steel**					**Mild Steel**				**Wood**		
1/16	1833	2445	3056	3667	4278	4889	5500	6111	5722	12222	18333	24444
1/8	917	1222	1528	1833	2139	2445	2750	3056	3361	6111	9167	12222
3/16	611	815	1019	1222	1426	1630	1833	2037	2241	4074	6111	8148
1/4	458	611	764	917	1070	1222	1375	1528	1681	3056	4584	6111
5/16	367	489	611	733	856	978	1100	1222	1345	2445	3666	4888
3/8	306	407	509	611	713	815	917	1019	1120	2037	3056	4074
1/2	229	306	382	458	535	611	688	764	840	1528	2292	3056
5/8	183	244	306	367	428	489	550	611	672	1222	1833	2445
3/4	153	203	255	306	357	407	458	509	560	1018	1527	2036
					Medium Hard Cast Iron					**Aluminum & Brass**		

*Carbon steel drills should be operated 40 percent to 50 percent of the the above speeds.

2.3.2 Pneumatic Hammers

Pneumatic hammers are normally used for **chipping**, **scaling**, riveting, and drilling. Large pneumatic hammers are also used for demolition work. The proper air pressure is critical if the hammer is to operate at maximum efficiency, so always check the manufacturer's recommendations. Also, make sure that the air supply is in good working order.

Most pneumatic hammers have a pistol grip for easy handling; however, the design of pneumatic hammers varies for specific jobs. While most pneumatic hammers are the straight-line blow type, certain types include a rotating motion in addition to delivering hammering blows.

A light-duty chipping hammer or scaler, as shown in *Figure 5*, is ideal for scaling. This type of pneumatic hammer typically delivers a stroke up to 1 inch long with enough **force** to dislodge thin layers of scale or other materials.

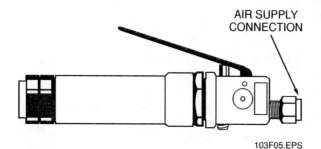

AIR SUPPLY
CONNECTION

103F05.EPS

Figure 5 ◆ Light-duty chipping hammer.

A heavy-duty chipping hammer, such as shown in *Figure 6*, is normally used for chipping. This type of pneumatic hammer typically delivers a stroke up to 4 inches long with enough force to dislodge large scale or other materials.

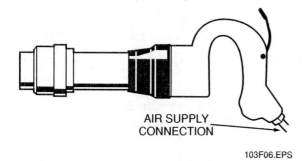

AIR SUPPLY
CONNECTION

103F06.EPS

Figure 6 ◆ Heavy-duty chipping hammer.

2.4.0 Drill Bits

Drill bits used with pneumatic hammers and drills are carbide-tipped bits of many designs. Two widely used types of masonry bits used with rotary hammers are the two-cutter head and four-cutter head (star) bits (*Figure 7A*). These bits, along with other types of hammer bits, are made in sev-

eral shank styles so that they are compatible for use with hammer drills made by different manufacturers. Some common drill bit shank styles include SDS, Universal SDS, spline, Hilti, hex, and A/B tapers (*Figure 7B*). It should be noted that most hammer drill manufacturers also make adapters (*Figure 7C*) that allow a drill bit with a different type of shank to be used with their hammer. For example, adapters are made that allow SDS or universal SDS bits to be used with a hex drive hammer. Another style adapter allows A or B taper bits to be used in a spline-drive hammer.

WARNING!
Carbide-tipped bits are not made to drill steel because they can break.

Some of the same drill bits can often be used for electric and pneumatic drills. Usually, a three-jaw chuck is used to hold the bits and adapters in both electric and pneumatic drills. The drill bit or an adapter is tightened in the chuck with a chuck key.

NOTE
Be sure to tighten all three sides of a three-jaw chuck.

Metal-boring bits differ from wood-boring bits in shape and in the type of steel from which they are made. A metal-boring drill bit will not be damaged when boring wood, but a wood-boring bit will be damaged if it is used to drill metal.

If drill bits are to be stored for long periods, coat them with light oil and store them in holders to prevent dulling caused by contact with each other.

2.5.0 Chisels

Chisels for electric and pneumatic hammers are typically used to chip, channel, and chisel brickwork, and for small demolition jobs. While these are not jobs that are frequently performed in the instrumentation craft, there are occasions when chiseling is necessary. There are several different types of chisels used with electric and pneumatic hammers. Each type of chisel is used to perform specific work. *Figure 8* shows four different types of chisels used with electric and pneumatic hammers.

The bull point chisel is mostly used for general demolition work. The bull point chisel can be started into the work at any angle, depending on the job. When chipping away unwanted material

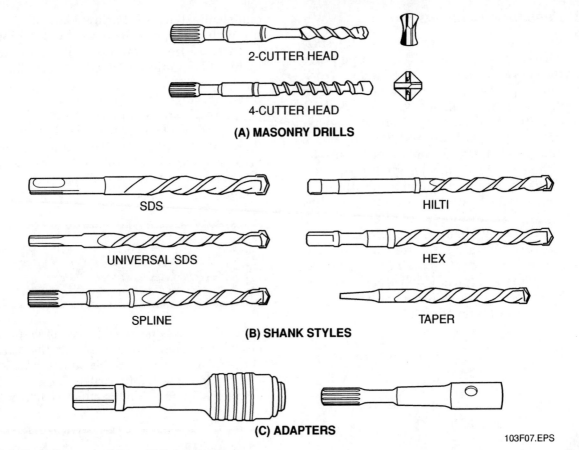

2-CUTTER HEAD

4-CUTTER HEAD

(A) MASONRY DRILLS

SDS

HILTI

UNIVERSAL SDS

HEX

SPLINE

TAPER

(B) SHANK STYLES

(C) ADAPTERS

103F07.EPS

Figure 7 ◆ Typical masonry bits and bit shank styles.

in the seams of parts, hold the bull point chisel at an angle of about 30 degrees to the seam and feed it into the seam along its length. Feed the chisel down and under the material with a forward motion.

The mortar chisel is primarily used to completely remove brickwork or to dig out old surface mortar. The mortar chisel is fed into the mortar between the bricks at about a 30-degree angle until the desired depth is reached, and then it is fed slowly under the material to dig it out. When using a mortar chisel, wipe or blow away the mortar as it loosens, so the chisel can work effectively.

A cold chisel is used as a general-purpose tool for edging, chipping, or channeling brickwork. When chipping, hold the chisel against the work at the bottom edge of the material to be removed and start the hammer. The chisel blade should be at an angle of 30 to 40 degrees to the work surface. Hold the hammer steady with both hands and feed the chisel into the work with an even, firm pressure, being careful not to allow the chisel to slip away from the work.

A scaling chisel is typically used to remove weld spatter or scale. The scaling chisel is held at an angle of about 30 to 40 degrees to the work. Be careful when feeding a scaling chisel, since it has a tendency to *walk* or break away from the work.

Other chisels and cutting tools for electric and pneumatic hammers and drills are made for cutting nuts, bolts, rivets, and metal panels. Regardless of the type of chisel used, be sure to inspect the cutting edge for cracks and nicks before beginning to work. Small defects in chisels can often be ground out, but more serious damage may require that the chisel be replaced.

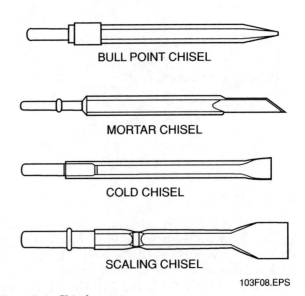

BULL POINT CHISEL

MORTAR CHISEL

COLD CHISEL

SCALING CHISEL

103F08.EPS

Figure 8 ◆ Chisels.

2.6.0 Procedure for Using an Electric Percussion Hammer

Before using an electric percussion hammer, you must know its applications and limitations. These can be found in the manufacturer's instructions. Electric percussion hammers can be used with drill bits, chisels, or other attachments. The procedure that follows uses a drill bit.

WARNING!
Make sure the hammer is unplugged before installing the bit. Connect to a GFCI-protected circuit or receptacle. Wear proper eye and ear protection.

Step 1   Select the correct drill bit for the job.

Step 2   Insert the drill bit in the chuck.

NOTE
If using a star drill, insert the chuck and handle assembly, lock it in place, and then insert the bit.

WARNING!
Check that the bit is secure in the chuck. A loose bit can cause personal injury or damage to the work.

Step 3   Position the hammer at the angle desired for the hole. Position the bit firmly on the center mark.

NOTE
Pull the trigger only after the bit is in position and firm pressure has been applied. The pressure holds the bit in place and prevents it from wandering. Never allow an electric hammer to idle. If there is no pressure being applied to the bit, the force of the **reciprocating** action of the bit is absorbed by the nose bushing. This can seriously damage the nose bushing.

Step 4   Squeeze the trigger, being sure to hold the hammer securely and straight while drilling to avoid jamming or binding the bit.

NOTE
Should the bit seize in the hole, reversing direction of the bit or using a rotating motion may loosen it.

Step 5   When finished drilling the hole, clean chips and debris out of the hole with a squeeze bulb.

WARNING!
In order to prevent particles from being blown back into your eyes, do not use an air hose to clean out the hole.

3.0.0 ◆ ELECTRIC SOLDERING GUNS AND IRONS

There are three basic types of soldering tools used in the instrumentation craft: the electric soldering gun, the electric soldering iron, and the soldering torch. The two basic types that will be discussed in this module are the electric soldering gun and the electric soldering iron. These soldering tools are used for making electrical connections. Occasionally they are used for removing and replacing electrical components, such as resistors and diodes, on printed circuit boards.

3.1.0 Electric Soldering Guns

Electric soldering guns can be purchased in kit form. These kits typically contain a soldering gun, soldering tips, a tip-changing wrench, and an all-purpose solder.

Most electric soldering guns, such as those shown in *Figure 9*, operate on 110/120V and are used for general soldering. For jobs away from electrical outlets, cordless rechargeable soldering guns are available.

Single-temperature soldering guns have only one temperature setting, while dual-temperature soldering guns can be switched from low to high temperature settings. The temperature range on multi-range soldering guns may be regulated by changing the tip or varying the trigger position. Soldering guns are usually operated by a trigger located in the front of the handle.

The tips of soldering guns are replaceable and can be changed by unscrewing the nuts from the front of the gun with a tip-changing wrench, or, on some models, by loosening the set screws that secure the tip in place. Tips used for sustained heavy-duty soldering are usually the plug-in tip/element type.

Many soldering guns have a built-in work light to illuminate the work piece.

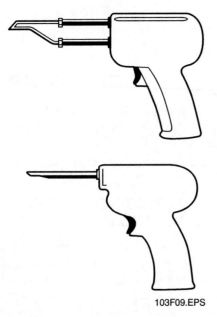

103F09.EPS

Figure 9 ◆ Electric soldering guns.

3.1.1 Soldering Tips for Soldering Guns

Soldering tips (*Figure 10*) for soldering guns come in different shapes (narrow, loop, or pencil), temperature ranges, and types (soldering, smoothing, and plastic cutting). The type of soldering gun and the job being done determine the shape, temperature range, and type of soldering tip to be used.

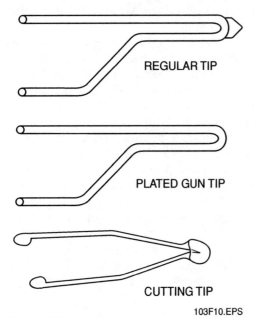

REGULAR TIP

PLATED GUN TIP

CUTTING TIP

103F10.EPS

Figure 10 ◆ Soldering gun tips.

3.2.0 Electric Soldering Irons

Electric soldering irons, such as those shown in *Figure 11*, are used primarily for removing and installing electronic components on printed circuit boards. Electric soldering irons run on 120/240VAC or DC. For jobs away from electrical outlets, cordless soldering irons are used.

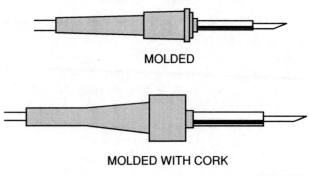

MOLDED

MOLDED WITH CORK

103F11.EPS

Figure 11 ◆ Electric soldering irons.

Electric soldering irons are typically available from 15W to 550W, and from 675°F to 1010°F. To change the watts and temperature on some soldering irons, heating elements are changed.

3.2.1 Soldering Tips for Soldering Irons

The tips of soldering irons are interchangeable so that one soldering iron can be used for several jobs. The basic types of soldering tips used with soldering irons are needle, diamond, and screwdriver (sometimes referred to as chisel tip), as shown in *Figure 12*. Other types of soldering tips are also available for special jobs.

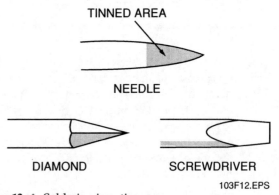

TINNED AREA

NEEDLE

DIAMOND

SCREWDRIVER

103F12.EPS

Figure 12 ◆ Soldering iron tips.

3.3.0 Solder

Solder is made in rolls, bars, or slugs. The instrumentation craft uses mostly roll solder, shown in *Figure 13*. Roll solder comes in various sizes. The size used depends on the job being done.

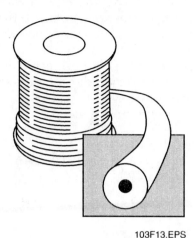

Figure 13 ◆ Roll of core solder.

The most common solder compound is tin and lead. Solder is identified by two numbers. The first number is the percent of tin in the solder, and the second number is the percent of other material in the solder. A tin-lead solder labeled 65/35 would contain 65 percent tin and 35 percent lead.

 WARNING!
Prolonged exposure to lead fumes can present a health hazard. Repeated exposures can result in a gradual accumulation of lead absorbed into the bloodstream and stored in bones and tissues.

The melting point of tin and lead solder is quite low, and at typical temperatures associated with soldering, the vapor of lead should not result in significant air concentrations.

There are several different types of solder: rosin-core solder, solid-wire solder, acid-core solder, lead-free solder, and aluminum solder.

New non-lead alloy solders have been developed and are now available to eliminate the hazards of lead, such as 97/3, which is an alloy of 97 percent tin and 3 percent silver.

Rosin-core solder with a tin-lead ratio of 65/35 is the most common type of solder used in the electrical and electronics industry. It can be used with most common metals (brass, copper, and clean mild steel), but not with aluminum or magnesium.

Solid-wire solder is used for dipping, tinning, and sheet metal work. It can also be used to solder motor commutators and armatures where a second solder joint of lower temperature is required after initial solder application.

Acid-core solder is primarily used in the plumbing industry to connect or sweat copper pipe and fittings together.

Lead-free solder is primarily used for food-sevice equipment, refrigeration, plumbing, heating, and air conditioning.

Aluminum solder is used for aluminum, copper, and stainless steel.

 CAUTION
It is important to select the right solder. Not all solders are compatible with all materials.

3.4.0 Safety Precautions

The following safety precautions should be followed when performing any soldering operation:

- Avoid breathing soldering fumes. If soldering for extended periods of time, soldering should be done in a fume hood.
- Never shake or sling a soldering gun or iron to remove solder from the tip. The pieces of solder that come off may cause serious burns to the skin or eyes and could ignite combustible materials in the work area.
- Always use a soldering tool tip cleaner such as a damp sponge or a cleaning cloth to clean the tip. Be careful not to touch the hot tip to your skin.
- Always place a hot soldering gun or iron on a nonflammable surface or in a stand made for the tool.
- Always turn off or unplug the soldering gun or iron when not in use.

3.5.0 Procedure for Using a Soldering Iron

Soldering is the process of joining together two metal parts with a heated metal or alloy. This process causes a surface fusion between two metal parts to form a solid connection.

 WARNING!
Eye protection and protective clothing covering exposed skin areas should be worn.

Step 1 Select the proper soldering gun or iron, tip, and temperature for the job.

Step 2 Thoroughly clean all metal surfaces that are to be soldered.

Step 3 If flux is to be used, select the proper flux.

Step 4 Have the work supported so that it does not move while the solder is cooling.

Step 5 Verify that the soldering tip is **tinned**. Tinning is normally required after installing a new tip, and is accomplished by applying a thin layer of solder on the tip. Wipe off any excess solder from the tip with a damp sponge or cloth.

Step 6 Heat up the work by touching it with the soldering tip.

> **NOTE**
>
> If soldering two wires together, place the tip under the joint, since the solder will flow toward the heated iron. Many electronic components require special **heat sinks** to protect them from the extreme heat.

Step 7 After heating the work, apply the flux, if necessary.

> **NOTE**
>
> The flux must wet the entire surface to be soldered.

Step 8 Touch the heated area with the solder, allow the solder to flow into the joint.

Step 9 Remove the tip from the work and let the joint cool.

> **NOTE**
>
> A properly soldered joint will be shiny when it cools. If the joint has a frosted look, reheat the joint, remove the melted solder using a **solder sucker**, and resolder the joint. The frosted look is known as a *chilled* or *cold* solder joint. This can be caused by insufficient heat or the work cooling too rapidly.

Step 10 When soldering is completed, clean the soldering tip and disconnect the power cord from the receptacle. Place the hot solder gun or iron on a nonflammable surface or in a stand until it cools.

4.0.0 ◆ HYDRAULIC KNOCKOUT PUNCHES

Hydraulic-power knockout punches are used to enlarge knockouts and punch holes for conduit in metal boxes, cabinets, and panels in stainless steel and mild steel up to 10 gauge. Hydraulic fluid is pumped into a cylinder attached to the punch. As the piston moves, it pulls the punch into the material being cut.

The hydraulic knockout punch consists of four parts: die, punch, cylinder adapter screw, and a porta-power jack system (consisting of a pump and ram), as shown in *Figure 14*.

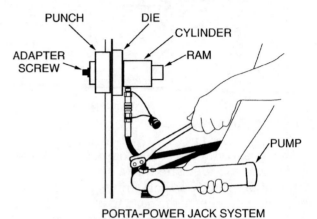

PORTA-POWER JACK SYSTEM

103F14.TIF

Figure 14 ◆ Hydraulic knockout punch.

4.1.0 Safety Precautions

The following safety precautions must be followed when using hydraulic knockout punches:

- Do not use an extension bar on the pump handle.
- Make sure that the hose is not twisted or kinked.
- Never use a jack that is leaking; replace the seals or hose before using the jack.
- Always select a jack that has a high enough rating for the job.

4.2.0 Procedure for Using a Hydraulic Knockout Punch

> **WARNING!**
>
> Wear proper eye protection. Be aware of the high pressures generated by a porta-power jack system.

Step 1 Select the proper size and type of knockout die for the work to be performed.

> **WARNING!**
>
> Make sure that the correct punch and die combination is used. A punch that is larger than the die cannot fit within the die housing and can shatter with the extreme hydraulic pressures applied to it.

Step 2 Inspect the porta-power jack, die, adapter screw, and punch for any defects that might make them unsafe to use.

Step 3 Drill a hole big enough to freely accommodate the cylinder adapter screw in the metal plate.

Step 4 Attach the adapter screw to the hydraulic cylinder hose.

Step 5 Place the required knockout die on the adapter screw.

Step 6 Insert the cylinder adapter screw with knockout die through the drilled hole.

Step 7 Carefully reach into the opposite side of the work and turn the knockout punch onto the adapter screw until it contacts the material being punched out.

Step 8 Operate the hydraulic pump to draw the knockout punch through the metal until the hole is cut.

NOTE
Normally the punch will cut through only one point of the cutter first. Slowly continue pumping the handle until the die and punch assembly is free in the knocked out hole, indicating a completed punch.

5.0.0 ◆ ELECTRIC THREADING MACHINES

Threading machines, also called *pipe cutting machines*, are used to cut, ream, and thread a wide range of sizes of pipe, rod, and conduit. Most threading machines can be loaded from the front or rear for easy access and quick changes; however, some threading machines only load from the rear. A typical electric threading machine is shown in *Figure 15*.

Most threading machines are designed with gear drives and chucks that hold and turn the work. During operation, the cutter, reamer, and threader are held still, and the work rotates.

Most threaders are operated by a three-position, switch with forward, off, and reverse positions, and a foot switch (not shown). The forward and reverse positions on the three-position switch allow the machine to rotate clockwise and counterclockwise. The forward and reverse positions start the threader motor in the selected direction, but the chuck doesn't start turning until the foot switch is pressed. The OFF position shuts off all power to the threading machine.

WARNING!
Due to the gear drive system that allows for greater torque, the threading machine doesn't stop immediately when turned off.

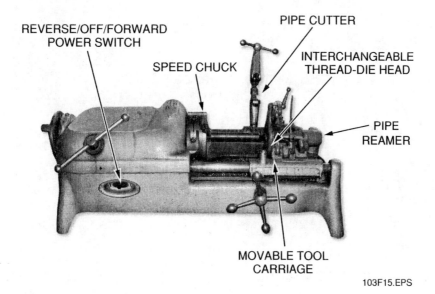

REVERSE/OFF/FORWARD POWER SWITCH

PIPE CUTTER

SPEED CHUCK

INTERCHANGEABLE THREAD-DIE HEAD

PIPE REAMER

MOVABLE TOOL CARRIAGE

103F15.EPS

Figure 15 ◆ Threading machine.

Threading machines are typically available for threading work ranging from ⅛ inch to 6 inches in diameter. Depending on the size of the threader, it may be mounted on a tripod, table, or special stand, or may be handheld. Those on tripods or stands are often equipped with wheels for portability in the field. A typical portable, stand-mounted threader is shown in *Figure 16A*, while a handheld threader, commonly referred to as a *power pony*, is shown in *Figure 16B*.

In a handheld power pony threader, the dies are inserted into a ring within the revolving power head and can thread pipe from ¼ inch to 2 inches. The work is normally supported within a stationary pipe vise. The operator holds the power pony with one hand in the handhold near the power head and the other hand operates the trigger assembly. The die ring revolves within the head, allowing the power pony to be held in a stationary position.

Most electric threading machines thread pipe ranging from ⅛ inch to 2 inches, and rod (bolt stock) from ¼ inch to 2 inches. Special threading machines are made to thread larger pipe and conduit up to 6 inches in diameter.

A cutter is usually attached to the carriage of the threading machine. It is used for cutting pipe, rod, and conduit. The cutter is swung out of the way when not in use.

Some portable threading machines are also equipped with a reamer. The reamer is used to remove the **burr** left on the inside of pipe or conduit after it has been cut. Like the cutter, it is also attached to the carriage and is swung out of the way when not in use.

WARNING!

The power pony generates tremendous torque and, like the other power pipe threading machines, does not immediately stop once the trigger is released. Power ponies must be used with extreme caution, including the use of eye protection and an understanding of the potential danger associated with a handheld, high-torque device. Never attempt to manually restrain a power pony that continues to run beyond the desired position.

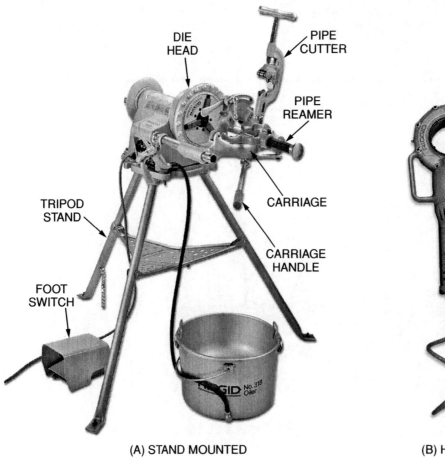

(A) STAND MOUNTED

(B) HAND-HELD

103F16.EPS

Figure 16 ◆ Stand mounted and hand-held portable threading machines.

5.1.0 Threading Dies

Before cutting threads with a threading machine, the proper size dies must be selected. The dies are usually installed in a die head. *Figure 17* shows a typical die head for an electric threading machine.

103F17.EPS

Figure 17 ◆ Die head.

Typically, four different sets of dies are used with threading machines to cut thread on different pipe sizes. Each die set can be used with a range of pipe or rod sizes. Once the dies are installed in the die head, the die head is adjusted to accept the particular size of pipe or rod being threaded. The manufacturer's instructions for a specific threading machine will explain how to install the dies in the die head and how to adjust the die head for different sizes of pipe or rod. Most dies are interchangeable and will vary depending on the type of thread being cut.

A nipple chuck with different sizes of adapters is often used for holding short, close pipe nipples, bolts, and studs during threading with an electric threading machine. *Figure 18* shows a nipple chuck with various adapters.

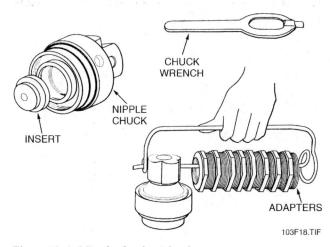

CHUCK WRENCH

NIPPLE CHUCK

INSERT

ADAPTERS

103F18.TIF

Figure 18 ◆ Nipple chuck with adapters.

A nipple chuck with the proper inserts and adapters is normally used to thread pipe nipples from ⅛ inch to 2 inches in diameter. The nipple chuck can also be used to thread bolts and studs from ¼ inch to 2 inches in diameter with the proper inserts and adapters. A special wrench is used to tighten the adapters in the nipple chuck.

5.2.0 Safety Precautions

The following safety precautions must be followed when using an electric threading machine:

- Make sure the power switch is off and the foot switch operates freely before plugging in the threading machine.
- Remove any tools or materials from the threading machine before starting.
- Do not use a threading machine as a vise or bench.
- Wear proper safety equipment when operating a threading machine.
- Operate the threading machine from the foot switch side only.
- Keep the area around the threading machine free of debris.
- Do not use the threading machine in damp or wet locations.
- Disconnect the power cord when adjusting, servicing, or changing accessories on the threading machine.
- Support long pipes with a pipe support. This will keep the end of the pipe from whipping as it turns and will also reduce the pressure on the centering device and chuck.

5.3.0 Procedures for Using a Threading Machine

The following procedures are for loading pipe, cutting pipe, threading pipe, and changing dies on a typical electric threading machine. The procedure for working with rods and conduits is basically the same as for pipe. Check the manufacturer's instructions on guidelines for using a specific type of threading machine. Refer to *Figure 19* while performing the following procedure.

5.3.1 Loading Pipe

On most electric threading machines, the pipe can be inserted from either end of the chuck. Before loading, the pipe should be measured and marked to length for the job to be done.

WARNING!

Use proper lifting techniques when loading heavy pipe. Get assistance as needed. Wear protective gloves.

Step 1 Verify that the three-position switch is in the OFF position.

Step 2 Swing the cutter, threader, and reamer out of the way.

Step 3 Verify that the chuck is open.

Step 4 Place the pipe in the threading machine by pushing or pulling it until it reaches the pipe stop, or until there is enough pipe sticking out through the chuck to be cut off.

NOTE

For long pipe, support the end of the pipe with an adjustable pipe support.

Step 5 Make sure the pipe is centered and tighten the chuck jaws by turning the chuck handwheel counterclockwise until the chuck is tightened enough that the pipe will not slip.

NOTE

Spin the chuck handwheel closed with a hard snap to make sure the pipe is centered, locked in place, and does not move.

5.3.2 Cutting and Reaming Pipe

After the pipe has been loaded into the threading machine, it can be cut and reamed according to the following procedure. Refer to *Figure 19* while performing the following steps:

WARNING!

Wear proper eye protection and protective gloves as required. Avoid sharp edges of newly cut and reamed pipe.

Step 1 Lower the cutter onto the pipe and line up the cutter with the mark where the pipe is to be cut by moving the carriage with the carriage handwheel.

Step 2 Place the three-position switch in the FORWARD position, and step on the foot switch.

Step 3 Direct the **cutting oil** to the cutting area.

Step 4 To prevent damage to the pipe, slowly tighten the cutter by turning the cutter feed screw T-handle clockwise in small increments of a turn until the pipe is cut completely through.

Step 5 Release the foot switch and place the three-position switch in the OFF position.

WARNING!

Make sure that the threading machine has come to a complete stop before continuing.

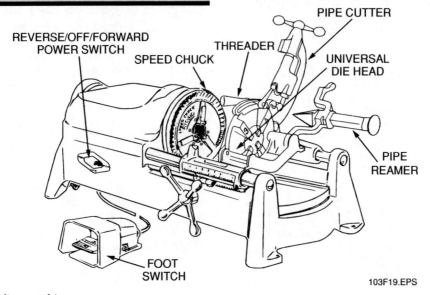

Figure 19 ◆ Threading machine.

Step 6   Swing the pipe cutter to the out-of-the-way position.

Step 7   Swing the reamer down into place so the blades barely touch the inside of the pipe.

Step 8   Place the three-position switch in the FORWARD position and step on the foot switch.

Step 9   Slowly and gradually move the reamer farther into the pipe by moving the carriage handwheel counterclockwise. Ream the burrs from inside the pipe, but don't ream beyond the inside diameter of the pipe.

 WARNING!
A reamer that has reaming blades in a spiral design versus a straight configuration has a tendency to grab the inner wall of the pipe and attempt to thread itself rapidly into the pipe. Use extreme caution when using a spiral reamer.

Step 10   Move the reamer out of the pipe by turning the carriage handwheel clockwise.

Step 11   Release the foot switch and place the three-position switch in the OFF position.

 WARNING!
Make sure that the threading machine has come to a complete stop.

Step 12   Return the reamer to the out-of-the-way position.

Step 13   If the job doesn't require threading, loosen the chuck by spinning the chuck handwheel clockwise, and remove the pipe.

5.3.3 Changing Threading Dies

The proper dies must be selected and installed in the die head before cutting threads on any pipe. Refer to *Figure 20* while performing the following steps.

 WARNING!
The machine must be disconnected from its electrical power source when removing or replacing the die head.

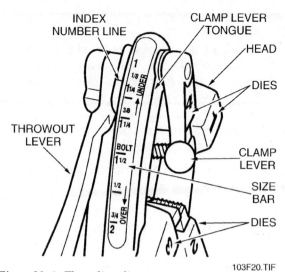

Figure 20 ◆ Threading dies.

103F20.TIF

Step 1   Lay the die head down. If the die has numbers on it, make sure that the numbers are facing up.

Step 2   Open the throwout lever by lifting the lever up.

Step 3   Loosen the clamp lever approximately three turns.

Step 4   Lift the clamp lever tongue out of the slot.

Step 5   Slide the throwout lever to the end of the slot in the OVER direction shown on the size bar.

Step 6   Remove the old dies from the die head.

Step 7   Insert the new dies in the die head in the correct order.

 NOTE
The numbers on the dies must match those on the die head.

Step 8   Place the clamp lever tongue back in the slot under the size bar.

Step 9   Tighten the clamp lever.

5.3.4 Die Head Adjustment for Pipe Size

Before threading the pipe, the die head must be adjusted to accept the size of pipe. Refer to *Figure 20* while performing the following steps.

Step 1   Verify that the proper dies are installed in the die head.

Step 2   Move the throwout lever to the open position.

WARNING!

Eye protection must be worn at all times when working with any part of the threading machine. Watch out for sharp edges on dies and cutters.

Step 3 Loosen the clamp lever by turning it counterclockwise.

Step 4 Slide the size bar until the pipe size number lines up with the index number line.

Step 5 Tighten and lock the clamp lever by turning the lever clockwise.

5.3.5 Threading Pipe

After the pipe has been loaded in the threading machine, cut, and reamed, the pipe can be threaded according to the following procedure. Refer to *Table 2* while performing the following steps.

WARNING!

Make sure eye protection is in place. Avoid wearing loose-fitting clothing that may become entangled with revolving parts.

Table 2 Thread Length Chart

Pipe I.D. Size (Inches)	Thread Length (Inches)
1/8	3/8
1/4	5/8
3/8	5/8
1/2	3/4
3/4	3/4
1	7/8
1 1/4	1
1 1/2	1
2	1
2 1/2	1 1/2
3	1 1/2
3 1/2	1 5/8
4	1 5/8
5	1 3/4
6	1 3/4
8	1 7/8
10	2
12	2 1/8

Step 1 Determine the length of threads to be cut. Refer to *Table 2*.

Step 2 Swing the die head and cutting oil line down into proper position.

Step 3 Adjust the die for the size pipe to be threaded, if necessary.

Step 4 Place the three-position switch in the FORWARD position and step on the foot switch.

Step 5 Move the die against the end of the pipe by turning the carriage handwheel counter-clockwise.

Step 6 Check the reading on the length gauge indicator at the start of threading and determine the desired stopping point.

NOTE

Add the desired length of the threads to the starting reading on the length gauge to determine where to stop cutting. Another way to determine when the correct length of threads have been cut is to stop cutting when the end of the pipe has gone completely through the dies.

Step 7 Make sure that cutting oil is flooding the cutting die during threading.

Step 8 Exert a slight pressure on the carriage handwheel to start cutting threads. Continue to cut the threads until the desired length is achieved.

Step 9 Release the foot switch and place the three-position switch in the OFF position.

WARNING!

Make sure that the threading machine has come to a complete stop.

Step 10 When finished cutting the threads, open the throwout lever, and retract the die by turning the carriage handwheel clockwise.

Step 11 Swing the die head and cutting oil line to the out-of-the-way position.

Step 12 Visually check the threads and verify with a thread gauge (*Figure 21*).

WARNING!

If the threads are too deep, it could weaken the pipe and present a safety hazard. The pipe should be discarded.

NOTE

If the threads are not deep enough, adjust the die and repeat the threading operation.

Step 13 Open the chuck by turning the chuck handwheel clockwise, and remove the pipe.

Step 14 Clean any chips or shavings from the carriage, die, and die head.

WARNING!

Don't brush the chips or shavings away with your bare hands. Wear protective gloves and use a brush or small broom.

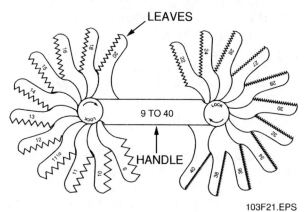

Figure 21 ◆ Thread gauge.

5.3.6 *Threading Nipples, Bolts, and Studs*

The nipple chuck, proper insert, and adapter must be installed in the threading machine before cutting threads on nipples, bolts, or studs. When threading a nipple, one end of the nipple should already be threaded on a pipe before being cut to nipple size. The following procedure is for threading a pipe nipple.

WARNING!

Follow the same safety precautions applied when threading pipe. Always wear eye protection and avoid loose-fitting clothing around revolving machinery.

Step 1 Place the nipple chuck in the threader's chuck.

Step 2 Insert the small end of the insert toward the outside when threading ⅛ inch to ¾

inch pipe. Place the large end of the insert toward the outside when threading 1 inch pipe. Do not use any insert when threading 1¼ inch and larger pipe.

Step 3 Select the proper size nipple chuck adapter and screw it into the nipple chuck with the proper wrench.

Step 4 Insert the nipple into the adapter.

Step 5 Tighten the adapter with the proper wrench.

Step 6 Thread the nipple using the procedure in a previous section for threading pipe.

6.0.0 ◆ POWDER-ACTUATED TOOLS

Another power tool that is often used in the instrumentation trade, as well as other construction trades, is the powder-actuated driver (*Figure 22*). This device uses factory-loaded ammunition shell casings, with different levels of gunpowder charges, to shoot fastening devices into hard materials such as steel and concrete. It is constructed much like a handgun, with the gunpowder charge causing an internal ram to strike the loaded fastener, shooting it out of the barrel and into the work.

Charges typically come preloaded in clips, with the color of casing designating the strength of the gunpowder charge. Charges are selected based on the material that is to be penetrated. Charges are not interchangeable between brands of tools but must only be loaded in the matching tool.

The fasteners used with powder-actuated tools are also designed specifically for these tools. Careful matching of tool, charge, and fastener must be adhered to in the selection and installation process associated with powder-actuated tools.

OSHA Standard 29CFR 1926.302(e) governs the use of powder-actuated tools and states that only those individuals who have been trained in the operation of a particular powder-actuated tool be allowed to operate it. Authorized instructors available from the various powder-actuated tool manufacturers generally provide such training and licensing.

WARNING!

Powder-actuated fastening tools are to be used only by trained and licensed operators and in accordance with the tools operator's manual. You must carry your license with you whenever you are using a powder-actuated tool.

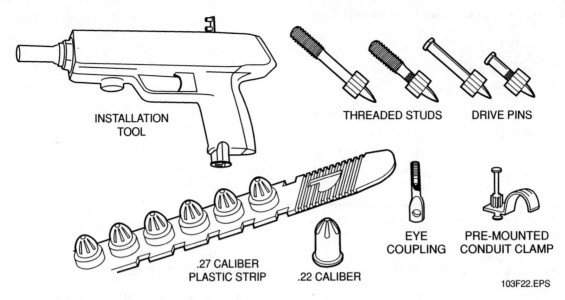

Figure 22 ◆ Powder-actuated driver and accessories.

Trained operators must take precautions to protect both themselves and others in the area when using a powder-actuated driver tool. Some guidelines are given here:

- Always use the tool in accordance with the published tool operation instructions. The instructions should be kept with the tool. Never attempt to override the safety features of the tool.
- Never place your hand or other body parts over the front muzzle end of the tool.
- Use only fasteners, powder loads, and tool parts specifically made for use with the tool. Use of other materials can cause improper and unsafe functioning of the tool.
- Operators and bystanders must wear eye and hearing protection along with hard hats. Other personal safety gear, as required, must also be used.
- Always post warning signs that state *Powder-Actuated Tool in Use* within 50 feet of the area where tools are used.
- Prior to using a tool, make sure it is unloaded, then perform a proper function test. Check the functioning of the unloaded tool as described in the published tool operation instructions.
- Do not guess before fastening into any base material; always perform a center punch test.
- Always make a test firing into a suitable base material with the lowest power level recommended for the tool being used. If this does not

set the fastener, try the next higher power level. Continue this procedure until the proper fastener penetration is obtained.

- Always point the tool away from operators or bystanders.
- Never use the tool in an explosive or flammable area.
- Never leave a loaded tool unattended. Do not load the tool until you are prepared to complete the fastening. Should you decide not to make a fastening after the tool has been loaded, always remove the powder load first, then the fastener. Always unload the tool before cleaning, servicing, and when changing parts, prior to work breaks, and when storing the tool.
- Always hold the tool perpendicular to the work surface and use the spall (chip or fragment) guard or stop spall whenever possible.
- Always follow the required spacing, edge distance, and base material thickness requirements.
- Never fire through an existing hole or into a weld area.
- In the event of a misfire, always hold the tool depressed against the work surface for at least 30 seconds. If the tool still does not fire, follow the published tool instructions. Never carelessly discard or throw unfired powder loads into a trash receptacle.
- Always store the powder loads and unloaded tool under lock and key.

SUMMARY

In this module, we have covered many of the basic power tools that are used in the instrumentation craft. Additional power tools are covered in other modules. Whatever job you do, select the proper tool, inspect it, maintain it, and use it safely. Proper use and care of power tools makes the job easier to perform, extends the life of the tool, and provides for a quality product.

Review Questions

1. Of the following statements concerning the safe use of power tools, which is correct?
   a. It is not necessary to inspect the power plug and cord for damage before using the tool.
   b. It is okay to wear loose clothing when operating a power tool to allow for unrestricted movement of your legs and arms.
   c. Eye protection must be worn and the lenses kept clean.
   d. It is okay to operate an electrical tool in areas containing flammable gases.

2. When drilling a hole with an electric hammer, position the bit firmly on the _____.
   a. chuck
   b. key
   c. center mark
   d. fitting

3. A(n) _____ is used to clean chips and debris out of a drilled hole.
   a. sponge
   b. wet rag
   c. squeeze bulb
   d. air hose

4. On a multi-range soldering gun, temperature is changed by _____.
   a. adjusting the voltage
   b. adjusting the built-in rheostat
   c. switching from high to low settings
   d. changing the tip or varying the trigger position

5. The shape, temperature range, and type of soldering tip used is determined by the _____.
   a. type of solder being used
   b. type of flux being used
   c. job being done
   d. voltage rating of the soldering iron or gun

6. Before using a soldering iron or gun that has a new tip installed, _____ the tip.
   a. tin
   b. wet
   c. flux
   d. lead

7. The pump assembly used with a hydraulic knockout set is called a _____.
   a. foot pump
   b. cylinder adapter
   c. punch and die
   d. porta-power jack

8. A power pony is a type of _____.
   a. soldering gun
   b. repercussion hammer
   c. portable threading machine
   d. powder-actuated tool

9. The proper position for operating a threading machine is _____.
   a. the opposite side from the foot switch
   b. the foot switch side
   c. dependent on the size of pipe to be threaded
   d. the opposite side from the attached cutter

10. Once you have been trained on the proper use of a particular brand and/or model of powder-actuated tool, you are authorized to operate _____.
    a. only that tool
    b. any powder-actuated tool
    c. all tools from that manufacturer
    d. all powder-actuated tools from that manufacturer

Trade Terms Introduced in This Module

bpm: Abbreviation for *blows per minute.*

Burr: A sharp, ragged edge on the inside or outside of pipe or conduit caused by cutting.

Chipping: The removal of large pieces of material.

Cutting oil: Fluid applied to tools to assist in the cutting or threading operation by cooling and lubricating.

Double-insulated tool: An electric tool that has a plastic casing designed to insulate the user from any fault inside the tool.

Force: A push or pull measured in units of weight.

Heat sink: A device attached between a soldering point and component to protect electronic components.

Percussion: To strike or pound.

Pneumatic oil: Non-detergent lubricant designed for lubricating air-operated tools.

Pressure: The amount of force against a specific area, usually measured in pounds per square inch (psi).

Reciprocating: Moving forward and backward alternately.

Rotary: To turn on an axis like a wheel.

rpm: Abbreviation for *revolutions per minute.*

Scaling: The removing of thin layers of paint scale, rust, flux, and weld spatter from smooth or rough surfaces.

Solder sucker: A spring-loaded or hand-operated vacuuming device designed to remove hot, liquid solder.

Tinned: A soldering tip coated with a thin layer of solder.

ACKNOWLEDGMENTS

Figure Credits

Gerald Shannon   103F15, 103F17

Ridge Tool Company   103F16

NCCER CRAFT TRAINING USER UPDATES

The NCCER makes every effort to keep these textbooks up-to-date and free of technical errors. We appreciate your help in this process. If you have an idea for improving this textbook, or if you find an error, a typographical mistake, or an inaccuracy in the NCCER's Craft Training textbooks, please write us, using this form or a photocopy. Be sure to include the exact module number, page number, a detailed description, and the correction, if applicable. Your input will be brought to the attention of the Technical Review Committee. Thank you for your assistance.

Instructors – If you found that additional materials were necessary in order to teach this module effectively, please let us know so that we may include them in the Equipment and Materials list in the Instructor's Guide.

Write: Curriculum Revision and Development Department
National Center for Construction Education and Research
P.O. Box 141104, Gainesville, FL 32614-1104

Fax: 352-334-0932

E-mail: curriculum@nccer.org

Craft _____ Module Name _____

Copyright Date _____ Module Number _____ Page Number(s) _____

Description _____

_____

_____

_____

_____

(Optional) Correction _____

_____

_____

(Optional) Your Name and Address _____

_____

_____

Electrical Systems for Instrumentation

COURSE MAP

This course map shows all of the modules in the first level of the Instrumentation curriculum. The suggested training order begins at the bottom and proceeds up. Skill levels increase as you advance on the course map. The local Training Program Sponsor may adjust the training order.

INSTRUMENTATION LEVEL ONE

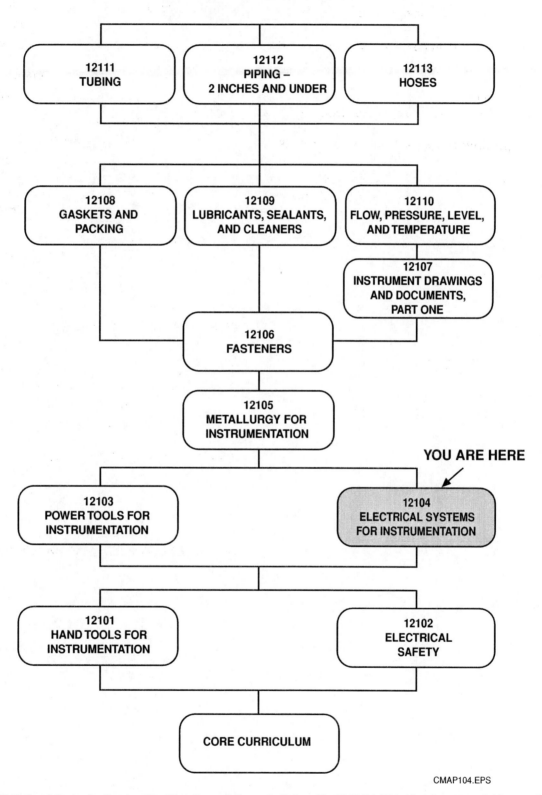

CMAP104.EPS

MODULE 12104 CONTENTS

Figures

Electrical Systems for Instrumentation

Objectives

When you have completed this module, you will be able to do the following:

1. Define the following terms:
   - Alternating current (AC)
   - Capacitance
   - Conductor
   - Current
   - Direct current (DC)
   - Electrical circuit
   - Inductance
   - Insulator
   - Ohm's law
   - Resistance
   - Voltage
2. State the two requirements for current flow in a circuit.
3. Use a multimeter and clamp-on ammeter to measure voltage, current, and resistance in a circuit.
4. State Ohm's law in equation form.
5. Use Ohm's law to calculate individual component values and total values for I, E, R, and P in a simple DC series circuit, given any two of the following properties: resistance, current, and voltage.
6. Demonstrate a knowledge of safety considerations when working with electricity.
7. Calculate the value and determine the tolerance of a resistor.

8. Identify correct wire sizes used for different instrumentation applications.
9. Identify various types of electrical fittings used for different instrumentation applications.

Prerequisites

Before you begin this module, it is recommended that you successfully complete the following modules: Core Curriculum; Instrumentation Level One, Modules 12101 through 12103.

Required Trainee Materials

1. Pencil and paper
2. Appropriate personal protective equipment
3. Calculator

1.0.0 ◆ INTRODUCTION

The fundamental relationships between **current, voltage, resistance,** and power in a simple **direct current (DC)** series circuit are basic to understanding all types of **electrical circuits.** This module provides a general introduction to the electrical concepts presented in **Ohm's law** and simple DC series circuitry. It includes the proper methods for measuring the electrical properties of voltage, current, and resistance in an electrical circuit. This module also covers identification of **resistors** and **capacitors,** wire sizes, and electrical fittings.

Throughout this module, you should observe all safety practices, especially those covered in the Instrumentation Level One Module, *Electrical Safety.*

Note: The designations "National Electrical Code," "NE Code," and "NEC," where used in this document, refer to the *National Electrical Code®,* which is a registered trademark of the National Fire Protection Association, Quincy, MA. *All National Electrical Code (NEC) references in this module refer to the 1999 edition of the NEC.*

2.0.0 ◆ TERMS AND DEFINITIONS

In order to understand basic principles of electricity, you must understand basic electrical terminology including the definitions of the following terms:

- *Alternating current (AC)* – Current that flows back and forth in a wire at regular intervals, going first in one direction peaking, stoping, and then flowing in the other direction until it peaks. AC power is used exclusively to power lighting circuits and to power appliances and/or equipment in homes and commercial/industrial businesses. Power-generating plants produce AC because it can be transmitted efficiently from the power-generating stations to the end users. This is because AC can be increased or decreased easily by **transformers,** without any appreciable power loss, to facilitate its transmission over long distances.

- *Capacitance* – The property of an electric circuit that enables it to store electric energy by means of an electrostatic field and to release this energy at a later time. Capacitance is measured in farads. Physically, a capacitor is formed whenever an insulating material separates two **conductors** that have a difference in potential between them.

- *Conductor* – A material such as copper or silver that offers very little resistance to current flow.

- *Current* – The flow of electrons (electricity) in a circuit. Current is measured in amperes (amps). Electric current can flow as long as the following two conditions are met:

  - There must be a force to push the electrons along.
  - There must be a path through which the electrons can flow. A path is formed when a conductor is connected to opposing poles.

  The electromotive force that pushes the electrons is measured in volts. The larger the force (that is, the larger the voltage source), the larger the amount of current. The path through which electrons flow is called an *electrical circuit*. An electrical circuit is often explained in terms of a water flow loop. A pump causes the water to flow through a pipe. If a larger pump is used, more water will flow through the pipe. If the voltage source (power supply) in an electrical circuit is compared to the pump, the same principle applies: if the size of the power supply (voltage) is increased, more current flows through the circuit.

- *Direct current (DC)* – Current that always flows in the one direction. Unlike AC power, DC power produced by a DC generator cannot easily be increased or decreased, and it is thus limited by the distance over which it can economically be transmitted. If DC is required for use by a motor or other equipment, it is common for the incoming AC power to be rectified (changed) from AC to DC by a **rectifier**. This is widely done in DC power supply circuits contained in radios, TVs, computers, and similar devices. DC power is also easily produced by batteries, making it useful for powering portable electronic devices, tools, and equipment.

- *Inductance* – The property of an electrical circuit that tends to oppose any change of current through the circuit. Inductance is measured in henrys. Physically, an inductor is made by coiling or winding a length of insulated conductor (wire) around a core (usually some type of magnetic material).

- *Insulator* – A material that offers a very high resistance to current flow, such as plastic or rubber.

- *Ohm's law* – A statement of the relationship between current, voltage, and resistance in an electrical circuit: current equals the voltage divided by the resistance. Ohm's law can be expressed by using several different mathematical formulas. It is generally expressed using the mathematical formula: $E = I \times R$

- *Path* – Formed when a conductor is connected between two opposing (+, –) poles.

- *Resistance* – An electrical property that opposes the flow of current through a material. Resistance is measured in **ohms** (Ω).

- *Series circuit* – A circuit with only one path for current flow.

- *Voltage* – The measure of the electromotive force that makes current flow in a circuit.

3.0.0 ◆ SIMPLE CIRCUIT

A simple circuit can be constructed using a battery and a length of wire. One end of the wire is connected to the positive terminal of the battery, and the other end is connected to the negative terminal of the battery. Current will flow through this circuit as long as there is a potential difference between the positive and negative charges. *Potential difference* means that the positive and negative charges are not equal. If they were equal, the charges would cancel each other out and current could not flow. This potential difference is voltage. The wire connects the negative terminal of the battery to the positive terminal and provides a path through which current can flow.

The wires (conductors) in an electrical circuit are made of such materials as copper, silver, and aluminum, which allow current to flow easily. Other materials (rubber, wood, and certain types of plastic) offer a great deal of resistance to the flow of current, and are called *insulators*.

If one end of the wire in the circuit were to be disconnected, current flow would stop because the circuit is no longer complete. Current cannot flow if its path has been interrupted. An incomplete current path is called an *open circuit*, or just an *open*.

In the water pump and pipe example, the total flow of the water is completely controlled by the pump. To change the amount of water flowing through the pipe, a larger pump is used, or the speed of the pump is changed. In an electric circuit, the same is true. To change the rate of current flow in a simple DC circuit, the size of the battery must be changed.

In the water system, a throttling valve can be added in the line to adjust the amount of water flowing through the pipe. Similarly, in an electric circuit, a resistor can be added to adjust the flow of current as shown in *Figure 1*.

If the resistor and the battery in an electric circuit have fixed values (that is, their values cannot change), there is only one possible rate of current flow through the circuit. However, if an adjustable resistor (like a rheostat, volume control, or light dimmer) is installed in the circuit, the rate of current flow in the circuit can be controlled just as the flow rate of water in the pipe can be adjusted with a throttling valve.

4.0.0 ◆ OHM'S LAW

The voltage across a component of a DC circuit is equal to the current (measured in amperes) through the component, multiplied by the resistance of the component (measured in ohms).

The illustration shown in *Figure 2* indicates the various possibilities of expressing Ohm's law. It is generally expressed using the mathematical formula:

$$E = I \times R$$

Where:

E = voltage
I = current
R = resistance

Ohm's law was developed by scientist George Simon Ohm. Ohm discovered that if the resistance in a DC circuit was kept constant and the source voltage was increased, there would be a corre-

sponding increase in current flow. In a DC circuit, current is directly proportional to voltage and inversely proportional to resistance. In other words:

- If E increases: I increases
- If E decreases: I decreases
- If R increases: I decreases
- If R decreases: I increases

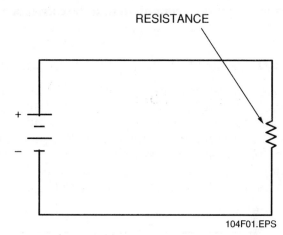

104F01.EPS

Figure 1 ◆ Simple circuit.

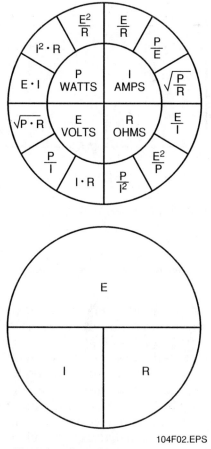

104F02.EPS

Figure 2 ◆ Ohm's law formulas.

5.0.0 ◆ SERIES DC CIRCUITS

A series circuit is an electrical circuit in which all of the resistors are connected in such a manner that there is only one path for current to flow through the resistors (refer to *Figure 1*).

Since a series circuit has only one path for current flow, the value of current flowing through each component in the circuit is equal throughout the circuit.

Ohm's law can be applied to each resistor individually in a series circuit to find the difference in potential, or voltage drop, across each resistor.

5.1.0 Current, Voltage, and Resistance

Current is the movement, or flow, of electrons in a circuit. Voltage is the electromotive force that makes current flow through a circuit, and resistance is an electrical property that opposes the flow of current through a circuit. The total resistance (RT) in a series circuit is the sum of resistances of all the resistors in the circuit (*Figure 3*)

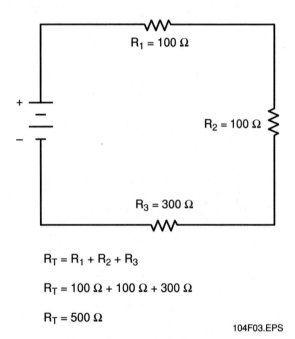

$$R_T = R_1 + R_2 + R_3$$

$$R_T = 100\ \Omega + 100\ \Omega + 300\ \Omega$$

$$R_T = 500\ \Omega$$

104F03.EPS

Figure 3 ◆ Calculating equivalent resistances.

To draw an equivalent circuit, a group of resistors connected in series may be replaced by a single resistor having a resistance which is equal to the sum of all the resistors in the circuit.

Once the total resistance (R_T) and total voltage (E_T) for a series circuit are known, an equivalent circuit may be drawn that represents these calculated quantities, and the total current (I_T) in the circuit can be calculated using another version of the formula for Ohm's law ($I = E/R$).

Use the sample circuit in *Figure 4* to determine R_T and I_T.

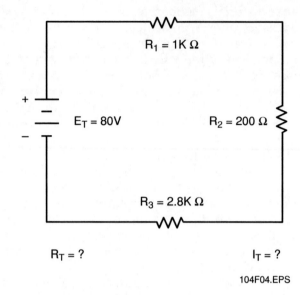

$R_T = ?$ $I_T = ?$

104F04.EPS

Figure 4 ◆ Series circuit.

The correct answers are:

$$R_T = 4,000\Omega\ (R_1 + R_2 + R_3$$
$$= 1,000\Omega + 200\Omega + 2,800\Omega)$$

and

$$I_T = .02\ \text{amps}\ (E_T \div R_T = 80V \div 4,000\Omega)$$

5.2.0 Power

Power is the term used to represent the amount of work that can be done by a load in an electrical circuit. The basic unit of power is the **watt.** Power is calculated by taking the voltage (E) across a device times the current (I) that flows through the device. Power in watts can be calculated using the formula:

$$P = E \times I$$

Where:

P = power
E = voltage
I = current

Other methods of calculating power are shown in *Figure 2*.

Total power (P_T) dissipated in a series circuit can be found by multiplying the source voltage by the total current (I_T) flowing in the circuit, or by adding the individual power dissipated by each resistor in the circuit. For the example shown in *Figure 4*, the source voltage is 80V and the total current is .02A. Therefore, total power (P_T) for this circuit is 1.6W.

$$PT = ET \times IT$$
$$PT = 80V \times .02A$$
$$PT = 1.6W$$

Example Problems:

Using the formulas $E = I \times R$, $I = E/R$, and $P = E \times I$, complete the following example problems. Make sure to indicate units on all answers.

1. $E =$ _____ when $I = 5A$ and $R = 10\Omega$

2. $I =$ _____ when $R = 25\Omega$ and $E = 100V$

3. $P =$ _____ when $R = 100\Omega$ and $I = 2A$

4. $R =$ _____ when $E = 120V$ and $I = 2A$

5. $P =$ _____ when $I = 10A$ and $E = 120V$

6.0.0 ◆ METHODS OF MEASURING ELECTRICAL PROPERTIES

There are three types of metering devices widely used to measure the electrical properties in a circuit:

- *Voltmeter* – Used to measure voltage
- *Ohmmeter* – Used to measure resistance
- *Ammeter* – Used to measure current flow

Voltmeters, ohmmeters, and ammeters are made as separate meters or they can be combined into one instrument called a *multimeter*. Separate meters are normally only used in electrical system monitoring panels or in development/research laboratory settings. The multimeter is the instrument normally used in the field to make voltage, resistance, and current measurements. There are two types of multimeters: analog and digital. However, the digital multimeter (*Figure 5*) is the type of multimeter currently being used by most instrumentation personnel. For this reason, the procedures given in the remainder of this section assume the use of a digital multimeter. If you are unfamiliar with the digital multimeter being used, read the manufacturer's instructions to familiarize yourself with the meter's capabilities and limitations.

 NOTE
Digital multimeters are battery operated. Aging of the batteries will affect the accuracy of the meter. If so equipped, the digital meter's internal battery test should be performed to check the condition of the battery. Otherwise, the batteries should be replaced periodically.

104F05.EPS

Figure 5 ◆ Digital multimeter.

6.1.0 Measuring Voltage With a Multimeter

Voltage measurements are typically made in circuits to determine the value of the voltage applied to the circuit or to determine the amount of voltage drop across a resistor, etc. When measuring voltage, always make sure to connect the multimeter in parallel with the circuit or component (for example, a resistor) being measured. Because it measures the difference in potential between two points in a circuit, it is always connected between the two points to be measured. Make voltage measurements as follows (*Figure 6*):

Step 1 Set the function/range switch to AC or DC volts, as appropriate. For the example shown in *Figure 6*, the function/range switch would be set to the DC volts position. Set the range control to AUTO (automatic ranging).

 WARNING!
Making voltage measurements requires that the circuit under test be energized. Observe all safety precautions when working on or near energized circuits.

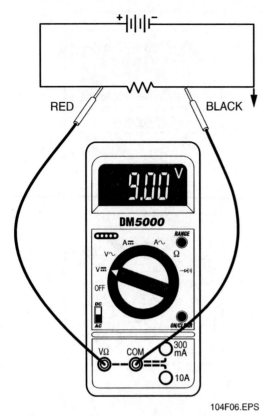

Figure 6 ◆ Digital multimeter connected to measure voltage.

Step 2 Plug the test probes into the meter jacks. The black probe is connected to the common (COM), or minus (−), jack and the red probe to the V-ohm, or plus (+), jack.

Step 3 Connect the test probe tips to the circuit in parallel with the load or power source. Good practice is to observe correct polarity when measuring DC voltages. Connect the red test probe to the positive side of the circuit and the black test probe to the negative side or circuit ground.

Step 4 Read the measured voltage on the meter display. Be sure to note the unit of measurement (volt, millivolt) indicated on the display. Note that if the test leads are reversed when measuring DC voltages, the reading will display a minus (−) sign to indicate negative polarity.

6.2.0 Measuring Resistance With a Multimeter

Resistance measurements are usually made to determine the resistance of an electrical component, such as a relay coil, relay contacts, diodes, or resistors (*Figure 7*), or to determine the continuity of a circuit or wire. Multimeters can be used to measure the resistance in ohms of all or any part of a circuit. Resistance values of components can vary greatly from a few ohms to several million ohms. Make resistance measurements as follows (*Figure 7*).

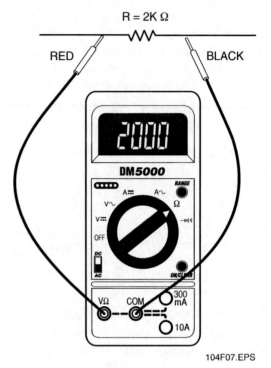

Figure 7 ◆ Digital multimeter connected to measure resistance.

Step 1 Turn off power to the equipment or circuit.

CAUTION
Resistance measurements must be made with the equipment power off, otherwise damage to the multimeter can result.

Step 2 Set the function/range switch to resistance (ohms or Ω). Set the range control to AUTO (automatic ranging).

NOTE
If other components are connected in parallel with the component to be measured, it is necessary to electrically isolate the component being measured by disconnecting at least one lead of the component from the circuit. This is important in order to get an accurate resistance reading. Otherwise, the meter will read the combined resistance of all components that are connected in parallel with the component to be measured.

Step 3   Plug the test probes into the meter jacks. The black probe is connected to the common (COM), or minus (–) jack, and the red probe to the V-ohm, or plus (+), jack.

Step 4   Connect the test probe tips across the component or portion of the circuit you want to measure.

Step 5   Read the measured resistance on the meter display. Be sure to note the unit of measurement: ohms (Ω), kilohms (kΩ), or megohms (MΩ) shown for the reading.

6.3.0 Measuring Current With a Multimeter

Current measurements are made to measure current flow through a circuit. Making current measurements with a multimeter is different than making other measurements with a multimeter. To measure current using a multimeter, the multimeter must always be connected in series with the current flow. This requires disconnecting or opening the normal circuit wiring to insert the multimeter. The use of a multimeter to make current measurements is usually limited to making low-level DC current measurements in electronic circuits. Make current measurements as follows (*Figure 8*).

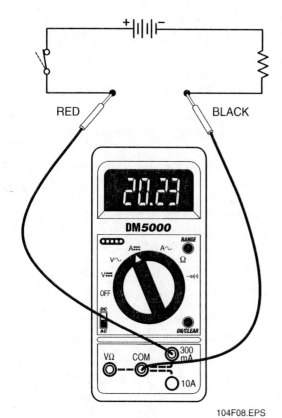

Figure 8 ◆ Digital multimeter connected to measure current.

104F08.EPS

 WARNING!
Making current measurements requires that the circuit under test be energized. Observe all safety precautions when working on or near energized circuits.

Step 1   Turn off power to the circuit. Disconnect one end of the component or circuit to make a place where the multimeter probes can be inserted in series with the circuit to be measured.

Step 2   Set the function/range switch to AC or DC amps, as appropriate. For the example shown in *Figure 8*, the function/range switch would be set to the DC amps position.

Step 3   Plug the test probes into the meter jacks. The black probe is connected to the common (COM), or minus (–), jack. Connect the red probe to the input jack marked for the DC current range of the expected reading; typically the jacks are marked 10 amperes (10A) or 300 milliamperes (300mA).

Step 4   Connect the test probe tips in series with the circuit so that all current flows through the meter. Good practice is to observe correct polarity (+/–) when measuring DC current. Connect the red test probe to the positive side of the circuit and the black test probe to the negative side. Measurement is easier if alligator clips are used to connect the meter leads to the circuit.

Step 5   Turn the circuit power on. Read the measured current on the display. Be sure to note the unit of measurement indicated: amps (A) or milliamps (mA). Note that if the test leads are reversed when measuring DC current, the reading will display a minus (–) sign to indicate negative polarity.

6.4.0 Measuring Alternating Current With a Clamp-on Ammeter

Clamp-on ammeters (*Figure 9*) can be used to measure alternating current in a circuit without the need to disconnect the circuit wires as is required with a multimeter and other types of ammeters. For this reason, they are the most widely used meter for measuring current in the field. Clamp-on ammeters have a movable set of jaws that can be opened and placed (clamped) around each of the wires to be measured, one wire at a time. Alternating current flowing through the wire creates lines of force that induce a current in the jaws. The induced current passes through the meter, providing an indication of how much AC current is passing through the wire.

Figure 9 ◆ Current measurement with a clamp-on ammeter.

NOTE

There are specialized clamp-on ammeters available that can be used to measure direct current in the milliamp range. These meters are used for checking electronic signals in the 4–20mA range.

7.0.0 ◆ RESISTORS AND COLOR CODES

Most resistors have their resistance value marked on them in some way. Most larger power resistors, precision resistors, and variable resistors are marked with numbers printed right on the resistor indicating the resistance value. Small, fixed-composition resistors are usually marked with colored bands as shown in *Figure 10*.

The positions of the bands and their color, making up what is called a *color code*, indicate the resistance values. A single standard color code (*Figure 11*) has been adopted by the United States Armed Forces and the Electronic Industries Association (EIA) for fixed composition, axial-lead resistors.

Refer to *Figure 11* while reading this explanation of the color coding system for determining the value of resistors.

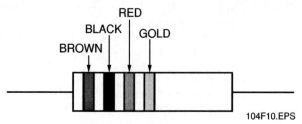

Figure 10 ◆ Resistor color coding.

The first color band indicates the first significant number of the resistance value (brown = 1; orange = 3). The second color band indicates the second significant number (black = 0; yellow = 4) of the resistance value. The third color band indicates the multiplier (black = the two significant numbers are multiplied by one; red = the first two significant numbers are multiplied by 100) to be used. If the third band is silver or gold, the multiplier is 0.01 or 0.1, respectively. The fourth color band indicates the tolerance, or accuracy rating, of the resistor (gold = ±5%; silver = ±10%). If there is no fourth color band, the tolerance of the resistor is ±20%.

The following example shows how the color code system for resistors works.

The first band is red (2)
The second band is violet (7)
The third band is orange (multiplier = 1,000)
The fourth band is gold (±5% tolerance)

The value of the resistor is:

$$27 \times 1,000 = 27,000\Omega, \pm5\% \text{ tolerance}$$

The examples shown in *Figure 11* should also help with mastering the ability to read resistor color codes.

In addition to being able to determine the value of a resistor by looking at its color code, the system can be used to identify and select a needed resistor of a known value. Practice reading the color codes on resistors by determining the color codes that correspond to the following resistor values.

1. 70Ω ±5%: _____
2. 4.4Ω ±5%: _____
3. 10KΩ ±20%: _____

The answers are:

1. 70Ω ±5%: *violet, black, black and gold*
2. 4.4Ω ±5%: *yellow, yellow, gold, gold*
3. 10KΩ ±20%: *brown, black, orange, no color*

COLOR CODE TABLE

Color	Significant Figures	Multiplier Value	Tolerance
Black	0	1	–
Brown	1	10	–
Red	2	100	–
Orange	3	1,000	–
Yellow	4	10,000	–
Green	5	100,000	–
Blue	6	1,000,000	–
Violet	7	10,000,000	–
Gray	8	100,000,000	–
White	9	1,000,000,000	–
Gold	–	0.1	±5%
Silver	–	0.01	±10%
No Color	–	–	±20%

Examples of the use of this table are shown below:

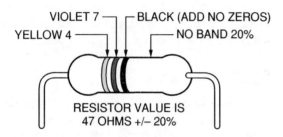
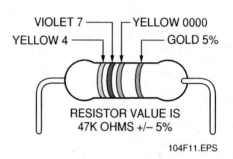

104F11.EPS

Figure 11 ◆ Resistor color code table.

8.0.0 ◆ CAPACITORS AND COLOR CODES

Capacitors come in various shapes and sizes. A color coding system very similar to that used for resistors is used to identify the value of capacitors.

Capacitance is measured in farads, which are very large units. To make the color coding system more practical, the color designations for capacitors represent picofarads (one millionth of one millionth of a farad) since most capacitors fall in this range. The color coding system for capacitors uses dots as well as bands (like resistors) on the body of the capacitor. Color designations for the significant numbers and multipliers used for capacitors are the same as those used for resistors. However, many of the tolerance designations are different for capacitors. For this reason, an appropriate capacitor color chart needs to be used to determine capacitor values for specific types of capacitors.

Exceeding a capacitor's maximum voltage rating can damage the capacitor. Some capacitors have the voltage rating and capacitance value printed on the body, or the voltage rating may be added to the color code.

Since the value of capacitors is also affected by temperature changes, an additional color code may also be printed on the capacitor to identify this property of the capacitor.

While the color codes for resistors and capacitors are generally similar, the color code system for capacitors is more complex as can be seen by the explanation just given. It is very difficult for most people to remember. In most cases, it is best to refer to the manufacturer's manual when identifying the value of capacitors.

9.0.0 ◆ INSTRUMENTATION CONTROL WIRING

Instrumentation control wiring links the field sensing, controlling, printout, and operating devices that form an electronic instrumentation control system. The type and size of instrumentation control wiring must be matched to a specific job.

Instrumentation control wiring is available in one to multiple conductors. These wires may also have shielding or grounding conductors. An outer layer, called the *jacket*, protects the conductors. An illustration of instrumentation control wiring is shown in *Figure 12*.

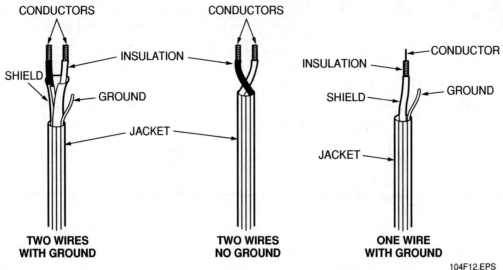

CONDUCTORS CONDUCTORS

INSULATION

SHIELD

GROUND

JACKET

CONDUCTOR

INSULATION

SHIELD

GROUND

JACKET

**TWO WIRES
WITH GROUND**

**TWO WIRES
NO GROUND**

**ONE WIRE
WITH GROUND**

104F12.EPS

Figure 12 ◆ Instrumentation control wiring.

Multi-conductor cable may be grouped in pairs. The multi-conductor cable may have as many as 50 or more pairs of conductor wires.

9.1.0 Shields

Shields (*Figure 13*) are provided on instrumentation control wiring to protect the electrical signals traveling through the conductors from external electrical interference or noise. Electrical noise may come from other electrical equipment operating in the area. Shields are usually constructed of aluminum foil bonded to a plastic film.

If the wiring is not properly shielded, electrical noise may cause erratic or inaccurate control signals, false indications, and improper operation of control devices.

9.2.0 Grounding

A grounding wire may be a bare or insulated wire used to provide continuous contact with a specified grounding terminal. Usually, insulated grounding wires are color coded green. A grounding wire allows connections of all the instruments within a loop to a common grounding system. In some electronic systems, the grounding wire is called a drain wire. Not all instrumentation systems are grounded. Always refer to the installation details to determine whether a grounding wire is to be terminated to a grounding terminal.

Usually, instrumentation is not grounded at both ends of the wire. This helps prevent unwanted ground loops in the system. If the ground is not to be connected at the end of the wire being installed, do not remove the grounding wire. Fold it back and tape it to the cable. This is done in case the ground at the other end develops a problem. If a problem

occurs, the ground that was not originally connected can be used for grounding the system.

9.3.0 Jackets

A synthetic plastic jacket, as shown in *Figure 14*, covers and insulates the components within the instrumentation control wiring. Polyethylene and PVC are the most common materials used for instrumentation control wiring jackets. Some jackets have a nylon rip cord that allows the jacket to be

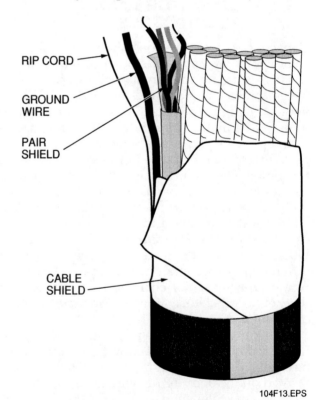

RIP CORD

GROUND
WIRE

PAIR
SHIELD

CABLE
SHIELD

104F13.EPS

Figure 13 ◆ Multi-conductor instrumentation control wiring with shields.

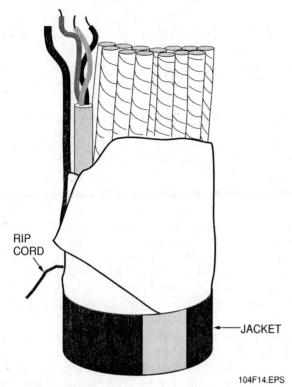

Figure 14 ◆ Wire jacket.

In the AWG system, the larger the number, the smaller the cross-sectional area of the wire. This practice originates from the original numbering system that determined the gauge number by the number of times the wire was fed through the machine that reduced it in size. As an example, 10 AWG was run through the machine 10 times, while 12 AWG was run through 12 times. Wire is no longer manufactured using these methods, but the numbering system remains. The AWG numbers range from 50 to 0; then 00, 000, and 0000. Any wire larger than 0000 is identified by its area in circular mils. Wire sizes smaller than 18 AWG are usually solid, but may be stranded in some cases. Wire sizes 6 AWG and larger are stranded.

For wire sizes larger than 16 AWG, the wire size is marked on the insulation. If a wire size is not marked on the insulation, the size can be found by using a standard wire gauge, as shown in *Figure 16*.

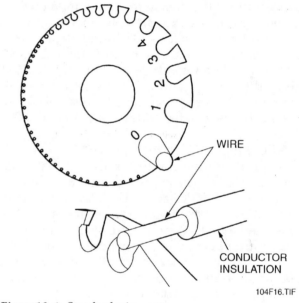

Figure 16 ◆ Standard wire gauge.

peeled back without the use of a knife or cable cutter. This reduces the possibility of nicking the conductor insulation when preparing for termination.

9.4.0 Wire Sizes

Wire sizes are expressed in gauge numbers. The standard system of wire sizes used in the United States is the American Wire Gauge (AWG) system. The AWG system uses numbers to identify the different sizes of wire and cable. An illustration of various AWG wire sizes is shown in *Figure 15*.

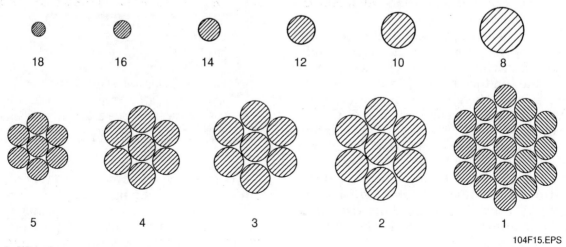

Figure 15 ◆ Wire sizes.

The most common sizes of wire used for instrumentation control wiring and their typical uses are listed below:

- 14-16 AWG – 120VAC supply
- 18 AWG – Low-voltage DC supply
- 18-22 AWG– Low-voltage DC signal

9.5.0 Wire Ratings

An important step in design of electrical circuits is selection of the type of conductor to be used, such as TW, THW, THWN, RHH, THHN, XHHW. The various types of conductors are covered in *NEC Article 310,* and the **ampacities** of conductors with the different insulation and temperature ratings are given in *NEC Tables 310-16* through *310-19* for the varying conditions of use in open air raceways, and at normal or higher-than-normal ambient temperatures. Conductors must be used in accordance with all the data in the tables and notes.

Temperature is an extremely important factor to consider in instrumentation control wiring. Temperature tolerance is the basis for safe operation of insulated conductors. *NEC Table 310-13* gives the ratings and applications for various types of conductors, including their suitability for use in different temperature ranges (i.e., 60°C, 75°C, 90°C).

NEC Tables 310-16 through *310-19,* which are used to determine conductor size for particular applications, are based on an assumed ambient temperature of 30°C (86°F). This means conductor ampacities are based on the ambient temperature plus the heat (I2R) produced by the conductor when current is flowing. Therefore, the size of the conductor in combination with the type of insulation used on the conductor determines the maximum permitted conductor ampacity.

The following is a simplified example used to show how these NEC tables are employed to determine the types of conductors required for a particular application:

A No. 3/0 THW copper conductor used in a raceway has an ampacity of 200, according to *NEC Table 310-16.* In a 30°C ambient temperature environment, the conductor is subjected to this ambient temperature when it carries no current. Since a THW-insulated conductor is rated at 75°C, there is a maximum of 45°C (75° – 30°) of allowable temperature increase due to current flow. If the ambient temperature exceeds 30°C, the conductor's maximum load current rating must be reduced proportionally so that the total temperature, ambient plus conductor temperature rise due to current flow, does not exceed the temperature rating of the conductor's insulation.

Where ambient temperatures do exceed 30°C, the correction factors at the bottom of the NEC tables must be used. The ampacity of the conductors must be derated according to *NEC Table 310-15(b)(2)(a).*

10.0.0 ◆ THERMOCOUPLES

Thermocouples are temperature-measuring devices that work on the principle that two dissimilar metals, when in contact with one another, will produce a measurable difference in potential (voltage). In simple terms, thermocouples are made by joining two wires at one end by twisting, welding with like material, or both. If a thermocouple is connected to an electrical circuit, the voltage generated by the thermocouple can be measured using a voltmeter. The voltage generated by the thermocouple changes as the temperature changes. A conversion chart for the particular type of thermocouple is used to convert the voltage reading to a temperature. Most instruments that use thermocouples as temperature sensors automatically convert the voltage to a temperature readout. *Figure 17* shows a thermocouple that is used to measure the temperature inside a pipe. There are many other types of thermocouples.

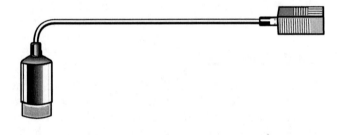

104F17.EPS

Figure 17 ◆ Typical thermocouple.

CAUTION

If thermocouple wires are to be welded, do not introduce another dissimilar metal during the welding. In other words, simply fuse the pair together. Introducing another metal will probably change the voltage output of the thermocouple.

Thermocouples come in a variety of types that measure different ranges of temperatures. The following are some examples of different types of thermocouples, the metals they are made of, and their respective temperature ranges.

- *Type J, Iron-Constantan:* 32° to 1400°F (white and red conductors)
- *Type K, Chromel-Alumel:* 32° to 2300°F (yellow and red conductors)
- *Type T, Copper-Constantan:* –300° to +700°F (blue and red conductors)

The wires themselves make up the thermocouple. Each of the thermocouple wires is made of one of the metals listed for the particular type of thermocouple. The wires are identified by colors, as listed above.

11.0.0 ◆ ELECTRICAL FITTINGS

There are various types of electrical fittings used in the instrumentation craft. Some of these fittings are described here.

11.1.0 Cable Tray Fittings

Cable trays are rigid structures used to support wire and cable. Cable tray fittings are part of the cable tray system and provide a means of chang-

ing the direction or dimension of the different type cable trays. *Figure 18* shows some uses of the different types of cable tray fittings, such as horizontal and vertical tees, horizontal and vertical bends, horizontal crosses, reducers, barrier strips, covers, and box connectors.

11.2.0 Conduit Fittings

Conduit is similar to pipe, and is used to protect conductors.

Conduit fittings are manufactured in two basic types: threaded and threadless. The type of conduit fittings used in a particular application depends upon the size and type of conduit, the type of fitting needed for the application, the location of the fitting, and the installation method.

Set screw couplings as shown in *Figure 19(A)* are threadless fittings. As the name implies, the set screw coupling relies upon a set screw to hold the conduit to the coupling. This type of coupling does not provide a seal and is not permitted by the NEC to be used in wet condition locations.

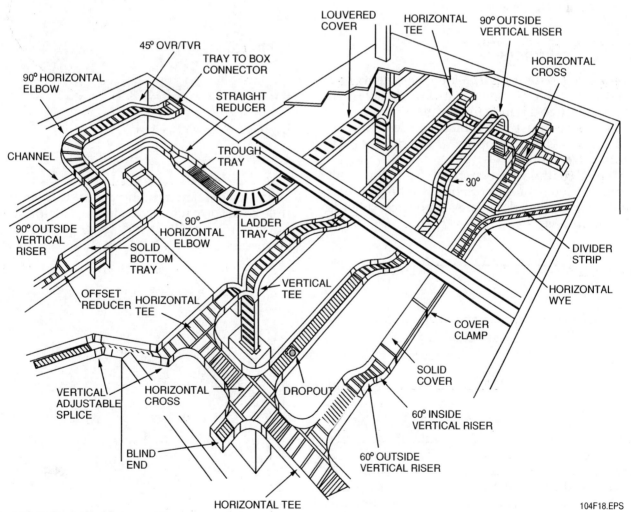

Figure 18 ◆ Typical cable tray system.

104F18.EPS

Compression couplings like the one shown in *Figure 19(B)* are also threadless fittings that provide a tight seal around the conduit and are permitted by the NEC to be used in wet locations.

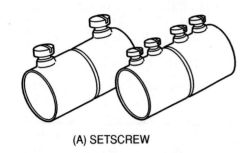

(A) SETSCREW

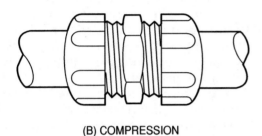

(B) COMPRESSION

104F19.EPS

Figure 19 ◆ Conduit couplings.

11.3.0 Condulets

Condulets (conduit bodies) are components of a conduit or tubing system that provide access to wiring through a removable cover.

Condulets must not contain splices, taps, or devices unless they comply with the rules of *NEC Section 370-16(c)(2)*.

Type C condulets may be used to provide a pull point in a long conduit run or a conduit run that has numerous bends in it. A Type C condulet is shown in *Figure 20*.

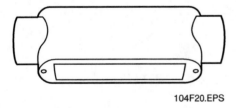

104F20.EPS

Figure 20 ◆ Type C condulet.

The letter L represents *elbow*. A Type L condulet is used as a pulling point for conduit that requires a 90-degree change in direction. Type L condulets are available with the cover on the back (Type LB), or on the sides (Type LL or LR), or on both sides (Type LRL). Several types of L condulets are shown in *Figure 21*.

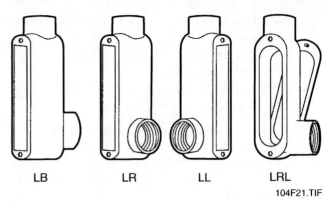

LB   LR   LL   LRL

104F21.TIF

Figure 21 ◆ Type L condulets.

A Type T condulet is used to provide a junction point for three intersecting conduits. Type T condulets are used extensively in rigid conduit systems. A Type T condulet is shown in *Figure 22*.

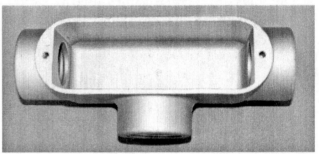

104F22.EPS

Figure 22 ◆ Type T condulet.

A Type X condulet is used to provide a junction point for four intersecting conduits. The removable cover provides access to the interior of the X so that wire pulling and splicing may be performed. A Type X condulet is shown in *Figure 23*.

104F23.EPS

Figure 23 ◆ Type X condulet.

Entrance ell SLB fittings are built with an offset so that they may be attached flush against the surface that is to have a conduit penetration. A cover on the back of the SLB permits wire to be pulled out and reinserted into the conduit (*Figure 24*).

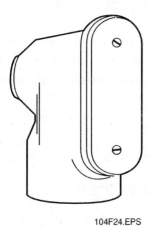

Figure 24 ◆ Entrance ell.

11.4.0 Insulating Bushing

An insulating bushing is made of nonmetal material or has an insulated insert. Insulating bushings are installed on the threaded end of conduit that enters a sheet metal enclosure. The purpose is to protect the conductors from being damaged by the sharp edges of the threaded conduit end. An insulating bushing is shown in *Figure 25*.

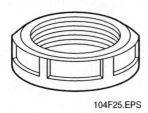

Figure 25 ◆ Insulating bushing.

11.5.0 Grounding Insulating Bushing

Grounding insulating bushings protect conductors and also have provisions for connection of a ground wire. The ground wire, once connected to the grounding bushing, may be connected to the enclosure to which the conduit is connected, and is considered part of the bonding system, according to *NEC Article 250, Part E.* A grounding bushing is shown in *Figure 26*.

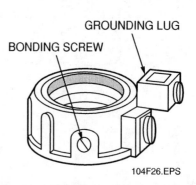

Figure 26 ◆ Grounding bushing.

11.6.0 Flex Connectors

Flex connectors (*Figure 27*) are used to connect flexible conduit to boxes or equipment. They are available in straight, 45-degree, and 90-degree configurations.

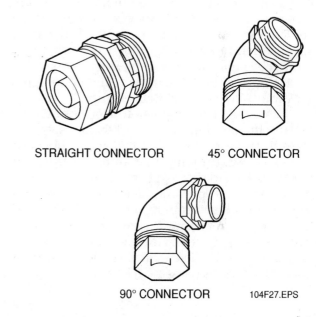

Figure 27 ◆ Flex connectors.

11.7.0 Coaxial Cable Connectors

Coaxial cable connectors come in a wide variety of sizes and designs to fit many different applications. Most of these connectors have three basic parts: the connector body (either male or female), the electrical contact (either male or female), and the inner connector assembly. Several different types of coaxial cable connectors are shown in *Figure 28*.

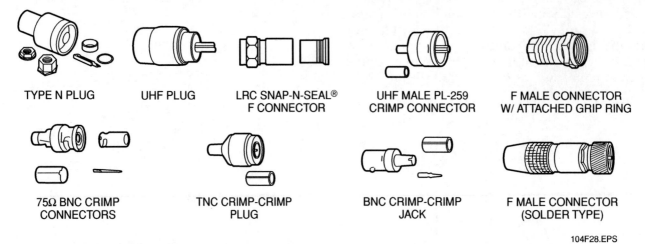

TYPE N PLUG　　UHF PLUG　　LRC SNAP-N-SEAL®
F CONNECTOR

UHF MALE PL-259
CRIMP CONNECTOR

F MALE CONNECTOR
W/ ATTACHED GRIP RING

75Ω BNC CRIMP
CONNECTORS

TNC CRIMP-CRIMP
PLUG

BNC CRIMP-CRIMP
JACK

F MALE CONNECTOR
(SOLDER TYPE)

104F28.EPS

Figure 28 ◆ Coaxial cable connectors.

12.0.0 ◆ EXPLOSION-PROOF HOUSINGS

Explosion-proof housings are made in a variety of materials, including cast metal or specially designed plastic. The housings are designed to contain explosions without rupture. If the atmosphere inside an explosion-proof housing is ignited by an arc or by heat, the explosion will be contained within the housing and will not ignite the atmosphere around the housing.

The cover of an explosion-proof housing is usually threaded to the body of the housing. The threads provide a long path that allows hot gases to cool below ignition temperatures before escaping to the outside atmosphere.

An explosion-proof system is only safe from explosion when properly installed and maintained. Before removing the cover of an explosion-proof housing, the electrical equipment inside the housing must be de-energized. *NEC Article 500* covers hazardous (classified) locations.

12.1.0 Seal Fittings

Hazardous locations in manufacturing plants and other industrial facilities involve a wide variety of flammable gases, vapors, and ignitable dusts. These hazardous substances have widely varying flash points and other flammability characteristics that require the installation of conduit seals. Conduit seals are installed in conduit runs to prevent the passage of gases, liquids, and vapors through the conduit. They are required by *NEC Section 501-5* in specific hazardous locations as outlined by this NEC section.

Seal fittings should be installed in accordance with *NEC Section 501-5.* Seal fittings are usually from 3 inches to 10 inches in length and are threaded on each end with either male or female threads. Each fitting has a plug that can be removed so that a fiber dam and sealing compound can be added. The fiber dam prevents the sealing compound from flowing into the conduit. Several types of seal fittings are shown in *Figure 29.*

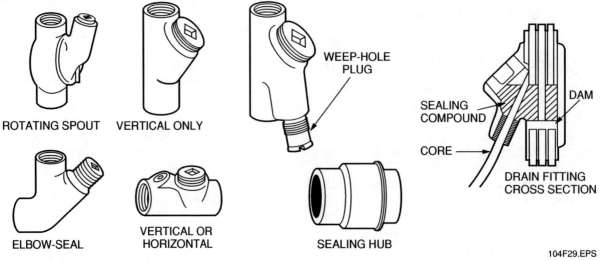

ROTATING SPOUT　VERTICAL ONLY

WEEP-HOLE
PLUG

SEALING
COMPOUND

CORE

DAM

ELBOW-SEAL

VERTICAL OR
HORIZONTAL

SEALING HUB

DRAIN FITTING
CROSS SECTION

104F29.EPS

Figure 29 ◆ Common types of seal fittings.

Summary

Trainees wishing to understand electrical circuits must know Ohm's law and the relationship of current, voltage, resistance, and power in simple DC series circuits. Good circuit analysis skills demand a mastery of resistor and capacitor color codes.

Proper identification of wiring and fittings permits proper and safe installation of instrumentation. Understanding and mastering these concepts will greatly improve your ability to work safely and efficiently around electrical circuits.

Review Questions

1. Current that flows in one direction until it peaks, stops, and then flows in the other direction until it peaks is called _____.
   a. direct current
   b. alternating current
   c. amp current
   d. ground current

2. A henry is the basic unit measurement for _____.
   a. resistance
   b. current
   c. capacitance
   d. inductance

3. Ohm's law is a statement of the relationship between _____ in an electrical circuit.
   a. resistance, voltage, and capacitance
   b. current, resistance, and capacitance
   c. voltage, inductance, and current
   d. current, voltage, and resistance

4. The mathematical formula for Ohm's law is expressed as _____.
   a. $E = I \times R$
   b. $E = I/R$
   c. $E = MC2$
   d. $E = R/I$

5. According to Ohm's law, if E decreases and R remains the same, I _____.
   a. increases
   b. decreases
   c. stays the same
   d. fluctuates

6. According to Ohm's law, if E = 200V, and I = 250mA, R = _____.
   a. 25Ω
   b. 800Ω
   c. $5,000\Omega$
   d. $8,000\Omega$

7. A digital multimeter get its power from _____.
   a. the voltage in the circuit
   b. the current in the circuit
   c. the resistance in the circuit
   d. a battery in the meter

8. The type of meter normally used to measure alternating current is the _____.
   a. VOM
   b. megger
   c. ohmmeter
   d. clamp-on ammeter

9. The value of a resistor may be determined by a(n) _____.
   a. color code marking
   b. amp rating
   c. AWG number
   d. UL rating

10. According to the NEC, if more than three conductors are to be installed in a raceway, you must _____.
    a. decrease the size of the conductors
    b. derate the conductors' ampacity
    c. increase the temperature coefficient
    d. remove at least one conductor

11. The ampacity of a conductor is determined by _____.
    a. the size of the conductor and the type of insulation
    b. the size of the conductor only
    c. the size of the raceway only
    d. the ambient temperature only

12. The colors of the conductors of a Type J thermocouple are _____.
    a. yellow and red
    b. blue and red
    c. white and red
    d. green and red

13. The temperature range of a Type K thermo-couple is _____.
    a. 32°F to 1400°F
    b. 32°F to 2300°F
    c. −300°F to +700°F
    d. 32°F to 5000°F

14. A device that provides access to conductors through a removable cover or covers is a(n) _____.
    a. coaxial connector
    b. seal
    c. coupling
    d. condulet

15. The fiber dam in a seal fitting _____.
    a. prevents the sealing compound from flow-ing into the conduit.
    b. ensures a proper grounding connection for the fitting
    c. insulates the conduit from an isolated ground
    d. protects the conductors from physical dam-age

Trade Terms Introduced in This Module

Alternating current (AC): Alternating current is a current that flows in one direction, stops, and then flows in the other direction.

Ampacity: The maximum amount of current, in amperes, that a conductor may carry under specific conditions of use.

Capacitance: The property of an electric circuit that enables it to store electric energy by means of an electrostatic field and to release this energy sometime later.

Capacitor: A device having two conducting surfaces (plates) separated by an insulating material such as air, paper, mica, glass, plastic film, or oil. It stores electrical energy, blocks the flow of direct current, and permits the flow of alternating current to a degree dependent upon the capacitance value and the frequency.

Conductor: A conductor is a material that offers very little resistance to current flow.

Continuity: A continuous path for the flow of an electric current, such as in a wire. Electrical tests called continuity tests are made to determine whether a connection or wire is broken.

Current: Current is the flow of electrons (electricity) in a circuit.

Direct current (DC): Direct current is a current that always flows in the same direction.

Electrical circuit: The path over which electrons (current) flow.

Inductance: A property of an electrical circuit that tends to oppose any change of current flow through the circuit.

Insulator: A material that offers a very high resistance to current flow.

Ohm (Ω): An ohm is the basic unit of measurement for resistance.

Ohm's law: A statement of the relationship between current, voltage, and resistance in an electrical circuit: current equals the voltage divided by the resistance.

Rectifier: A device that converts alternating current (AC) to direct current (DC).

Resistance: An electrical property that opposes the flow of current through a material.

Resistor: A resistor is any device in a circuit that resists the flow of electrons.

Transformers: Electrical devices that, by electromagnetic induction, transform AC electric energy applied at its input to an AC output at the same frequency, but usually at a different voltage and current value.

Voltage: A measurement of the electromotive force which makes current flow in a circuit.

Watt: The basic unit of measurement for electrical power.

Additional Resources

This module is intended to present thorough resources for task training. The following reference works are suggested for further study. These are optional materials for continued education rather than for task training.

Crouse-Hinds Catalogs of Fittings, Syracuse, NY: Crouse-Hinds.

Electrical Standards and Product Guide, National Electric Manufacturer's Association (NEMA).

National Electrical Code 1999. Quincy, MA: Delmar Publishers, Inc.

National Electrical Code Handbook, 1996. Brian J. McPartland and Joseph F. McPartland, Saddle River, NJ: McGraw-Hill Publishing Company.

Ugly's Electrical References, 1999. George V Hart and Sammie Hart. Houston, TX: United Printing Arts.

Figure Credits

Veronica Westfall   104F22, 104F23

The NCCER makes every effort to keep these textbooks up-to-date and free of technical errors. We appreciate your help in this process. If you have an idea for improving this textbook, or if you find an error, a typographical mistake, or an inaccuracy in the NCCER's Craft Training textbooks, please write us, using this form or a photocopy. Be sure to include the exact module number, page number, a detailed description, and the correction, if applicable. Your input will be brought to the attention of the Technical Review Committee. Thank you for your assistance.

Instructors – If you found that additional materials were necessary in order to teach this module effectively, please let us know so that we may include them in the Equipment and Materials list in the Instructor's Guide.

Write: Curriculum Revision and Development Department
National Center for Construction Education and Research
P.O. Box 141104, Gainesville, FL 32614-1104

Fax: 352-334-0932

E-mail: curriculum@nccer.org

Craft _____ Module Name _____

Copyright Date _____ Module Number _____ Page Number(s) _____

Description _____

_____

_____

_____

(Optional) Correction _____

_____

_____

(Optional) Your Name and Address _____

_____

_____

Metallurgy for Instrumentation

COURSE MAP

This course map shows all of the modules in the first level of the Instrumentation curriculum. The suggested training order begins at the bottom and proceeds up. Skill levels increase as you advance on the course map. The local Training Program Sponsor may adjust the training order.

INSTRUMENTATION LEVEL ONE

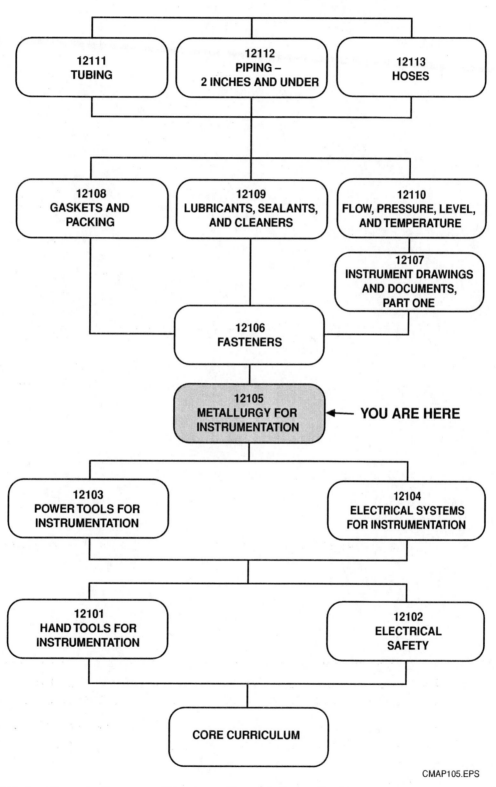

CMAP105.EPS

MODULE 12105 CONTENTS

Figures

Tables

Metallurgy for Instrumentation

OBJECTIVES

When you have completed this module, you will be able to do the following:

1. Define metallurgy.
2. Identify types of common metals.
3. Describe uses and applications of metals in instrumentation.

Prerequisites

Before you begin this module, it is recommended that you successfully complete the following modules: Core Curriculum; Instrumentation Level One, Modules 12101 through 12104.

Required Trainee Materials

1. Pencil and paper
2. Appropriate personal protective equipment

1.0.0 ◆ INTRODUCTION

Metallurgy involves an understanding of the types, properties, and heat treatment methods of metals. There are two types of metallurgy: chemical metallurgy and physical metallurgy. Chemical metallurgy deals with the separation of metals from their ores and with the mixture of metals to form **alloys**. Physical metallurgy deals with how metals behave during various operations.

Many metals and chemicals do not have **compatibility** with one another and must never be combined or come in contact with one another. Reactions can occur which can be injurious or even fatal to personnel. This includes combining metals with metals or metals with chemicals. Some incompatible mixtures include:

- *Acetylene* – Acetylene is incompatible with chlorine, bromine, copper, fluorine, silver, and mercury.
- *Copper* – Copper is incompatible with acetylene and hydrogen peroxide.
- *Hydrocarbons* – Hydrocarbons are incompatible with fluorine, chlorine, bromine, chromic acid, and sodium peroxide.
- *Mercury* – Mercury is incompatible with acetylene, fulminic acid, and ammonia.
- *Silver* – Silver is incompatible with acetylene, oxalic acid, tartaric acid, ammonium compounds, and fulminic acid.
- *Alkali metals* – Alkali metals are incompatible with water, carbon tetrachloride or other chlorinated hydrocarbons, carbon dioxide, and halogens (fluorine, chlorine, bromine, iodine, astatine).

This listing represents only a few of the incompatible materials and is for basic information only. Always refer to the Material Safety Data Sheet (MSDS) for the particular material before assuming its compatibility or incompatibility with another material, and read any information provided by the manufacturer of the material.

A form of corrosion known as galvanic corrosion occurs when two dissimilar metals are placed together in a corrosive environment. The combination of the metals and the corrosive environment forms an electrical circuit that will cause one of the metals to corrode.

The most commonly used metals today are **ferrous metals**, or those which contain iron. Steel is the most common ferrous metal. The composition and properties of ferrous metals may be changed by the addition of various alloying elements to impart the desired qualities.

Nonferrous metals (containing no iron) include aluminum, copper, lead, nickel, tin, and zinc, as well as steel that contains little or no iron. Nonferrous metals are resistant to corrosion and are nonmagnetic.

2.0.0 ◆ FERROUS METALS

Cast iron, machine steel, tool steel, alloy steel, high-speed steel, and high-strength, low-alloy (HSLA) steels are all ferrous metals. Each of these metals has different properties which make it suitable or unsuitable for particular applications.

In its pure form, iron is soft. Because it is so soft, pure iron has very few uses. Different ferrous metals are made by adding elements such as carbon, manganese, or silicon to molten iron. The amount of carbon added to pure iron determines many of the properties of ferrous metals. Cast iron and steel are two of the most common ferrous metals. Cast iron is made by adding carbon, silicon, and manganese to iron. Cast iron has between 2 percent and 4 percent carbon. The difference between cast iron and steel is that steel has less than 2 percent carbon. The amount of carbon in steel primarily determines its **hardness** and **strength**.

Alloy steels are formed by the addition of such elements as chromium, molybdenum, nickel, tungsten, or vanadium, in addition to carbon. The temperature of steel during forming also has a great effect on the properties of the finished steel.

2.1.0 Cast Iron

Cast iron is an alloy of iron, carbon, silicon, and manganese. Cast iron is a brittle metal. It will break rather than bend under shock or impact. Types of cast iron include white cast iron and gray cast iron.

White cast iron is very hard and resists wear and abrasion. It is used for making pulverizing equipment, crushers, and machinery used for handling abrasive materials.

Gray cast iron contains graphite flakes that reduce the strength of the iron. It is used where strength and **toughness** are not required. Gray cast iron can be machined more easily than white cast iron. It is commonly used for making machine bases, engine blocks, and machine parts.

2.2.0 Low-Carbon Steel

Low-carbon steels, commonly called *machine* or *mild steel*, contain from 0.10 to 0.30 percent carbon. Because low-carbon steel is easily forged, welded, and machined, it is used for making auto body frames, I-beams, chains, rivets, bolts, nails,

screws, washers, and fencing wire. Low-carbon steel is easily recognized by its black color.

2.3.0 Medium-Carbon Steel

Medium-carbon steel contains from 0.30 percent to 0.60 percent carbon and is stronger and harder than low-carbon steel. However, the higher carbon content makes it more difficult to form. Different heat-treating processes are used with medium-carbon steels to allow them to be formed and then hardened to achieve strength.

Medium-carbon steel is used for heavy forgings and for making such items as car axles, rails, gears, and drive shafts.

2.4.0 High-Carbon Steel

High-carbon steel, commonly called *tool steel*, contains from 0.60 percent to 1.7 percent carbon. The additional carbon in high-carbon steel makes it even harder and more difficult to form than medium-carbon steel. However, its hardness and strength are important qualities for making a variety of items requiring strength and durability, such as dies, taps, chisels, crowbars, hammers, bridge cables, and machining tools.

2.5.0 Stainless Steel

Alloy steels, such as stainless steels, are formed by the addition of elements such as chromium, molybdenum, nickel, tungsten, and vanadium, as well as carbon. In order for a steel to be called stainless steel, it must contain at least 12 percent chromium by weight.

The **American Iron and Steel Institute (AISI)** recognizes more than 40 different **alloys** as stainless steels. The different types of stainless steel have different properties. Most stainless steel alloys are resistant to rust, corrosion, heat, abrasion, shock, and **fatigue**. Stainless steel is often used in applications that require corrosion resistance and where it is necessary to reduce scaling caused by high temperatures.

Stainless steel alloys are commonly used to make pipe, tubing, and fittings used in instrumentation work. The most common stainless steels (AISI Type 304 and 316) contain chromium and nickel, but not manganese.

2.6.0 High-Speed Steel

High-speed steels are formed by the addition of various amounts and combinations of tungsten, chromium, vanadium, cobalt, and molybdenum. Cutting tools made from high-speed steel maintain a cutting edge at temperatures where most steels would break down. Because of this, high-speed cutting tools are used for machining hard materials at high speeds.

2.7.0 High-Strength, Low-Alloy Steel

High-strength, low-alloy (HSLA) steels contain a maximum carbon content of 0.28 percent and small amounts of vanadium, columbium, copper, and other alloying elements. HSLA steel has a higher strength than medium-carbon steel and is less expensive than other alloy steels. It has strength properties built into the steel and requires no further heat treating. In addition, it has a higher hardness and toughness than carbon steel, and has higher fatigue failure limits. High-strength, low-alloy steel may be used unpainted because it develops a protective oxide coating on exposure to the atmosphere.

3.0.0 ◆ NONFERROUS METALS

Nonferrous metals contain little or no iron. They are resistant to corrosion and are nonmagnetic. Nonferrous metals are used where ferrous metals would be unsuitable. Most nonferrous metals and alloys can be cast or worked into shape by ordinary metalworking processes. They can also be heat treated to produce special properties.

The most common nonferrous metals used are aluminum, magnesium, copper, brass, lead, nickel, and tin. Aluminum, copper, and brass piping are commonly used in instrumentation for pneumatic supply lines and signal lines.

Iron, steel, and aluminum are in common use and are considered standard metals. Specialty metals or alloys are seldom used except when needed for a specific application requiring special metal properties. Specialty metals include magnesium, titanium, nickel alloys, lead, and tantalum.

3.1.0 Aluminum

Aluminum is made from bauxite ore that contains aluminum oxide, iron, and silicon. It is a white, lightweight, soft metal used where a light, non-corrosive metal is required. Aluminum is usually alloyed with silicon, iron, and copper to increase its strength and stiffness. Aluminum alloys are strong, resist corrosion, and are easy to cut and shape.

When exposed to air, the outer layer of aluminum combines with oxygen from the air. This forms a thin film of aluminum oxide on the surface. This film keeps oxygen away from the aluminum underneath, preventing further corrosion. For this reason, aluminum is used extensively in

the manufacturing of aircraft, automotive parts, and cans for food products.

Oxidation is a film that forms on the surface of aluminum when it is exposed to air. This film is what gives aluminum its good corrosion resistance. Oxidation is not apparent, as it leaves the metal bright and clean appearing. Once an oxide film has been cleaned from aluminum, an antioxidant compound must be immediately applied to prevent the oxide from reforming.

Aluminum is sometimes used as an electrical conductor. However, oxidation reduces its conductivity and must be removed if the metal is to be used for that purpose.

3.2.0 Copper

Copper is a soft, **ductile**, **malleable** metal which is very tough and strong. Copper is easy to form and resists corrosion. Cold working copper can cause it to harden. Hardened copper can be **annealed** to make it softer. When hard copper is annealed, it is heated to about 1100°F (600°C), and then cooled to room temperature. This process restores the copper to its original softness and ductility.

Copper is reddish in color and is second only to silver as an effective electrical conductor.

Copper that is 99.9 percent pure is used mostly as an electrical conductor. Sometimes copper is combined with certain other metals to make alloys that conduct electricity as well as pure copper does and with better mechanical properties. Some of these alloys are leaded copper, sulfur copper, and tellurium copper.

Pipe, tubing, fittings and other products are made by casting copper alloys rather than pure copper. Pure copper does not cast well and is more expensive than most copper alloys. For example, brass is a copper alloy that has good mechanical properties and is low in cost.

There are several types of copper pipe and tubing used in instrumentation work. These are described in detail in other training modules.

3.3.0 Brass

Brass is a copper and zinc alloy. Brass is easy to cold form. It can be electroplated with nickel or chromium to improve its appearance. As the percentage of zinc increases in brass, the alloy becomes more yellow due to corrosion. This corrosion process is called *dezincification*.

Red casting brass contains tin as a hardener and lead to improve its machinability. It is often used for valves in high-pressure lines. Yellow casting brass contains zinc plus aluminum, manganese, silicon, nickel, and iron. It is used for plumbing fixtures, machine parts, and ornamental castings.

3.4.0 Magnesium

WARNING!

Pure magnesium explodes when exposed to water.

Magnesium is an element. It is always combined with other elements to form metals. Magnesium is weaker, more brittle, and has poorer high-temperature properties than aluminum. Magnesium is often alloyed with aluminum or zinc. The addition of aluminum to magnesium produces a hardenable alloy. The addition of zinc results in a metal with good corrosion resistance.

Magnesium alloys are lightweight and easily machinable. They can be die-cast or extruded easily. Magnesium alloys are used primarily where lightweight material is required. They are used extensively in the aircraft industry and for household appliances. In fact, one of the first household appliances built with magnesium alloy castings to appear on the market was an upright vacuum cleaner created by Henry Dreyfuss for the Hoover Company in 1936.

3.5.0 Titanium

Titanium is a strong, lightweight, ductile metal with a high resistance to acid corrosion. It remains strong at temperatures of 300°F to 700°F (150°C to 370°C). Titanium is not used extensively in industrial applications because it is expensive. However, titanium and titanium alloys are used in making rivets, nuts, bolts, screws, and other fasteners.

3.6.0 Nickel Alloys

Nickel alloys are corrosion resistant and have good cold-working properties. Some of the more commonly used nickel alloys are described here.

- Monel® is the trade name that International Nickel Corporation uses for its various nickel-copper alloys. Monel® is highly resistant to corrosion from the atmosphere. It also shows good resistance to salt water, lye, sulfuric acid, most foods, and many chemicals. It is similar to stainless steel in appearance, **brittleness**, and other properties. Monel® is often used where high strength and ductility are required. It can also be cold worked. Although Monel® alloys are difficult to machine, their ability to resist corrosion is not decreased by welding.
- Nickel-chromium steels are made from nickel, iron, chromium, and carbon. The strength and

toughness of low-alloy steels are increased with the addition of nickel. Nickel also increases the **hardenability** of low-alloy steels. Nickel-chromium steels are designated by the American Iron and Steel Institute (AISI) and **Society of Automotive Engineers (SAE)** as AISI 3100-9800 and SAE 3200-3400.

- Nickel steels are made from nickel, carbon, and iron. The strength, toughness, hardness, and fatigue resistance of low-alloy steels are increased with the addition of nickel. Nickel steels, unlike other steels, resist brittleness at temperatures below 0°F (−18°C).
- Inconel® is a trade name that International Nickel Corporation uses for its various nickel-iron-chromium alloys. Inconel® consists of nickel, chromium, and iron. Inconel® is often used in high-temperature applications since it remains strong at very high temperatures in normal atmosphere.
- Hastelloy® is a trade name that Union Carbide Corporation uses for its various nickel-based alloys. Hastelloy® contains nickel plus molybdenum or silicon. Hastelloy® is highly resistant to corrosion, especially corrosion by hot, concentrated acids or liquors.
- Nichrome™ consists of nickel and chromium. It has a high resistance to electrical current and oxidation. When electrical current is run through Nichrome™, a large amount of heat is produced. For this reason, heating elements for equipment such as hair dryers and toasters are often made from Nichrome™.

3.7.0 Lead

WARNING!

Exposure to lead fumes can present a health hazard. Repeated exposure can result in a gradual accumulation of lead absorbed into the bloodstream and stored in bones and tissues. Consult your MSDS data sheet for more information on hazards associated with lead.

Lead is commonly used in many industrial applications. It is used in piping systems to carry acids and other corrosive chemicals, for insulation, to shield against radiation, to make paint, to make bronze and babbitt bearings, and as the primary metal in some types of solders.

Alloys of lead, tin, and silver are used extensively for making solder. The type of solder alloy used for a particular job depends primarily on the temperature conditions of the work. The melting temperatures of solder vary with the ratio of alloys in the solder. Solder having a tin content of 50 percent with a lead content of 50 percent has a melting temperature of 425°F, while solder having a tin content of 37 percent with a lead content of 63 percent, has a melting temperature of 361°F. In comparison, solder having a silver content of 5.5 percent with a lead content of 94.5 percent has a melting range of 579°F to 689°F, depending on other ambient conditions.

3.8.0 Tantalum

WARNING!
Tantalum components react with chlorine by creating toxic vapors. Tantalum should not be exposed to processes that involve chlorine use.

Tantalum is a hard metallic element that is resistant to many chemicals. Tantalum loses its chemical resistance to many elements when the temperature exceeds 302°F (150°C), but has a melting temperature of nearly 3000°C.

Tantalum is used in special light bulb filaments, electrolytic capacitors, heat exchangers, and some nuclear reactor parts.

4.0.0 ◆ METAL PROPERTIES

The properties of metals determine their use. It is important to understand the mechanical properties of metals: hardness, ductility, malleability, toughness, strength, **tensile strength**, and **elasticity**. These terms describe the behavior of a metal when acted upon by external forces. Organizations such as the **American Society for Testing Materials (ASTM)** publish standards and specifications describing the properties of various metals.

4.1.0 Hardness

The hardness of a metal is defined as its ability to resist forcible penetration or bending by another substance. Hard metals resist denting and scratching.

Various methods of heat treatment may increase or decrease the hardness of metals. Hardenability is the ability of a metal to be hardened by heat treatment. In many cases, a machine or its parts are hardened after they are fabricated. For example, it is usually easier, faster, and less expensive to forge and machine a gear while the metal is soft. Heat treatment then hardens the metal.

A hardness test determines the degree of hardness of a metal. One standard hardness test is the Brinell Hardness Test. An accurately ground 10mm steel ball is forced into the metal by a hydraulic press. The hydraulic press does this by exerting a predetermined force on the steel ball for a specific period of time. The **diameter** of the dent made in the metal by the steel ball determines the degree of penetration or hardness value of the metal. *Figure 1* shows a comparison of the size of dents made in hard and soft metal resulting from a Brinell Hardness Test.

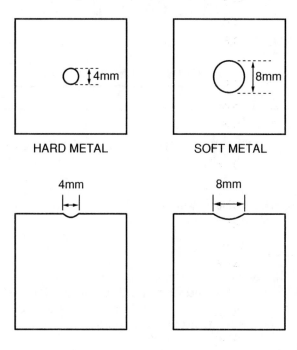

Figure 1 ◆ Brinell hardness test comparison.

Brittleness is a condition in metal that results from over-hardening the metal. A metal is brittle if it cracks or breaks when only a small amount of force is applied. As a rule, the harder the metal, the more brittle it is. A brittle metal, such as gray cast iron, breaks apart or shatters if struck a heavy blow with a hammer. Soft metals bend or distort when hit with a hammer.

4.2.0 Ductility

Ductility is the ability of a metal to be stretched into thin wire without breaking. Three types of **ductile** metals are copper, aluminum, and soft steel.

Ductility can be measured by stretching a metal sample and then comparing the amount of stretch to the original length of the material, as shown in *Figure 2*. This measurement is expressed as a percentage of stretch.

Another way to measure ductility is by comparing a cross section of the stretched material to a cross section of the material before it was stretched. This measurement is expressed as a percentage of area reduction.

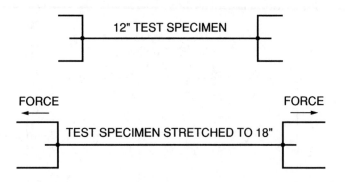

RESULTS: 50% STRETCH, HIGHLY DUCTILE

105F02.EPS

Figure 2 ◆ Ductility measurement.

4.3.0 Malleability

Malleability is the property of a metal that permits it to be hammered or rolled into other sizes and shapes. **Malleable** metals can be shaped or formed easily. Lead is a very malleable metal.

4.4.0 Toughness

Toughness is the ability of a metal to withstand sudden, high-impact shocks without breaking. Soft metals are usually tougher than hard metals. Toughness is the opposite condition of brittleness. Hammers, chisels and other tools are made from metals that are tough. Annealing can also be used to achieve the proper toughness.

4.5.0 Strength

Strength is the ability of a metal to resist distortion. Strength can be measured by exerting a predetermined force in a specific direction on the sample. The resistance to distortion from this force determines the strength of the metal. *Figure 3* shows the three ways to test strengths of a metal: tension strength, compression strength, and shear strength.

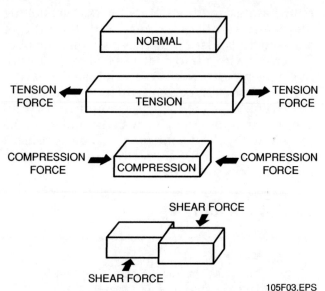

105F03.EPS

Figure 3 ◆ Tests for distortion of metals.

4.6.0 Tensile Strength

Tensile strength is the force in a metal that resists being pulled apart. A tensile-strength test can be performed on a metal by fastening a precise test sample of the metal (*Figure 4*) through holes drilled in the sample into a tensile testing machine. The test sample must be of a specific diameter so that the area of the sample can be calculated. The tensile testing machine stretches the sample until it pulls it apart. The resistance force exerted by the sample against being pulled apart is recorded by the testing machine.

The resistance force or tensile yield strength is expressed in thousands of pounds per square inch. *Figure 5* shows a tensile-strength test.

4.7.0 Elasticity

Elasticity is the ability of a metal to regain its original shape after deformation. For example, pulling on a spring with a flywheel and slider stretches the spring, as shown in *Figure 6*.

After the flywheel completes one rotation, the spring returns to its original shape. By increasing the size of the flywheel, the spring will be stretched beyond its elastic limit. If the spring is stretched too far (**yield point**), it will not return to its original shape.

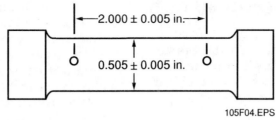

Figure 4 ◆ Example of a metal tensile test sample.

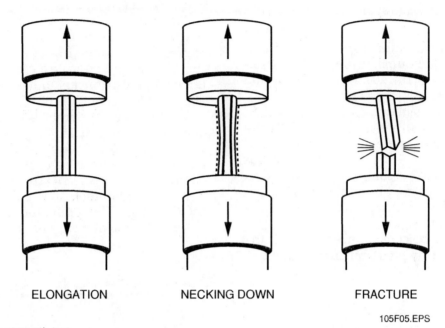

ELONGATION   NECKING DOWN   FRACTURE

105F05.EPS

Figure 5 ◆ Tensile-strength test.

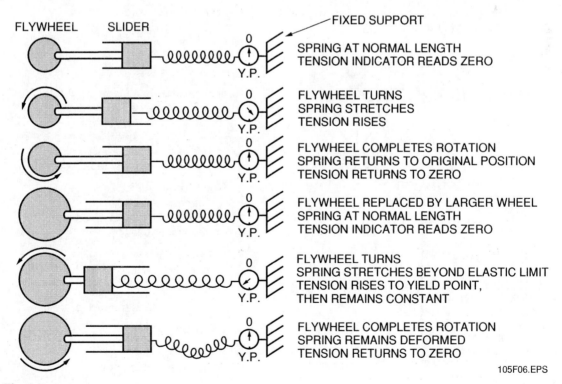

FIXED SUPPORT

SPRING AT NORMAL LENGTH
TENSION INDICATOR READS ZERO

FLYWHEEL TURNS
SPRING STRETCHES
TENSION RISES

FLYWHEEL COMPLETES ROTATION
SPRING RETURNS TO ORIGINAL POSITION
TENSION RETURNS TO ZERO

FLYWHEEL REPLACED BY LARGER WHEEL
SPRING AT NORMAL LENGTH
TENSION INDICATOR READS ZERO

FLYWHEEL TURNS
SPRING STRETCHES BEYOND ELASTIC LIMIT
TENSION RISES TO YIELD POINT,
THEN REMAINS CONSTANT

FLYWHEEL COMPLETES ROTATION
SPRING REMAINS DEFORMED
TENSION RETURNS TO ZERO

105F06.EPS

Figure 6 ◆ Elasticity test.

5.0.0 ◆ CLASSIFICATION OF METALS

Designers and engineers select the best metals for particular applications depending on factors such as temperature, pressure, corrosiveness, and suitability to process characteristics. Several classification systems are used to identify different types of metals.

5.1.0 Steel

In order to ensure that the composition of various types of steel remains constant and that certain types of steel meet the required specifications, two main systems of code numbers are used in classifying steels. One system was developed by the AISI. The other was developed by SAE.

The classification systems designed by the AISI and SAE are similar in most respects. Both the AISI and the SAE use a series of four or five numbers to designate the type of steel. Each code number specifies the chemical composition of one kind of steel. The AISI system also indicates the steel-making process by a letter prefix preceding the number, as shown in *Figure 7*.

The first digit in the code number indicates the basic kind of steel (the predominant alloying ele-ment). For example, 4 indicates molybdenum steels and 3 indicates nickel-chrome steels. These designations can be found in *Table 1*.

The second digit in the code number specifies the approximate percentage by weight of the alloying element. For example, 20XX would indicate a nickel steel with about .50 percent nickel, and 22XX would indicate a nickel steel with about 2 percent nickel. The percentage of the major alloying elements for designated code numbers can be found in *Table 1*.

The last two digits indicate the average carbon content in the steel (the carbon content is expressed in hundredths of a percent). For example, 2530 would indicate a nickel steel containing about 5 percent nickel and a carbon content of about 0.30 percent (30/100 of 1 percent).

When the code numbers have five digits, the last three digits indicate the percentage of carbon. for example, 20110 would indicate a nickel steel containing about .50 percent nickel and a carbon content of over 1 percent (110 in the code number).

AISI code numbers include a prefix in front of the first digit. This prefix indicates what method was used in making the steel, as shown in *Figure 7*.

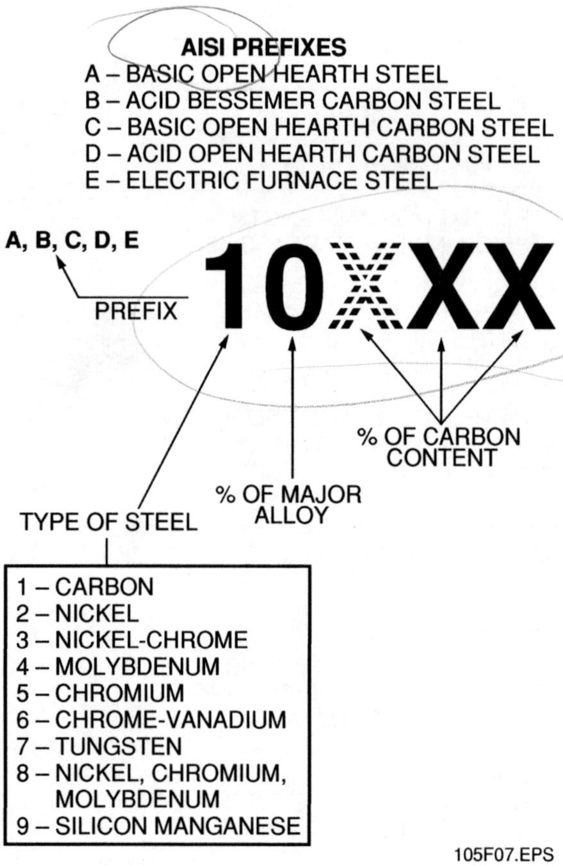

AISI PREFIXES
A – BASIC OPEN HEARTH STEEL
B – ACID BESSEMER CARBON STEEL
C – BASIC OPEN HEARTH CARBON STEEL
D – ACID OPEN HEARTH CARBON STEEL
E – ELECTRIC FURNACE STEEL

A, B, C, D, E

PREFIX

10XXX

% OF CARBON CONTENT

% OF MAJOR ALLOY

TYPE OF STEEL

1 – CARBON
2 – NICKEL
3 – NICKEL-CHROME
4 – MOLYBDENUM
5 – CHROMIUM
6 – CHROME-VANADIUM
7 – TUNGSTEN
8 – NICKEL, CHROMIUM, MOLYBDENUM
9 – SILICON MANGANESE

105F07.EPS

Figure 7 ◆ SAE and AISI system of classifying steel.

Table 1 Steel Classifications

Carbon steels	1xxx
Plain carbon	10xx
Free-cutting (resulphurized screw stock	11xx
Nickel steels	2xxx
0.50% nickel	20xx
1.50% nickel	21xx
3.50% nickel	23xx
5.00% nickel	25xx
Nickel-chromium steels	3xxx
1.25% nickel, 0.60% chromium	31xx
1.75% nickel, 1.00% chromium	32xx
3.50% nickel, 1.50% chromium	33xx
3.00% nickel, 0.80% chromium	34xx
Corrosion and heat-resisting steels	30xxx
Molybdenum steels	4xxx
Chromium-molybdenum	41xx
Chromium-nickel-molybdenum	43xx
Nickel-molybdenum	46xx and 48xx
Chromium steels	5xxx
Low-chromium	51xx
Medium-chromium	52xxx
Chromium-vanadium steels	6xxx
Triple-alloy steels (nickel, chromium, molybdenum)	8xxx
Manganese-silicon steels	9xxx

5.1.1 Identification of Steel Stock

It is often necessary to identify a type of metal by its physical appearance. *Table 2* describes the physical characteristics of some common metals, including several types of steel.

In addition to their physical appearance, metals are often identified by a manufacturer's stamp or a color code painted on the end of the stock.

> **NOTE**
>
> All steel manufacturers do not use the same color-coding system for particular grades of steel stock, so be sure that you know the color-coding system used by the manufacturer of the stock.

When cutting steel from color-coded stock, always cut from the unpainted end. That way, the color coding will remain on the stock that is left for later identification.

One way to determine the carbon content of steel is known as the file test. Because carbon content is a factor in hardness and resistance to cracking, the steel with the highest carbon content will be most resistant to filing, as shown in *Table 3*. The table lists the type of steel in the left-hand column, carbon content in the center column, and the reactions of a flat file when applied to the metal. From the information in the table, it can be verified that steel with a higher carbon content causes more resistance to the file's biting effect, indicating a harder metal.

Table 2 Identification of Metals

Metal	Carbon Content (%)	Appearance	Method of Processing	Uses
Cast iron (C.I.)	2.50 – 3.50	Gray, rough sandy surface	Molten metal poured into sand molds	Parts of machines, such as lathe beds, etc.
Machine steel (M.S.)	0.10 – 0.30	Black, scaly surface	Put through rollers while hot	Bolts, rivets, nuts, machine parts
Cold rolled or cold drawn (C.R.S.); (C.D.S)	0.10 – 0.30	Dull silver, smooth surface	Put through rollers or drawn through dies while cold	Shafting, bolts, screws, nuts
Tool steel (T.S.)	0.60 – 1.5	Black, glossy	Same as machine steel	Drills, taps, dies, tools
High-speed steel (H.S.S.)	Alloy steel	Black, glossy	Same as machine steel	Dies, tools, taps, drills, toolbits
Brass		Yellow (various shades); rough if cast, smooth if rolled	Same as cast iron, or rolled to shape	Bushings, pump parts, ornamental work
Copper		Red-brown; rough if cast, smooth if rolled	Same as cast iron, or rolled to shape	Soldering irons, electric wire, water pipes

Table 3 File Test for Steel

Steel Type	Carbon Content	Reaction of File
Mild steel	< 0.15 percent	Bites into surface easily, requiring minimal pressure or force applied to file
Medium carbon steel	0.15 to 0.25 percent	Bites into surface when slight pressure is applied to file
High alloy steel	0.26 to 0.35 percent	Bites into surface when force and pressure are applied to file
Tooling steel	0.36 to 0.45 percent	Minimal bite when force and pressure are applied to file
Hardened tooling steel	<0.45 percent	No bite, file slides over surface

5.2.0 Aluminum

Aluminum is classified into different grades according to the aluminum content, impurity limits, and the alloy modification. Two code systems were developed by the Aluminum Association. One system uses a four-digit numbering system to designate wrought aluminum grades. The other system uses a three-digit numbering system to designate cast aluminum grades.

In the four-digit code system, the predominant alloying element is designated by the first digit. The second digit designates alloy modifications or impurity limits. The purity of the aluminum or a particular alloy is designated by the last two digits. *Table 4* shows the designations for the main alloying elements in the four-digit code system.

In the 1XXX column (99.00 percent minimum aluminum), the minimum aluminum content above 99.00 percent is specified by the last two dig-

its (in tenths and hundredths of a percent above 99 percent). For example, 1060 would indicate a minimum aluminum content of 99.60 percent.

The second digit of the four-digit code system indicates the impurity limits. For example, if the second digit is 0, it means that individual impurities were not controlled. If the second digit is between 1 and 9, it indicates that there was some control of one or more impurities.

In the 2XXX through 8XXX group, the first digit designates the metal as an aluminum alloy. The second digit in the code number indicates whether the aluminum has any alloy modification. The last two digits further specify the different types of alloys in the group. Some of the most typical wrought aluminum alloy designations are listed in *Table 5*.

The code numbers may also include a letter or letter and number after the last digit. The **temper** of the aluminum is indicated by a letter or a letter and a number separated from the four-digit code number by a dash. For example, 5050-W is an aluminum-magnesium alloy. The W indicates that the alloy is a solution heat-treated (unstable temper) aluminum alloy. The aluminum alloy temper designations and their meanings are listed in *Table 6*.

In *Table 6*, some of the particular alloy temper designations listed apply only to wrought aluminum products. Others apply only to cast aluminum. However, most of the designations apply to both wrought and cast aluminum. When a second digit is added to the alloy temper designation, it is used to indicate the degree of hardness.

Table 4 Aluminum Alloy Numbering System

Main Alloying Element	Number
None (99.00%) aluminum, min.	1xxx
Copper	2xxx
Silicon w/copper and/or magnesium	3xxx
Silicon	4xxx
Magnesium	5xxx
Magnesium and silicon	6xxx
Zinc	7xxx
Other elements	8xxx

Table 5 Wrought Aluminum Alloy Designations

Alloy Number	Silicon	Copper	Manganese	Magnesium	Chromium	Zinc
1060		0.12	99.60 percent (minimum) aluminum			
1100			99.00 percent (minimum) aluminum			
1350			99.50 percent (minimum) aluminum			
2011		5.50				
2014	0.80	4.40	0.80	0.50		
2024		4.40	0.60	1.50		
3003		0.12	1.10			
3004			1.10	1.00		
4032	12.20	0.90		1.10	0.10	0.25
4043	5.50	0.30				
5050				1.20		
5052				2.50	0.25	
5154				3.50	0.25	
6053	0.70			1.30	0.25	
6061				1.00	0.20	
6063	1.30	0.10	0.10	0.80	0.40	
6201	0.70			0.80		
7004		2.10		3.00	0.30	7.40
7039			2.70	2.80	0.20	4.00

Table 6 Aluminum Alloy Temper Designations

F	As fabricated
O	Annealed and recrystallized (wrought only)
H	Strain-hardened (wrought only)
H1, plus a second digit	Strain-hardened only
H2, plus a second digit	Strain-hardened, then partially annealed
H3, plus a second digit	Strain-hardened, then stabilized
W	Solution heat-treated (unstable temper)
T	Treated to produce stable tempers other than F, O, or H
T2	Annealed (cast only)
T3	Solution heat-treated, then cold-worked
T4	Solution heat-treated and naturally aged to a stable condition
T5	Artificially aged only
T6	Solution heat-treated, then artificially aged
T7	Solution heat-treated, then stabilized
T8	Solution heat-treated, cold-worked, then artificially aged
T9	Solution heat-treated, artificially aged, then cold-worked
T10	Artificially aged, then cold-worked

For example, if H12 was used, the 2 indicates quarter-hard; a 4 would indicate half-hard; a 6 would indicate three-quarters hard; and an 8 would indicate full-hard.

In the three-digit numbering system for cast aluminum, the alloy is indicated by the first digit, as shown in *Table 7*.

Table 7 Aluminum Alloy Casting Designations

Alloying Elements	Number
Aluminum (99% min.)	1xx
Copper	2xx
Silicon, plus copper or magnesium	3xx
Silicon	4xx
Magnesium	5xx
(Not used)	6xx
Zinc	7xx
Tin	8xx
Others	9xx

In the 1XX group (99.00 percent minimum aluminum), the minimum aluminum content above 99.00 percent is specified by the last two digits (in tenths and hundredths of a percent above 99 percent). The second and third digits in the 2XX through 9XX series further define the elements in the particular alloy family. Sometimes a fourth digit is added to the group. This digit specifies the form of the metal.

- 0 – Casting specification
- 1 – Ingot, chemically similar to a casting alloy
- 2 – Ingot, chemically slightly different than No.1

In the 1XX group, a letter appearing to the left of the 1 indicates that one or more of the elements included in the alloy were controlled. A letter appearing to the left of the first digit indicates a variant of the original standard alloy using slightly different combinations of alloying elements. Examples are included in *Table 8*.

Table 8 Examples of Aluminum Casting Alloys

Alloy Number	Method	PERCENT OF ALLOYING ELEMENTS				
		Silicon	Copper	Magnesium	Zinc	Others
208.0	Sand casting	3.0	4.0			
213.0	Perm. mold	2.0	7.0			
295.0	Sand casting	1.1	4.5			
B295.0	Perm. mold	2.5	4.5			
A332.0	Perm. mold	12.0	1.0	1.0		2.5 Nickel
F332.0	Perm. mold	9.5	3.0	1.0		
C355.0	Sand casting & perm. mold	5.0	1.3	0.05		
A356.0	Sand casting & perm. mold	7.0		0.3		
A514.0	Perm. mold			4.0		
520.0	Sand casting			10.0		
A712.0	Sand casting		0.5	0.7	6.5	
A850.1	Sand casting & perm. mold	2.5	1.0			6.5 Tin
B850.0	Sand casting & perm. mold	0.4	2.0			6.5 Tin

If an aluminum casting alloy can be tempered, it will have a dash and a letter following the number to indicate the amount of temper. If an aluminum casting alloy has an F or no letter at all following the group number, it means that the alloy cannot be heat treated. *Table 8* shows the composition of aluminum casting alloys.

5.3.0 Magnesium Alloys

The classification system designed by the ASTM for magnesium alloys is shown in *Table 9*. The code letters, conditions, and properties for different alloying metals are shown at the bottom of the table.

Table 9 ASTM Magnesium Alloys Designations

Alloy and Form	Characteristics	Remarks
AZ31B (3Al, 1 Zn) Sheet and plate extrusions, forgings	Moderate strength; good formability, dent resistance, and good weldability; stress relief required.	General-purpose alloy; wide variety of uses to about 300°F (149°C).
AZ91B (9Al, 0.6 Zn) Die castings	Good strength, ductility, and castability; difficult to weld.	AZ91A differs from AZ91B only in its lower copper content.
EZ91C (8.7 Al, 0.7 Zn) Sand and permanent-mold castings	Good castability; moderately high-strength property levels; good pressure tightness and weldability.	Stable properties to about 200°F (93°C); often satisfactory to 350°F (177°C) if operating stresses are not high.
EZ33A (3 rare earths, 2.7 Zn, 0.7 Zr) Sand and permanent-mold castings	Good tensile and creep strengths; good weldability; excellent pressure tightness and damping capacity; somewhat less castability than AZ91C.	Used at 300° to 500°F (149° to 260°C).
HK31A (3 Th, 0.7 Zr) Sand and permanent-mold castings sheet and plate	Good short-time elevated-temperature properties; good formability; excellent weldability; no stress relief required; low microporosity.	Engine, airframe, and missile castings; missile and aircraft skins; used at 400°F to 700°F (204°C to 371°C).
HM21A (2 Th, 0.6Mn) Sheet and plate, forgings	Exceptionally stable at elevated temperatures; better creep strength than HK31A; good formability; excellent weldability; no stress relief required.	Primarily missile and aircraft uses; used at 400°F to 800°F (204°C to 427°C); plate properties higher than those of sheet.
OE22A (2.5 Ag, 2 Didymium, 0.7 Zr) Sand and permanent-mold castings, forgings	Superior tensile-yield strength plus excellent creep resistance and fatigue strength up to approximately 500°F (260°C).	Used in aircraft, missiles, and space vehicles.
ZK60A (5.7 Zn, 0.5 Zr) Extrusions, forgings	High strength; good toughness; limited arc weldability; good spot weldability.	Room-temperature alloy; for highly stressed parts, primarily in aircraft and military uses; wide use as forging alloy.

First Two Code Letters

A – Aluminum	L – Beryllium
B – Bismuth	M – Manganese
C – Copper	N – Nickel
D – Cadmium	P – Lead
E – Rare-Earth element	Q – Silver
F – Iron	R – Chromium
H – Thorium	S – Silicon
K – Zirconium	T – Tin
	Z – Zinc

Conditions and Properties

F – As fabricated
O – Annealed
H10 and H11 – Slightly strain hardened
H23, H24, and H26 – Strain hardened and partially annealed
T4 – Solution heat-treated
T5 – Artificially aged only
T6 – Solution heat-treated and artificially aged

Letter Following the Two Digits
Chronological order of the standardization of the alloy containing the two main elements.

The two main alloying elements are indicated by the first two letters in the series. These letters indicate the percentage by weight of the alloying elements, the larger percentage represented by the first letter and the smaller percentage shown by the second letter. If the percentages are the same, they are arranged in alphabetical order.

The two digits following the letters indicate the approximate percentage of the alloying elements. Again, the first digit defines larger percentage and the smaller percentage is designated by the second digit.

The letter following the two digits indicates that the alloy is a variant of the original alloy of the group. Conditions and properties are indicated by a letter and number. A hyphen separates the letter and number from the rest of the designation. For example, AZ31B-T4 means that aluminum and zinc (AZ) are the two main alloying elements. The 31 indicates that the alloy contains 3 percent aluminum and 1 percent zinc. The B indicates that this is the second (B) alloy with the same principal alloying elements to become a standard alloy. The T4 means that it has been solution heat-treated.

5.4.0 Gray Cast Iron

ASTM designations for gray cast iron are given in *Table 10*. The class number indicates the tensile strength of the different grades of cast iron.

5.5.0 Stainless Steel

Stainless steels are metals that are used where corrosion resistance is important. Stainless steel contains at least 12 percent chromium. Many types of stainless steel contain more than 12 percent chromium and other alloys.

Stainless steels are grouped in three major categories: austenitic, ferritic, and martensitic (classified by AISI).

- Austenitic stainless steels are part of the AISI 200 and 300 series and contain at least 16 percent chromium and small amounts of nickel, carbon, and manganese. AISI 200 series austenitic stainless steels contain chromium, nickel, and manganese. AISI 300 series austenitic stainless steels contain chromium and nickel. Austenitic stainless steel is widely used in construction, oil refineries, and chemical processing.

Table 10 Gray Cast Iron Designations

ASTM Specification and General Description	Class Number	Tensile Strength Minimum (1000 PSI)
A 48 For general-purpose parts where strength is a major consideration	20	20
	25	25
	30	30
	35	35
	40	40
	45	45
	50	50
	55	55
	60	60
A 159 **(Also SAE J 431a)** Castings for automotive and allied industries	G2000	20
	G3000	30
	G3000a	30
	G4000b	40
	G3500c	35
	G3500	35
	G4000	40
	G4500	45
	G4000d	40
	G4000e	40
	G4000f	40
A 278 **(Also ASME SA278)** Castings for pressure-containing parts for service to 650°F	40	40
	50	50
	70	70
	80	80
A 319 Castings for nonpressure-containing parts for elevated temperatures	I	Low
	II	30
	III	to 40
A 436 High-alloy austenitic gray iron for parts requiring resistance to heat, corrosion, and water	1	25
	1b	30
	2	25
	2b	30
	3	25
	4	25
	5	20
	6	25

- Ferritic stainless steels are part of the AISI 400 series and contain 12 percent to 27 percent chromium and very little carbon. Ferritic stainless steel is the most corrosion resistant and has the greatest machinability of the three types of stainless steels.
- Martensitic stainless steels are part of the AISI 400 series and contain between 11.5 percent and 18 percent chromium and small amounts of other alloys. Martensitic stainless steel is magnetic and can be hardened by heat treating. It does not resist corrosion as well as ferritic and austenitic stainless steels do.

6.0.0 ◆ APPLICATIONS OF METALS IN THE INSTRUMENTATION CRAFT

Applications of metal products used in the instrumentation craft, such as fasteners, tubing, and piping, are covered in detail in the task modules that focus on these items.

At this point, you should know that metal fasteners, pipe, and tubing have various identification codes and markings which must be checked to determine if a particular metal product is appropriate for a specific job. Usually, the type of metal product to be used is designated in the project specifications. Your job will be to check the actual product identification to make sure that it matches the specifications, before installation.

For example, the strength and quality of a bolt or screw is important in many instrumentation jobs. You may have to check the bolt or screw identification against the specifications for the job. SAE and ASTM have developed a system of special markings that appear on the heads of bolts and screws. These marks are called grade, or line markings. The greater the number of marks on the head, the higher the quality of the steel. Unmarked fasteners are usually considered to be made of mild steel (low-carbon steel). The grade markings may also indicate the type of metal from which the fastener is made. *Figure 8* shows the ASTM and SAE grade markings for steel bolts and screws.

GRADE MARKING	SPECIFICATION	MATERIAL
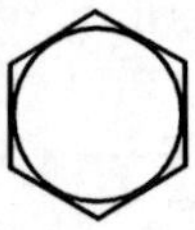	SAE – Grade 0	Steel
	SAE – Grade 1 ASTM – A 307	Low-Carbon Steel
	SAE – Grade 2	Low-Carbon Steel
	SAE – Grade 3	Medium-Carbon Steel, Cold Worked
	SAE – Grade 5	Medium-Carbon Steel, Quenched and Tempered
	ASTM – A 449	
 A 325	ASTM – A 325	Medium-Carbon Steel, Quenched and Tempered
 BB	ASTM – A 354 Grade BB	Low-Alloy Steel, Quenched and Tempered
 BC	ASTM – A 354 Grade BC	Low-Alloy Steel, Quenched and Tempered
	SAE– Grade 7	Medium-Carbon Alloy Steel, Quenched and Tempered, Roll Threaded After Heat Treatment
	SAE– Grade 8	Medium-Carbon Alloy Steel, Quenched and Tempered
	ASTM – A 354 Grade BD	Alloy Steel Quenched and Tempered
 A 490	ASTM – A 490	Alloy Steel Quenched and Tempered

ASTM SPECIFICATIONS
A 307 – Low-carbon steel externally and internally threaded standard fasteners.
A 325 – High-strength steel bolts for structural steel joints, including suitable nuts and and plain hardened washers.
A 449 – Quenched and tempered steel bolts and studs.
A 354 – Quenched and tempered alloy steel bolts and studs with suitable nuts.
A 490 – High-strength alloy steel bolts for structural steel joints, including suitable nuts and plain hardened washers.
ASTM SPECIFICATION
J 429 – Mechanical and quality requirements for threaded fasteners.

105F08.EPS

Figure 8 ◆ ASTM and SAE grade markings.

Summary

Understanding the properties of metals is important in performing quality instrumentation work. In this training module, you learned about various types and properties of common ferrous and nonferrous metals. The applications of different types of metal in the instrumentation craft were introduced, along with identification systems for particular metals.

The knowledge and skills covered in this module provide basic and fundamental competencies required to work with different metals. Metal products are used in a variety of instrumentation jobs. At this point, you need to be able to identify particular metals so that you are sure that the correct materials are being used for a job. In your day-to-day work activities, take the time to practice the skills learned in this module. It takes a lot of practice, study, and on-the-job experience to develop the skills needed to be expert in working with different metal products.

Review Questions

1. Cast iron contains _____ percent carbon.
   a. less than 2
   b. 2½
   c. between 2 and 4
   d. more than 5

2. The element in steel that primarily determines its hardness and strength is_____.
   a. silicon
   b. carbon
   c. nickel
   d. manganese

3. Low-carbon steels usually contain less than _____ percent carbon.
   a. 0.010
   b. 0.090
   c. 0.003
   d. 0.35

4. Hard copper is annealed to make it _____.
   a. harder and stronger
   b. softer and stronger
   c. softer and more ductile
   d. harder and less brittle

5. The test sample used in a tensile strength test must be of a specific _____.
   a. length
   b. diameter
   c. material
   d. temperature

6. The resistance force or tensile yield strength of a metal product is expressed in _____ per square inch.
   a. thousands of pounds
   b. thousandths of one pound
   c. fractional pounds
   d. liters

7. The carbon content of the steel with an SAE code number of 8720 is about _____ percent.
   a. 0.20
   b. 2.0
   c. 20
   d. 87

8. When cutting steel from color-coded stock, always cut from the _____ .
   a. painted end
   b. tapered end
   c. end with the arrow on it
   d. unpainted end

9. A file test can be used to determine the _____ of steel.
   a. zinc content
   b. carbon content
   c. tensile strength
   d. toughness

10. The type of metal product to be used on a job is usually designated in the project _____.
    a. site plan
    b. metals-to-be-used catalog
    c. supplier's preference listing
    d. specifications

Trade Terms Introduced in This Module

Alloy: A metal made up of two or more different metals melted together.

American Iron and Steel Institute (AISI): An organization that publishes information about research, development, use, specifications and standards relating to metals.

American Society for Testing Materials (ASTM): An organization that publishes information about specifications, standards and practices relating to the testing of metals.

Anneal: A heating process followed by slow cooling that makes a metal softer and less brittle.

Brittleness: The property of a metal which permits no permanent distortion before breaking.

Compatibility: The capability of two materials to be placed in contact or in close proximity without affecting the physical or chemical properties of either material.

Diameter: The distance across a circle at its widest point.

Ductile: The ability of a metal to be stretched into thin wire without breaking.

Elasticity: The property of a metal to return to its original shape after deformation, once the force acting upon it has been removed.

Fatigue: The prolonged effect of repeated straining action which causes the metal to strain or break.

Ferrous metal: A metal that contains iron.

Hardenability: The ability of a metal to be hardened by heat treatment.

Hardness: The property of a metal to resist forcible penetration or bending by another substance.

Malleable: The property of a metal which permits it to be hammered or rolled into other sizes and shapes.

Nonferrous metal: A metal that contains no iron.

Society of Automotive Engineers (SAE): An organization that publishes specifications and standards relating to metals used in motorized vehicles.

Strength: The ability of a metal to resist deformation.

Temper: The degree of hardness and elasticity of a metal.

Tensile strength: The force with which a metal resists being pulled apart.

Toughness: The property of a metal to withstand sudden shock or high-impact forces without fracturing or breaking. Toughness is the opposite condition to brittleness.

Yield point: The point at which a stretched piece of metal will not return to its original shape or size.

Additional Resources

This module is intended to present thorough resources for task training. The following reference works are suggested for further study. These are optional materials for continued education rather than for task training.

Ferrous Materials Standards Manual 2000. Warrendale, PA: Society of Automotive Engineers (SAE).

Machinery's Handbook, 2000. Erik Oberg. New York, NY: Industrial Press Inc.

Standards and Specifications for Metals Washington, DC: American Iron and Steel Institute (AISI).

Standards and Specifications for Metals. New York, NY: American National Standards Institute (ANSI).

Standards and Specifications for Metals. Philadelphia, PA: American Society for Testing and Materials (ASTM).

NCCER CRAFT TRAINING USER UPDATES

The NCCER makes every effort to keep these textbooks up-to-date and free of technical errors. We appreciate your help in this process. If you have an idea for improving this textbook, or if you find an error, a typographical mistake, or an inaccuracy in the NCCER's Craft Training textbooks, please write us, using this form or a photocopy. Be sure to include the exact module number, page number, a detailed description, and the correction, if applicable. Your input will be brought to the attention of the Technical Review Committee. Thank you for your assistance.

Instructors – If you found that additional materials were necessary in order to teach this module effectively, please let us know so that we may include them in the Equipment and Materials list in the Instructor's Guide.

Write: Curriculum Revision and Development Department
National Center for Construction Education and Research
P.O. Box 141104, Gainesville, FL 32614-1104

Fax: 352-334-0932

E-mail: curriculum@nccer.org

Craft _____   Module Name _____

Copyright Date _____   Module Number _____   Page Number(s) _____

Description _____

_____

_____

_____

(Optional) Correction _____

_____

_____

(Optional) Your Name and Address _____

_____

_____

Fasteners

COURSE MAP

This course map shows all of the modules in the first level of the Instrumentation curriculum. The suggested training order begins at the bottom and proceeds up. Skill levels increase as you advance on the course map. The local Training Program Sponsor may adjust the training order.

INSTRUMENTATION LEVEL ONE

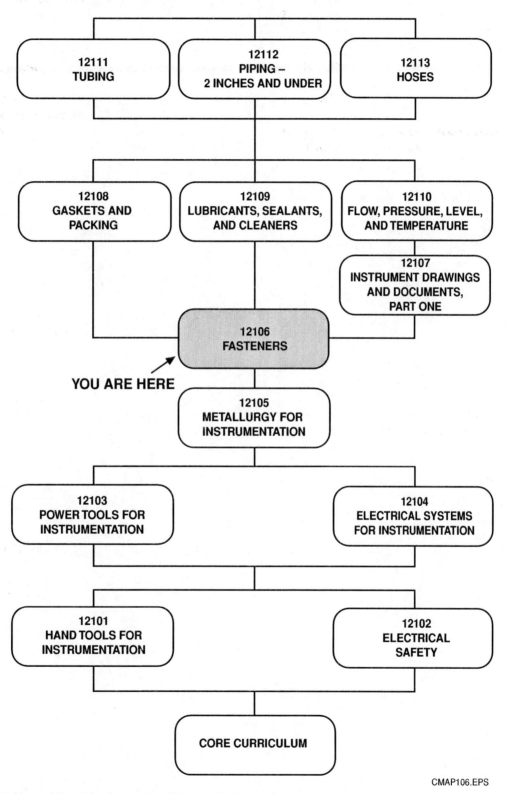

YOU ARE HERE

CMAP106.EPS

Figures

Tables

Fasteners

OBJECTIVES

When you have completed this module, you will be able to do the following:

1. Identify and explain the use of threaded fasteners.
2. Identify and explain the use of non-threaded fasteners.
3. Describe various types of fasteners.
4. Demonstrate the correct applications for fasteners.
5. Install fasteners.

Prerequisites

Before you begin this module, it is recommended that you successfully complete the following modules: Core Curriculum; Instrumentation Level One, Modules 12101 through 12105.

Required Trainee Materials

1. Pencil and paper
2. Appropriate personal protective equipment

1.0.0 ◆ INTRODUCTION

Fasteners are used to assemble and install many different types of equipment, parts, and materials. Fasteners include screws, bolts, nuts, pins, clamps, retainers, tie wraps, rivets, and **keys**. Fasteners are used extensively in the instrumentation craft. You need to be familiar with the many different types of fasteners in order to identify, select, and properly install the correct fastener for a specific application.

The two primary categories of fasteners are threaded fasteners and non-threaded fasteners.

Within each of these two categories, there are numerous different types and sizes of fasteners. Each type of fastener is designed for a specific application. The kind of fastener used for a job may be listed in the project specifications, or you may have to select an appropriate fastener.

Fastener failure can result in a number of different problems. To perform quality instrument work, it is important to use the correct type and size of fastener for the particular job. It is equally important that the fastener be installed properly.

In this training module, you will be introduced to fasteners commonly used in instrumentation work.

2.0.0 ◆ THREADED FASTENERS

Threaded fasteners are the most commonly used type of fastener. Many threaded fasteners are assembled with nuts and washers. The following sections describe standard threads used on threaded fasteners, as well as different types of bolts, screws, nuts, and washers. *Figure 1* shows several types of threaded fasteners.

2.1.0 Thread Standards

There are many different types of threads used for manufacturing fasteners. The different types of threads are designed to be used for different jobs. Threads used on fasteners are manufactured to industry established **thread standards** for uniformity. The most common standard is the Unified standard, sometimes referred to as the *American* standard. Unified standards are used to establish thread series and classes.

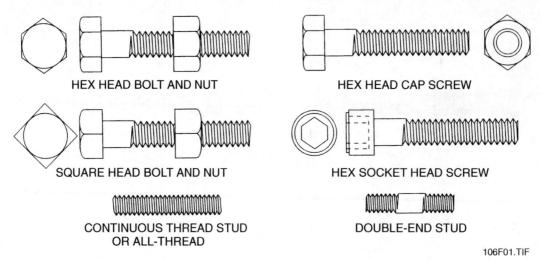

HEX HEAD BOLT AND NUT

HEX HEAD CAP SCREW

SQUARE HEAD BOLT AND NUT

HEX SOCKET HEAD SCREW

CONTINUOUS THREAD STUD
OR ALL-THREAD

DOUBLE-END STUD

106F01.TIF

Figure 1 ◆ Threaded fasteners.

2.1.1 *Thread Series*

Unified standards are established for three series of threads, depending on the number of threads per inch for a certain diameter of fastener. These three series and their abbreviations are as follows:

- *Unified National Coarse (UNC) Thread* – Used for bolts, screws, nuts and other general purposes. Fasteners with UNC threads are commonly used for rapid assembly or disassembly of parts and where corrosion or slight damage may occur.

- *Unified National Fine (UNF) Thread* – Used for bolts, screws, nuts, and other applications where a finer thread for a tighter fit is desired.

- *Unified National Extra Fine (UNEF) Thread* – Used on thin-walled tubes, nuts, ferrules, and couplings.

2.1.2 *Thread Classes*

The unified standards also establish **thread classes**. Classes 1A, 2A, and 3A apply to external threads only. Classes 1B, 2B, and 3B apply to internal threads only. Thread classes are distinguished from each other by the amounts of **tolerance** provided. Classes 3A and 3B provide a minimum **clearance** and classes 1A and 1B a maximum clearance.

Classes 2A and 2B are the most commonly used. Classes 3A and 3B are used when close tolerances are needed. Classes 1A and 1B are used where quick and easy assembly is needed and a large tolerance is desired.

2.1.3 *Thread Identification*

Screw threads are identified by a standard **thread identification** method. *Figure 2* shows how screw threads are designated for a common fastener.

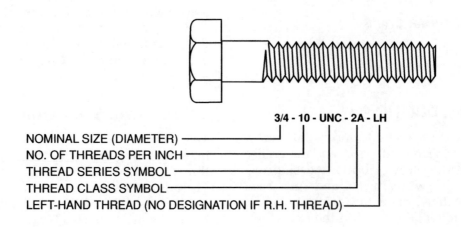

3/4 - 10 - UNC - 2A - LH

NOMINAL SIZE (DIAMETER) ——————
NO. OF THREADS PER INCH ——————
THREAD SERIES SYMBOL ——————
THREAD CLASS SYMBOL ——————
LEFT-HAND THREAD (NO DESIGNATION IF R.H. THREAD) ——————

106F02.EPS

Figure 2 ◆ Screw thread designations.

- *Nominal size* – The approximate diameter of the fastener.
- *Number of threads per inch (TPI)* – TPI is standard for all diameters.
- *Thread series symbol* – The unified standard thread type (UNC, UNF, or UNEF).
- *Thread class symbol* – The closeness of fit between the bolt threads and nut threads.
- *Left-hand thread symbol* – Specified by the symbol LH. Unless threads are specified with the LH symbol, the threads are right-hand threads.

NOTE

Left-hand threads tighten in a counterclockwise direction. Right-hand threads tighten in a clockwise direction.

2.1.4 Power Transmission Threads

Several types of threads are used for moving machine parts for adjusting, setting, and transmitting power. These special threads are referred to as power transmission threads. Three special types of power transmission threads are the square, acme, and buttress forms (*Figure 3*).

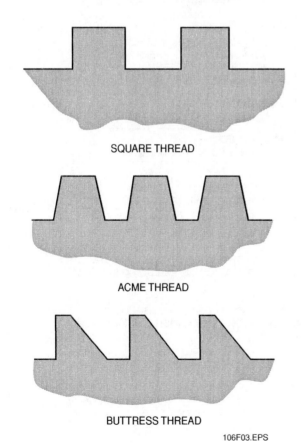

SQUARE THREAD

ACME THREAD

BUTTRESS THREAD

106F03.EPS

Figure 3 ◆ Power transmission threads.

- *Square thread* – The square thread is the strongest and most useful of all thread forms. It is also the most difficult to make because its parallel sides must be accurately machined.
- *Acme thread* – The acme thread has replaced the square thread for most uses because it is easier to machine than the square thread.
- *Buttress thread* – The buttress thread has one side cut square and the other side cut at a slant. It has great strength along the thread axis in one direction only. This thread form is used to screw thin tubular parts together.

2.1.5 Grade Markings

Special **grade markings** on the head of a bolt or screw can be used to determine the strength of the fastener. The **Society of Automotive Engineers (SAE)** and the **American Society of Testing Materials (ASTM)** have developed the standards for these markings. These grade or line markings for steel bolts and screws are shown in *Figure 4*.

Generally, the higher strength steel fasteners have a greater number of marks on the head. If the head is unmarked, the fastener is usually considered to be made of mild steel (low carbon content).

2.2.0 Types of Bolts and Screws

Bolts and screws are made in many different sizes and shapes and from a variety of materials. They are usually identified by the head type or other special characteristics. The following sections describe several different types of bolts and screws.

NOTE

The appropriate drill sizes for tapping holes for different sizes of bolts and screws will be discussed later in this module.

2.2.1 Machine Screws

Machine screws differ from machine bolts in that they are typically installed or removed using a shank-type device like a screwdriver or other tool that is inserted into the head of the machine screw. Machine screws are available in a range of diameters, with the smaller diameters (0.0600 through 0.2160) designated by using a numbering system from zero through twelve.

ASTM AND SAE GRADE MARKINGS FOR
STEEL BOLTS & SCREWS

GRADE MARKING	SPECIFICATION	MATERIAL
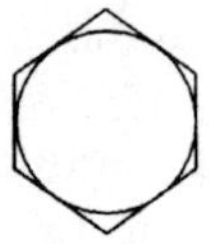	SAE-GRADE 0	STEEL
	SAE-GRADE 1 ASTM-A 307	LOW CARBON STEEL
	SAE-GRADE 2	LOW CARBON STEEL
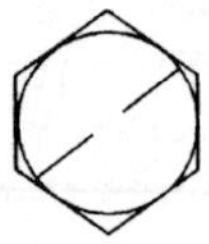	SAE-GRADE 3	MEDIUM CARBON STEEL, COLD WORKED
	SAE-GRADE 5	MEDIUM CARBON STEEL, QUENCHED AND TEMPERED
	ASTM-A 449	
	ASTM-A 325	MEDIUM CARBON STEEL, QUENCHED AND TEMPERED
	ASTM-A 354 GRADE BB	LOW ALLOY STEEL, QUENCHED AND TEMPERED
	ASTM-A 354 GRADE BC	LOW ALLOY STEEL, QUENCHED AND TEMPERED
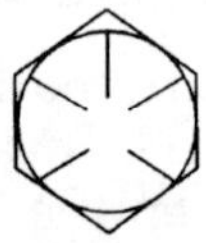	SAE-GRADE 7	MEDIUM CARBON ALLOY STEEL, QUENCHED AND TEMPERED ROLL THREADED AFTER HEAT TREATMENT
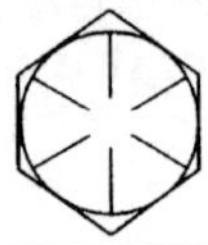	SAE-GRADE 8	MEDIUM CARBON ALLOY STEEL, QUENCHED AND TEMPERED
	ASTM-A 354 GRADE BD	ALLOY STEEL, QUENCHED AND TEMPERED
	ASTM-A 490	ALLOY STEEL, QUENCHED AND TEMPERED

ASTM SPECIFICATIONS
    A 307 - LOW CARBON STEEL EXTERNALLY AND INTERNALLY THREADED STANDARD FASTENERS.
    A 325 - HIGH STRENGTH STEEL BOLTS FOR STRUCTURAL STEEL JOINTS, INCLUDING SUITABLE
           NUTS AND PLAIN HARDENED WASHERS.
    A 449 - QUENCHED AND TEMPERED STEEL BOLTS AND STUDS.
    A 354 - QUENCHED AND TEMPERED ALLOY STEEL BOLTS AND STUDS WITH SUITABLE NUTS.
    A 490 - HIGH STRENGTH ALLOY STEEL BOLTS FOR STRUCTURAL STEEL JOINTS, INCLUDING
           SUITABLE NUTS AND PLAIN HARDENED WASHERS.
SAE SPECIFICATION
    J 429 - MECHANICAL AND QUALITY REQUIREMENTS FOR THREADED FASTENERS.

106F04.TIF

Figure 4 ◆ Grade markings for steel bolts and screws.

For example, a 10-32 machine screw has a diameter of 0.190, with 32 threads per inch. Those in the larger range (above 0.2160) are typically sized by their respective nominal sizes, such ¼ inch and ³⁄₁₆ inches. The length of machine screws range from ⅛ inch (very small diameter) to over 3 inches. *Figure 5* shows different types of machine screws.

2.2.2 *Machine Bolts*

Machine bolts are generally used to assemble parts where close tolerances are not required. Machine bolts have square or hexagonal shaped heads. They are generally available in diameters ranging from ¼ inch to 3 inches. The length of machine bolts typically varies from ½ inch to 30 inches. Nuts for machine bolts are similar in shape to the bolt heads. The nuts are usually furnished along with the bolts. *Figure 6* shows two different types of machine bolts. The square head machine bolt is not generally used in applications requiring **torque** specifications.

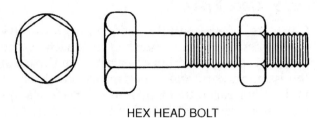

HEX HEAD BOLT

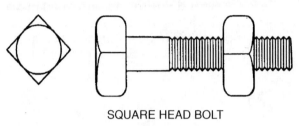

SQUARE HEAD BOLT

106F06.TIF

Figure 6 ◆ Machine bolts.

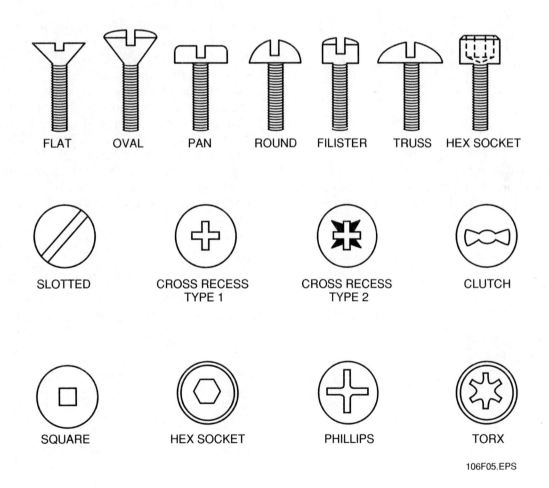

106F05.EPS

Figure 5 ◆ Machine screws.

2.2.3 Cap Screws

Cap screws are usually used on high-quality assemblies requiring a finished appearance. The cap screw passes through a clearance hole in one of the assembly parts and screws into a threaded hole in the other part rather than into a nut. The clamping action occurs by tightening the cap screw.

Cap screws are made to close tolerances and are provided with a machined or semi-finished bearing surface under the head. They are normally made in coarse and fine thread series and in diameters from ¼ inch to 2 inches. Lengths may range from ⅜ inch to 10 inches. Metric sizes are also available. *Figure 7* shows typical cap screws.

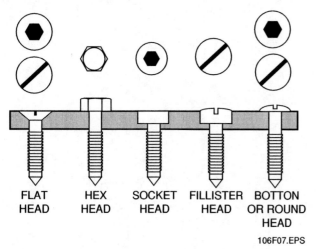

| FLAT HEAD | HEX HEAD | SOCKET HEAD | FILLISTER HEAD | BOTTON OR ROUND HEAD |

106F07.EPS

Figure 7 ◆ Cap screws.

2.2.4 Set Screws

Set screws are normally made from heat-treated steel. They typically screw through threads in one part, with the specially machined end being forced against the other part, keeping either part from moving in relationship to one another. Some typical uses include preventing pulleys from slipping on shafts, holding collars in place on shafts, and holding shafts in place.

The head style, in conjunction with the style of machined end, are typically used to classify set screws. *Figure 8* shows several styles of set screws.

2.2.5 Carriage Bolts

Carriage bolts are used in assembly where a smooth, tamper-proof bolt head is required. Directly under the bolt head is a machined square area that, in the case of fastening metal parts together, fits into a square hole. This prevents the bolt from inadvertently loosening. Securing or tightening a carriage bolt must always be done by turning the nut. This is because the carriage bolt head is dome-shaped and offers no means of tightening. *Figure 9* shows the features of a carriage bolt.

2.2.6 Stud Bolts

Stud bolts are headless bolts that are threaded over the entire length of the bolt or for a length on both ends of the bolt. One end of the stud bolt is screwed into a tapped hole. The part to be clamped is placed over the remaining portion of the stud, and a nut and washer are screwed on to clamp the two parts together. Stud bolts are used for several purposes, including holding together inspection covers on equipment and bearing caps. *Figure 10* shows a typical stud bolt. It is not unusual for double-end stud bolts to have different types of threads on each end.

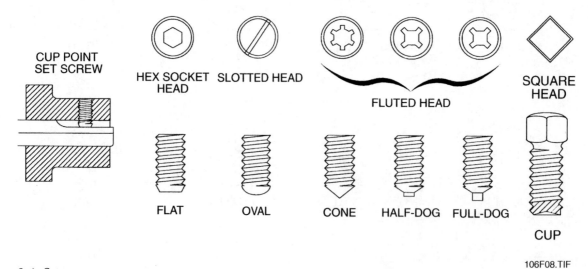

Figure 8 ◆ Set screws.

106F08.TIF

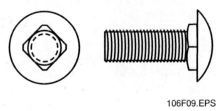

Figure 9 ◆ Carriage bolt.

106F09.EPS

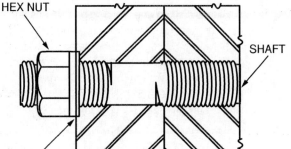
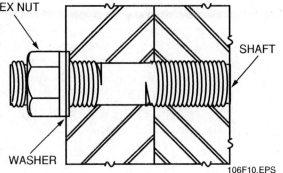

HEX NUT

SHAFT

WASHER

106F10.EPS

Figure 10 ◆ Stud bolt.

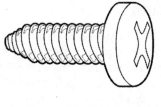

STANDARD THREAD FORMING SCREW

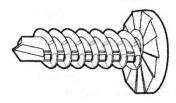

SELF-DRILLING SCREWS

106F11.TIF

Figure 11 ◆ Thread-forming screws.

2.2.7 Thread-Forming Screws

Thread-forming screws are made of hard metal. They form a thread as they are driven into the work. This thread-forming action eliminates the need to tap a hole before installing the screw. Some thread-forming screws also drill their own holes, eliminating drilling, punching, and aligning of parts. Thread-forming screws are primarily used to fasten light-gauge metal parts together. *Figure 11* shows two types of thread-forming screws. Often thread-forming screws are referred to as *sheet metal screws*.

2.2.8 Thread-Cutting Screws

Thread-cutting screws actually cut threads into the metal as they are driven into a pilot hole. Thread-cutting screws are made of hardened steel that is harder than the metal being tapped. Thread-cutting screws are primarily used to join heavy-gauge sheet metal and nonferrous metal parts. *Figure 12* shows some typical thread-cutting screws.

2.2.9 Drive Screws

Drive screws do not require that the hole be tapped. They are installed by hammering the screw into a drilled or punched hole of the proper size. Drive screws are mostly used to fasten parts that will not be exposed to much pressure. A typical use of drive screws is attaching permanent name plates on electric motors and other types of equipment. *Figure 13* shows typical drive screws.

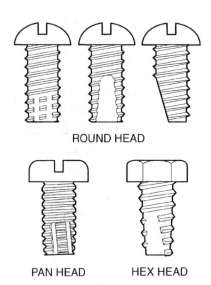

ROUND HEAD

PAN HEAD   HEX HEAD

106F12.TIF

Figure 12 ◆ Thread-cutting screws.

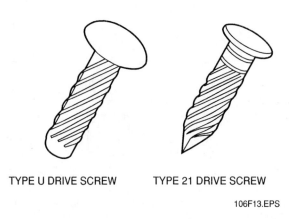

TYPE U DRIVE SCREW   TYPE 21 DRIVE SCREW

106F13.EPS

Figure 13 ◆ Drive screws.

2.3.0 Nuts

Most nuts used with threaded fasteners are hexagonal or square-shaped. They are usually used with bolts having the same shaped head. *Figure 14* shows several different types of nuts used with threaded fasteners.

Nuts are typically finished as regular, semi-finished, or finished. The only machining done on regular nuts is to the threads. In addition to the threads, semi-finished nuts are also machined on the bearing face. Machining the bearing face makes a truer surface for fitting the washer. The only difference between semi-finished and finished nuts is that finished nuts are made to closer tolerances.

The standard machine screw nut has a regular finish. Regular finished and semi-finished nuts are shown in *Figure 15*.

2.3.1 Jam Nuts

A jam nut is used to lock a standard nut in place. A jam nut is a thin nut installed on top of the standard nut. *Figure 16* shows an example of a jam nut installation.

NOTE

A standard sized nut can also be used as a jam nut atop another standard sized nut. To properly install a jam nut, tighten the first nut down to the desired tightness or torque, then while holding that nut with a wrench to prevent it from turning, install and tighten the jam nut with a second wrench until it forcefully contacts the first nut.

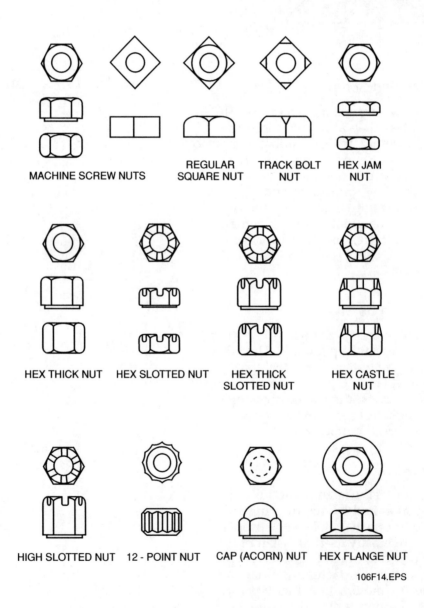

MACHINE SCREW NUTS   REGULAR SQUARE NUT   TRACK BOLT NUT   HEX JAM NUT

HEX THICK NUT   HEX SLOTTED NUT   HEX THICK SLOTTED NUT   HEX CASTLE NUT

HIGH SLOTTED NUT   12 - POINT NUT   CAP (ACORN) NUT   HEX FLANGE NUT

106F14.EPS

Figure 14 ◆ Nuts.

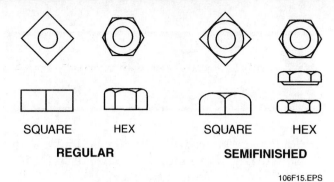

Figure 15 ◆ Nut finishes.

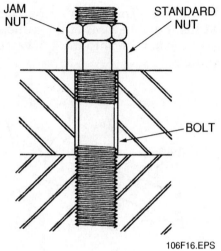

Figure 16 ◆ Jam nut.

2.3.2 Castellated, Slotted, and Self-Locking Nuts

Castellated (castle) and slotted nuts are slotted across the flat part of the nut. They are used with specially manufactured bolts in applications where little or no loosening of the fastener can be tolerated. After the nut has been tightened, a cotter pin is fitted in through a hole in the bolt and one set of slots in the nut. The cotter pin keeps the nut from loosening under working conditions.

Self-locking nuts are also used in many applications where loosening of the fastener cannot be tolerated. Self-locking nuts are designed with nylon inserts, or they are slightly deformed in such a manner so they cannot work loose. An advantage of self-locking nuts is that no hole in the bolt is needed. *Figure 17* shows typical castellated, slotted, and self-locking nuts.

2.3.3 Acorn Nuts

When appearance is important or exposed and sharp thread edges on the fastener must be avoided, acorn (cap) nuts are used. The acorn nut tightens on the bolt and covers the ends of the threads. The tightening capability of an acorn nut is limited by the depth of the nut. *Figure 18* shows a typical acorn nut.

2.3.4 Wing Nuts

Wing nuts are designed to allow rapid loosening and tightening of the fastener without the need for a wrench. They are used in applications where limited torque is required and where frequent adjustments and service are necessary. Figure 19 shows a typical wing nut.

> **NOTE**
> Wing nuts should be used for applications where hand tightening is sufficient.

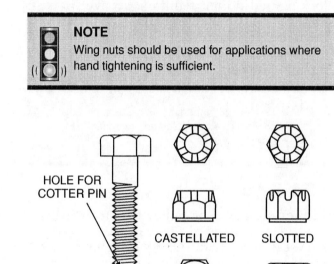

Figure 17 ◆ Castellated, slotted, and self-locking nuts.

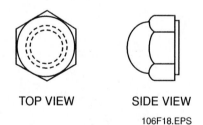

Figure 18 ◆ Acorn nut.

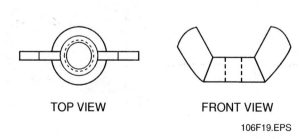

Figure 19 ◆ Wing nut.

3.0.0 ◆ NON-THREADED FASTENERS

Non-threaded fasteners have many uses in instrumentation. Different types of non-threaded fasteners often used in instrumentation include retainers, keys, pins, clamps, washers, rivets, and tie wraps.

3.1.0 Retainer Fasteners

Retainer fasteners, also called *retaining rings*, are used for both internal and external applications. Some retaining rings are seated in grooves in the fastener. Other types of retainer fasteners are self-locking and do not require a groove. To easily remove internal and external retainer rings without damaging the ring or the fastener, special pliers are used. *Figure 20* shows several types of retainer fasteners.

 NOTE
External retainer fasteners are sometimes called *clips*.

3.2.0 Keys

To prevent a gear or pulley from rotating on a shaft, keys are inserted. One half of the key fits into a keyseat on the shaft. The other half fits into a **keyway** in the hub of the gear or pulley. The key fastens the two parts together, stopping the gear or pulley from turning on the shaft. *Figure 21* shows several types of keys, keyways, and their uses. Some different types of keys include:

- *Square key* – A square key is usually one-fourth the shaft diameter. It may be slightly tapered on the top for easier fitting.

 CAUTION
Shaft keyseats typically have razor-sharp edges.

- *Pratt and Whitney key* – This key is similar to the square key, but rounded at both ends. It fits into a keyseat of the same shape.

- *Gib head key* – This key is interchangeable with the square key. The head design allows easy removal from the assembly.

- *Woodruff key* – This key is a semi-circular shape that fits into a keyseat of the same shape. The top of the key fits into the keyway of the mating parts.

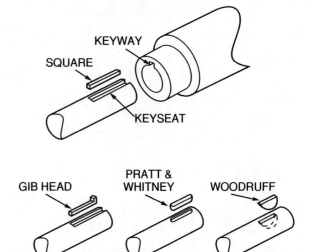

106F21.EPS

Figure 21 ◆ Keys and keyways.

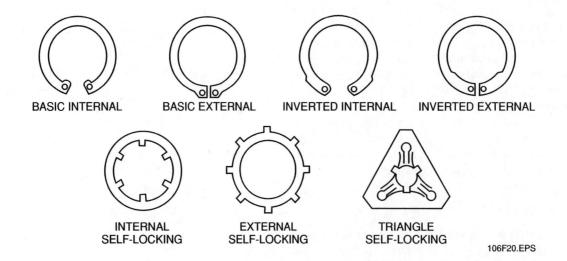

106F20.EPS

Figure 20 ◆ Retainer fasteners (rings).

3.3.0 Pin Fasteners

Pin fasteners come in several types and sizes. They have a variety of applications. Common uses of pin fasteners include holding moving parts together, aligning mating parts, fastening hinges, holding gears and pulleys on shafts, and securing slotted nuts. *Figure 22* shows several typical pin fasteners.

3.3.1 Dowel Pins

Dowel pins are fitted into holes to position mating parts. They may also support a portion of the load placed on the parts. *Figure 23* shows an application of dowel pins used to position mating parts.

3.3.2 Taper and Spring Pins

Taper and spring pins are used to fasten gears, pulleys, and collars to a shaft. *Figure 24* shows how taper and spring pins are used to attach a component to a shaft. The groove in a spring pin allows it to compress against the walls in a spring-like fashion.

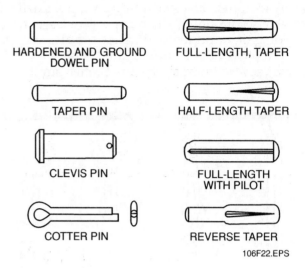

Figure 22 ◆ Pin fasteners.

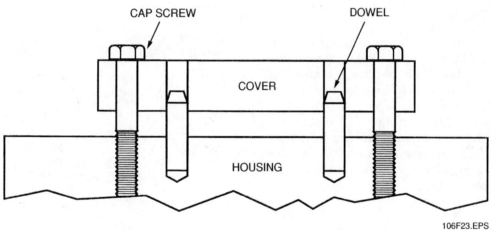

Figure 23 ◆ Dowel pins.

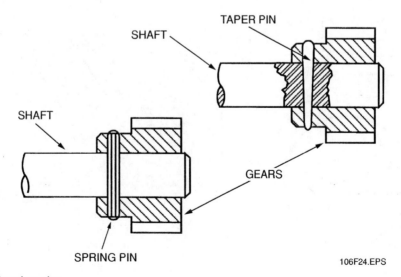

Figure 24 ◆ Taper and spring pins.

3.3.3 Cotter Pins

There are several different types of cotter pins. They are used for a variety of applications. Cotter pins are often inserted through a hole drilled crosswise through a shaft to prevent parts from slipping on or off the shaft. They are also used to keep slotted nuts from working loose. *Figure 25* shows several common types of cotter pins.

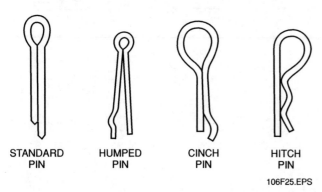

STANDARD PIN   HUMPED PIN   CINCH PIN   HITCH PIN

106F25.EPS

Figure 25 ◆ Cotter pins.

3.4.0 Yoke Clamps

Yoke clamps are precision manufactured clamps with smooth, rounded edges. Yoke clamps are used with carriage bolts to hold tubing securely in place. The yoke clamp is held in place by the carriage bolt with a hex nut. When in place, the square shoulder of the carriage bolt fits into a square hole in the bottom of the tubing tray. This keeps the bolt from turning when tightening the hex nut. Yoke clamps have large smooth surfaces to prevent damage to parts. *Figure 26* shows a typical yoke clamp and its use.

3.5.0 Spacer Clamps

Spacer clamps are used to separate tubing in multi-directional tubing runs. They are available with either two-directional or three-directional holding action. Spacer clamps are normally supplied in solid stainless steel or solid acetyl plastic. Spacer clamps may also be supplied in fabricated stainless steel clamps. *Figure 27* shows three types of spacer clamps.

> **NOTE**
> Strong acetyl clamps have excellent corrosion resistance, but are not recommended for high-temperature applications.

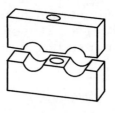
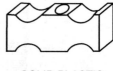

SOLID STAINLESS SPACER CLAMP   FABRICATED STAINLESS SPACER CLAMP

SOLID PLASTIC SPACER CLAMP

106F27.EPS

Figure 27 ◆ Spacer clamps.

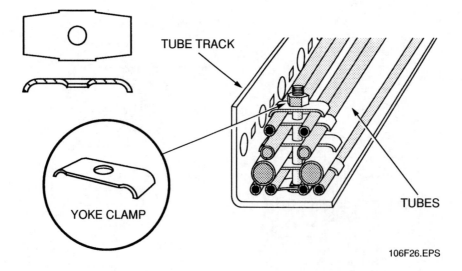

TUBE TRACK

YOKE CLAMP

TUBES

106F26.EPS

Figure 26 ◆ Yoke clamp.

3.6.0 Bundle-Lock Clamps

Bundle-lock clamps hold a bundle of tubing in an efficient manner in horizontal or vertical tubing runs. Most bundle-lock clamps come complete with band, screw, and nut. Bundle-lock clamps are typically made of stainless steel. *Figure 28* shows a bundle-lock clamp application.

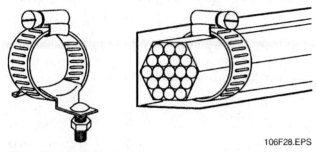

106F28.EPS

Figure 28 ◆ Bundle-lock clamp.

3.7.0 Blind Rivets

When only one side of a joint can be reached, blind rivets can be used to fasten the parts together. Some applications of blind rivets include fastening light-to-heavy-gauge sheet metal, fiberglass, plastics, and belting.

Blind rivets are made of a variety of materials and come in several sizes and lengths. They are installed with special riveting tools. *Figure 29* shows a typical blind rivet installation.

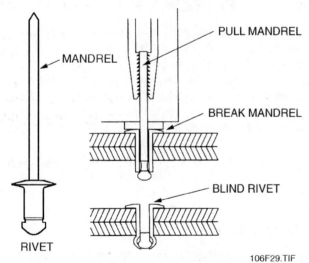

106F29.TIF

Figure 29 ◆ Blind rivets.

3.8.0 Inserts

Inserts are fitted into soft metals, woods, and plastics to provide high-strength internal threads for a fastener. They may also be used to replace damaged or stripped threads in a tapped hole. The threads of inserts are standard sizes and types. *Figure 30* shows a typical thread insert.

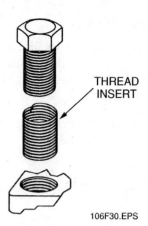

106F30.EPS

Figure 30 ◆ Thread insert.

3.9.0 Washers

There are several different types and sizes of washers. Flat washers or fender washers fit over a bolt or screw to provide an enlarged surface for bolt heads and nuts. Washers also serve to distribute the fastener load over a larger area and to prevent **marring** of the surfaces. Standard washers are made in light-duty, medium-duty, heavy-duty, and extra heavy-duty series. *Figure 31* shows different types of washers.

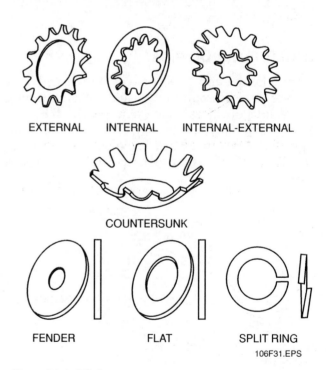

106F31.EPS

Figure 31 ◆ Washers.

> **NOTE**
>
> The threads of the bolt or screw should have minimal clearance from the hole in the washer.

3.9.1 Lock Washers

Lock washers, shown in *Figure 31*, are specially designed to keep bolts or nuts from working loose. There are various types of lock washers for different applications.

- *Split-ring lock washer* – Commonly used with bolts and cap screws
- *External type* – Used for the greatest resistance
- *Internal type* – Used with small screws
- *Internal-external type* – Used for oversized mounting holes
- *Counter sunk type* – Used with flat or oval-head screws

3.9.2 Fender Washers

Fender washers, shown in *Figure 31*, are used to keep bolts or nuts from pulling through the material being fastened. They are flat washers that have a larger diameter and surface area than regular washers. They may also be thinner than a regular washer. Fender washers do not lock nuts in place. They are used when it is necessary to cover a larger surface area to help dissipate the pulling force of a nut so that it doesn't pull through the material being fastened.

3.10.0 Gang Clamps

Gang clamps and back plates, shown in *Figure 32*, are devices commonly used to fasten tubing to various surfaces. Gang clamps are deburred to eliminate any sharp edges which could damage coated tubing. They are also used in long, multiple tubing runs to keep tubing neat and orderly.

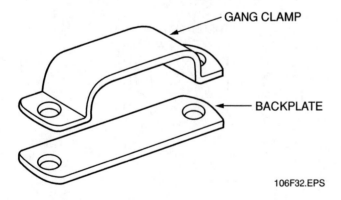

106F32.EPS

Figure 32 ◆ Gang clamp.

3.11.0 Tie Wraps

A tie wrap is a one-piece cable tie, usually made of nylon, that is used to save time on wire and cable bundling. Tie wraps can be quickly installed and are self-locking. Black tie wraps resist ultraviolet light and are good for outdoor use. Some types of tie wraps come with a release lever molded into the one-piece head. *Figure 33* shows a typical tie wrap.

Some tie wraps are available with a molded-in mounting hole (shown in *Figure 33*) in the head for inserting a rivet, screw, or bolt after the tie wrap has been installed around the bundle.

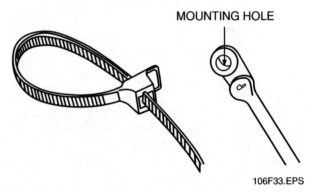

106F33.EPS

Figure 33 ◆ Tie wrap.

4.0.0 ◆ SPECIAL THREADED FASTENERS

Special threaded fasteners consist of hardware manufactured in several shapes and sizes designed to perform specific jobs. Certain types of nuts may be considered special threaded fasteners if they are designed especially for a particular application. In the instrumentation craft, special threaded fasteners are used on a number of different jobs.

Three types of special threaded fasteners are described in this section: eye bolts, toggle bolts, and J-bolts.

4.1.0 Eye Bolts

Eye bolts get their name from the loop, or eye, at one end. The other end of an eye bolt is threaded. There are many types of eye bolts. The eye on some eye bolts is formed and welded while the eyes on other types are forged. Shoulder forged eye bolts are typically inserted to the shoulder and are commonly used as lifting devices and guides for wires, cables, and cords. *Figure 34* shows some typical eye bolts.

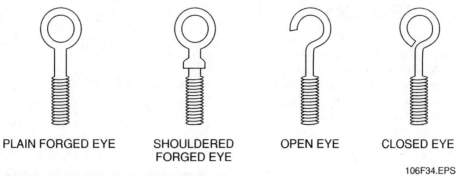

PLAIN FORGED EYE   SHOULDERED FORGED EYE   OPEN EYE   CLOSED EYE

106F34.EPS

Figure 34 ◆ Eye bolts.

4.2.0 Toggle Bolts

A toggle bolt is used to fasten a part to a hollow wall or panel. Toggle bolts have a hinged, spring-acting mechanism attached to a standard thread nut. To use a toggle bolt, the bolt or machine screw is first threaded part way into the nut. The hinged mechanism is then squeezed together and inserted into a pre-drilled hole. Once the spring mechanism extends into the hollow area of the wall or panel, it opens to provide an anchor for tightening the bolt. The bolt or machine screw is then tightened, and the mechanism holds tightly against the back of the wall or panel.

Figure 35 shows three types of toggle bolts.

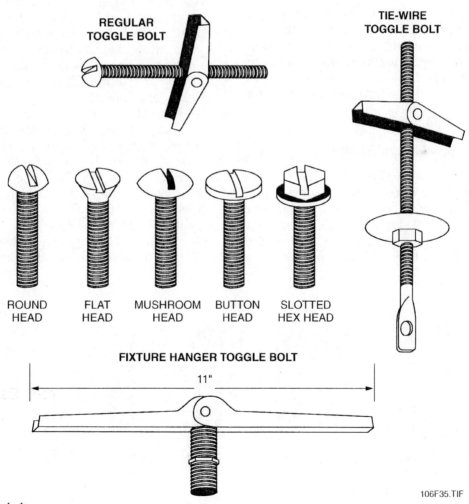

Figure 35 ◆ Toggle bolts.

4.3.0 Anchor-Type Fastening Devices

Anchor-type fastening devices differ from most other fasteners in that the fastener is installed permanently. There are various types of anchoring devices, depending on the material and the strength requirements of the attachment. *Figure 36* shows some of these anchoring devices.

4.3.1 Wet Concrete Anchors

In new construction, structural anchors are often installed in concrete slabs prior to the concrete being poured. Anchors installed at this stage of the project usually are large in size and secure such parts as structural steel, lamp or light poles, and other parts that require precise specifications regarding anchor support and strength. The L-shaped wet concrete anchor (*Figure 36*) may be installed so that the L portion hooks under a section of bar reinforcement (rebar) in the slab, while the ring-type may encircle a section of bar reinforcement, providing extreme anchoring strength.

Most anchoring other than structural components, however, is installed after the concrete slab is poured, allowing for precise location. Such anchoring may be accomplished using any of several dry-type anchors, such as plastic anchors, drop-in anchors, lead shields, or wedge anchors.

4.3.2 Plastic Anchors or Shields

Plastic shields (*Figure 36*) are normally used for attaching something to concrete, masonry block, or brick, and not for anchoring. The installation involves drilling a hole large enough to insert the plastic sleeve, lightly tapping the sleeve until it is flush with the edge of the hole, then attaching the part using a sheet metal-type screw. Long-term reaction to changes in humidity and temperature makes plastic shield usage very limited.

4.3.3 Drop-In Anchors

Drop-in anchors (*Figure 36*) are typically comprised of two parts: a zinc-plated steel expansion shield and a solid, cone-shaped expanding plug. The shield has four equally spaced slots along a portion of its length. The shield may be installed either flush or countersunk into the hole. The bottom of the shield is tapered to allow maximum depth and holding power. The expanding plug has internal threads, and, as the bolt is tightened in the plug, the plug is pulled further into the shield, forcing the shield against the walls of the drilled hole in the concrete. Its application is typically for anchoring that requires medium, non-structural anchoring strength.

4.3.4 Lead Shield

A lead shield (*Figure 36*) is a zinc alloy sleeve separated into two halves that are mechanically, but lightly, joined together to keep the sleeve as one piece until it is installed in a pre-drilled hole. The interior of the sleeve is threaded in a spiraled downward slant, while the exterior of the sleeve is ribbed to allow maximum gripping strength. The lead shield accepts a lag screw, which resembles a very large wood screw, as its fastener. As the lag screw is threaded into the shield, the shield expands in the hole and grips the walls of the hole, anchoring the part. The hole must be drilled at least 1/2 inch deeper than the length of the shield to allow space for the end of the lag shield once it is tightened into the shield. If the hole is not drilled deep enough, the lag screw will bottom out and will not tighten down on the part being anchored.

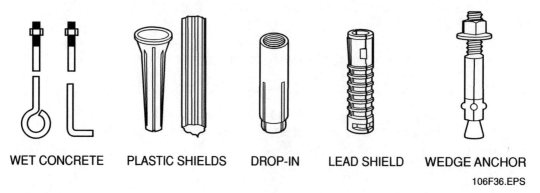

WET CONCRETE   PLASTIC SHIELDS   DROP-IN   LEAD SHIELD   WEDGE ANCHOR

106F36.EPS

Figure 36 ◆ Anchors.

4.3.5 Wedge Anchor

A wedge anchor (*Figure 36*) is an assembly that contains its own stud bolt that works on the same principal as the drop-in anchor, with the expanding wedge constructed as the bottom part of the stud bolt. Once the wedge anchor is inserted into a precisely drilled hole, the part being anchored may be placed over the protruding stud bolt. A washer is then applied, followed by a nut. As the nut is tightened, the stud bolt, with its wedge-shaped bottom end, is drawn into its sleeve, securing the sleeve in the hole. The nut may then be removed, as well as the part being anchored, without disturbing the anchored stud. This system allows for flexibility in that once the wedge anchor is cinched into place, it provides the ease of frequent part removal and replacement without the need to install a new anchor.

4.4.0 J-Bolts

J-bolts get their name from the curve on one end that gives them a J shape. The other end of a J-bolt is threaded. There are many types of J-bolts. Some J-bolts are used to hold tubing bundles and include a plastic jacket to protect the tubing. Others are used to attach instrumentation to existing grating. Most J-bolts used in tubing racks are attached using two nuts. The upper nut allows for adjustment. The tubing bundle is clamped firmly, but not flattened. Both nuts are tightened against tube track for positive holding. *Figure 37* shows a typical J-bolt.

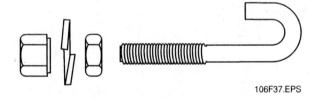

106F37.EPS

Figure 37 ◆ Typical J-bolt.

5.0.0 ◆ INSTALLING FASTENERS

Different types of fasteners require different installation techniques. However, there are some work practices which apply to many installations, including knowing the proper installation methods, tightening sequence, and torque specification for the type of fastener being used.

Some bolts and nuts require special safety wires or pins to keep them from working loose. Anchor bolts must be properly aligned and grouted. The following sections explain how to tighten and install several common types of fasteners.

One of the most important factors in quality fastener installation is to make sure that the correct size of pilot hole is drilled for the fastener being used. Most fastener manufacturers provide charts that specify the size of pilot hole for their products. *Table 1* shows an example of a chart indicating the proper size of drill bit to use for various bolts, screws, and wood screws.

5.1.0 Torque Tightening

To properly tighten a fastener, two primary factors must be considered:

- The strength of the fastener material
- The degree to which the fastener is tightened

A torque wrench is used to control the degree of tightness. The torque wrench measures how much a fastener is being tightened. **Torque** is the turning force applied to the fastener. Torque is normally expressed in **inch-pounds (in. lbs)** or **foot-pounds (ft. lbs)**. In instrumentation work, most fasteners are tightened to torque values expressed in inch-pounds. A one-pound force applied to a wrench one foot long exerts one foot-pound, or twelve inch-pounds, of torque. The torque reading is read from the indicator on the torque wrench as the fastener is being tightened. *Figure 38* shows two types of torque wrenches.

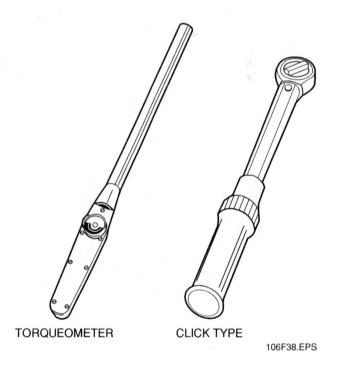

TORQUEOMETER   CLICK TYPE

106F38.EPS

Figure 38 ◆ Torque wrenches.

Table 1 Fastener Hole Guide Chart

DRILL THIS SIZE HOLE		To Tap For This Size Bolt or Screw	For This Size Wood Screw Pilot in Hard Wood
Drill Size	Dec. Equiv.		
60	.0400		
59	.0410		
58	.0420		
57	.0430		
56	.0465	0 × 80	
3/64	.0469		
55	.0520		
54	.0550	1 × 56	No. 3
53	.0595	1 × 64-72	
1/16	.0625		
52	.0635		No. 4
51	.0670		
50	.0700	2 × 56-64	
49	.0730		No. 5
48	.0760		
5/64	.0781		
47	.0785	3 × 48	No. 6
46	.0810		
45	.0820	3 × 56	
44	.0860	4 × 36	No. 7
43	.0890	4 × 40	
42	.0935	4 × 48	
3/32	.0937		
41	.0960		
40	.0980	5 × 36	No. 8
39	.0995		
38	.1015	5 × 40	
37	.1040	5 × 44	No. 9
36	.1069		
7/64	.1094		
35	.1100	6 × 32	
34	.1110	6 × 36	
33	.1130	6 × 40	No. 10
32	.1160		
31	.1200		No. 11
1/8	.1250	7 × 36	
30	.1285	8 × 30	No. 12
29	.1360	8 × 32-36	
28	.1405	8 × 40	
27	.1440	9 × 30	
26	.1470	3/16 × 24	
25	.1495	10 × 24	No. 14
24	.1520		
23	.1540	10 × 28	
5/32	.1562		
22	.1570	10 × 30	
21	.1590	10 × 32	
20	.1610	3/16 × 32	
19	.1660		
18	.1695		No. 16
11/64	.1719		
17	.1730		
16	.1770	12 × 24	
15	.1800		
14	.1820	12 × 28	
13	.1850	12 × 32	No. 18
3/16	.1875		
12	.1890		

DRILL THIS SIZE HOLE		To Tap For This Size Bolt or Screw	For This Size Wood Screw Pilot in Hard Wood
Drill Size	Dec. Equiv.		
11	.1910		
10	.1935	15 × 20	
9	.1960		
8	.1990		
7	.2010	1/4 × 20	
13/64	.2031		
6	.2040		
5	.2055		
4	.2090	1/4 × 24	No. 20
3	.2130	1/4 × 28	
7/32	.2187	1/4 × 32	
2	.2210		
1	.2280		No. 24
A	.2340		
15/64	.2344		
B	.2380		
C	.2420		
D	.2460		
1/4	.2500		

DRILL THIS SIZE HOLE		To Tap For This Size Bolt or Screw
Drill Size	Dec. Equiv.	
E	.2500	
F	.2570	5/16 × 18
G	.2610	
17/64	.2656	5/16 × 18
H	.2660	
I	.2720	5/16 × 24-32*
J	.2770	
K	.2810	
9/32	.2812	5/16 × 24-32*
L	.2900	
M	.2950	
19/64	.2969	
N	.3020	
5/16	.3125	3/8" × 16-1/8" P
O	.3160	
P	.3230	
21/64	.3281	3/8 × 20-24
Q	.3332	
R	.3390	
11/32	.3437	
S	.3480	
T	.3580	
23/64	.3594	
U	.3680	
3/8	.3750	7/16 × 14
V	.3770	
W	.3860	
25/64	.3906	7/16 × 14
X	.3970	
Y	.4040	
13/32	.4062	
Z	.4130	
27/64	.4219	1/2 × 12-13
7/16	.4375	1/4" Pipe
29/64	.4531	1/2 × 20-24
15/32	.4687	1/2 × 27
31/64	.4844	9/16 × 12
1/2	.5000	

* All tap drill sizes are for 75% full thread except asterisked sizes which are 60% full thread.

106T01.EPS

Different types of bolts, nuts, and screws are torqued to different values depending on the application. Always check the project specifications and manufacturer's manual to determine the proper torque for a particular type of fastener. *Figure 39* shows selected torque values for various graded steel bolts.

5.2.0 Tightening Sequence

To avoid misalignment of parts when multiple fasteners are used, the fasteners must be tightened in small increments, and in the proper sequence. *Figure 40* shows the proper tightening sequence for several different bolt arrangements.

TORQUE IN FOOT POUNDS

FASTENER DIAMETER	THREADS PER INCH	MILD STEEL	STAINLESS STEEL 18-8	ALLOY STEEL
1/4	20	4	6	8
5/16	18	8	11	16
3/8	16	12	18	24
7/16	14	20	32	40
1/2	13	30	43	60
5/8	11	60	92	120
3/4	10	100	128	200
7/8	9	160	180	320
1	8	245	285	490

SUGGESTED TORQUE VALUES FOR GRADED STEEL BOLTS

GRADE		SAE 1 OR 2	SAE 5	SAE 6	SAE 8
TENSILE STRENGTH		64000 PSI	105000 PSI	130000 PSI	150000 PSI
GRADE MARK					
BOLT DIAMETER	THREADS PER INCH	FOOT POUNDS TORQUE			
1/4	20	5	7	10	10
5/16	18	9	14	19	22
3/8	16	15	25	34	37
7/16	14	24	40	55	60
1/2	13	37	60	85	92
9/16	12	53	88	120	132
5/8	11	74	120	169	180
3/4	10	120	200	280	296
7/8	9	190	302	440	473
1	8	282	466	660	714

106F39.TIF

Figure 39 ◆ Torque value chart.

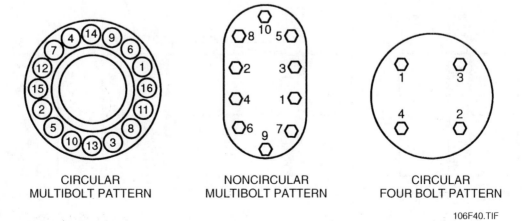

CIRCULAR MULTIBOLT PATTERN

NONCIRCULAR MULTIBOLT PATTERN

CIRCULAR FOUR BOLT PATTERN

106F40.TIF

Figure 40 ◆ Flange tightening sequence.

Each bolt should be lightly tightened the first time around in the sequence shown on the chart. The same sequence should be repeated several times until the bolts are snug and torqued to the specified value.

5.3.0 Installing Threaded Fasteners

The following procedure can be used to install threaded fasteners in a variety of applications.

NOTE

When installing threaded fasteners for a specific job, make sure to check all installation requirements.

WARNING!

Always wear proper eye protection when drilling holes for fasteners and when cleaning out holes in concrete for fasteners. Always know what is behind the surface you are drilling if the surface is not solid, as in the case of installing blind rivets or hollow wall fasteners.

Step 1   Select the proper bolts or screws for the job.

Step 2   Check for damaged or dirty internal and external threads.

Step 3   Clean the bolt or screw threads. Do not lubricate the threads if a torque wrench is to be used to tighten the nuts.

Step 4   Insert the bolts through the pre-drilled holes and tighten the nuts by hand, or insert the screws through the holes and start the threads by hand.

NOTE

Turn the nuts or screws several turns by hand and check for cross threading.

Step 5   Following the proper tightening sequence, tighten the bolts or screws until they are snug.

Step 6   Check the torque specification. Following the proper tightening sequence, tighten each bolt, nut, or screw several times, approaching the specified torque. Tighten to the final torque specification.

Step 7   If required to keep the bolts or nuts from working loose, install jam nuts, cotter pins, or safety wire. *Figure 41* shows fasteners with safety wires installed.

5.4.0 Installing Blind Rivets

Blind rivets are installed through drilled or punched holes with a special blind (pop) rivet tool. *Figure 42* shows a typical pop rivet tool. Use the following general procedure to install blind rivets.

Step 1   Select the correct length and diameter of blind rivet to be used.

Step 2   Select the appropriate drill bit for the size of rivet being used.

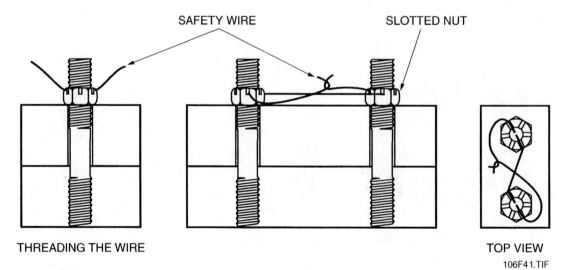

SAFETY WIRE   SLOTTED NUT

THREADING THE WIRE   TOP VIEW

106F41.TIF

Figure 41 ◆ Safety-wired fastener.

NOTE

Blind rivets should only be installed in situations where no other means of attachment is possible due to the dangers of contacting hazardous materials or electrical circuits during penetration. Never install blind rivets into an unknown source. If you do not know what lies behind the surface, do not drill into it. Make sure to wear proper eye and face protection when riveting.

Step 3   Drill a hole through both parts being connected.

Step 4   Inspect the rivet gun for any defects that might make it unsafe for use.

Step 5   Place the rivet mandrel into the proper sized setting tool.

Step 6   Insert the rivet end into the pre-drilled hole.

Step 7   Install the rivet by squeezing the handle of the rivet gun, causing the jaws in the setting tool to grip the mandrel. The mandrel is pulled up, expanding the rivet until it breaks at the shear point. *Figure 43* shows the rivet and tool positioned for joining parts together.

Step 8   Inspect the rivet to make sure the pieces are firmly riveted together and that the rivet is properly installed. *Figure 44* shows a properly installed blind rivet. Properly dispose of all sheared mandrels.

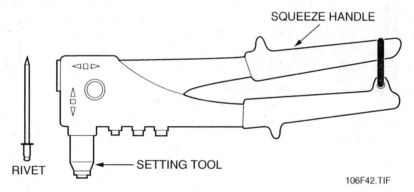

Figure 42 ◆ Rivet gun.

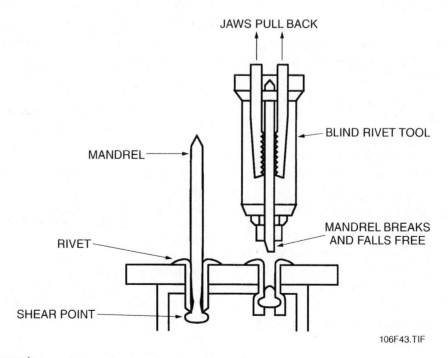

Figure 43 ◆ Joining parts.

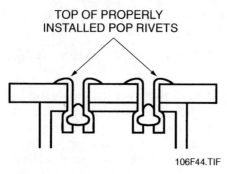

TOP OF PROPERLY INSTALLED POP RIVETS

106F44.TIF

Figure 44 ◆ Blind rivet.

5.5.0 Installing Toggle Bolts

Toggle bolts are used to fasten a part to hollow block, wallboard, plaster, panel, or tile.

The following general procedure can be used to install toggle bolts.

> **WARNING!**
>
> Always wear proper eye protection when drilling holes for toggle bolts. Always know what is behind the hollow surface you are drilling. Be aware of electrical circuits behind the walls.

Step 1   Select the proper size of drill bit or punch and toggle bolt for the job.

Step 2   Check the toggle bolt for damaged or dirty threads and malfunctioning wing mechanism.

Step 3   Clean and lightly lubricate the threads of the bolt.

Step 4   Using the correct size of drill bit, drill a hole completely through the surface to which the part is to be fastened.

Step 5   Insert the toggle bolt through the opening in the item to be fastened.

Step 6   Screw the toggle wing onto the end of the toggle bolt, ensuring that the flat side of the toggle wing is facing the bolt head.

Step 7   Fold the wings completely back and push them through the drilled hole until the wings spring open.

Step 8   Pull back on the item to be fastened in order to hold the wings firmly against the inside surface to which the item is being attached.

Step 9   Tighten the toggle bolt with a screwdriver until it is snug.

5.6.0 Installing Anchor Bolts

Anchor bolts are used to fasten equipment to a foundation, floor, or other surface. They are also used to hold sills, plates, and structural steel in place. Anchor bolts come in different sizes and shapes for different jobs. It is important to install anchor bolts with proper alignment to the anchor holes in equipment and bedplates. To properly locate anchor bolts on a surface, templates are used to mark the position of the bolts.

General procedures for installing anchor bolts in wet and hardened concrete are presented in the following sections.

5.6.1 Wet Concrete Installation

One common method used to install anchor bolts in wet concrete involves making a wooden template to locate the anchor bolts. The template positions the anchor bolts so that they correspond to those in the equipment to be fastened. *Figure 45* shows a wooden template that has been made to locate anchor bolts.

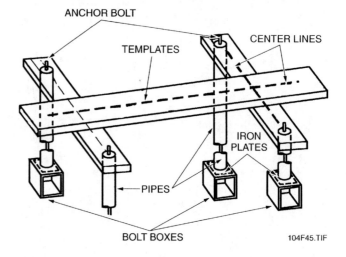

Figure 45 ◆ Anchor bolt template.

Pipes at least two inches larger than the J-type anchor bolt diameter are suspended down to the bolt boxes. These pipes allow a margin of space around each bolt for small errors in layout measurements.

Another type of wet concrete installation uses a bent-end or hook on the bolt. The anchor bolts are located by a special template suspended in the wet concrete. *Figure 46* shows a typical template and anchor bolt.

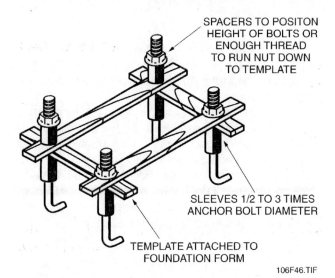

SPACERS TO POSITON HEIGHT OF BOLTS OR ENOUGH THREAD TO RUN NUT DOWN TO TEMPLATE

SLEEVES 1/2 TO 3 TIMES ANCHOR BOLT DIAMETER

TEMPLATE ATTACHED TO FOUNDATION FORM

106F46.TIF

Figure 46 ◆ Template and anchor bolts.

5.6.2 Hardened Concrete Installation (Wedge Anchors)

After laying out the position for each hole, the following general procedure can be used to install wedge anchor bolts in hardened concrete. Refer to *Figure 47* as you study the procedure.

Step 1   Drill the anchor bolt hole the same size as the anchor bolt. The hole must be deep enough for six threads of the bolt to be below the surface of the concrete.

See Step 1 in *Figure 47*.

WARNING!
Follow all safety precautions, including wearing safety glasses. Do not use compressed air to blow out holes.

NOTE
Clean out the hole using a squeeze bulb.

Step 2   Drive the anchor bolt into the hole with a hammer. See Step 2 in *Figure 47*.

NOTE
Protect the threads of the bolt with a nut that does not allow any threads to be exposed.

Step 3   Put a washer and nut on the bolt, and tighten the nut with a wrench until the anchor is secure in the concrete. See Step 3 in *Figure 47*.

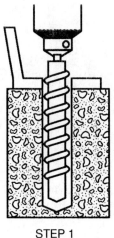

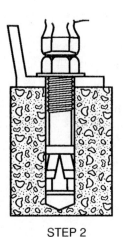

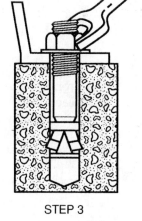

STEP 1   STEP 2   STEP 3

106F47.EPS

Figure 47 ◆ Installing anchor bolt in hardened concrete.

Summary

Fasteners are used for a variety of tasks in the instrumentation craft. In this training module, you learned about various types of threaded and non-threaded fasteners and their uses. Basic installation procedures for fasteners were also included in the module. Selecting the correct fastener for a particular job is required in order to perform high quality work. In the instrumentation craft, it is important to be familiar with the correct terms used to describe fasteners. Using the proper technical terms helps avoid confusion and improper selection of fasteners. Installation techniques for fasteners may vary depending on the job. Make sure to check the project specifications and manufacturer's information when installing any fastener.

The knowledge and skills covered in this module provide basic and fundamental competencies required to identify, select, and install different types of fasteners. In your day-to-day work activities, take the time to practice the skills learned in this module. It takes a lot of practice, study, and on-the-job experience to develop the skills needed to be expert in working with fasteners.

Review Questions

1. The most commonly used threads classes are _____.

   a. classes 1A and 1B
   b. classes 2A and 2B
   c. classes 1A and 3B
   d. classes 3A and 3B

2. The number of threads per inch on a bolt with a designation of 3/4-10-UNC-2A-RH is _____.

   a. 3 to 4
   b. 2
   c. ¾
   d. 10

3. The buttress thread _____.

   a. is the strongest and most useful of all threads
   b. has threads on one side cut square and the other side cut at a slant
   c. has both sides of the threads cut square
   d. is the easiest thread to machine

4. The SAE grade of the bolt shown here is _____.

   a. grade 3
   b. grade 5
   c. grade 7
   d. grade 0

5. The approximate diameter of a 10-32 machine screw is _____ inch(es)

   a. 0.190
   b. 1.0
   c. ⅝
   d. 0.32

6. Set screws are normally made from _____.

   a. soft carbon steel
   b. aluminum
   c. nonferrous metal
   d. heat-treated steel

7. When a smooth, tamper-proof bolt head is required, a _____ is used.

   a. wedge anchor bolt
   b. carriage bolt
   c. J-bolt
   d. toggle bolt

8. A(n) _____ keeps a castle or slotted nut from loosening on the bolt it is threaded on.

   a. acorn nut
   b. dowel pin
   c. cotter pin
   d. keyway

9. A(n) _____ is often used to obtain good appearance and avoid the possibility of sharp edges.
   a. anchor bolt
   b. toggle bolt
   c. castellated nut
   d. acorn nut

10. Dowel pins are used to _____.
   a. join heavy gauge sheet metal
   b. lock nuts in place
   c. position mating parts
   d. allow expansion and contraction of materials

11. Washers are used to _____.
   a. distribute the load over a larger area
   b. attach an item to a hollow surface
   c. anchor materials that expand due to temperature changes
   d. allow the bolts to expand with temperature changes

12. _____ are commonly used as lifting devices.
   a. Toggle bolts
   b. Anchor bolts
   c. J-bolts
   d. Eye bolts

13. Each of the following anchors are designed for use in hardened concrete installation *except* the _____.
   a. wedge anchor
   b. drop-in anchor
   c. toggle bolt
   d. lead shield

14. Torque is normally expressed in _____.
   a. pounds per square inch (psi)
   b. gallons per minute (gpm)
   c. foot-pounds (ft. lbs)
   d. cubic feet per minute (cfm)

15. When torque tightening bolts, nuts, or screws, always use the proper _____.
   a. tightening sequence
   b. drill bit
   c. set screw
   d. cotter pin

Trade Terms Introduced in This Module

Clearance: The amount of space between the threads of bolts and their nuts.

Foot-pounds (ft lbs): The normal method used for measuring the amount of torque being applied to bolts or nuts.

Grade markings: A set of markings that identifies the strength and quality of a fastener.

Inch-pounds (in. lbs): A method of measuring the amount of torque applied to small bolts or nuts that require measurement in smaller increments than foot-pounds.

Key: A machined metal part that fits into a keyway and prevents parts such as gears or pulleys from rotating on a shaft.

Keyway: A machined slot in a shaft and on parts such as gears and pulleys that accepts a key.

Marring: Damaging or defacing threads or a surface.

Nominal size: Approximate or rough size by which screws, bolts, lumber, block and other building materials are commonly known and sold. It is normally slightly larger than the actual size.

Thread classes: Threads are distinguished by three classifications according to the amount of tolerance the threads provide between the bolt and nut.

Thread identification: Standard symbols used for the identification of threads.

Thread standards: An established set of standards for machining threads.

Tolerance: The amount of difference allowed from a standard. For example, the standard size may be 1.5 inches, but a difference of up to .1 inches is tolerated.

Torque: The turning force applied to a fastener.

Unified National Coarse Thread Series (UNC): The thread series most commonly used for screws, bolts, and nuts. It is used for producing threads in low strength materials such as cast iron, softer copper alloys, aluminum, etc.

United National Extra Fine Thread Series (UNEF): The thread series used to fasten materials with thin walls. It can be used in all applications where the fine thread series can be used.

United Fine Thread Series (UNF): The thread series used for applications that require a higher strength than the coarse thread series. It can be used for fastening materials with thinner walls.

Additional Resources

This module is intended to present thorough resources for task training. The following reference works are suggested for further study. These are optional materials for continued education rather than for task training.

ISO Standards Handbook: Fasteners and Screw Threads, Volume 1, 1998. Warrendale, PA: Society of Automotive Engineers (SAE).

Specifications and Standards for Fasteners, 2000. New York, NY: American National Standards Institute (ANSI).

Specifications and Standards for Fasteners, Volume 01.08, 2000. Philadelphia, PA: American Society for Testing and Materials (ASTM).

NCCER CRAFT TRAINING USER UPDATES

The NCCER makes every effort to keep these textbooks up-to-date and free of technical errors. We appreciate your help in this process. If you have an idea for improving this textbook, or if you find an error, a typographical mistake, or an inaccuracy in the NCCER's Craft Training textbooks, please write us, using this form or a photocopy. Be sure to include the exact module number, page number, a detailed description, and the correction, if applicable. Your input will be brought to the attention of the Technical Review Committee. Thank you for your assistance.

Instructors – If you found that additional materials were necessary in order to teach this module effectively, please let us know so that we may include them in the Equipment and Materials list in the Instructor's Guide.

Write: Curriculum Revision and Development Department
National Center for Construction Education and Research
P.O. Box 141104, Gainesville, FL 32614-1104

Fax: 352-334-0932

E-mail: curriculum@nccer.org

Craft _____ Module Name _____

Copyright Date _____ Module Number _____ Page Number(s) _____

Description _____

_____

_____

_____

(Optional) Correction _____

_____

_____

(Optional) Your Name and Address _____

_____

_____

_____

Instrument Drawings and Documents, Part One

COURSE MAP

This course map shows all of the modules in the first level of the Instrumentation curriculum. The suggested training order begins at the bottom and proceeds up. Skill levels increase as you advance on the course map. The local Training Program Sponsor may adjust the training order.

INSTRUMENTATION LEVEL ONE

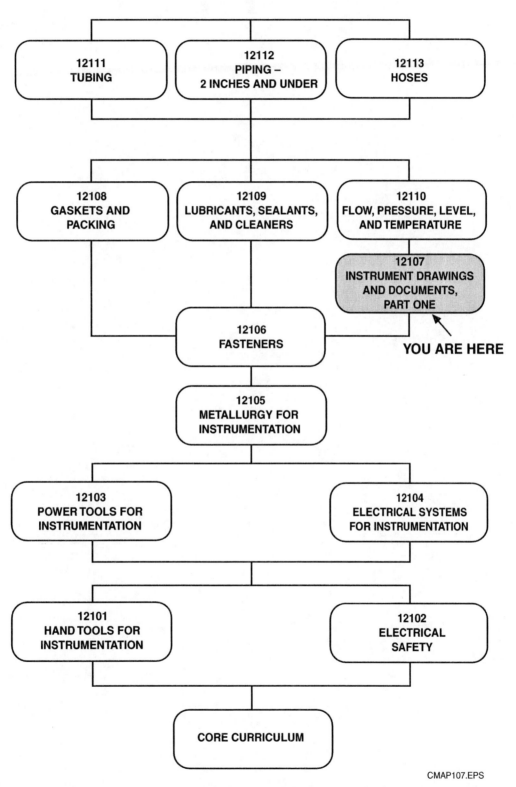

YOU ARE HERE

CMAP107.EPS

MODULE 12107 CONTENTS

Figures

Tables

Instrument Drawings and Documents, Part One

OBJECTIVES

When you have completed this module, you will be able to do the following:

1. Identify and describe standard Instrument Society of America (ISA) instrument symbols and abbreviations.
2. Read and interpret instrument indexes.
3. Read and interpret general instrument specifications.
4. Read and interpret general notes and details included on instrument drawings and documents.
5. Read and interpret installation detail drawings.
6. Read and interpret location drawings.

Prerequisites

Before you begin this module, it is recommended that you successfully complete the following modules: Core Curriculum; Instrumentation Level One, Modules 12101 through 12106.

Required Trainee Materials

1. Pencil and paper
2. Appropriate personal protective equipment

1.0.0 ◆ INTRODUCTION

The information needed to identify, locate, install, repair, maintain, and troubleshoot instrument systems and equipment is included in several types of drawings and documents. To safely and effectively perform quality instrument work, you need to be able to read and understand these drawings and documents.

Being able to quickly and effectively use instrument drawings and documents takes a combination of knowledge and on-the-job experience. Those who master the art are valuable contributors to the success of projects. This training module covers instrument symbols and abbreviations, **installation detail drawings**, **location drawings**, general notes and details, **instrument indexes**, and **general instrument specifications**. Later modules in your training program will expand on what you learn in this program.

2.0.0 ◆ INSTRUMENT SYMBOLS AND IDENTIFICATION

The Instrument Society of America (ISA) has established a standard set of symbols and identification techniques that are widely used for instrument drawings and documents. ISA symbols, abbreviations, and identification techniques are published in ISA Standard S5.1, entitled *Instrumentation Symbols and Identification*. It is recommended that you have a copy of this standard, or access to it, so you can look up information that you may need when reading instrument diagrams and documents.

While most companies use ISA standards as the basis for preparing their drawings and documents, a company may make some modifications to satisfy particular needs. It is always important to make sure that you understand the terminology, symbols, and abbreviations used in drawings and documents for each project.

2.1.0 Instrument Symbols

A circle, often called an instrument **balloon** or instrument bubble, has traditionally been used to represent an instrument on drawings. However, with more and more computers and other **digital** electronic equipment being used in instrument systems, some changes to the traditional circular instrument symbol have been made to help identify this new equipment.

Letters, numbers, and lines drawn inside instrument balloons provide information about the type of instrument, its location, and its **function**. The meanings of the letters and numbers will be explained later. *Figure 1* shows typical instrument symbols used in most types of drawings. It includes the meanings for the lines, or absence of a line, in each symbol.

The definitions for the different types of devices referenced next to the symbols shown in Figure 1 are listed here:

- **Behind the panel** (*behind the board*) – The location containing an instrument panel (board) and its associated rack-mounted hardware, or devices enclosed within a panel. Devices mounted behind the panel are not normally accessible for the operator's use.

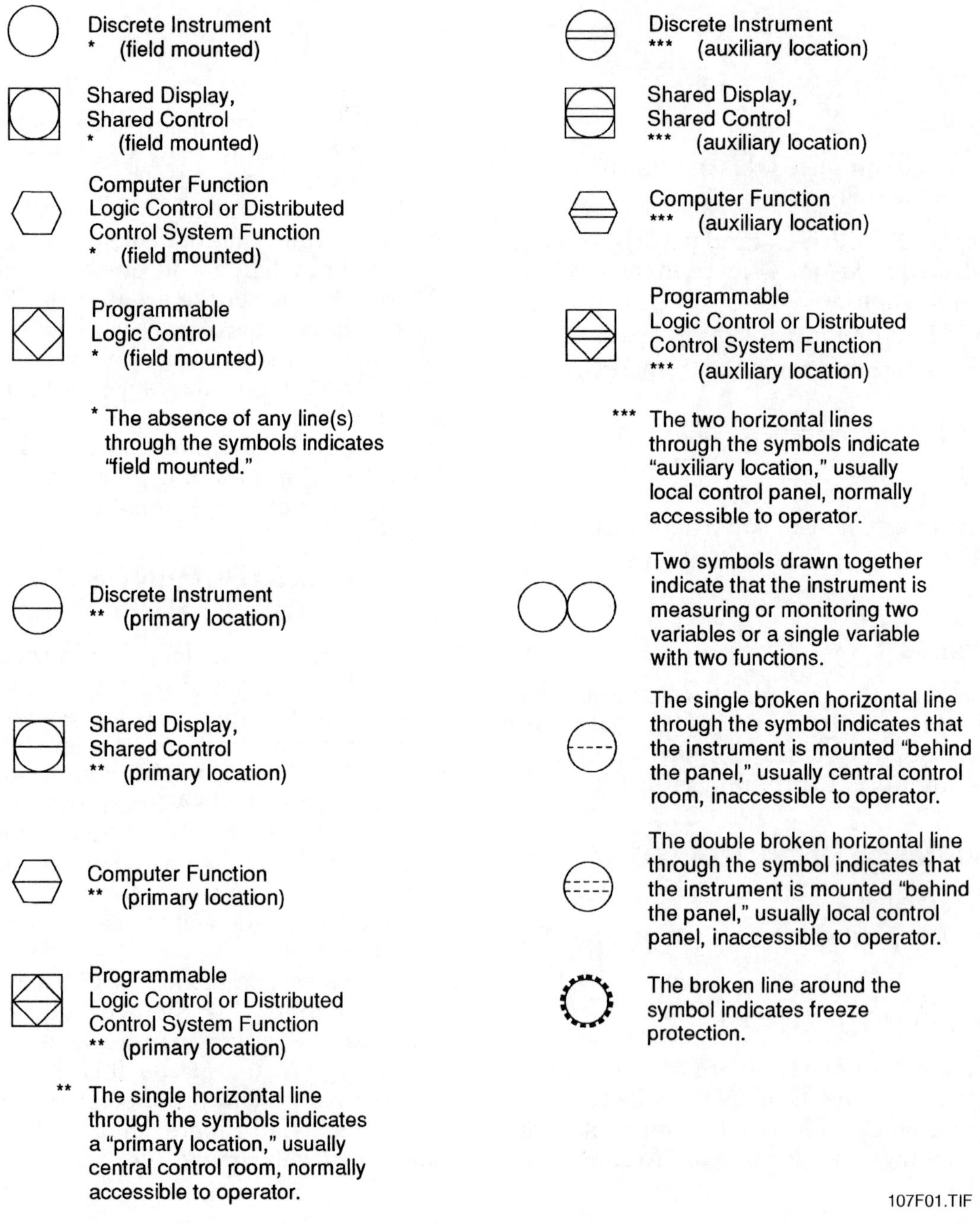

Discrete Instrument
*   (field mounted)

Shared Display,
Shared Control
*   (field mounted)

Computer Function
Logic Control or Distributed
Control System Function
*   (field mounted)

Programmable
Logic Control
*   (field mounted)

*   The absence of any line(s) through the symbols indicates "field mounted."

Discrete Instrument
**   (primary location)

Shared Display,
Shared Control
**   (primary location)

Computer Function
**   (primary location)

Programmable
Logic Control or Distributed
Control System Function
**   (primary location)

**   The single horizontal line through the symbols indicates a "primary location," usually central control room, normally accessible to operator.

Discrete Instrument
***   (auxiliary location)

Shared Display,
Shared Control
***   (auxiliary location)

Computer Function
***   (auxiliary location)

Programmable
Logic Control or Distributed
Control System Function
***   (auxiliary location)

***   The two horizontal lines through the symbols indicate "auxiliary location," usually local control panel, normally accessible to operator.

Two symbols drawn together indicate that the instrument is measuring or monitoring two variables or a single variable with two functions.

The single broken horizontal line through the symbol indicates that the instrument is mounted "behind the panel," usually central control room, inaccessible to operator.

The double broken horizontal line through the symbol indicates that the instrument is mounted "behind the panel," usually local control panel, inaccessible to operator.

The broken line around the symbol indicates freeze protection.

107F01.TIF

Figure 1 ◆ Common instrument symbols.

- *Computer function* – An action controlled by or performed by a computer.
- *Discrete instrument* – A specific type of instrument such as a pressure or temperature gauge.
- ***Distributed control system (DCS)*** – A functionally integrated system that consists of subsystems which may be physically separate and remotely located from one another.
- ***Programmable logic controller (PLC)*** – A controller, usually with multiple inputs and outputs, that can be programmed to perform a variety of functions.
- *Shared control* – A single controller that can process information from a number of different sources.
- *Shared display* – A single display that can display information from a number of different sources.

With some practice reading and interpreting instrument symbols like those shown in *Figure 1*, you should be able to identify several important points about an instrument simply by looking at its symbol.

Exercise One

Match the type of instrument and/or function listed here to the correct symbol (A through J) shown in *Figure 2*.

1. Symbol ____ identifies a discrete instrument with freeze protection.
2. Symbol ____ identifies a computer function in a primary location.
3. Symbol ____ identifies a discrete instrument mounted behind the panel located in a central control room.
4. Symbol ____ identifies a **field**-mounted discrete instrument.
5. Symbol ____ identifies a shared-display instrument mounted in an auxiliary location.

6. Symbol ____ identifies a field-mounted programmable logic control function.
7. Symbol ____ identifies a field-mounted shared control device.
8. Symbol ____ identifies a distributed control system function mounted in a primary location.
9. Symbol ____ identifies an instrument mounted behind a **local panel**.
10. Symbol ____ identifies an instrument that is measuring two variables.

2.2.0 Instrument Tag Numbers and Identification Abbreviations

Instruments are identified on drawings and documents by **identification numbers** or tag numbers. Tag numbers consist of numbers and letters usually placed inside the instrument balloon. These numbers:

- Designate the plant area where the instrument is located
- Identify the function of the instrument
- Indicate the instrument **loop** in which the instrument is located

Regardless of how many instruments are used on a project, each will have a different tag number. *Figure 3* shows the place within an instrument balloon where specific tag number information is commonly placed.

2.2.1 Area Designation in Tag Numbers

When a project includes instruments in more than one building or area, the tag number may include an area designation number. Some companies place the area designation number above the functional identification number, while others place it in front of the functional identification number (prefix) as shown in *Figure 4*.

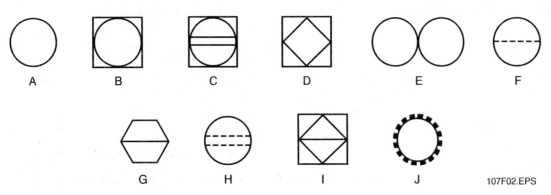

Figure 2 ◆ Symbols for Exercise One.

107F02.EPS

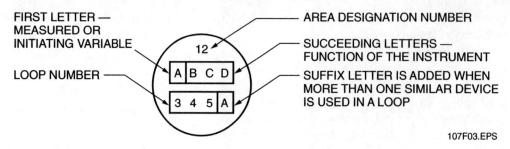

Figure 3 ◆ Placement of instrument tag numbers.

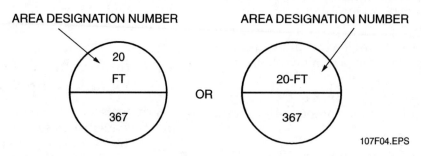

Figure 4 ◆ Area designation in tag number.

If all the tag numbers for instruments on a drawing are located in the same area, the area number is often not included in the instrument balloons on the drawing. In such cases, a note is usually placed on the drawing indicating that all tag numbers are preceded by the same area number, such as 12, unless otherwise noted.

2.2.2 First Letters in Tag Numbers

The first letter of the tag number identifies the measured or **initiating variable** in the loop. For example, in *Figure 5*, the first letters represent:

- *F* = flow rate
- *P* = pressure or vacuum
- *T* = temperature
- *L* = level

The following is a list of letters commonly used as the first letter in tag numbers to identify the measured or initiating variable in the loop in which the instrument is installed.

- *A* – analysis
- *B* – burner, combustion
- *C* – conductivity (electrical) or user's choice
- *D* – density (mass) or specific gravity or user's choice
- *E* – voltage
- *F* – flow rate
- *G* – gauging (dimensional)
- *H* – hand (manually initiated)
- *I* – current (electrical)
- *J* – power
- *K* – time, time schedule
- *L* – level
- *M* – moisture or humidity or user's choice
- *N* – user's choice
- *O* – user's choice
- *P* – pressure or vacuum
- *Q* – quantity or event
- *R* – radiation or radioactivity
- *S* – speed or frequency

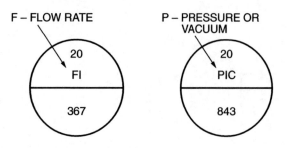
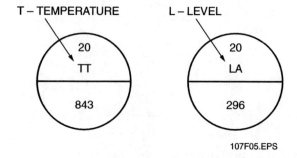

Figure 5 ◆ First letters in tag numbers.

- *T* – temperature
- *U* – multi-variable
- *V* – vibration, mechanical analysis (also viscosity)
- *W* – weight or force
- *X* – unclassified
- *Y* – event, state, or presence
- *Z* – position or dimension

> **NOTE**
> Sometimes first-letter designations are modified to reflect the needs of a particular project. You will need to check the **legend** on the instrument drawings and documents for each project to verify the use of each first-letter designation for the instrument tag numbers.

The first letters *C, D, M, N,* and *O,* which are classified as *user's choice,* are normally used to identify unlisted measured or initiating variables that are used repetitively on a project. For example, *N* = thickness or *O* = stress.

When user's choice letters appear on instrument drawings for a project, their meanings are generally defined only once in the legend to indicate how they are being used. A user's choice letter may also have one meaning as a first letter and another meaning as a second letter. Their definitions as to position must be defined on the drawings.

The first letter X, which is designated as *unclassified,* is also used for unlisted measured or initiating variables. It is normally used only once, or to a limited extent, to identify a particular variable.

The first letter X may also be used to identify a number of different unlisted variables on instrument drawings for the same project. When the first letter X is used in this manner, an explanation of its meaning is generally defined on the drawing, outside the tagging balloon.

2.2.3 Succeeding Letters in Tag Numbers

The succeeding letter or letters in a tag number (letters that follow the first letter in a tag number) may have different functions or designations, depending on their location in the tag number. Normally the second letter in a tag number that only contains two letters is used to identify the function of the instrument. For instance, an instrument with a tag number of 20 PR 237 would indicate that this instrument is a pressure instrument as indicated by the letter P, and its function is to record, as indicated by the second letter, R. For example, in *Figure 6* the letter *I* in *FI* describes the function of the flow instrument as indicating or indicator; however, the letter *I* in *PIC* identifies the passive function of this instrument as indicating or indicator, while the letter *C* identifies the output function as control or controller. *TT* represents a temperature instrument (first letter denotes process as temperature) with the second letter *T* identifying the function as transmitting or transmitter.

If the tag number contains more than two letters, the second letter may be used to modify or better define the first letter in the tag number, or it may also identify the function of the instrument. The third letter may also denote function or it may modify or better describe the second letter function. For examples, an instrument with a tag number of 20 PDT 237 would identify a Pressure Differential Transmitter. The second letter, *D,* in this case modifies or better describes the pressure instrument as a differential pressure instrument. The third letter, *T,* in this case now describes the function of the instrument as transmitting. In a situation where an instrument has a tag lettering of PAL (Pressure Alarm Low), the second letter identifies the function of the instrument as an alarm, while the third letter modifies or better describes the second letter function as a low alarm.

Special tag numbers containing more than three letters may even be required in certain installations to better identify or describe an instrument in

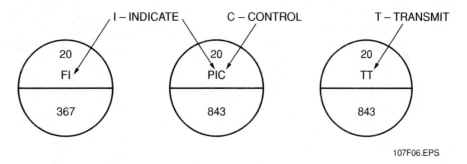

Figure 6 ◆ Succeeding letters in tag numbers.

a loop, but the succeeding letter designations should follow the same general pattern as those tag numbers containing two or three letter designations. The grammatical form of the succeeding-letter definitions may be modified as needed. For example, *indicator* may be applied as *indicate* or *indicating*, while *transmitter* may be applied as *transmit* or *transmitting*.

Table 1 gives a list of letters that are typically used as succeeding letters in tag numbers. The columns in the table identify the usage of the letter depending on its location in the tag number. As shown, the letter may have a different meaning depending on its location in the tag number. Remember, process modifiers or descriptors are typically found as the second letter in a tag number; however, the second letter may also describe a function of the instrument. The third letter may identify a function of the instrument or it may be a modifier or descriptor of the function found in the second position. Also note in *Table 1* that the letters B and N are designated as user choices for functions or functions modifiers only.

When used as a first-letter modifier, the letter S (safety) applies only to emergency protective **primary elements** and emergency protective **final control elements**. If the device is intended to protect against emergency conditions, the letter S is used to modify the first letter. This is true even if the normal function of the device is not emergency protection. For example, a pressure control valve (PCV) which controls the flow of fluid in a system would be designated as PSV (pressure safety valve) if, in addition to its control function, it was also intended to protect against emergency conditions, such as high pressure.

Table 1 Common Designations for Tag Number Succeeding Letters

Succeeding Letter	First-Letter Modifier	Readout/Pass.	Output Function	Modifier Function
A		Alarm		
B		User's Choice	User's Choice	User's Choice
C		Control		
D	Differential			
E		Sensor (Primary Element)		
F	Ratio (Fraction)			
G		Glass(Viewing Device)		
H				High
I		Indicate		
J	Scan			
K	Time (Rate of Change)		Control Station	
L		Light (Pilot)		Low
M	Momentary			Middle
N		User's Choice	User's Choice	User's Choice
O		Orifice Restriction		
P		Point (Test Connection)		
Q	Integrate, Totalize			
R		Record or Print		
S	Safety		Switch	
T			Transmit	
U		Multifunction	Multifunction	Multifunction
V			Valve, Damper, Louver	
W		Well		
X	X Axis	Unclassified	Unclassified	Unclassified
Y	Y Axis		Relay, Compute, or Convert	
Z	Z Axis		Driver, Actuator, Unclassified Final Control Element	

User's choice letters *B* and *N* and unclassified letter *X* designations for succeeding letters on instrument drawings and documents are used in the same manner explained for first letters. Succeeding letters *B* and *N* (user's choice) are normally used to identify unlisted functions or modifiers that are used repetitively on a project. For example, *N* = oscilloscope. If used, user's choice letters may have one meaning for a first letter and a different meaning for succeeding letters in the tag number. When user's choice letters appear on instrument drawings for a project, their meanings are generally defined only once in the legend to indicate how they are being used.

The succeeding letter *X*, which is designated as *unclassified*, is also used for unlisted modifiers or functions. It is normally used only once, or to a limited extent, to identify a particular modifier or function. The succeeding letter *X* may also be used to identify a number of different unlisted modifiers or functions on instrument drawings for the same project. When the succeeding letter *X* is used in this manner, an explanation of its meaning is generally defined next to each instrument symbol that it is being used to identify.

2.2.4 Loop Identification in Tag Numbers

An instrument loop consists of one or more interconnected instruments arranged to measure and/or control a process variable. To identify all instruments in a particular loop, a loop identification number is assigned. This loop number becomes part of the tag number.

Loop numbering may be parallel or serial. In parallel numbering, instrument numbering involves starting a numerical sequence for each new first letter; for example, TIC-200, FRC-200, or LIC-200. In serial numbering, instrument numbering can be set up using a single sequence of numbers for a project or for relatively large sections of a project, regardless of the first-letter of the loop identification, for example, TIC-200,

FRC-201, LIC-202, etc. *Figure 7* shows a typical instrument loop using parallel tag numbers for each instrument.

If more than one of a similar type instrument is used in a loop, a suffix letter is added at the end of the loop number of each similar instrument as shown in *Figure 8*.

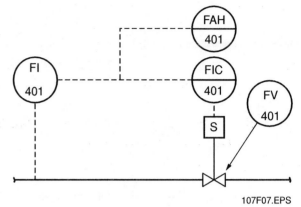

107F07.EPS

Figure 7 ◆ Loop identification numbers.

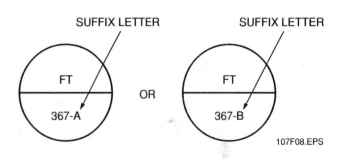

107F08.EPS

Figure 8 ◆ Suffix letter in loop number.

2.3.0 Graphic or Pictorial Instrument Symbols

In addition to general instrument symbols that appear on drawings, numerous graphic or pictorial instrument symbols are also used to represent specific types of equipment or devices. With practice, you will learn to recognize graphic or pictorial instrument symbols when reading drawings. The most commonly used graphic or pictorial instrument symbols are shown in *Figure 9*. Note that the slashes shown on the signal lines for some symbols represent the type of signal line, such as electric or pneumatic. Signal lines are covered later in this section.

Air Regulator Symbols

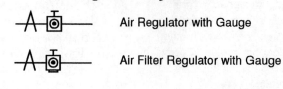

Air Regulator with Gauge

Air Filter Regulator with Gauge

Valve Symbols

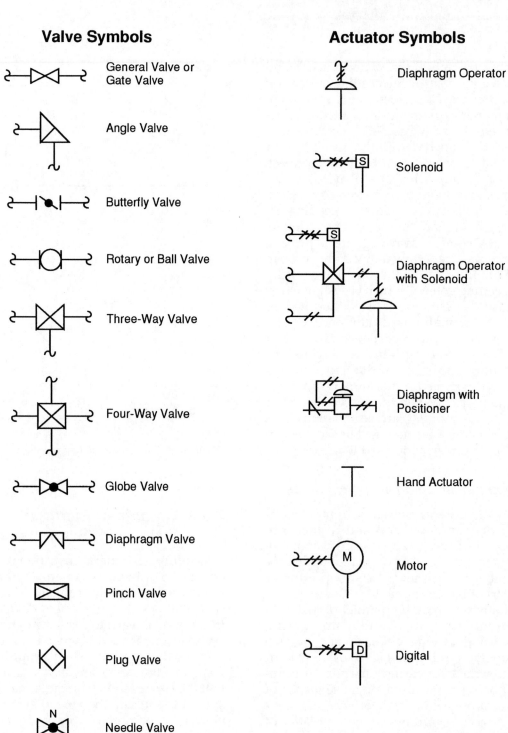

General Valve or Gate Valve

Angle Valve

Butterfly Valve

Rotary or Ball Valve

Three-Way Valve

Four-Way Valve

Globe Valve

Diaphragm Valve

Pinch Valve

Plug Valve

Needle Valve

Actuator Symbols

Diaphragm Operator

Solenoid

Diaphragm Operator with Solenoid

Diaphragm with Positioner

Hand Actuator

Motor

Digital

107F09A.TIF

Figure 9 ◆ Instrument symbols (1 of 4).

Actuator Symbols - Continued

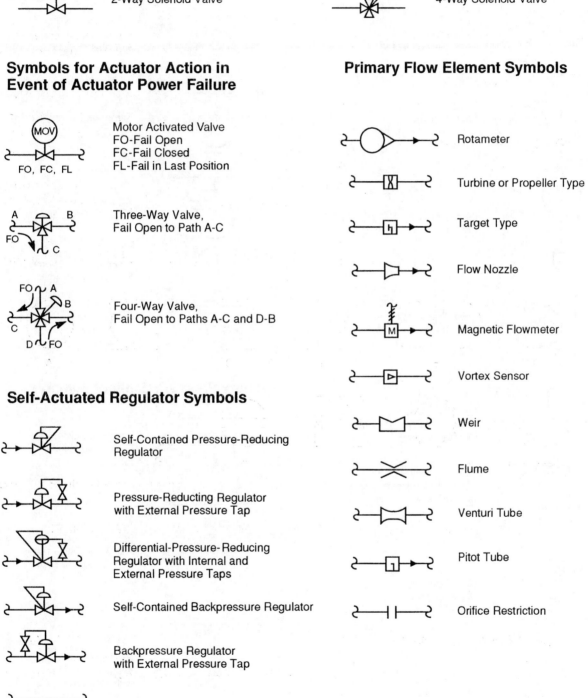

Electrohydraulic

2-Way Solenoid Valve

3-Way Solenoid Valve

4-Way Solenoid Valve

Symbols for Actuator Action in Event of Actuator Power Failure

Motor Activated Valve
FO-Fail Open
FC-Fail Closed
FL-Fail in Last Position

FO, FC, FL

Three-Way Valve,
Fail Open to Path A-C

Four-Way Valve,
Fail Open to Paths A-C and D-B

Self-Actuated Regulator Symbols

Self-Contained Pressure-Reducing Regulator

Pressure-Reducting Regulator with External Pressure Tap

Differential-Pressure-Reducing Regulator with Internal and External Pressure Taps

Self-Contained Backpressure Regulator

Backpressure Regulator with External Pressure Tap

Trap

Primary Flow Element Symbols

Rotameter

Turbine or Propeller Type

Target Type

Flow Nozzle

Magnetic Flowmeter

Vortex Sensor

Weir

Flume

Venturi Tube

Pitot Tube

Orifice Restriction

107F09B.TIF

Figure 9 ◆ Instrument symbols (2 of 4).

Primary Level Element Symbols

Gauge Glass, mounted on tank

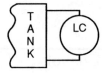

Gauge Glass, externally connected

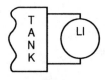

Level Indicator, with two connections

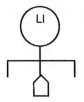

Level Indicator, Float Type

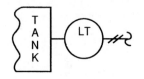

Level Transmitter, one connection

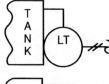

Level Transmitter, Differential Pressure Type, mounted on tank

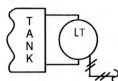

Level Transmitter, Differential Pressure Type, with two connections

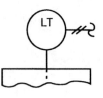

Level Transmitter, Capacitance or Dielectric Type

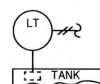

Level Switch, Paddle Wheel or Lever Type

Primary Level Element Symbols

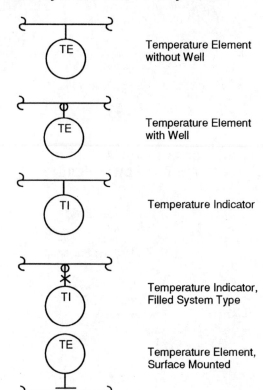

Temperature Element without Well

Temperature Element with Well

Temperature Indicator

Temperature Indicator, Filled System Type

Temperature Element, Surface Mounted

Primary Pressure Element Symbols

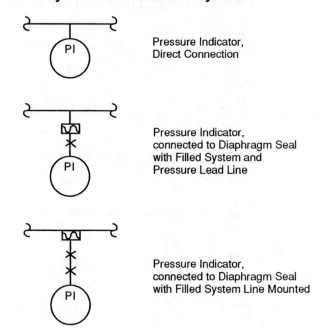

Pressure Indicator, Direct Connection

Pressure Indicator, connected to Diaphragm Seal with Filled System and Pressure Lead Line

Pressure Indicator, connected to Diaphragm Seal with Filled System Line Mounted

107F09C.TIF

Figure 9 ◆ Instrument symbols (3 of 4).

Miscellaneous Primary Element Symbols

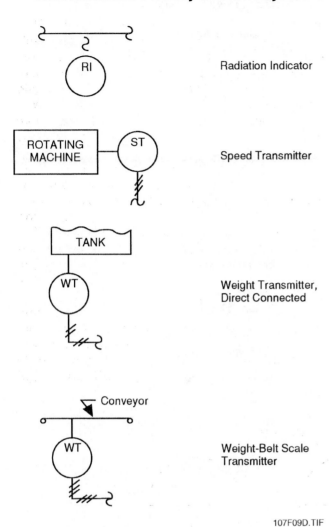

Radiation Indicator

Speed Transmitter

Weight Transmitter, Direct Connected

Weight-Belt Scale Transmitter

107F09D.TIF

Figure 9 ◆ Instrument symbols (4 of 4).

2.4.0 Line Symbols

There are several types of line symbols used on instrument drawings. They identify such things as process piping, process connections, and signal lines. Process piping lines are usually dark and bold as shown in *Figure 10*.

Process piping lines represent the piping that carries working process fluids such as steam, water, or gases. Also shown in *Figure 10* is a process connection line. Process connection lines are fine lines used to represent different types of connections such as mechanical links between two parts of an instrument system, a connection between an instrument and the process, or a connection indicating the supply line to an instrument.

For an instrument system to function, different types of signals are sent from one instrument to another. *Figure 11* shows the symbols for common types of instrument signal lines.

3.0.0 ◆ INSTRUMENT INDEX

The instrument index (*Figure 12*) is one of the most used and most important documents in instrumentation. It lists every instrument used on a project by tag number. It also provides a means to locate related drawings and documents containing information needed for installation, service, troubleshooting, or maintenance of instruments. Without an instrument index, locating the information needed to do instrumentation work would be difficult.

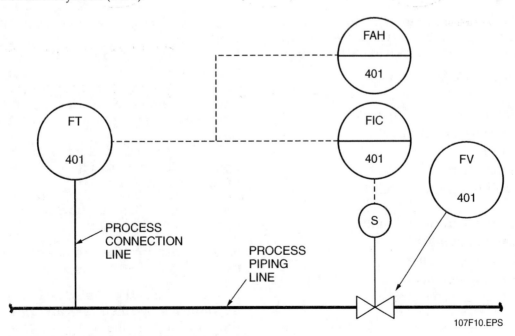

Figure 10 ◆ Process piping and connection lines.

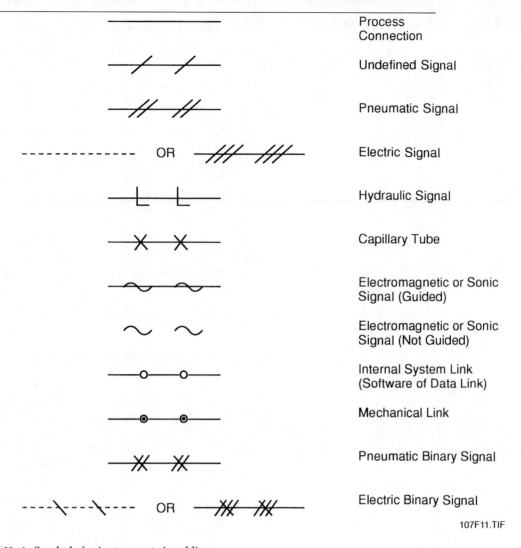

	Process Connection
	Undefined Signal
	Pneumatic Signal
OR	Electric Signal
	Hydraulic Signal
	Capillary Tube
	Electromagnetic or Sonic Signal (Guided)
	Electromagnetic or Sonic Signal (Not Guided)
	Internal System Link (Software of Data Link)
	Mechanical Link
	Pneumatic Binary Signal
OR	Electric Binary Signal

107F11.TIF

Figure 11 ◆ Symbols for instrument signal lines.

In addition to listing all the instruments used for a project by tag number, a typical instrument index includes information such as the following:

- Instrument service function
- Location
- Manufacturer
- Specification sheet number
- P&ID number
- Loop diagram number
- Location and routing or panel drawing number
- Installation detail drawing number
- **Piping drawing** number
- Electrical drawing number
- Vendor drawing number
- Notes relating to each instrument

You may use an instrument index often in your work, so become familiar with how it is organized for each project. It is an important document that you will use to identify instruments, locate instruments, find appropriate drawings, identify specifications, reference documents, and find other information relating to specific instruments used on a project.

The following is an explanation of the information included in each of the columns on the sample instrument index.

Tag no. – Lists the tag number for every instrument used on the project.

Service – Identifies the instrument and the type of process in which it is being used.

Location – Lists the code describing where the instrument is installed. A location legend is sometimes included at the bottom of each page of the instrument index.

TAG NO.	SERVICE	LOCATION	MFR	SPEC SHEET NO.	P & I D NO.	LOOPSHEET DWG NO	LOCATION & ROUTING OR PANEL DWG N	INSTL DETAIL DWG NO.	PIPING DWG NO	ELECT. DWG NO	VENDER DWG NO	NOTES
LAH-1	Cooling Tower Level	PV	ACME	03-LA-1	03-P-100	03-L-1	------	------	------	------	------	P.O. NO. 249-126
LAL-1	Cooling Tower Level	PV	ACME	03-LA-1	03-P-100	03-L-1	------	------	------	------	------	P.O. NO. 249-126
LIC-1	Cooling Tower Level	L	Jones	03-C-2	03-P-100	03-L-1	03-I-600	65-I-502	------	------	------	P.O. NO. 249-290
LSH-1	Cooling Tower Level	L	US Inst.	03-LS-1	03-P-100	03-L-1	03-I-600	------	------	------	------	P.O. NO. 249-423
LT-1	Cooling Tower Level	F	Smith	03-LT-1	03-P-100	03-L-1	03-I-600	03-I-600	03-P-200	------	------	P.O. NO. 249-612
LV-1	Cooling Tower Level	F	Honey	03-V-2	03-P-100	03-L-1	03-I-600	65-I-523	03-P-200	------	------	P.O. NO. 249-612
PC-1	Cooling Tower Recirculation Water Pressure	F	Fisher	03-V-005	03-P-100	03-P-002	03-I-600	65-I-502 65-I-540A	03-P-200	------	------	P.O. NO. 249-083
PCV-2	Cooling Tower Recirculation Water Pressure	F	Fisher	03-V-005	03-P-100	03-P-002	03-I-600	65-I-524	03-P-200	------	------	P.O. NO. 249-083
VAH-3A	Cooling Tower Fan Vibration	PV	Roberts	03-VA-1	03-P-100	66-I-301	------	------	------	------	------	P.O. NO. 249-016
VT-3A	Cooling Tower Fan Vibration	PV	Roberts	03-VA-1	03-P-100	03-V-003	03-I-600	------	------	------	------	P.O. NO. 249-016
VAH-3B	Cooling Tower Fan Vibration	PV	Roberts	03-VT-1	03-P-100	66-I-301	------	------	------	------	------	P.O. NO. 249-018
VT-3B	Cooling Tower Fan Vibration	PV	Roberts	03-VS-1	03-P-100	03-V-003	03-I-600	------	------	------	------	P.O. NO. 249-018
VS-3A	Cooling Tower Fan Vibration	PV	Roberts	03-VS-1	03-P-100	03-V-003	03-I-600	------	------	------	------	P.O. NO. 249-020

			LOCATION LEGEND	DRAWN BY Word Process.	DATE 4/26/92	X Y Z ENGINEERING	No. 2 Cooling Tower
			A - ANALOG SOFTWARE	DESIGNED BY	DATE 3/29/92		
			B - BACK OF PANEL D - DIGITAL SOFTWARE	CHECKED BY	DATE 5/05/92		
			E - EXISTING F - FIELD	APPROVED BY	DATE		CONTRACT NO.
1	8/5/92	ADDED HEAT TRACE I.D.	L - LOCAL PANEL P - FRONT OF PANEL				SHEET 1 OF 3
0	5/7/92	RELEASED FOR CONSTRUCTION	B - BACK				ABC-249
NO.	DATE	REVISIONS	V - VENDOR PACKAGE	RELEASED BY	DATE 5/07/92		INSTRUMENT INDEX

107F12.TIF

Figure 12 ◆ Example of an instrument index.

MFR – Identifies the manufacturer of the instrument.

Spec sheet no. – Identifies the specification sheet number for the instrument that describes the physical characteristics of the instrument. Some instruments do not have a specification sheet.

P&ID no. – Identifies the **piping and instrument drawing** number on which the instrument appears.

Loop sheet dwg no. – Identifies the **loop sheet drawing** number on which the instrument appears.

Location and routing or panel dwg no. – Identifies the location and routing or panel drawing number on which the instrument appears, if applicable.

Instl detail dwg no. – Identifies the installation detail drawing number that provides directions for installing the instrument.

Piping dwg no. – Identifies the piping drawing number that shows the piping line and related instrument that is to be installed, if applicable.

Elect dwg no. – Identifies the electrical drawing number that shows how the instrument is to be electrically connected, if applicable.

Vendor dwg no. – Identifies any vendor drawing number relevant to the type of instrument.

Notes – Describe any additional information relating to the instrument. The notes section may be used to explain any notations made in the index. It is often used to list the purchase order number for the instrument.

4.0.0 ◆ GENERAL INSTRUMENT SPECIFICATIONS

On every project, there are usually several specifications that have wide applications for instrument work. These **general instrument specifications** may be found in the general piping specifications for a project. If instrument specifications are different from those in the general piping specifications, you may find the information in another document such as:

• A detail or note on the appropriate piping diagram

• An instrument, mechanical, or process connection detail drawing for the instrument

• The instrumentation installation detail drawing for the instrument

You must locate all the documents necessary to find the proper specifications for instrument work. If you have all of the drawings and documents, you can do the job right the first time.

Some examples of types of information you might find in the general instrument specifications for a project are listed here:

• Field-mounted liquid-level controllers will be located where the gauge glass is visible. The level control valve will be located where the operator can see the gauge glass while operating the control valve by-pass.

• Level gauges and level controllers are to be accessible.

• Control valves are to be located at grade.

• Pressure gauge connections to piping and equipment will be ¾-inch threadolet or sockolet.

• Temperature instrument connections to piping and equipment will be 1 inch threadolets. When the flow sheet calls for a flanged connection, it will be ½ inch-long welding neck. The instrument department will purchase the companion flange with the thermowell welded in. The piping department will supply the bolts and gaskets.

• The minimum requirement for meter runs for orifice flanges will be computed according to American Gas Association (AGA) standards. A 0.75-diameter ratio will be used for determining the upstream and downstream straight pipe requirements.

• Orifice flange taps will be vertical for vapor service and horizontal for liquid service. Taps can be 45 degrees to the vertical. Piping will furnish the two valves and nipples connected to the orifice flange. These valves will not show on the piping plans and elevations, but will show on the isometric drawings.

• Instruments shall be located so as to be accessible for repair, calibration, and adjustment from the ground or permanent ladder or platform. It is not intended that this requirement apply to transmitters close coupled to the points of measurement.

• Wherever possible, locally mounted instruments shall be mounted at approximately 4 feet 6 inches above the floor, ground, or platform in an accessible and visible position.

NOTE

Always consult the general instrument specifications for your specific project.

5.0.0 ◆ GENERAL NOTES AND DETAILS

Notes and details are included on most instrument drawings to provide special information or directions about the process or instruments in the drawings. You need to pay close attention to the notes or details appearing on any drawing. This information is often vital to the safe and successful completion of the work. Sometimes notes and details are included in a special section of a drawing, or they may be presented on the drawing itself.

6.0.0 ◆ INSTALLATION DETAIL DRAWINGS

Installation detail drawings (*Figure 13*) provide the information and requirements for proper mounting of an instrument, connecting the instrument to the process, and/or positioning the instrument for correct operation. Installation detail drawings usually include a materials list that describes items and parts needed to install the instrument. These items may include tubing, fittings, bolts, and flanges.

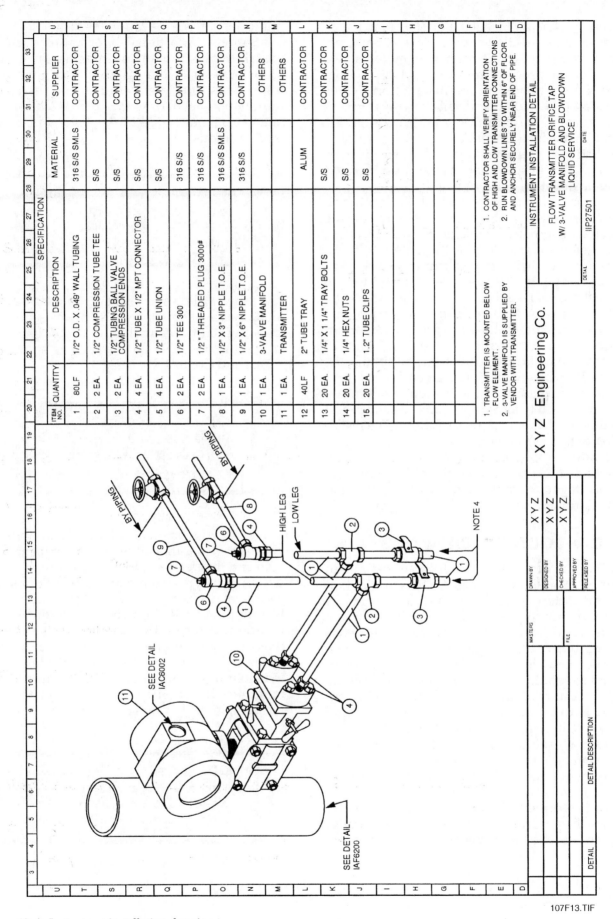

The table in the drawing reads:

ITEM NO.	QUANTITY	DESCRIPTION	SPECIFICATION		SUPPLIER
			MATERIAL		
1	80LF	1/2" O.D. X .049' WALL TUBING	316 S/S SMLS		CONTRACTOR
2	2 EA.	1/2" COMPRESSION TUBE TEE	S/S		CONTRACTOR
3	2 EA.	1/2" TUBING BALL VALVE COMPRESSION ENDS	S/S		CONTRACTOR
4	4 EA.	1/2" TUBE X 1/2" MPT CONNECTOR	S/S		CONTRACTOR
5	4 EA.	1/2" TUBE UNION	S/S		CONTRACTOR
6	2 EA.	1/2" TEE 300	316 S/S		CONTRACTOR
7	2 EA.	1/2" THREADED PLUG 3000#	316 S/S		CONTRACTOR
8	1 EA.	1/2" X 3" NIPPLE T.O.E.	316 S/S SMLS		CONTRACTOR
9	1 EA.	1/2" X 6" NIPPLE T.O.E.	316 S/S		CONTRACTOR
10	1 EA.	3-VALVE MANIFOLD			OTHERS
11	1 EA.	TRANSMITTER			OTHERS
12	40LF	2" TUBE TRAY	ALUM		CONTRACTOR
13	20 EA.	1/4" X 1 1/4" TRAY BOLTS	S/S		CONTRACTOR
14	20 EA.	1/4" HEX NUTS	S/S		CONTRACTOR
15	20 EA.	1.2" TUBE CLIPS	S/S		CONTRACTOR

NOTES:
1. TRANSMITTER IS MOUNTED BELOW FLOW ELEMENT.
2. 3-VALVE MANIFOLD IS SUPPLIED BY VENDOR WITH TRANSMITTER.

1. CONTRACTOR SHALL VERIFY ORIENTATION OF HIGH AND LOW TRANSMITTER CONNECTIONS
2. RUN BLOWDOWN LINES TO WITHIN 6" OF FLOOR AND ANCHOR SECURELY NEAR END OF PIPE.

X Y Z Engineering Co.

INSTRUMENT INSTALLATION DETAIL

FLOW TRANSMITTER ORIFICE TAP W/ 3-VALVE MANIFOLD AND BLOWDOWN LIQUID SERVICE

IIP27501

DRAWN BY	X Y Z
DESIGNED BY	X Y Z
CHECKED BY	X Y Z
APPROVED BY	
RELEASED BY	

MASTERS

DETAIL DESCRIPTION

DETAIL

DATE

107F13.TIF

Figure 13 ◆ Instrument installation drawing.

You can use an installation detail drawing to determine the position of the instrument in reference to the process line, such as mounted above or below the process line, or to find any special instructions related to the installation. Notes included on installation detail drawings present any special information or directions for installing the instrument. A list of reference drawings and documents relating to the instrument or any installation specifications may also be listed on an installation detail drawing.

The callout numbers on installation detail drawings relate to the numbered items on the materials list. For example, in *Figure 13*, callout No. 2 refers to item No. 2 on the materials list. In this example, there are two stainless steel, compression-type, tee fittings (size – ½ inch) used to make these connections.

The notes and references on installation detail drawings and other drawings provide important information. For example, Note 1 in *Figure 13* describes the correct position for mounting the transmitter (below the flow **element**).

References listed on installation detail drawings allow you to locate applicable drawings and documents that may be needed during the installation of the instrument.

If additional information is needed, you should also check the instrument index for the specific tag number of the instrument or the general instrument specifications for the project.

7.0.0 ◆ LOCATION DRAWINGS

Finding the exact location where an instrument is to be installed may require that you look at several different drawings and documents. A location drawing, sometimes referred to as a location and routing drawing, is helpful in determining where an instrument is to be installed. Location drawings may show where an instrument tap should be located in the process piping or the location of the vessel on which the instrument is to be mounted. However, the actual physical location of the instrument is often decided by the instrument field personnel, the superintendent, foreman, or other experienced instrument person. You may need to check with one of them.

An instrument location drawing typically shows the general location of the instrument in reference to the plan view of the area. It usually

indicates a given elevation for installation of the instrument. Additional information needed to install the instrument, such as height from the floor or permissible distance from the process pipe lines, may be found in the instrument installation detail drawings. These requirements may also be included in the general instrument specifications.

NOTE

Check all appropriate drawings and documents if you are not sure exactly where the instrument is to be installed.

Figure 14 shows an example of a typical location drawing showing a mix tank close to where building column centerlines A1 and 2 intersect. It also shows the position of a White Water Storage Chest and Control Room C.

NOTE

In some cases, the numbers 0 and 1, and the letters I, O, and Q, are omitted from location drawings to avoid confusion.

The drawing shown in *Figure 14* indicates the approximate location of several instruments in the plan and their elevations, where appropriate. The drawing also references applicable loop sheets, P&IDs, and piping drawings that could provide helpful information, if needed. Additional information relating to the location of these instruments may be found by using the instrument index. The instrument index will identify the installation specification drawings and **instrument specification sheets** for the instruments included in the location drawing.

NOTE

Be sure to analyze and cross reference all instrument drawings to make sure that you have a complete understanding of the job.

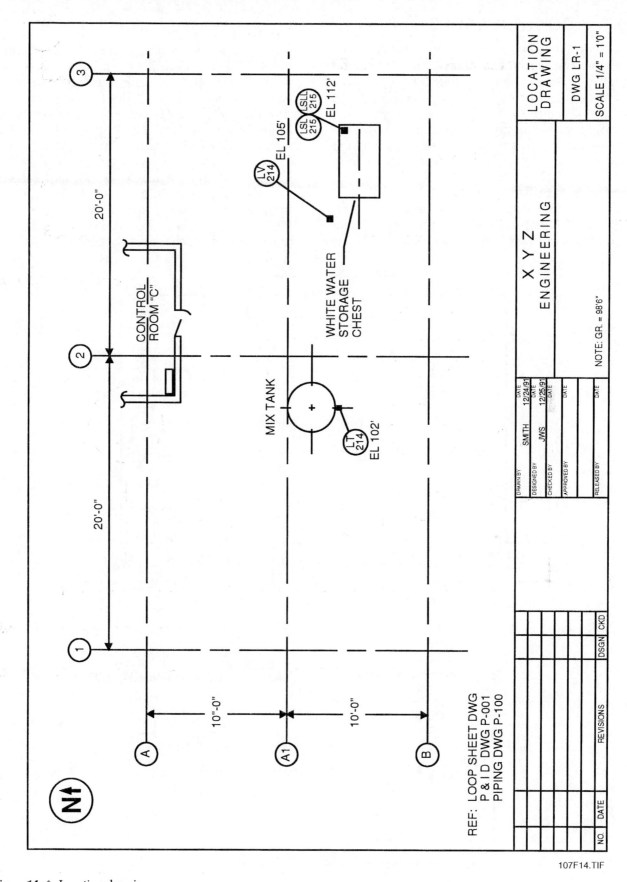

Figure 14 ◆ Location drawing.

8.0.0 ◆ CONTROL LOOPS

A control loop is a combination of two or more instruments or control functions arranged so that signals pass from one to another for the purpose of measurement or control of a process variable. The top of *Figure 15* shows a block diagram of a control loop. The bottom of the figure shows the same control loop as it might be drawn on a loop drawing for a specific facility. For the control loop shown, the flow in the process line is the measured and controlled property.

There are four instruments or control functions in the control loop shown. The primary element represents an orifice plate (FE2) mounted in the process line downstream from the flow control valve (FE2). FE2 provides the input to a flow transformer (FT2) that controls the signal to control valve FV2 according to a desired set point on the controller (FIC2). FV2 operates to regulate the flow in the process line, which is again monitored and measured by FE2, which continues to supply the loop. This arrangement is referred to as a feedback loop since all four devices in the loop depend on the preceding device in the loop for feedback (information) to allow it to function. Notice that controller FIC2 is the only discreet instrument located in a primary location, probably in the control room.

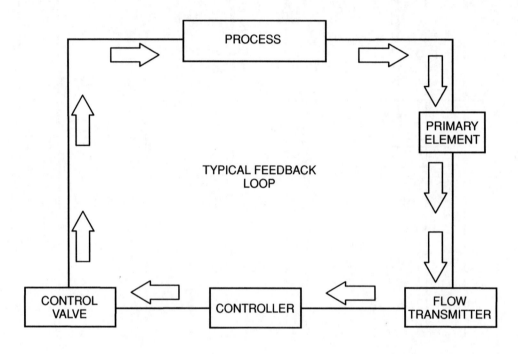

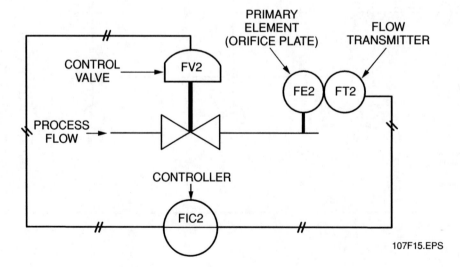

107F15.EPS

Figure 15 ◆ Example of a typical feedback control loop.

Summary

In this training module, you were introduced to the following:

- Instrument symbols and abbreviations
- Instrument indexes
- General instrument specifications
- General notes and details that appear on drawings and in documents
- Installation detail drawings
- Location drawings
- Loop drawings

These drawings and documents, along with others that will be covered in later modules, provide information needed to perform safe and high quality instrument work. In your day-to-day activities, take time to analyze the drawings for each project. It takes practice, study, and plenty of on-the-job experience to be able to effectively read and interpret all of the drawings and documents related to instrument work.

Review Questions

1. The organization that established a standard set of symbols and identification techniques that are widely used for instrument drawings and documents is _____.
   a. ANSI
   b. SAE
   c. ISA
   d. ASIE

2. A single solid line drawn through the instrument balloon indicates that _____.
   a. the instrument is in a primary location, normally accessible to the operator
   b. the instrument is mounted in an auxiliary location, normally accessible to the operator
   c. the instrument is field-mounted, near the point of measurement or a final control element
   d. the instrument accepts a digital input signal

3. A programmable logic controller (PLC) and a _____ share the same instrument symbol, which is a hexagon.
   a. shared control device (SCD)
   b. distributed control system (DCS)
   c. motorized control valve (MCV)
   d. self-contained pressure regulator (SPR)

4. A(n) _____ letter may have one meaning as a first letter and another meaning as a second letter.
   a. user's choice
   b. unclassified
   c. safety
   d. succeeding

5. If the first letter of the tag number for all the instruments in a loop is *F*, the measured or initiating variable is _____.
   a. burner flame
   b. pressure
   c. temperature
   d. flow rate

6. A succeeding letter *I* may be defined as all of the following *except* _____.
   a. indicate
   b. indicator
   c. indicating
   d. inversing

7. When used as a first-letter modifier, the letter _____ applies only to emergency protective elements and emergency protective final control elements.
   a. E
   b. P
   c. T
   d. S

8. Sometimes succeeding-letter designations are modified to reflect the _____.
   a. needs of a particular project
   b. choices of the installer
   c. equipment manufacturer
   d. international standards

9. Loop numbering may be parallel or _____.
   a. random
   b. selective
   c. optional
   d. serial

10. A primary flow element symbol that looks like a square box with an inverted L in it is used to represent a _____.
    a. flow nozzle
    b. pitot tube
    c. vortex sensor
    d. venturi tube

11. The instrument signal line symbol that consists of a single solid line with Ls drawn through it represents a(n) _____ signal.
    a. pneumatic
    b. hydraulic
    c. internal system link (software or data link)
    d. electric

12. _____ lines represent the piping that carries working process fluids.
    a. Capillary tube
    b. Pneumatic binary
    c. Process piping
    d. Signal

13. _____ signal line symbols have groups of three slashes across the main line.
    a. Process
    b. Pneumatics
    c. Electric
    d. Hydraulic

14. If you wanted to find the manufacturer of an instrument with a specific tag number, the best place to locate that information is in the _____.
    a. P&ID
    b. instrument index
    c. flow sheet
    d. general instrument specifications

15. Each one of the following is typically found on an instrument index *except* _____.
    a. location
    b. manufacturer
    c. P&ID
    d. list of symbols

16. _____ are included on most instrument drawings to provide special information or directions about the process or instruments in the drawings.
    a. Symbols
    b. Addendum sheets
    c. Notes and details
    d. Designer contact numbers

17. The callout numbers on an installation detail drawing relate to the numbered items on the _____.
    a. instrument index
    b. location drawing
    c. materials list
    d. purchase order

18. To get a complete understanding of the job, you should analyze and _____ all instrument drawings.
    a. memorize
    b. copy
    c. cross reference
    d. disregard

19. The elevation at which an instrument is to be installed is likely to be found on the _____.
    a. loop sheet
    b. location drawing
    c. P&ID
    d. instrument index

20. A drawing that illustrates the interconnection of devices from the primary element in the field, to the board-mounted instruments on the control panel, to the final control devices is called a(n) _____.
    a. instrument index
    b. location drawing
    c. detail drawing
    d. loop drawing

Trade Terms Introduced
in This Module

Balloon: The circular symbol used to denote and identify the purpose of an instrument or function. It may contain a tag number. Also referred to as a *bubble*.

Behind the panel: A term applied to a location containing the instrument panel and its associated rack-mounted hardware. These devices can either be behind the panel, enclosed within the panel, or both. Devices mounted behind the panel are not normally accessible for the operator's use. Also referred to as *behind the board*.

Board: A structure that has a group of instruments mounted on it. Also referred to as *panel*.

Digital: A term applied to a signal or device that uses binary (0,1) digits to represent continuous values or discrete states.

Distributed control system (DCS): A functionally integrated system that consists of subsystems which may be physically separate and remotely located from one another.

Element: A component of a device or system.

Field: The location of an instrument that is neither in nor on a panel or console, nor is it mounted in a control room. Local or field instruments are commonly in the vicinity of the primary element or final control element. Also referred to as *local*.

Final control element: The device that directly changes the value of the manipulated variable of a control loop. A control valve is often the final control element in a loop.

Function: The purpose of, or an action performed by, a device.

General instrument specifications: A written description of the general criteria for installing instruments for a particular project.

Identification number: The sequence of letters or digits, or both, used to designate an individual instrument and/or loop. Also referred to as *tag number*.

Initiating variable: A quantity, property, or condition that is measured (such as temperature, pressure, flow, etc.). Also referred to as *measured variable*.

Installation detail drawing: A drawing that shows how a device is mechanically installed, and includes a materials list.

Instrument Index: A document that lists all pertinent information regarding each separate instrument on a project by tag number. It is also a directory for locating the necessary drawings and documents associated with each instrument.

Instrument specification sheet: A document that outlines the functional and process requirements of an instrument along with physical and chemical specifications.

Legend: A section of a drawing that provides explanatory information such as lists of symbols, abbreviations, location codes, and other designations used on the drawing.

Local panel: A panel that is not a central or main panel. Local panels are commonly in the vicinity of plant sub-systems or sub-areas.

Location drawing: A drawing showing general locations of instruments in relation to physical plant layouts. Sometimes used to route wire and other utilities to the general area of the plant. Usually includes elevation, column grid line coordinates, and North orientation. Also referred to as *location and routing drawing*.

Loop: A combination of two or more instruments or control functions arranged so that signals pass from one to another for the purpose of measurement or control of a process variable.

Loop sheet drawing: A drawing illustrating the interconnection of devices in a loop from the primary element in the field to the board-mounted instruments on the control panel to the final control devices. Illustrates all tubing and wiring for the complete loop and shows where the instruments are located: panel front, panel rear, field junction, and field process area. Calibration parameters and specific termination points, by name and number, are also normally included on loop drawings. Also referred to as *loop sheet*.

Piping drawing: A drawing made to scale showing all process piping and equipment connected to the process piping. These drawings (plans, sections, details) may show instrument locations.

Piping and instrument drawing: A detailed drawing that shows equipment, piping, and instrumentation required on a project. Also referred to as *P&ID, P&I drawing*, or *P&I diagram*.

Primary element: The system element in contact with measured variable that converts the measured variable energy into a form suitable for measurement.

Programmable logic controller (PLC): A controller, usually with multiple inputs and outputs, that can be programmed to perform a variety of functions.

Shared control: A single device (controller) that can control a number of process variables.

Shared display: A device (usually a video screen) that can display process information from a number of different sources.

Additional Resources

This module is intended to present thorough resources for task training. The following reference works are suggested for further study. These are optional materials for continued education rather than for task training.

ISA Standards. Research Triangle Park, NC: Instrument Society of America.

- ISA Standard S5.1 – *Instrumentation Symbols and Identification*
- ISA Standard S5.2 – *Binary Logic Diagrams for Process Operations*
- ISA Standard S5.3 – *Graphic Symbols for Distributed Control/ Shared Display Instrumentation, Logic, and Computer Systems*
- ISA Standard S5.4 – *Instrument Loop Diagrams*
- ISA Standard S51.1 – *Process Instrumentation Terminology*

NCCER CRAFT TRAINING USER UPDATES

The NCCER makes every effort to keep these textbooks up-to-date and free of technical errors. We appreciate your help in this process. If you have an idea for improving this textbook, or if you find an error, a typographical mistake, or an inaccuracy in the NCCER's Craft Training textbooks, please write us, using this form or a photocopy. Be sure to include the exact module number, page number, a detailed description, and the correction, if applicable. Your input will be brought to the attention of the Technical Review Committee. Thank you for your assistance.

Instructors – If you found that additional materials were necessary in order to teach this module effectively, please let us know so that we may include them in the Equipment and Materials list in the Instructor's Guide.

Write: Curriculum Revision and Development Department
National Center for Construction Education and Research
P.O. Box 141104, Gainesville, FL 32614-1104

Fax: 352-334-0932

E-mail: curriculum@nccer.org

Craft _____ Module Name _____

Copyright Date _____ Module Number _____ Page Number(s) _____

Description _____

_____

_____

_____

(Optional) Correction _____

_____

_____

(Optional) Your Name and Address _____

_____

_____

Gaskets and Packing

COURSE MAP

This course map shows all of the modules in the first level of the Instrumentation curriculum. The suggested training order begins at the bottom and proceeds up. Skill levels increase as you advance on the course map. The local Training Program Sponsor may adjust the training order.

INSTRUMENTATION LEVEL ONE

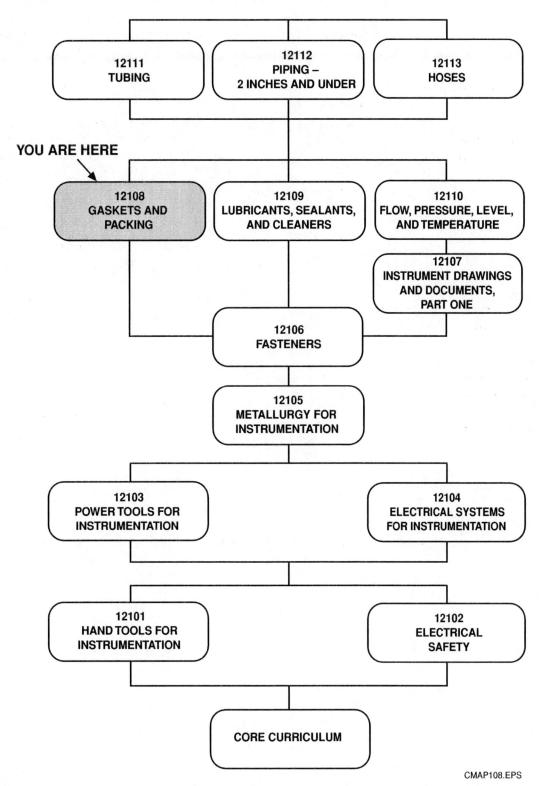

YOU ARE HERE

12111
TUBING

12112
PIPING –
2 INCHES AND UNDER

12113
HOSES

12108
GASKETS AND
PACKING

12109
LUBRICANTS, SEALANTS,
AND CLEANERS

12110
FLOW, PRESSURE, LEVEL,
AND TEMPERATURE

12107
INSTRUMENT DRAWINGS
AND DOCUMENTS,
PART ONE

12106
FASTENERS

12105
METALLURGY FOR
INSTRUMENTATION

12103
POWER TOOLS FOR
INSTRUMENTATION

12104
ELECTRICAL SYSTEMS
FOR INSTRUMENTATION

12101
HAND TOOLS FOR
INSTRUMENTATION

12102
ELECTRICAL
SAFETY

CORE CURRICULUM

CMAP108.EPS

MODULE 12108 CONTENTS

Figures

Gaskets and Packing

OBJECTIVES

When you have completed this module, you will be able to do the following:

1. Identify the different types of gaskets and gasket material.
2. Identify the different types of packing.
3. Describe uses of packing.
4. Describe uses of O-rings.
5. Describe uses of gaskets.
6. Fabricate gaskets.

Prerequisites

Before you begin this module, it is recommended that you successfully complete the following modules: Core Curriculum; Instrumentation Level One, Modules 12101 through 12107.

Required Trainee Materials

1. Pencil and paper
2. Appropriate personal protective equipment

1.0.0 ◆ INTRODUCTION

Different types of gaskets, O-rings, and packing are used extensively in instrumentation work. Gaskets and O-rings are used to form a seal at the joint of two parts. Gaskets are made of material that can be compressed to fill irregularities in the mating surfaces of the parts. The gasket material conforms to the shapes of the surfaces and makes a seal between them.

There is one major difference between the way that gaskets and O-rings form seals. A gasket usu-ally forms a seal between two flat surfaces. An O-ring fits into a groove on a shaft or surface and is made to protrude slightly from the groove. When another surface is brought in contact with the O-ring, the O-ring compresses to make a seal.

Packing is used to form seals around various shafts that turn, such as valve stems, faucets, pumps, compressors, and other equipment. Packing is made of a variety of materials and is extremely versatile. It is used for numerous applications to ensure a leakproof system.

1.1.0 Compatibility

The information given in this module is general in nature. It is important to know that selecting gaskets and O-rings for a particular application involves more than just finding one that is the right size and shape. The properties of the material from which a particular gasket or O-ring is made must also be compatible with the process and environment to which the gasket or O-ring will be exposed. Use of the wrong type gasket can cause leaks to occur. It can also result in a hazardous condition for people, equipment, or both, depending on the type of fluid or other material that is leaking from a damaged seal into the environment.

Gaskets or O-rings made of natural rubber have a limited resistance to petroleum products. Some others made of synthetic rubber compounds will degrade when exposed to specific kinds of chemicals. This degradation can cause the gaskets or O-rings to either shrink or swell, causing a leak to occur at the seal. O-ring and gasket materials can also be affected by the process temperature and ambient temperature to which they are exposed. Subjecting gaskets or O-rings to the wrong range of temperatures can cause them to shrink or swell. These temperatures can also cause the associated flange bolts to elongate or shrink. One or more of these conditions can result in a leaking seal.

In general, the higher the operating temperature of the process or environment, the more attention should be given to the selection of the gasket or O-ring material. Fluids are generally easier to seal than gases. However, ambient or process temperatures can cause some fluids to have an increased deteriorating effect on polymers, a common material used in many gaskets or O-rings. Some tests have shown that concentrations of oxygen at relatively high temperatures (above 200°F /93°C) have a deteriorating affect on some elastomers, another material used in the construction of gaskets or O-rings.

Manufacturers of seals, O-rings, and gaskets typically provide compatibility tables in their catalogs and product literature that list the composite materials from which their gaskets or O-rings are made and their compatibility or noncompatibility with certain application processes. Always check these compatibility charts whenever replacing or installing a gasket or O-ring in any process.

2.0.0 ◆ GASKETS AND GASKET MATERIAL

Gaskets are available in a variety of types and materials. The type of gasket used must be matched to the process characteristics and operating conditions to which it will be exposed. For example, different gasket materials are capable of withstanding different temperature and pressure ranges. Certain gasket materials are compatible with different process fluids.

When replacing a gasket, it is considered good work practice to use a replacement gasket that is identical in properties to the gasket that has been removed. Replacement gaskets are generally supplied by the manufacturer of the equipment. However, in some cases, the replacement gasket will have to be fabricated.

In many instruments, gaskets are used to form a seal between two parts of the instrument. The gasket might be used to prevent air from leaking between parts of a pneumatic instrument. There are also many applications where gaskets are used to form a seal when connecting instruments to the process piping.

In piping systems, gaskets are placed between two **flanges** to make the joint leakproof. There are different types of gaskets that must be matched to different types of flanges. The general rule is to use a full-face gasket with a flat-face flange and a ring-joint gasket with a raised-face flange. Gaskets may also be regularly or irregularly shaped. Irregularly shaped gaskets are often cut to fit around openings and fasteners. Gaskets are normally sized by the thickness of the gasket material in fractions of an inch, such as $\frac{1}{16}$ inch or $\frac{1}{8}$ inch. Some of the more common types of gaskets are shown in *Figure 1*.

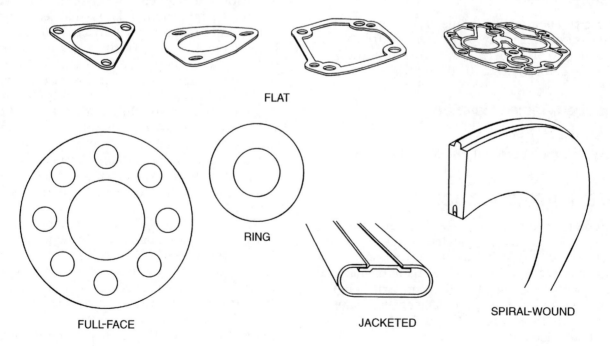

FLAT

FULL-FACE

RING

JACKETED

SPIRAL-WOUND

108F01.TIF

Figure 1 ◆ Common gasket types.

2.1.0 Gaskets

In order to ensure that the composition of various types of gaskets, gasket material, and some packing meets the required specifications, the American Society for Testing Materials (ASTM) devised a method of identifying different types of gasket material. Gaskets are made of many different types of materials to meet the demands of the particular process system in which they are installed. Generally, one of the following four conditions will exist in a process system. These conditions affect the types of gaskets that can be used in the system:

- *High temperature/low pressure* – Generally includes temperatures from 500°F to 1200°F and pressures up to 600 psi.
- *High temperature/high pressure* – Generally includes temperatures from 500°F to 1200°F and pressures from 600 to 2,500 psi.
- *Low temperature/low pressure* – Generally includes temperatures up to 500°F and pressures up to 600 psi.
- *Low temperature/high pressure* – Generally includes temperatures up to 500°F and pressures from 600 to 2,500 psi.

NOTE

Usually the types of gaskets and gasket materials to be used on a project are listed in a special section of the piping specifications. Gasket materials are rated by the **American National Standards Institute (ANSI)** specifications for applicable pressures.

2.2.0 Gasket Materials

Since most process systems are subject to a combination of chemicals, temperature, and pressure, it is extremely important to match the proper gasket material to the operating conditions of the process system. Different gasket materials have different pressure and temperature ratings. These ratings reflect the ability of a gasket material to withstand forces in a process system.

2.2.1 Teflon® Gaskets

Teflon® flange gaskets provide a nonporous, leak-free, reusable nongalvanic gasket. They are usually white in color and are available in several pressure/temperature limits. For example, various Teflon® gaskets are rated at 500 psi at 250°F,

400 psi at 280°F, 300 psi at 340°F, and 200 psi at 380°F. Teflon® gaskets are good for use in processes where temperature extremes exist in the range of –300°F to +450°F. However, Teflon® has a very low elasticity, which limits its usage in many processes.

2.2.2 Fiberglass Gaskets

Fiberglass gaskets are treated to remain soft and pliable. They sometimes include wire inserts for use with boiler handhole and manhole covers, as well as for tank heads and other high-pressure applications. Fiberglass gaskets are usually white in color. They can typically be used in applications up to 380°F and 180 psi.

2.2.3 Acrylic Non-Asbestos Fiber Gaskets

Many acrylic non-asbestos fiber flange gaskets are used with oil, fuel, solvents, steam, weak acids, **caustics**, and **alkalis**. They are usually off-white in color. Acrylic fiber gaskets can typically be used in applications with temperature ranges of –100°F to +750°F and pressures to 1,500 psi.

2.2.4 Metal Gaskets

Metal gaskets are used for machine flanges and where metal-to-metal fits are required. They are good for applications where higher temperature fluctuations and pressures are normal. When using metal gaskets, the material must be suitable for use within the process system. There are several different types of metal gaskets:

- Solid-metal gaskets are used in processes suitable for the metal or alloy used to make the gasket. Common materials are copper, Monel®, steel, and iron. Copper gaskets are not used in high-pressure/high-temperature systems. Monel®, steel, and iron gaskets can be used in a variety of pressure and temperature applications.
- Ring-joint metal gaskets are generally available in two types: octagonal and oval cross section. Both are standardized. The octagonal is considered superior. The rings are made of the softest carbon steel or iron available. Ring joint gaskets are generally used in high-pressure systems.
- Serrated metal gaskets are solid metal gaskets having concentric ribs machined into their surfaces. With the contact area reduced to a few concentric lines, the required bolt load is reduced considerably. This design forms an efficient joint. Serrated gaskets are used with smooth-finished flange faces and can be used in high-temperature/high-pressure systems.

- Corrugated metal gaskets are generally used on low-pressure systems where the flanges are smooth and bolt pressure is low. The ridges of the corrugations tend to concentrate the gasket loading along the concentric ridges.
- Laminated metal gaskets are made of metal with a soft filler. The laminate can be parallel to the flange face or spiral wound. Laminated gaskets require less bolt load to compress them than solid metal gaskets. Laminated gaskets can be used in high-pressure, high-temperature applications.
- Corrugated metal with asbestos-inserted gaskets are used for a variety of pressure and temperature applications in steam, water, gas, air, oil, oil vapor, and refrigerant systems.
- Corrugated metal jacket gaskets with heat-resistant synthetic filler are used for the same applications as corrugated metal with asbestos-inserted gaskets.

NOTE

Synthetic replacements for asbestos are often referred to as non-asbestos.

- Flat-metal jacket gaskets with asbestos gasket material are used in the same applications as corrugated metal gaskets with asbestos inserted.
- Spiral-wound metal gaskets with heat-resistant synthetic filler are used for a variety of pressure and temperature applications in the same systems as corrugated metal jacket gaskets with heat-resistant, synthetic filler.

2.2.5 Rubber Gaskets

Rubber gaskets are made in a variety of pressure and temperature ratings. Rubber gaskets generally come in thicknesses from $\frac{1}{16}$ inch to 1 inch. Rubber gaskets are used in low-pressure/low-temperature water, gas, air, and refrigerant systems.

- Standard black or red rubber gaskets are used for saturated steam up to 100 psi. They have an approximate temperature range of –20°F to 170°F.
- Reinforced rubber gaskets are strengthened by using polyester fabric plies. They are commonly used for saturated steam and low-pressure steam. Reinforced rubber gaskets have an approximate temperature range of –40°F to 200°F. They are typically black in color.
- High-test reinforced rubber gaskets are used for pressures up to 500 psi. They have an approximate temperature range of –40°F to 200°F, and they are black.

2.2.6 Cork Gaskets

Cork gaskets are **compressible**, flexible, lightweight, **resilient**, and **nonabsorbent**. They resist most oils, petroleum products, and chemicals. Cork is widely used in industry as a vibration-absorbing material. Cork is moisture resistant. It can be used for most liquids, even when boiling, except for strong alkalis. Cork gaskets are generally available in thicknesses from $\frac{1}{16}$ inch to $\frac{1}{2}$ inch.

2.2.7 Treated-Paper Gaskets

Treated-paper gaskets are made from a water-resistant material comprised of cellulose with a styrene butadiene rubber (SBR) binder. Treated-paper gaskets are commonly used in hot and cold water and antifreeze systems. Treated-paper gaskets are generally available in thicknesses from $\frac{1}{64}$ inch to $\frac{1}{16}$ inch.

2.2.8 Vinyl Gaskets

Vinyl gaskets are specially fabricated for use as oil-resistant gaskets. They also have a good resistance to water, chemicals, **oxidizing** agents, ozone, and abrasion. Vinyl gaskets are black in color. They have an approximate temperature range of 20°F to 160°F.

2.2.9 Ceramic Gaskets

Ceramic gaskets are used for high-temperature air applications, such as boiler systems, where other types of materials would fail due to the high temperature. Ceramic gaskets can typically be used for temperatures exceeding 1500°F.

2.2.10 Asbestos Gaskets

Asbestos gaskets are no longer installed in new installations and those that are installed in existing applications requiring replacement must be replaced with a non-asbestos type gasket suited for the application.

WARNING!

Asbestos is classified as a hazardous material. For this reason, removal of existing asbestos gaskets must be performed by authorized personnel only and under the supervision of the proper authority. All standards and safety regulations set forth by all jurisdictions having authority in the matter of the proper handling and disposal of asbestos products must be followed.

2.2.11 Fiber Gaskets

Fiber gaskets are not designed to be used when temperatures exceed 500°F. Fiber gaskets are used in low-pressure/low-temperature water, gas, air, and refrigerant systems.

3.0.0 ◆ FABRICATING GASKETS

The easiest way to make a gasket is to use the existing flange or the old gasket to make a template to cut out the new gasket. If this is not possible, the following section describes the procedures for laying out and cutting a new gasket.

3.1.0 Laying Out a New Gasket

The following procedure describes how to lay out and cut a new gasket for a pipe flange.

 WARNING!
Approved eye protection should be worn to protect the eyes from airborne gasket fibers or metal shards when fabricating gaskets. Hand protection should also be worn to protect the hands from injury when sharp gasket cutter blades are being used and/or sharp metal gasket edges are present.

Step 1 Select the proper gasket material for the conditions and process.

Step 2 Take three measurements (draw as concentric circles):

— Diameter of pipe opening
— Outside diameter of flange
— Diameter of the bolt hole circle

The diameter of the bolt circle is found by measuring from the edges of opposite holes, as shown in *Figure 2*. To get a center measurement, measure either from the inside edge of one hole to the outside edge of the opposite hole, or from the outside edge of one hole to the inside edge of the opposite hole.

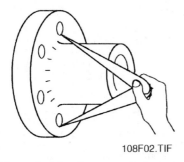
108F02.TIF

Figure 2 ◆ Measuring the diameter of a bolt circle.

Step 3 Find the radius of the bolt circle as shown in *Figure 3*. The radius of the bolt circle is equal to half of the diameter.

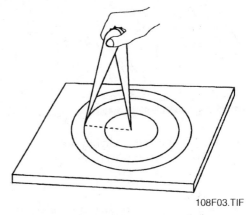
108F03.TIF

Figure 3 ◆ Radius of bolt circle.

Step 4 Draw a line through the circle's center for opposite holes.

Step 5 On a six-hole flange, the radius is equal to the distance between bolt holes as shown in *Figure 4*.

Step 6 To check the distance, walk the dividers around the circle.

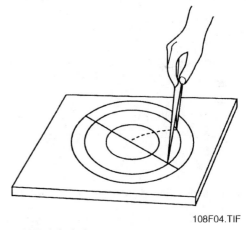
108F04.TIF

Figure 4 ◆ Bolt hole layout.

 NOTE
Lay out holes a little larger than their actual size as shown in *Figure 5*. Gaskets with an even number of holes (4, 8, 16) can also be laid out using the *swing arc* method. This method uses the divider to bisect distances. Flanges with an odd number of holes can be laid out using a protractor by simply dividing 360 degrees by the number of holes.

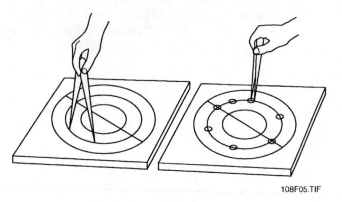

Figure 5 ◆ Lay out bolt hole slightly larger than actual size.

Step 7   Cut out the inside circle and outside circle of the gasket using a gasket cutter, as shown in *Figure 6*.

 NOTE

The gasket cutter blade should not protrude more than ⅟₃₂ inch more than the thickness of the gasket material. Never hammer the gasket, as hammering may cause lumps in the gasket.

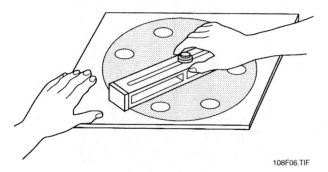

Figure 6 ◆ Using a gasket cutter.

Step 8   Place the gasket material on hard wood to protect the punch edge. Then, punch out the holes using the proper size hole punch as shown in *Figure 7*.

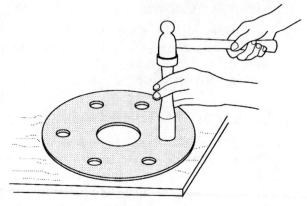

Figure 7 ◆ Using a hole punch.

3.2.0 Tracing a New Gasket

The following procedure describes how to trace and cut a new metal gasket for a pipe flange.

Step 1   Spread bluing ink on the pipe flange face, as shown in *Figure 8*.

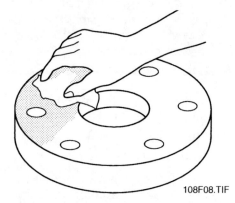

Figure 8 ◆ Bluing ink tracing.

Step 2   Place the gasket material on the flange face and make an impression, as shown in *Figure 9*.

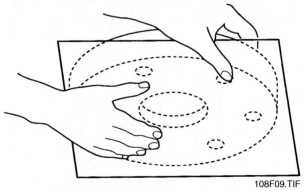

Figure 9 ◆ Making a bluing ink impression.

Step 3 Lift the gasket material off of the flange face. You should have an impression of the gasket, as shown in *Figure 10*.

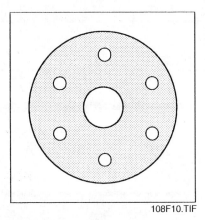
108F10.TIF

Figure 10 ◆ Bluing ink impression.

Step 4 Cut out the gasket using tin snips, as shown in *Figure 11*.

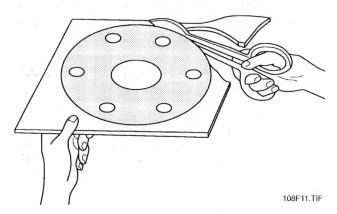
108F11.TIF

Figure 11 ◆ Cutting out the gasket with tin snips.

NOTE

Never hammer the gasket. Hammering may cause lumps in the gasket.

Step 5 Place the gasket material on hard wood to protect the punch edge, and then punch out the holes with the proper size hole punch.

Step 6 Clean any loose particles or wet ink off of the gasket using the appropriate cleaner. It is not necessary to clean the dried bluing ink from the surfaces.

4.0.0 ◆ PACKING

Packing is commonly used to form a seal around shafts, stems, or mandrels that either rotate or turn, yet require a sealing point. Uses in revolving equipment or devices include valve stems, faucets, pumps, compressors, and other equipment. Packing is sometimes used as gaskets for piping couplings, flange facings, and gear cases, with the packing installed in a packing groove. Various types of packing are shown in *Figure 12*.

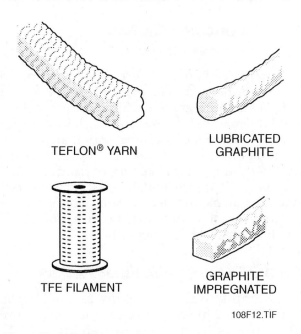

TEFLON® YARN

LUBRICATED GRAPHITE

TFE FILAMENT

GRAPHITE IMPREGNATED

108F12.TIF

Figure 12 ◆ Packing.

Commonly used types of packing include Teflon® yarn and filament, lubricated graphite yarn, lubricated carbon yarn (graphite impregnated), and **tetrafluoroethylene (TFE)**/synthetic fiber.

4.1.0 Teflon® Yarn Packing

Teflon® yarn packing is a cross-braided yarn impregnated with Teflon®. Teflon®-impregnated packing resists concentrated acids, such as sulfuric acid and nitric acid, sodium hydroxide, gases, alkalis, and most solvents. It is good for use in applications of up to approximately 550°F.

4.2.0 Teflon® Filament Packing

Teflon® filament (cord) packing is a braided packing made from TFE filament. It is impregnated with Teflon® and an inert softener lubricant. It is often used on rotating pumps, mixers, agitators, kettles, and other equipment.

4.3.0 Lubricated Graphite Yarn Packing

Lubricated graphite yarn packing is an intertwined braid of pure graphite yarn impregnated with inorganic graphite particles. The graphite particles dissipate heat. Lubricated graphite yarn packing also contains a special lubricant that provides a film to prevent wicking and reduce friction. It is good for use in high-temperature applications.

4.4.0 Lubricated Carbon Yarn Packing

Lubricated carbon yarn (graphite impregnated) packing is made from an intertwined braid of carbon fibers impregnated with graphite particles and lubricants to fill voids and block leakage. It is used in systems containing water, steam, and solutions of acids and alkalis. When used for packing pumps, it is capable of handling shaft speeds up to approximately 3,000 rpm. It is considered suitable for steam application with temperatures up to approximately 1200°F, and up to 600°F where oxygen is present.

4.5.0 TFE/Synthetic Fiber Packing

TFE/synthetic fiber packing is made from braided yarn fibers saturated and sealed with TFE particles before being woven into a multi-lock braided packing. TFE/synthetic fiber packing protects against a variety of chemical actions. It is used in applications where caustics, mild acids, gases, and many chemicals and solvents are present. It is often used in general service for rotating and reciprocating pumps, agitators, and valves.

4.6.0 Removing and Installing Packings

Packing rings used on revolving equipment shafts are usually installed in a packing gland, similar to the one shown in *Figure 13*. In this example, the packing gland is shown with four packing rings installed. The number of rings used normally depends on the pressure of the process that needs to be contained by the packing rings. The following procedure describes how to remove and replace packing rings in a packing gland on a pump.

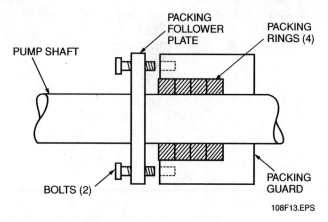

Figure 13 ◆ Packing gland.

 WARNING!

If repacking an operational process-connected piece of equipment, follow all safety procedures according to the standards, practices, and rules that apply to the specific location, equipment, and situation. Always wear approved eye protection when repacking a pump.

Step 1 De-energize/de-activate and lockout/tagout the equipment if operational or if connected to a process.

Step 2 Remove the packing follower plate, then use a packing extractor tool (*Figure 14*) to hook and pull out the old packing rings from inside the packing gland cavity.

Figure 14 ◆ Packing extractor tool.

Step 3 Inspect and clean the packing gland cavity and examine the pump shaft for any damage, burrs, or pitting. If any of these conditions exist, the equipment must be repaired; otherwise, the new packings can become damaged and will not properly seal.

Step 4 Size the new packing rings according to the old rings and cut new rings from a roll of matching packing material.

Step 5 Place the rings into the packing gland one at a time until the gland contains the correct number of rings. The last ring installed should extend slightly beyond the outer edge of the packing gland. When installing each ring, make sure to stagger its cut end 180 degrees from the cut end of the ring installed before it. Staggering the packing cut ends is important in order to prevent leaks from occurring.

Step 6 Secure the packing follower plate in place with the plate bolts and tighten just enough to apply a slight pressure on the packing rings.

Step 7 Momentarily operate the pump at its normal speed while checking for any leaks around the shaft. If no leaks are visible, slightly loosen the packing plate bolts until minimal leakage is visible around the pump shaft, then slightly tighten the bolts again until the leakage stops. This gradual but slight tightening procedure prevents undue pressure from being applied to the shaft by excessive compression of the packing rings, while still maintaining proper sealing.

5.0.0 ◆ O-RINGS

O-rings (*Figure 15*) are rugged and extremely dependable. They are used to seal against conditions ranging from strong vacuum to high pressure. O-rings are made from a variety of materials for different applications. Like gaskets, O-rings are often used to seal a mechanical connection between two parts of an instrument. O-rings that are used in instruments are often made of rubber or of a synthetic material. Occasionally, high-temperature or pressure applications may require the use of a metal O-ring.

Some of the more common O-rings are made from Buna-N (Nitrile), ethylene propylene, Viton®, Teflon®, silicone, Teflon®-encapsulated silicone, and polyurethane. O-rings are used in both static and dynamic seals. A static seal is not subjected to flow but may have system pressure. A dynamic seal has both flow and pressure.

The sizes of O-rings are set by Aerospace Standard AS568A published by the Society of Automotive Engineers (SAE). Sizes are designated by dash numbers, such as AS568 Dash No. 006 and AS568 Dash No. 216.

108F15.TIF

Figure 15 ◆ O-rings.

5.1.0 Buna-N O-Rings

Buna-N O-rings are widely used. They are made of an elastomeric-sealing material. They are used with a variety of petroleum and silicone fluids, hydraulic and nonaromatic fuels, and solvents. Buna-N O-rings are not compatible with phosphate esters, ketones, brake fluids, strong acids, or ozone. They have an approximate temperature range of –65°F to 275°F. Buna-N O-rings do not weather well, especially in direct sunlight.

5.2.0 Ethylene Propylene O-Rings

Ethylene propylene O-rings resist automotive brake fluids, hot water, steam to approximately 400°F, silicone fluids, dilute acids, and phosphate esters. They are not compatible with petroleum fluids and diester lubricants. Ethylene O-rings have a good compression set plus high abrasion resistance, and they are weather resistant. They have an approximate temperature range of –70°F to 250°F.

5.3.0 Viton® O-Rings

Viton® O-rings offer excellent resistance to petroleum products, diester lubricants, silicone fluids, phosphate esters, solvents, and acids, except fuming nitric acid. They have a low compression set and low gas permeability. Viton® O-rings are often used for hard vacuum service. They should never be used with acetates, methyl alcohol, ditones, brake fluids, hot water, or steam. The approximate temperature range of Viton® O-rings is –31°F to 400°F.

5.4.0 Teflon® O-Rings

Teflon® O-rings lubricate well and have excellent chemical and temperature resistance. They make fine static seals, but need mechanical loading when used as dynamic seals. They have an approximate temperature range of –300°F to 500°F.

5.5.0 Silicone O-Rings

Silicone O-rings are used where long-term exposure to dry heat is expected. Due to poor abrasion resistance, silicone O-rings perform best in static sealing applications. Silicone O-rings resist brake fluids and high aniline point oil. They are not recommended for use with ditones and most petroleum oils. They have an approximate temperature range of –80°F to 400°F.

5.6.0 Teflon®-Encapsulated Silicone O-Rings

Teflon®-encapsulated silicone O-rings are used in most of the same applications as silicone O-rings. The Teflon® coating makes them resistant to most solvents and chemicals. These O-rings have an extremely low coefficient of friction and low compression set. They are primarily used as seals in static applications. They have an approximate temperature range of –75°F to 400°F.

5.7.0 Polyurethane O-Rings

Polyurethane O-rings have high tensile strength, are abrasion resistant, and have excellent tear strength. Polyurethane is the toughest of the elastomers. Polyurethane O-rings can be used with petroleum fluids, ozone, and solvents, except ketones. Polyurethane O-rings are noncompatible with hot water, brake fluids, acids, and high temperature. They have poor compression set. Polyurethane O-rings have an approximate temperature range of –40°F to 200°F.

5.8.0 Removing and Installing O-Rings

The removal and installation of an O-ring seal is a relatively simple procedure. To achieve a proper seal and protect the new O-ring from damage, follow these guidelines:

- The equipment must be properly prepared to receive the new O-ring. The groove(s) that the O-ring fits into must be clean and free of any sharp edges.
- The type and size of the O-ring must be right for the application.
- As applicable, lubricate the shaft, O-ring, and O-ring groove(s) using a lubricant specified by the O-ring manufacturer.
- During assembly, protect the O-ring from being damaged by the sharp edges of threads, keyways, or the end of a shaft.
- Follow the proper bolt-tightening procedure.

CAUTION

Do not overtighten O-ring face seals. Overtightening can distort the O-ring, resulting in a leak.

Summary

In this training module, you learned about various types of gaskets, O-rings, and packing, and how to lay out and fabricate a gasket. Gaskets, O-rings, and packing are used with a variety of equipment and systems in the instrumentation craft. Different types of gaskets, O-rings, and packing are designed to accommodate various pressure and temperature conditions and process characteristics.

The knowledge and skills covered in this module provide basic and fundamental competencies required to identify gaskets, O-rings, and packing and to effectively work with different gasket, O-ring, and packing materials. In your day-to-day work activities, take the time to practice the skills learned in this module. It takes a lot of practice, study, and on-the-job experience to develop the skills needed to be expert in working with gaskets and packing.

Review Questions

1. Once the size of a gasket or O-ring is determined, _____ factors must be considered before choosing a gasket or O-ring.
   a. cost
   b. availability
   c. compatibility
   d. maintenance

2. Natural rubber has a limited chemical resistance to _____.
   a. petroleum products
   b. water
   c. organic substances
   d. saturated steam

3. Serrated and corrugated gaskets are made of _____.
   a. Teflon®
   b. neoprene
   c. rubber
   d. metal

4. Copper gaskets are _____.
   a. not used in high-pressure/high-temperature steam systems
   b. used in high-pressure/low-temperature steam systems
   c. used in low-pressure/high-temperature steam systems
   d. not used in low-pressure/low-temperature steam systems

5. Rubber gasket material is used in _____ water, gas, air, and refrigerant systems.
   a. high-pressure/high-temperature
   b. high-pressure/low-temperature
   c. low-pressure/low-temperature
   d. low-pressure/high-temperature

6. The radius of a bolt circle is equal to _____ of the diameter.
   a. ¼
   b. ⅓
   c. ½
   d. ⅔

7. When using a gasket cutter, the blade should not protrude more than _____ beyond the thickness of the gasket.
   a. ¹⁄₆₄ inch
   b. ¹⁄₃₂ inch
   c. ¹⁄₁₆ inch
   d. ⅛ inch

8. Packing rings are usually installed in a _____ on revolving equipment.
   a. motor housing
   b. seal unit
   c. packing gland
   d. groove

9. _____ O-rings are used with most petroleum and silicone fluids, hydraulic and nonaromatic fuels, and solvents.
   a. Buna-N
   b. Silicone
   c. Ethylene propylene
   d. Neoprene

10. The approximate temperature range of _____ O-rings is –31°F to 400°F.
    a. Teflon®
    b. ethylene propylene
    c. Viton®
    d. silicone

Trade Terms Introduced in This Module

Alkali: Any chemical substance that forms soluble soaps with fatty acids. Alkalis are also referred to as *bases*. Strong alkalis may cause severe burns to the skin. Alkalis turn litmus paper blue and have a pH value greater than 7.0.

American National Standards Institute (ANSI): An organization that publishes specifications and standards relating to materials and products, including gaskets and packing.

Caustic: A material that is corrosive by chemical action or that can burn, eat away, or destroy living tissue.

Compressible: Capable of being pressed or squeezed together.

Flange: A projecting rim or collar on a pipe used to hold it in place, give it strength, or attach it to something else.

Nonabsorbent: The ability of a material to resist absorbing a liquid or gas.

Oxidizing: The ability of a material to combine with oxygen.

Resilient: Capable of withstanding shock without permanent deformation or rupture.

Tetrafluoroethylene (TFE): The material from which Teflon® is made. Teflon® is the registered trademark of the DuPont Company

Additional Resources

This module is intended to present thorough resources for task training. The following reference works are suggested for further study. These are optional materials for continued education rather than for task training.

Specifications for Gaskets, O-Rings, and Packing. 1819 L Street NW, Washington, DC: American National Standards Institute (ANSI).

Specifications for Gaskets, O-Rings, and Packing. 100 Barr Harbor Drive, West Conshohoken, PA: American Society for Testing and Materials.

Specifications for Gaskets, O-Rings, and Packing. 400 Commonwealth Drive, Warrendale, PA: Society of Automotive Engineers.

NCCER CRAFT TRAINING USER UPDATES

The NCCER makes every effort to keep these textbooks up-to-date and free of technical errors. We appreciate your help in this process. If you have an idea for improving this textbook, or if you find an error, a typographical mistake, or an inaccuracy in the NCCER's Craft Training textbooks, please write us, using this form or a photocopy. Be sure to include the exact module number, page number, a detailed description, and the correction, if applicable. Your input will be brought to the attention of the Technical Review Committee. Thank you for your assistance.

Instructors – If you found that additional materials were necessary in order to teach this module effectively, please let us know so that we may include them in the Equipment and Materials list in the Instructor's Guide.

Write: Curriculum Revision and Development Department
              National Center for Construction Education and Research
              P.O. Box 141104, Gainesville, FL 32614-1104

Fax: 352-334-0932

E-mail: curriculum@nccer.org

Craft _____   Module Name _____

Copyright Date _____   Module Number _____   Page Number(s) _____

Description _____

_____

_____

_____

_____

(Optional) Correction _____

_____

_____

(Optional) Your Name and Address _____

_____

_____

Lubricants, Sealants, and Cleaners

COURSE MAP

This course map shows all of the modules in the first level of the Instrumentation curriculum. The suggested training order begins at the bottom and proceeds up. Skill levels increase as you advance on the course map. The local Training Program Sponsor may adjust the training order.

INSTRUMENTATION LEVEL ONE

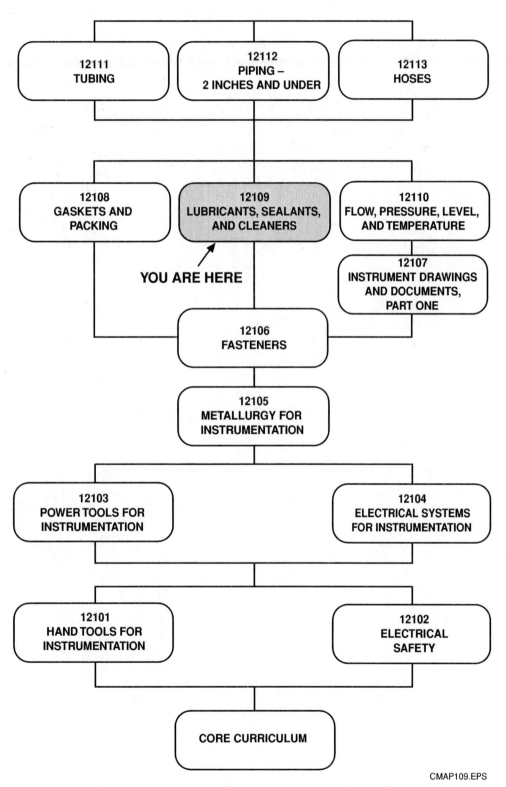

Figures

Tables

Lubricants, Sealants, and Cleaners

OBJECTIVES

When you have completed this module, you will be able to do the following:

1. Identify and select the appropriate lubricants for use in specific applications.
2. Identify and select the appropriate sealants for use in specific applications.
3. Identify and select the appropriate cleaners for specific applications.
4. Describe the differences between lubricants, sealants, and cleaners.
5. Describe proper applications of lubricants, sealants, and cleaners.
6. Properly handle and store lubricants, sealants, and cleaners.
7. Explain Material Safety Data Sheets (MSDSs).

Prerequisites

Before you begin this module, it is recommended that you successfully complete the following modules: Core Curriculum; Instrumentation Level One, Modules 12101 through 12108.

Required Trainee Materials

1. Pencil and paper
2. Appropriate personal protective equipment

1.0.0 ◆ INTRODUCTION

Lubricants, sealants, and cleaners are often used in performing instrumentation work. Lubricants are used for a variety of purposes, including reducing friction between moving parts of equipment, threading pipe, lubricating pipe, and fitting threads for easier joining. Sealants are used for bonding materials together. For example, in some higher-pressure piping systems, a sealant is applied to the pipe threads to prevent leaking. Different types of cleaners are used to remove dirt, grease, or other contaminants from equipment, tools, materials, circuit boards, and other items.

>
> **WARNING!**
> When working with hazardous materials, there are certain safety precautions that must be observed. This module covers only a few hazardous substances. For additional information on hazardous materials, read the **Material Safety Data Sheet (MSDS)** that is supplied with each hazardous material.

Since many lubricants, sealants, and cleaners contain potentially **hazardous chemicals**, it is important to know the properties of each substance. Before using any type of lubricant, sealant, or cleaner, read the MSDS and the manufacturer's instructions.

The MSDS and even some manufacturers' brochures for lubricants, sealants, and cleaners do not address the issue of **compatibility** with certain O-rings, gaskets, and other materials that are produced using **chemical** compounds. It is often necessary to review the compatibility tables for these items, along with the chemical makeup of the lubricants, sealants, and cleaners to ensure that they are compatible. For example, natural rubber products have a limited chemical resistance to petroleum products, which are often the prime ingredients in many lubricants, sealants and cleaners. Some synthetic rubber compounds used in various O-rings and some gasket materials will degrade when exposed to specific chemicals contained in many lubricants, sealants, and cleaners.

Because they can contain hazardous chemicals, it is important to properly dispose of lubricants, sealants, and cleaners in accordance with **Occupational Safety and Health Administration (OSHA)** regulations, project guidelines, and other applicable regulations.

> **NOTE**
> The information given in this module is general in nature. When selecting lubricants, sealants, and cleaners, it is important to make sure that your selection is compatible with the process or application where it is to be used. When in doubt, always consult the manufacturer.

Normally, the type of lubricant, sealant, or cleanser selected depends on one or more of the following (as applicable):

- System operating temperatures
- System operating pressures
- The type of fluid or other media the system or equipment handles
- The composition of the system components
- The environment where it is to be installed

2.0.0 ◆ MATERIAL SAFETY DATA SHEET (MSDS)

When using lubricants, sealants, and cleaners, always check the manufacturer's instructions, MSDSs, and other information for appropriate and safe application of these materials.

The MSDS is a detailed information bulletin prepared by the manufacturer, distributor, or importer of a chemical. It describes the physical and chemical properties, physical and health hazards, routes of exposure, precautions for safe handling and use, emergency and first-aid procedures, and control measures for a hazardous material. Information on an MSDS aids in the selection of safe products and helps prepare employers and employees to respond effectively to daily exposure situations as well as to emergency situations.

MSDSs are a comprehensive source of information for all types of hazardous substances. Although there may be information on a particular MSDS that is not of use to you or not important to safety and health in your particular operation, always pay attention to the information on the MSDS that is applicable to your situation. Generally, the hazard information and protective measures presented on the MSDS should be the focus of your concern.

2.1.0 Sections of an MSDS and Their Significance

OSHA specifies the types of information that must be contained in an MSDS describing a specific product. However, they do not mandate the method of presenting the required information. For this reason, MSDSs produced by different manufacturers will look different. All MSDSs must contain the same basic information in at least nine required sections. Some may have more sections covering subjects such as transportation and environmental issues, as deemed necessary by the manufacturer. *Figure 1* shows an MSDS produced by one major manufacturer. The information required in the nine sections of an MSDS is described here. Note that manufacturers may list information on their MSDSs with slightly different section titles, and in a different order, than given here. MSDSs must be written in English; however, some employers may also maintain copies in other languages.

Section I. Product Identification – This section lists the trade name of the product, the same name as found on the **label** attached to the product container. It will list the manufacturer's name, address, telephone numbers, date of MSDS preparation, and signature of the author. It may also contain the chemical name, chemical formula, and other information for the product.

Section II. Hazardous Ingredients – The chemical ingredients of the product are listed in this section with the relative percentage of each, either by weight or volume.

- For a hazardous chemical mixture that has been tested as a whole, the common name of the mixture and the chemical name and common names of each hazardous ingredient are listed.
- For a hazardous chemical mixture that has not been tested as a whole, the chemical and common names of each hazardous ingredient comprising 1 percent or greater of the composition are listed.
- Chemical and common names of **carcinogens** are listed if they are present in the mixture at levels of 0.1 percent or greater.
- All components determined to present a physical hazard are listed.
- Chemical and common names of all ingredients determined to be health hazards and comprising less than 1 percent (0.1 percent for carcinogens) of the mixture are also listed if they exceed an established **permissible exposure limit (PEL)** or **threshold limit value (TLV)**, or present a health risk to exposed employees in these concentrations.

MATERIAL SAFETY DATA SHEET

— SECTION I —
PRODUCT IDENTIFICATION

THE SHERWIN - WILLIAMS CO.
101 PROSPECT AVE. N.W.
CLEVELAND, OH 44115

EMERGENCY TELEPHONE NO.
(216) 566-2917
INFORMATION TELEPHONE NO.
(216) 566-2902

DATE OF PREPARATION
1 - MAY - 95

©1995, The Sherwin-Williams Co.

SOL/2

Reducers

SECTION II HAZARDOUS INGREDIENT (percent by weight)	CAS No.	ACGIH TLV <STEL>	OSHA PEL <STEL>	Units	Vapor Pressure (mm Hg)	Toluene R2 K1	Xylene R2 K4	H. Fl. Naphtha - 100 R2 K5 R7K100	High Flash Naphtha - 150	Acrylic Enamel Reducer R4 K 35	Acrylic Enamel Reducer R4 K 36
						154-2364 154-8668 (153-7547) (153-7737) (153-7851) (153-7976) (153-8222) 154-2372 (153-7554) (153-7745) (153-7869) (153-7964) (153-8230)	154-2380 154-8684 (153-7562) (153-7752) (153-7877) (153-7992) (153-8248) 154-2398 (153-7570) (153-7760) (153-7885) (153-8008) (153-8255)	154-4576 154-4584 154-8767	154-4592 154-4600 154-8809		
Lt. Aliphatic Hydrocarbons	64742-89-8	100	100	PPM	53.0					29	
§ Toluene	108-88-3	50 <150>	100 <150>	PPM (Skin)	22.0	100				38	29
§ Ethylbenzene	100-41-4	100 <125>	100 <125>	PPM	7.1		15	1			7
§ Xylene	1330-20-7	100 <150>	100 <150>	PPM	5.9		85	5		5	42
Light Aromatic Hydrocarbons	64742-95-6	Not Established			3.8			22			
§ Cumene	98-82-8	50	50	PPM (Skin)	10.0			5			
§ 1,3,5-Trimethylbenzene	108-67-8	25	25	PPM	10.0			27	1		
§ 1,2,4-Trimethylbenzene	95-63-6	25	25	PPM	2.0			40	2		
Med. Aromatic Hydrocarbons	64742-94-5	Not Established			0.1				84		
§ Naphthalene	91-20-3	10 <15>	10 <15>	PPM	1.0				13		
§ 2-Butoxyethanol	111-76-2	25	25	PPM (Skin)	0.6					6	
§ Acetone	67-64-1	750 <1000>	750 <1000>	PPM	180.0					15	
§ Methyl Ethyl Ketone	78-93-3	200 <300>	200 <300>	PPM	70.0						4
§ 2-Butoxyethyl Acetate	112-07-2	Not Established			1.0					3	16
Weight per Gallon (lbs.)						7.18	7.17	7.24	7.40	6.76	7.25
Volatile Organic Compounds (VOC) - lbs./gal.						7.18	7.17	7.24	7.40	6.76	7.25
Photochemically Reactive						Yes	Yes	Yes	Yes	Yes	Yes
Flash Point (°F)						40	80	105	140	10	10
DOL Storage Category						1B	1C	2	3A	1B	1B
Flammability Classification						Flammable	Flammable	Combustible	Combustible	Flammable	Flammable
HMIS (NFPA) Rating (health - flammability - reactivity)						2 3 0	2 3 0	3 2 0	3 2 0	2 3 0	2 3 0

§ Ingredient subject to the reporting requirements of the Superfund Amendments and Reauthorization Act (SARA) Section 313, 40 CFR 372.65 C

➤➤➤ MSDS Text Page Follows ➤➤➤

FRONT (SECTIONS 1 AND 2)

109F01A.TIF

Figure 1 ◆ Example of a Material Safety Data Sheet (MSDS) (1 of 2).

Reducers

Section III — PHYSICAL DATA

PRODUCT WEIGHT	– See TABLE	EVAPORATION RATE	– Slower than Ether
SPECIFIC GRAVITY	– 0.79-0.81	VAPOR DENSITY	– Heavier than Air
BOILING RANGE	– 132-395 °F	MELTING POINT	– N.A.
VOLATILE VOLUME	– 100 %	SOLUBILITY IN WATER	– N.A.

Section IV — FIRE AND EXPLOSION HAZARD DATA

FLAMMABILITY CLASSIFICATION   FLASH POINT   See TABLE   LEL 0.5   UEL 36.5
See TABLE
EXTINGUISHING MEDIA
    Carbon Dioxide, Dry Chemical, Foam
UNUSUAL FIRE AND EXPLOSION HAZARDS
    Keep containers tightly closed. Isolate from heat, electrical equipment, sparks, and open
flame. Closed containers may explode when exposed to extreme heat. Application to hot
surfaces requires special precautions. During emergency conditions overexposure to
decomposition products may cause a health hazard. Symptoms may not be immediately apparent.
Obtain medical attention.
SPECIAL FIRE FIGHTING PROCEDURES
    Full protective equipment including self-contained breathing apparatus should be used.
Water spray may be ineffective. If water is used, fog nozzles are preferable. Water may be
used to cool closed containers to prevent pressure build-up and possible autoignition or
explosion when exposed to extreme heat.

Section V — HEALTH HAZARD DATA

ROUTES OF EXPOSURE
    Exposure may be by INHALATION and/or SKIN or EYE contact, depending on conditions of use.
To minimize exposure, follow recommendations for proper use, ventilation, and personal
protective equipment.
ACUTE Health Hazards
EFFECTS OF OVEREXPOSURE
    Irritation of eyes, skin and respiratory system. May cause nervous system depression.
Extreme overexposure may result in unconsciousness and possibly death.
SIGNS AND SYMPTOMS OF OVEREXPOSURE
    Headache, dizziness, nausea, and loss of coordination are indications of excessive exposure
to vapors or spray mists.
    Redness and itching or burning sensation may indicate eye or excessive skin exposure.
MEDICAL CONDITIONS AGGRAVATED BY EXPOSURE
    None generally recognized.
EMERGENCY AND FIRST AID PROCEDURES
    If INHALED: If affected, remove from exposure. Restore breathing. Keep warm and quiet.
    If on SKIN: Wash affected area thoroughly with soap and water.
                 Remove contaminated clothing and launder before re-use.
    If in EYES: Flush eyes with large amounts of water for 15 minutes. Get medical attention.
    If SWALLOWED: Never give anything by mouth to an unconscious person. DO NOT INDUCE
                 VOMITING. Give several glasses of water. Seek medical attention.
CHRONIC Health Hazards
    No ingredient in these products is an IARC, NTP or OSHA listed carcinogen.
    Methyl Ethyl Ketone may increase the nervous system effects of other solvents.
    Prolonged overexposure to solvent ingredients in Section II may cause adverse effects to
the liver, urinary, blood-forming, cardiovascular, and reproductive systems.
    Reports have associated repeated and prolonged overexposure to solvents with permanent brain
and nervous system damage.

Section VI — REACTIVITY DATA

STABILITY - Stable
CONDITIONS TO AVOID
    None known.
INCOMPATIBILITY
    None known.
HAZARDOUS DECOMPOSITION PRODUCTS
    By fire: Carbon Dioxide, Carbon Monoxide
HAZARDOUS POLYMERIZATION — Will Not Occur

Section VII — SPILL OR LEAK PROCEDURES

STEPS TO BE TAKEN IN CASE MATERIAL IS RELEASED OR SPILLED
    Remove all sources of ignition. Ventilate and remove with inert absorbent.
WASTE DISPOSAL METHOD
    Waste from these products may be hazardous as defined under the Resource Conservation and
Recovery Act (RCRA) 40 CFR 261. Waste must be tested for ignitability to determine the
applicable EPA hazardous waste numbers. Waste from products containing Methyl Ethyl Ketone may
also require testing for extractability.
    Incinerate in approved facility. Do not incinerate closed container. Dispose of in
accordance with Federal, State, and Local regulations regarding pollution.

Section VIII — PROTECTION INFORMATION

PRECAUTIONS TO BE TAKEN IN USE
    Use only with adequate ventilation. Avoid breathing vapor and spray mist. Avoid contact
with skin and eyes. Wash hands after using.
VENTILATION
    Local exhaust preferable. General exhaust acceptable if the exposure to materials in
Section II is maintained below applicable exposure limits. Refer to OSHA Standards 1910.94,
1910.107, 1910.108
RESPIRATORY PROTECTION
    If personal exposure cannot be controlled below applicable limits by ventilation, wear
a properly fitted organic vapor/particulate respirator approved by NIOSH/MSHA for protection
against materials in Section II.
PROTECTIVE GLOVES
    Wear gloves which are recommended by glove supplier for protection against materials in
Section II.
EYE PROTECTION
    Wear safety spectacles with unperforated sideshields.

Section IX — PRECAUTIONS

DOL STORAGE CATEGORY — See TABLE
PRECAUTIONS TO BE TAKEN IN HANDLING AND STORING
    Keep away from heat, sparks, and open flame. Vapors will accumulate readily and may
ignite explosively.
    During use and until all vapors are gone: Keep area ventilated - Do not smoke -
Extinguish all flames, pilot lights, and heaters - Turn off stoves, electric tools and
appliances, and any other sources of ignition.
    Consult NFPA Code. Use approved Bonding and Grounding procedures.
    Keep container closed when not in use. Transfer only to approved containers with complete
and appropriate labeling. Do not take internally. Keep out of the reach of children.
OTHER PRECAUTIONS
    Intentional misuse by deliberately concentrating and inhaling the contents can be harmful
or fatal.

Section X — OTHER REGULATORY INFORMATION

CALIFORNIA PROPOSITION 65
    WARNING: These products, except High Flash Naphtha - 150, contain chemicals known to the
State of California to cause cancer and birth defects or other reproductive harm.

    The above information pertains to these products as currently formulated, and is based on
the information available at this time. Addition of additives or other coatings materials to
these products may substantially alter the composition and hazards of the products. Since
conditions of use are outside our control, we make no warranties, express or implied, and assume
no liability in connection with any use of this information.

BACK (SECTIONS 3 THROUGH 10)

Figure 1 ◆ Example of a Material Safety Data Sheet (MSDS) (2 of 2).

109F01B.TIF

Section III. Physical Data – The physical and chemical characteristics of the hazardous substances are listed, including items such as boiling points, freezing points, density, vapor pressure, specific gravity, evaporation rate, solubility, volatility, and the product's general appearance and odor. These characteristics provide important information to industrial hygienists, safety engineers, and similar professionals for designing safe and healthful work practices.

Section IV. Fire and Explosion Hazard Data – If applicable, the compound's potential for fire and explosion is described. The fire hazards of the chemical and the conditions under which it could ignite or explode are also identified. Recommended extinguishing agents and fire-fighting methods are described.

Section V. Health Hazards – The acute and chronic health hazards of the chemical are listed with signs and symptoms of exposure. In addition, any medical conditions that are aggravated by exposure to the compound are included. The specific types of chemical health hazards defined in the standard include carcinogens, **corrosives**, toxins, irritants, sensitizers, mutagens, teratogens, and effects on target organs (liver, kidney, nervous system, blood, lungs, mucous membranes, reproductive system, skin, and eyes).

The route of entry data describes the primary pathway by which the chemical enters the body. There are three principal routes of entry: inhalation, absorption through the skin, and ingestion. This section of the MSDS supplies the OSHA permissible exposure limit (PEL), the **American Conference of Governmental Industrial Hygienists (ACGIH)** threshold limit value (TLV), and other exposure levels used or recommended by the chemical manufacturer. If the compound is listed as a carcinogen by OSHA, the National Toxicology Program (NTP), or the International Agency for Research on Cancer (IARC), this information is indicated on the MSDS.

Section VI. Reactivity Data – This section presents information about other chemicals and substances with which the chemical is incompatible or with which it reacts. Information on any hazardous decomposition products, such as carbon monoxide, is included.

Section VII. Spill or Leak Procedures – This section lists the steps to be taken in the event the chemical is accidentally released or spilled.

Section VIII. Control Measures – This section lists any generally applicable control measures. These include engineering controls, safe handling procedures, and personal protective equipment. Information is often included on the use of goggles, gloves, body suits, respirators, and face shields.

Section IX. Precautions for Safe Handling and Use – This section describes the precautions for safe handling and use. These include recommended industrial hygiene practices and precautions to be taken during repair and maintenance of equipment. Some manufacturers also use this section to include useful information not specifically required by the standard, such as **Environmental Protection Agency (EPA)** waste disposal methods and state and local requirements.

2.2.0 Employer Responsibilities

Employers must ensure that each employee has a basic knowledge of how to find information on an MSDS and how to properly make use of that information. Employers also must ensure the following:

- Complete and accurate MSDSs are made available during each work shift to employees when they are in their work areas.

- Information is provided for each hazardous chemical.

3.0.0 ◆ LUBRICANTS

Lubricants are substances capable of reducing friction, heat, and wear when used as a film between two surfaces. Lubricants do not cement or seal a joint. In instrumentation work, lubricants are often used in machining operations, for threading pipe, and for loosening frozen, rusted, or corroded parts.

When using lubricants on pipe joints, always place the lubricant or sealant on the male threads. This prevents any lubricant or sealant from getting into the piping system. Do not use excessive amounts of lubricant when threading, and avoid putting lubricant on the first thread to prevent contamination.

The lubricants described in the following sections are commonly used in instrumentation work. You should be familiar with the proper and safe use of each type of lubricant used on a project.

3.1.0 Cutting Fluids

 WARNING!
Cutting fluids react violently with strong oxidizers, creating a fire hazard. Avoid breathing the vapor or mist.

Cutting fluids are essential in most metal-cutting, drilling, reaming, and threading operations. During a cutting process, considerable heat and friction are created. This heat and friction causes metal to adhere to the cutting edge of the tool, and the tool may break down. The result is a poor finish and inaccurate work.

The correct selection and application of cutting fluids, as shown in *Table 1*, can reduce the effects of heat by effectively cooling the work and reducing friction. Cutting fluids fall into three categories:

- Cutting oils
- **Emulsifiable** oils
- Chemical (synthetic) cutting fluids

Cutting oils are classified under two types: active or inactive. This classification relates to the oil's chemical ability to react with the metal surface at elevated temperatures to protect it and improve cutting action.

3.1.1 *Active Cutting Oils*

Active cutting oils contain sulfur that is not firmly attached to the oil. The sulfur is released to react with the work surface during cutting, enhancing lubrication. Active cutting oils may be dark or transparent in color and fall into three categories:

- Sulfurized mineral oils
- Sulfochlorinated mineral oils
- Sulfochlorinated fatty oil blends

Only sulfurized mineral oils are discussed here, as the other two types are used mainly for machining operations. Sulfurized mineral oils contain from 0.5 percent to 0.8 percent sulfur. They are generally light-colored, transparent, and

Table 1 Recommended Cutting Fluids

Material	Drilling	Reaming	Threading	Turning	Milling
Aluminum	Soluble oil Kerosene Kerosene and lard oil Water	Soluble oil Kerosene Mineral oil Water	Soluble oil Kerosene and lard oil Water	Soluble oil Water	Soluble oil Lard oil Mineral oil Dry Water
Brass	Dry Soluble oil Kerosene and lard oil	Dry Soluble oil	Soluble oil Lard oil	Soluble oil	Dry Soluble oil
Bronze	Dry Soluble oil Mineral oil Lard oil	Dry Soluble oil Mineral oil Lard oil	Soluble oil Lard oil	Soluble oil	Dry Soluble oil Mineral oil Lard oil
Cast iron	Dry Air jet Soluble oil	Dry Soluble oil Mineral lard oil	Dry Sulphurized oil Mineral lard oil	Dry Soluble oil	Dry Soluble oil
Copper	Dry Soluble oil Mineral lard oil Kerosene	Soluble oil Lard oil	Soluble oil Lard oil	Soluble oil	Dry Soluble oil
Malleable iron	Dry Soda water	Dry Soda water	Lard oil Soda water	Soluble oil	Dry Soda water
Monel® Metal	Soluble oil Lard oil	Soluble oil Lard oil	Lard oil	Soluble oil	Soluble oil
Steel alloys	Soluble oil Sulphurized oil Mineral lard oil	Soluble oil Sulphurized oil Mineral lard oil	Sulphurized oil Lard oil	Soluble oil	Soluble oil Mineral lard oil
Steel, machine	Soluble oil Sulphurized oil Lard oil Mineral lard oil	Soluble oil Mineral lard oil	Soluble oil Mineral lard oil	Soluble oil	Soluble oil Mineral lard oil
Steel, tool	Soluble oil Sulphurized oil Mineral lard oil	Soluble oil Sulphurized oil Lard oil	Sulphurized oil Lard oil	Soluble oil	Soluble oil Lard oil

Note: Chemical cutting fluids can be used successfully for most of the cutting operations above. These concentrates are diluted with water in proportions ranging from 1 part cutting fluid to 15 and as high as 100 parts of water, depending on the metal being cut and the type of machining operation. When using chemical cutting fluids, it is wise to follow the manufacturer's recommendations for use and mixture.

have good cooling, lubricating, and antiweld properties. Sulfurized mineral oils are used for drilling, reaming, and threading tool steel and steel alloys, and for threading cast iron.

3.1.2 Inactive Cutting Oils

Inactive cutting oils are oils in which the sulfur is so firmly attached to the oil that very little is released to react with the work surface during the cutting action. Inactive cutting oils fall into four categories:

- Straight mineral oils
- Fatty and mineral oil blends
- Sulfurized fatty-mineral oil blends
- Fatty oils

Straight mineral oils have faster wetting and penetrating factors because of their low **viscosity**. Straight mineral oils are used in the tapping and threading of white metal.

Mineral/lard oil blends are combinations of fatty oils, such as lard and mineral oil. These blends result in better wetting and penetrating qualities than straight mineral oils. They are used for drilling steel alloys, machine steel, and tool steel. They are also used for reaming steel alloys and cast iron and threading cast iron and machine steel.

Sulfurized fatty-mineral oil blends are made by combining sulfur with fatty oils. This combination is then mixed with certain mineral oils. They are used for machining ferrous and nonferrous metal at the same time.

Fatty oils, such as lard, are used for drilling, threading, and reaming nonferrous metals such as aluminum, copper, brass, bronze, and Monel® where a sulfurized oil might cause discoloration.

3.1.3 Emulsifiable (Soluble) Oils

A cutting fluid should have a high heat conductivity. Neither mineral oils nor fatty oils are very effective as coolants. Water is a very good cooling medium. However, when water is used as a cutting fluid for ferrous metals, it causes rust and has little lubricating value. By adding emulsifiable (soluble) oils to water, it is possible to add rust resistance and lubrication qualities to the cooling capabilities of water.

Soluble oils are used for drilling, reaming, and threading a variety of nonferrous metals such as aluminum, brass, bronze, copper, Monel®, cast iron, steel alloys, machine steel, and tool steel. Soluble oils are also used for threading machine steel.

Water is commonly used as a cutting fluid for aluminum and other soft nonferrous materials.

3.1.4 Chemical Cutting Fluids

WARNING!
Wear protective clothing to prevent skin contact with chemical cutting fluids. Suitable washing and changing facilities should also be available. Breathing of vapors or mists from chemical cutting oils should be avoided.

Chemical (synthetic) cutting fluids are stable, preformed emulsions which contain very little oil and mix easily with water. Some types of synthetic cutting fluids contain extreme-pressure (EP) lubricants. These cutting fluids react with the machined metal under heat and pressure to form a solid lubricant.

Synthetic cutting fluids are generally used on both ferrous and nonferrous metals. When using chemical cutting fluids, always follow the manufacturer's recommendations for use and mixture.

WARNING!
Due to the possibility of an adverse chemical reaction, do not use synthetic cutting fluids on alloys of magnesium, zinc, cadmium, or lead.

3.2.0 Penetrating Oil

Penetrating oils are used where frozen, rusted, and corroded parts are a problem. Penetrating oils are used to loosen rust and corrosion, and to free frozen bolts and connectors. Most penetrating oils also protect against rust and corrosion.

3.3.0 Aluminum Oxidizing Compound

When aluminum is exposed to air, an oxide is formed on the surface. Some instrumentation projects require the installation of aluminum conduit in environments that are not compatible with ferrous metal conduits or require greater physical protection than afforded by non-metal (PVC) conduit. Aluminum conduit is typically manufactured with a thin antioxidant coating that protects its outer surface from the effects of oxidation. However, when aluminum conduit is cut and threaded, the raw aluminum material becomes exposed to air and forms oxidation. This white, chalky substance can cause aluminum conduit threaded joints to become very difficult to disconnect should the need arise. Seized aluminum conduit joints and fasteners, such as bolts and nuts, are a common problem.

Oxidation in aluminum conduit joints can act as an insulator between conduit joints. Metal conduit installations, including aluminum conduit, are designed according to the requirements of *National Electrical Code (NEC), Article 250*, to provide a continuous, effective path for fault current should a fault occur. This continuous, effective path is referred to as *bonding*. Severe oxidation on aluminum conduit threads can disrupt this continuous path and interfere with the effective bonding qualities of the conduit system.

In order to prevent oxidation from forming on aluminum conduit threads or on aluminum bolts or nuts, an antioxidant compound must be applied to the threads prior to joining. There are several products available that offer oxidation protection, but not all products are suited for electrical installations. Make sure the anti-oxidizing compound is suited for the particular application before using it, and check its compatibility with the process or environment to which it will be exposed.

3.4.0 Silicone Lubricants

Silicone lubricants are usually clear, nonstaining, and odorless. They provide a slippery, long-wearing, nondrying film. They come in three grades:

- *Food grade* – Food-grade silicone lubricant prevents plastic, metal, and rubber parts from sticking on conveyors, heat sealers, mixers, slicers, and other machinery. It is also safe as a lubricant on plastics. It has an approximate temperature range of –40°F to 400°F.

- *General purpose* – General-purpose silicone lubricant provides noncorrosive, long-lasting lubrication for general use. It is sometimes used as a releasing agent for rubber molds. It is often used as a lubricant on doors, windows, hinges, conveyors, and sliding wood surfaces. General-purpose silicone lubricant is considered safe as a lubricant on plastics. It has an approximate temperature range of –50°F to 500°F.

- *Extreme duty* – Extreme-duty silicone lubricant reacts chemically with metals to provide lubrication properties superior to conventional silicones. It is used on metals, rubber, wood, glass, and painted surfaces. It has an approximate temperature range of –100°F to 500°F and a pressure rating of 1,200 psi.

3.5.0 Teflon® Tape

There is much confusion about Teflon® and its applications as a lubricant and/or sealant. Teflon® is a DuPont trade name for polytetrafluoroethylene (PTFE or TFE). It is a synthetic plastics product that resists most chemicals and has a maximum usage temperature of approximately 260°C.

500° F

WARNING!
Do not use Teflon® tape on oxygen service connections since it can present an explosion hazard.

There are many products used in the field of instrumentation that contain some percentage of TFE. Two products that are frequently used are tape and paste. Most instrument personnel can be seen with a least one roll of Teflon® tape hanging from their tool pouch or belt. It is freely applied to the threads of most tubing fittings (*Figure 2*). However, there is some debate as to whether the use of this type of tape on threads actually seals the connection or only affords lubrication for ease of connection or disconnection.

Teflon® tape thread lubricant is often applied on the threads of conduit and tubing fittings as a potential sealant because of its ease and convenience in application. However, Teflon® tape should not be used as a thread sealant for a permanent seal, but should be used only as a thread lubricant. Because of its thinness and its inherent non-stick characteristics, it does not adhere to the thread surfaces as true sealant does and only provides limited sealing effects. What sealing capabilities it does have result from its tendency to clog the thread path, thus preventing most leaks. Since Teflon® tape is so thin and does not adhere to the threads, it may even become dislodged from the threads during movement or vibration, causing leaks to occur. Tape particles may be released into the process material or substance.

CAUTION
Always check the manufacturer's information for safe applications to determine where Teflon® products can be used.

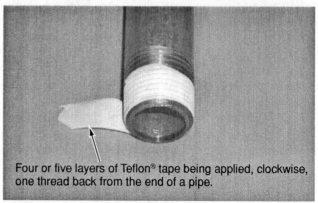
Four or five layers of Teflon® tape being applied, clockwise, one thread back from the end of a pipe.

109F02.EPS

Figure 2 ◆ Wrapping threads with Teflon® tape.

INSTRUMENTATION LEVEL ONE — TRAINEE MODULE 12109

3.6.0 Special Coolants

Special coolants, such as solid-form lubricants and air, are used for special machining operations such as tapping, honing, threading, and metal forming.

3.6.1 Solid-Form Lubricants

Solid-form lubricants, such as graphite, molybdenum disulfide, pastes, soaps, and waxes are usually used in operations where heavy metal forming is performed. Solid-form lubricants are particularly useful at high and low temperatures, in high vacuums, and in applications where oil is not suitable.

3.6.2 Air

Air is the most common gaseous coolant. Sometimes air is compressed to provide better cooling. A stream of air directed at the cutting surface removes heat. The advantages of using compressed air-machining and metal-cutting operations include good cooling ability; a clear view of the operation; elimination of mist; and noncontamination of the workpiece, chips, or machine lubricants.

3.7.0 Storing and Handling Lubricants

There are special storing and handling requirements for different types of lubricants. The MSDS and manufacturer's information should be checked to determine the proper storage and handling requirements for a particular lubricant.

Most lubricants used in the instrumentation craft come in small containers or tubes like the one shown in *Figure 3*. Storage and handling of large quantities of lubricants require special precautions.

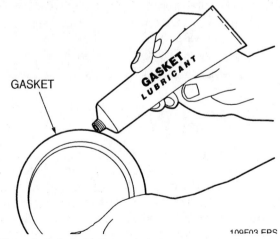

Figure 3 ◆ Lubricating a gasket.

Many lubricants are flammable, so precautions must be taken to avoid the possibility of ignition. Some lubricants give off harmful vapors that should be avoided. The general storage and handling precautions for cutting oils listed here provide some minimum guidelines for proper storage and handling of most common lubricants.

When storing and handling cutting oils, use the following guidelines and precautions:

- Be familiar with all data in the MSDS for the oil being used.
- Minimum feasible handling temperatures should be maintained.
- Periods of exposure to high temperatures should be minimized.
- Water contamination should be avoided.
- Chemical-type goggles or a face shield should be worn to prevent eye contact.
- Wash exposed skin with soap and water. Contaminated clothing should be removed and appropriately cleaned.
- If vapor, mist, or dust is generated, use a respirator approved by the **Mine Safety and Health Administration (MSHA)** or the **National Institute for Occupational Safety and Health (NIOSH)**, as appropriate.

4.0.0 ◆ SEALANTS

Sealants are used to prevent leaks in piping, ducts, flanges, lids, and other places where leaks may occur. High-pressure pipelines often leak when threaded connections are made solely with the aid of lubricants. On most high-pressure piping systems, an expanding type lubricant-sealant (or cement) is used to prevent leaks. Some, but not all, sealants are applied as a paste. The paste hardens as it dries to form a seal. On threaded piping systems, there are designed-in gaps between male and female threads that accommodate the sealant. Sealants also prevent galling of threads (localized welding of male and female threads caused by excessive friction during fastening).

The following sealants are commonly used in instrumentation work. You should be familiar with the proper and safe use of each type of sealant used on a project.

4.1.0 Teflon® Paste

Teflon® paste, unlike Teflon® tape, is manufactured for the purpose of sealing. These pastes may contain other ingredients besides polytetrafluoroethylene that provide the sealing characteristics along with the lubricating properties of TFE. For this reason there are many varieties of Teflon® paste, each suited for a particular service or application.

WARNING!

Teflon® paste must not be used on any oxygen services or applications, as it can present an explosion hazard. Seal oxygen applications and services with sealers specifically designed for use with oxygen.

General-purpose Teflon® pastes are generally lead-free, nontoxic, and nonseparating. They can withstand temperatures in a range of approximately –200°F to 500°F and gas pressures to 2500 psi. They provide a positive leakproof seal on most piping material and can be used for all liquids and gases except oxygen. Most general-purpose Teflon® pastes are safe to use for drinking water lines.

4.2.0 Other Sealant Pastes

There are many products that can be applied to prevent leaks in various processes and piping systems. Two other types of pastes used as sealants are solvent-based sealants and anaerobic resin compounds.

4.2.1 Solvent-Based Paste

Solvent-based pipe thread compound (*Figure 4*), which is normally applied using a brush or spatula, is commonly referred to as *pipe dope*. The sealer components in this paste use a **solvent** as a carrier base. The solvent soon evaporates, leaving the hardened sealer in place to block any leak paths.

Pipe dope is generally not used in applications of high temperatures, pressures, or vibrations, because it has a tendency to shrink over time,

Pipe thread compound (dope) applied one thread back from the end of a pipe and just covering the threads.

109F04.EPS

Figure 4 ◆ Using pipe thread compound.

allowing leaks to develop. It is inexpensive, easy to use, and compatible with most piping materials. As with any sealant, it should only be applied in those applications that specifically recommend that a solvent-based sealant paste be used.

4.2.2 Anaerobic Resin Compound

Anaerobic resin compounds do not contain solvents and use a different curing chemistry than solvent-based sealant pastes. Instead of using a carrier that evaporates, the curing or sealing begins when the sealant is confined within the threads of the metal pipe connection and air is blocked out. The cured material does not shrink or crack, and maintains its sealing properties even after aging. Unlike solvent-based sealants, anaerobic resin compounds can be used in applications of high temperatures, pressures, and vibrations. It has a slow cure time, which allows for adjustments and reconnections in the piping installation.

Because of the chemical elements found in anaerobic resin compounds, including TFE in some variations, caution must be exercised in applying these compounds. Do not use any sealant without first reviewing and understanding the MSDS and the compatibility tables associated with the process and/or product.

4.3.0 Silicone

In instrumentation work, **room temperature vulcanizing (RTV)** silicone sealants are the most widely used type of silicone sealant. Most RTV silicone sealants are one-component compounds that cure to a tough, rubbery solid when exposed to the moisture in the air.

WARNING!

Avoid breathing the vapor from silicone. Use silicone only in well-ventilated areas. When using RTV silicone sealants in a confined area, use an appropriate respirator and other personal protective equipment in accordance with the MSDS recommendations.

4.3.1 Single-Component Paste RTV Silicone

Single-component paste RTV silicone is used for general-purpose sealing, bonding, and gasketing. It can be applied overhead or on sidewalls without running off. It has an approximate temperature range of –80°F to 450°F. It is recommended for corrosion-sensitive materials where acid-curing types of sealants cannot be used.

4.3.2 High-Temperature RTV Silicone

High-temperature RTV silicone is used for critical bonding applications where parts must perform at high temperatures. It has an approximate temperature range of –85°F to 500°F for continual use and up to 600°F for intermittent use.

High-temperature RTV silicone is good for sealing and enclosing heating elements in appliances and for use on aerospace gasketing, moving oven belts, industrial ovens, and bag filters on smoke stacks. It has a tensile strength of approximately 350 psi.

4.3.3 Noncorrosive Neutral Cure RTV Silicone

Noncorrosive neutral cure RTV silicone adhesive is used for electrical and electronic bonding, sealing, and insulation where neutral cure byproducts are necessary to prevent corrosion.

4.4.0 Epoxy

WARNING!
Epoxies give off hazardous vapors and can cause skin damage. Use latex or vinyl gloves. Do not allow epoxy to come in contact with eyes. Wear approved eye protection and other appropriate personal protective equipment in accordance with the MSDS recommendations.

An epoxy is a resin that forms a hard, strong, resistant adhesive when its components are mixed. Epoxies comes in a variety of colors, setting times, and applications. Some of the common types are:

- Copper bonding epoxy
- Two-part epoxy putty
- Underwater epoxy
- High-temperature epoxy
- Aluminum epoxy

NOTE
Always read the manufacturer's instructions before using epoxies to determine the setup time. Plan the job accordingly.

4.4.1 Copper-Bonding Epoxy

Copper-bonding epoxy contains no lead and can be used as a replacement for soldering copper pipe connections. It is a fast-curing epoxy which forms leakproof joints in minutes with a shear strength of approximately 1,525 psi. It is high-impact resistant, heat resistant, and water resistant. It can be used for industrial assembly, solar heating, air conditioning and refrigeration work, and hot and cold potable water service.

4.4.2 Two-Part Epoxy Putty

Two-part epoxy putty can be molded by hand. It bonds metals, including copper, aluminum, steel, and brass, as well as glass, ceramics, plastics, wood, concrete, and plaster. It resists temperatures up to 300°F. It also resists **acid** and will cure underwater. It can be used to fill gaps and repair cast plastics. It is nonslumping and nonshrinking, and is good for high-vacuum and cryogenic applications.

4.4.3 Underwater Epoxy

Underwater epoxy is used where surfaces are wet or under water. It will bond metals, wood, fiberglass, concrete, ferro cement, and most plastics. It is used to repair pipe fittings, valves, pumps, and tanks. Underwater epoxy plugs and fills gouges, cracks, dry rot, and holes. It is resistant to acids, alkalis, solvents, gasoline, and oil.

4.4.4 High-Temperature Epoxy

High-temperature epoxy is used for high-performance bonding, potting, and sealing applications. It is good for temperatures up to approximately 525°F. It is used in applications involving nitric acids, caustic, and chromic acid solutions.

4.4.5 Aluminum Epoxy

Aluminum epoxy is made up of approximately 80 percent aluminum and 20 percent epoxy. It is non-rusting and bonds aluminum, iron, steel, glass, and wood. It resists temperatures up to approximately 250°F. Heat-resistant aluminum epoxy can be used in temperatures up to about 400°F.

4.5.0 Graphite Paste

Graphite paste is used to seal pipe joints where the process fluids are petroleum products, acid, or high-pressure steam. The graphite in graphite paste also lubricates the joint. It has an approximate temperature range of –30°F to 750°F.

WARNING!
Do not use graphite paste for water service since it will contaminate the water.

4.6.0 PVC-Solvent Cement

PVC-solvent cement (*Figure 5*) is a cement specifically designed to join PVC pipe and fittings for a tight, leakproof joint. There are several types of PVC cement, including:

- *PVC medium-duty cement* – PVC medium-duty cement is used to join potable water pipes, drain pipes, waste pipes, vent pipes, and fittings up to 6 inches in diameter.
- *PVC heavy-duty cement* – PVC heavy-duty cement is basically the same as PVC medium-duty cement, except that it is suitable for use on pipes up to 12 inches in diameter.
- *CPVC cement* – CPVC cement is used for joining CPVC plastic pipe and fittings. It is ideal for hot/cold water plumbing and industrial piping.
- *ABS cement* – ABS cement is specially formulated for joining rigid ABS pipe and fittings. It is used for drain pipes, waste pipes, vent pipes, and fittings.

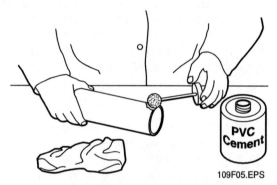

109F05.EPS

Figure 5 ◆ Applying PVC solvent cement.

4.7.0 Storing and Handling Sealants

There are special storing and handling requirements for different types of sealants. The MSDS and manufacturer's information should be checked to determine proper storage and handling requirements for particular sealants. Most sealants used by the instrumentation craft come in small containers or tubes. Storage and handling of large quantities of sealants require special precautions.

Many sealants are flammable, so precautions must be taken to avoid the possibility of ignition. Some sealants give off harmful vapors that should be avoided. The general storage and handling precautions for sealants listed here provide some minimum guidelines for proper storage and handling.

- Store sealants in a cool, dry, well-ventilated area, out of direct sunlight.
- Store sealants away from sources of heat or flame, such as lighted cigarettes, matches, welding operations, or any other ignition sources.

- Keep sealant containers tightly closed when not in use and protect them from damage.
- Most silicone and epoxy sealants give off vapors as they cure. Care should be taken not to breathe the vapors.
- Wash skin exposed to sealants with soap and water. Contaminated clothing must be removed and appropriately cleaned.

5.0.0 ◆ CLEANERS

Cleaners are used to remove dirt, grease, or other contaminants from pipe, relays, tube fittings, printed circuit boards, and other equipment and materials. Like lubricants and sealants, some cleaners are considered to be hazardous chemicals and should be treated as such.

The cleaners described below are commonly used in instrumentation work. You should be familiar with the proper and safe use of each type of cleaner used on a project.

5.1.0 Metal Wool

Metal wool is constructed of continuous strands of clean resilient metal. It comes in several grades from 0000 Ultra Fine to 4 Extra Coarse. Metal wool is used to clean metal surfaces in preparation for welding, lubricating, sealing, threading, or general-purpose cleaning. There are several types of metal wool cleaners, including:

- *Bronze wool* – Bronze wool is corrosion resistant and can be used to polish or refinish. It is also used as a chemical filter or as a dry filter around fire hazards.
- *Aluminum wool* – Aluminum wool is three times lighter than metal wool. It does not rust or burn. Aluminum wool can be used to clean and prepare aluminum surfaces for welding. It can also be used as a filter.
- *Stainless steel wool* – Stainless steel wool is highly rust and corrosion resistant. It is used for plant maintenance, filtration, cleaning stainless steel, and for cleaning with strong chemicals and solvents. It will withstand high temperatures in industrial processes.

5.2.0 Sandpaper

Sandpaper comes in a variety of abrasive grains, weight backings, and in sheet, belt, and disc forms (*Figure 6*). In general, the lighter the backing, the greater the flexibility; the heavier the paper, the greater the resistance to tearing. Sandpaper is used on wood and metal surfaces to clean and smooth the material in preparation for painting, sealing, and general cleaning. Some of the common types of sandpaper include:

- *Silicon carbide sandpaper* – Silicon carbide sandpaper is used for stock removal and finishing hard, brittle, low-tensile-strength metals. It can be used on aluminum, brass, magnesium, titanium, glass, rubber, plastics, fibrous wood, and enamel.
- *Flint sandpaper* – Flint sandpaper is a quartz abrasive that is good for general maintenance and cleanup. It is nonconductive, so it is often used on commutator surfaces of electrical equipment.
- *Emery cloth* – Emery cloth cuts slowly and has a good polishing action on most metals. It is used for general maintenance and polishing.
- *Crocus cloth* – Crocus cloth is used primarily for cleaning corroded surfaces of polished metals and for polishing gold and other soft metals where minimal stock removal is desired.

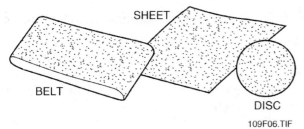

Figure 6 ◆ Sheet, belt, and disc types of sandpaper.

5.3.0 Rags

Rags are often used to clean equipment and to remove excess lubricants, sealants, and cleaners. Lint-free rags should be used to clean electric or electronic equipment, instruments, and instrument air lines.

 WARNING!
After using rags with lubricants, sealants, or cleaners, always dispose of the rags by putting them in an approved metal container. If left out in the atmosphere, rags may ignite by spontaneous combustion, causing a fire. Dispose of waste rags in accordance with the prevailing environmental laws and regulations.

5.4.0 Wire Brushes

Wire brushes are made from a variety of materials, including carbon steel and stainless steel.

Carbon steel wire brushes are used for cleaning welds and pipe threads, and for removing scale, paint, and rust from metal. Stainless steel wire brushes are good for cleaning castings and for removing scale, paint, and rust from metal. Stain-

less steel wire brushes are also ideal for cleaning hot metal and for use with corrosive solutions.

 NOTE
Always use a stainless steel wire brush when cleaning stainless steel.

5.5.0 Petroleum-Based Cleaners

Petroleum-based cleaners include gasoline, kerosene, and various other solvents. They should only be used in well-ventilated areas and only when specified. Petroleum-based cleaners are used primarily as degreasing agents.

 WARNING!
Petroleum-based cleaners must never be used to clean air or oxygen systems because of the danger of an explosion. The explosion is caused by what is known as the *diesel effect*. The diesel effect occurs when fuel/oxygen mixture is ignited by a sudden increase in pressure.

5.6.0 Acids and Bases

Acids and **bases** (sometimes referred to as *caustics*) are used in industry for etching, as chemical reagents, for wastewater neutralization, as grease and dirt dissolvers, and in many processes.

 WARNING!
Acids and bases are highly corrosive. They can irritate or burn the skin, eyes, and respiratory tract. Exposure to acids and caustic substances can cause serious eye injury and damage to the skin, nose, sinus, and lungs. When handling acids and bases, always wear the recommended protective clothing, a respirator, and a face shield, and use the recommended tools for handling acids and bases. Safeguards such as emergency showers and eyewashes should also be available. Acid and caustic mists should be controlled to prevent inhalation. Always follow proper procedures for disposing of acids and bases.

5.6.1 Acids

Acids exist in several forms. They may be liquid solutions, solid granules, powders, gases, or vapors. A few commonly used acids are hydrochloric acid, hydrofluoric acid, nitric acid, phosphoric acid, and sulfuric acid.

WARNING!

The gases and vapors from many acids, such as hydrochloric acid and hydrofluoric acid, dissolve readily in water. When they are inhaled, these gases and vapors are quickly absorbed by the moisture in throat and nose tissue. Some vapors, such as those from nitric acid, do not dissolve in water. These vapors can reach and damage the lungs without any early warning symptoms.

5.6.2 Bases

Bases are substances that burn or erode other materials. Bases feel slippery or soapy to the touch. Like some acids, the gases and vapors of ammonia and many other bases dissolve readily in water.

Sodium hydroxide (caustic soda or lye) can be used to unclog drains because it dissolves many different types of materials. Caustics such as ammonium hydroxide and potassium hydroxide (caustic potash) are often used to clean metal parts.

WARNING!

Wear a respirator, face shield, and protective clothing when handling caustic materials. When inhaled, caustic gases and vapors may irritate the nose and throat. Dry bases, powders, and solid granules will react with the moisture of the skin, eyes, and respiratory tract to produce severe burns. Concentrated bases dissolve tissue and can cause severe burns. Always follow the manufacturer's instructions when using caustics.

5.7.0 Acetone

WARNING!

Acetone is a highly volatile and explosive substance. When using acetone, use **nonsparking tools** and avoid high temperatures and open flames. Acetone must not be used with oxidizing agents (peroxides, nitrates, and perchlorates) or chlorinated solvent/alkali mixtures (chloroform and sodium hydroxide) since it reacts violently with these chemicals. It also reacts vigorously with hexachloromelamine, sulfur dichloride, and potassium tert-butoxide.

Acetone is used as a solvent in processes involving resins, lacquers, fats, waxes, adhesives, print-

ing inks, plastics, and varnishes. It is also used as a degreasing agent and in the manufacture of paints, varnishes, varnish removers, rubbers, plastics, dyes, explosives, artificial silk, synthetic rubber, and photographic chemicals.

5.8.0 Isopropyl Alcohol

Isopropyl alcohol is a volatile, flammable alcohol used as a solvent and rubbing alcohol. As a solvent, it can be used to clean grease and dirt from printed circuit board assemblies and other surfaces.

WARNING!

When using isopropyl alcohol, avoid high temperatures, sparks, or open flames since these conditions may cause an explosion.

5.9.0 Aerosol Cleaners

Aerosol cleaners are sometimes used to clean electrical and electronic equipment and components such as contacts and relays. Some aerosol cleaners are not recommended for use on certain types of plastics.

WARNING!

Aerosol cans can be hazardous and must be handled with care. Aerosol hazards include explosions caused by high temperatures, explosions caused by punctured cans, burning contents or propellants, poisonous contents or propellants, and chemical burns. Always read the instructions, warning statements, and environmental considerations before using any aerosol.

6.0.0 ◆ STORING AND HANDLING CLEANERS

There are special storing and handling requirements for different types of cleaners. The MSDS and manufacturer's information should be checked to determine proper storage and handling requirements for particular cleaners.

Many cleaners are flammable, so precautions must be taken to avoid the possibility of ignition. Some cleaners give off harmful vapors that should be avoided. The general storage and handling precautions for various types of cleaners listed here provide some minimum guidelines for proper storage and handling.

6.1.0 Storing Acids and Bases

When storing acids and bases, these minimum guidelines and precautions should be followed:

- Store acids separately from bases, solvents, and certain other **toxic** materials.
- Store inorganic acids (such as hydrochloric acid, hydrofluoric acid, nitric acid, phosphoric acid, and sulfuric acid) in glass or plastic containers.
- Store the least amount possible.
- Keep in a cool, well-ventilated area.
- Clean up any spills to prevent the acid or base from being mistaken for water.

6.2.0 Handling Acids and Bases

When handling acids and bases, these minimum guidelines and precautions should be followed:

- Ventilate the work area properly and avoid breathing the vapors.
- Wear appropriate protective clothing, such as gloves, aprons, safety glasses, and face shields.
- Use a respirator fitted with an appropriate cartridge, if necessary.
- Know the reactions that will occur when substances are mixed to avoid an explosion or release of toxic gases.
- Always add acid to water—not water to acid. Water added to acid may heat up and splatter.
- Know the effects of the acids and bases with which you are working.
- Use appropriate controls and work practices.
- Learn the location and use of emergency equipment.

6.3.0 Storing Acetone

When storing acetone, these minimum guidelines and precautions should be followed:

- Store in a cool, dry, well-ventilated area, out of direct sunlight.
- Store away from heat and ignition sources.
- Store away from incompatible materials, such as materials that support combustion (oxidizing material) and corrosive materials (strong acids or bases).
- Use grounded, non-sparking ventilation systems and electrical equipment that does not provide a source of ignition.
- Store in suitable, labeled containers.
- Keep containers tightly closed when not in use and when empty.

- Use suitable, approved storage cabinets, tanks, rooms, and buildings.
- Have appropriate fire extinguishers available in and near the storage area.
- Comply with all applicable regulations for the storage and handling of flammable materials.

6.4.0 Handling Acetone

When handling acetone, the following minimum guidelines and precautions should be followed:

- Only use approved flammable-liquid storage containers in the work area.
- Keep away from sources of heat or flame. Lighted cigarettes, matches, or any other ignition sources should not be allowed in and around indoor or outdoor areas where acetone is being used.
- Do not use near welding operations or hot surfaces.
- Containers should be grounded during transfer or mixing.
- Whenever possible, fire-resistant containers should be used.
- Use the smallest possible amounts, and only in designated areas with adequate ventilation.
- Have emergency equipment (for fires, spills, leaks) readily available.
- Keep empty containers closed when not in use. Empty containers may contain residues which are hazardous.

6.5.0 Storing Aerosols

When storing aerosols, the following minimum guidelines and precautions should be followed:

- Always keep the container in a cool place.
- Never store the container in direct sunlight or close to radiators, stoves, or other heat sources.
- Store in an approved cabinet or storage area.

6.6.0 Handling Aerosols

When handling aerosols, the following minimum guidelines and precautions should be followed:

- Ventilate the work area properly and avoid breathing the vapors or mist.
- When using aerosols, keep away from sources of heat or flame. Lighted cigarettes, matches, or any other ignition sources should not be allowed in and around indoor or outdoor areas where aerosols are being used.
- Wash exposed parts of the body after using.

Summary

Lubricants, sealants, and cleaners are widely used in the instrumentation field. There are numerous types of lubricants, sealants, and cleaners designed for many different jobs. Several types were described in this module to provide a basic understanding of the uses of these substances and the precautions necessary to safely use them. Make sure you understand the compatibility of the chemical you are using with the process or environment.

Safety is an extremely important consideration when using any lubricant, sealant, or cleaner. When selecting lubricants, sealants, and cleaners, always be aware of the chemical process, the working pressure, and the temperature at which the substances are going to be used. Read the MSDS and manufacturer's information on how to safely use, handle, and store particular types of lubricants, sealants, and cleaners.

Review Questions

1. Natural rubber has a limited chemical resistance to _____ products.
   a. petroleum
   b. aqueous
   c. organic
   d. petroleum, aqueous, and organic

2. The Material Safety Data Sheet contains written or printed information concerning _____.
   a. a hazardous material
   b. how to use lubricants
   c. the difference between lubricants, sealants, and cleaners
   d. the proper applications of lubricants

3. Cutting oils are used to reduce _____ during threading.
   a. explosion hazards
   b. contamination
   c. thread gap
   d. heat and friction

4. Active and inactive cutting oils both contain _____.
   a. acetone
   b. graphite
   c. sulphur
   d. silicone

5. When aluminum is exposed to air, _____ is formed on the surface.
   a. rust
   b. oxide
   c. moisture
   d. pitting

6. An abbreviation for polytetrafluoroethylene is _____.
   a. PET
   b. ETF
   c. FET
   d. TFE

7. Teflon® tape should be used as a _____ because its thinness and inherent non-sticking characteristics will prevent it from sticking to threaded surfaces.
   a. lubricant
   b. sealant
   c. cleaner
   d. marking tape

8. Solvent-based sealant paste is commonly referred to as _____.
   a. pipe chalk
   b. solopaste
   c. pipe dope
   d. plumbing putty

9. Flint sandpaper is often used for _____.
   a. general maintenance and cleanup
   b. cleaning corroded surfaces of polished metals
   c. fast cutting action on metals and woods
   d. removing excess lubricants and sealants from the surfaces of electrical equipment

10. The first thing you should do before using an aerosol is to _____.
    a. shake the can vigorously
    b. put on a respirator
    c. open all doors and windows, if inside
    d. read the instructions and warning statements

Trade Terms Introduced in This Module

Acid: Any chemical that undergoes dissociation in water with the formation of hydrogen ions. Acids have a sour taste and strong acids may cause severe skin burns. Acids turn litmus paper red and have pH values of less than 7.0.

Aerosol: A gaseous suspension of fine solid or liquid particles. A substance such as a cleaner or lubricant packaged under pressure with a gaseous propellant for release as an aerosol.

American Conference of Governmental Industrial Hygienists (ACGIH): An organization of professional personnel in governmental agencies or educational institutions engaged in occupational safety and health programs. ACGIH establishes recommended occupational exposure limits for chemical substances and physical agents.

Base: A substance that (1) liberates hydroxide (OH) ions when dissolved in water, (2) receives hydrogen ions from a strong acid to form a weaker acid, and (3) neutralizes an acid. Bases react with acids to form salts and water. Bases have a pH greater than 7.0 and turn litmus paper blue. Bases are also referred to as *alkalis*.

Carcinogen: A substance or agent capable of causing or producing cancer in mammals, including humans. A chemical is considered to be a carcinogen if it has been evaluated by the International Agency for Research on Cancer (IARC) and found to be a carcinogen or potential carcinogen; is listed as a carcinogen or potential carcinogen in the *Annual Report on Carcinogens* published by the National Toxicology Program (NTP) (latest edition); or is regulated by OSHA as a carcinogen.

Chemical: An element such as chlorine or a compound such as sodium bicarbonate, produced by a chemical reaction.

Corrosive: A chemical that causes visible destruction of or irreversible alterations in living tissue by chemical action at the site of contact is said to be corrosive.

Emulsifiable: Capable of being dissolved in water when a soap-like material (an emulsifier) is added.

Environmental Protection Agency (EPA): A government agency whose goal is to protect the environment. EPA duties include issuing regulations regarding the use of lubricants, sealants, and cleaners.

Hazardous chemical: Any chemical whose presence or use is a physical hazard or health hazard.

Label: Notice attached to a container bearing information concerning its contents.

Material Safety Data Sheet (MSDS): Provides information on the use of hazardous materials. Chemical manufacturers and distributors must provide purchasers of hazardous chemicals with an MSDS for the substance.

Mine Safety and Health Administration (MSHA): The government agency that enforces compliance with mandatory safety and health standards at all mining and mineral processing operations in the United States.

National Institute for Occupational Safety and Health (NIOSH): The government agency responsible for conducting research and making recommendations for the prevention of work-related disease and injury. Among other activities, NIOSH tests and certifies respiratory protective devices and air sampling detector tubes, recommends occupational exposure limits for various substances, and assists OSHA and MSHA in occupational safety and health investigations and research.

Nonsparking tools: Tools made from beryllium-copper or aluminum-bronze that greatly reduce the possibility of igniting dusts, gases, or flammable vapors.

Occupational Safety and Health Administration (OSHA): The government agency responsible for creating and enforcing workplace safety and health regulations.

Permissible exposure limit (PEL): PEL is an occupational exposure limit to a specific material or substance established by OSHA's regulatory authority. It may be a time-weighted average (TWA) limit or a maximum concentration exposure limit.

Room temperature vulcanizing (RTV): A silicone-based adhesive/sealant that cures with exposure to moisture in the air. Different types of RTV silicone materials are used as sealants.

Solvent: A substance, usually a liquid, in which other substances are dissolved. The most common solvent is water.

Threshold limit value (TLV): A term used by ACGIH to express the airborne concentration of materials to which nearly all persons can be exposed day after day without adverse effects.

Toxic: Any substance or material that can cause acute or chronic injury to the human body or which is suspected of being able to cause diseases or injury under some conditions.

Viscosity: The property of a fluid to resist flow without regard to its density. A fluid with a high viscosity is thick and flows slowly, while a fluid with a low viscosity flows readily.

Additional Resources

This module is intended to present thorough resources for task training. The following reference works are suggested for further study. These are optional materials for continued education rather than for task training.

Hazard Communication Standards. 200 Constitution Ave. NW, Washington, DC.: Occupational Safety and Health Administration (OSHA).

Figure Credits

Gerald Shannon	109F02, 109F04
Sherwin Williams	109F01A-B

NCCER CRAFT TRAINING USER UPDATES

The NCCER makes every effort to keep these textbooks up-to-date and free of technical errors. We appreciate your help in this process. If you have an idea for improving this textbook, or if you find an error, a typographical mistake, or an inaccuracy in the NCCER's Craft Training textbooks, please write us, using this form or a photocopy. Be sure to include the exact module number, page number, a detailed description, and the correction, if applicable. Your input will be brought to the attention of the Technical Review Committee. Thank you for your assistance.

Instructors – If you found that additional materials were necessary in order to teach this module effectively, please let us know so that we may include them in the Equipment and Materials list in the Instructor's Guide.

Write: Curriculum Revision and Development Department
National Center for Construction Education and Research
P.O. Box 141104, Gainesville, FL 32614-1104

Fax: 352-334-0932

E-mail: curriculum@nccer.org

Craft _____ Module Name _____

Copyright Date _____ Module Number _____ Page Number(s) _____

Description _____

_____

_____

_____

(Optional) Correction _____

_____

_____

(Optional) Your Name and Address _____

_____

_____

_____

Flow, Pressure, Level, and Temperature

COURSE MAP

This course map shows all of the modules in the first level of the Instrumentation curriculum. The suggested training order begins at the bottom and proceeds up. Skill levels increase as you advance on the course map. The local Training Program Sponsor may adjust the training order.

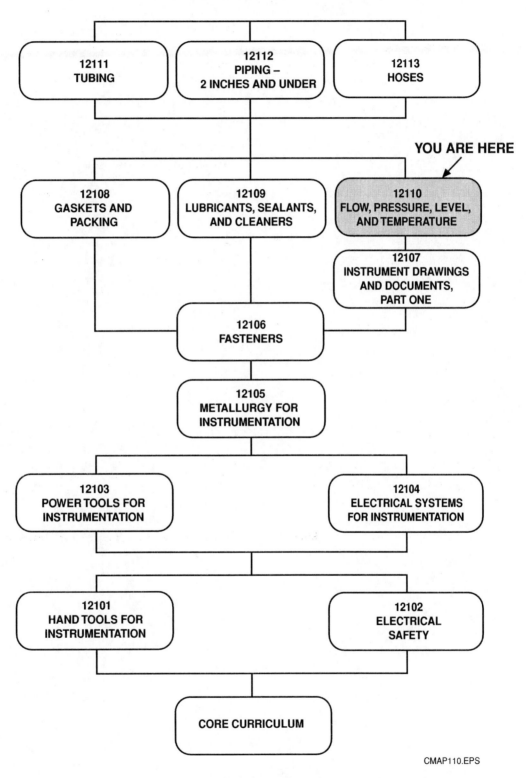

INSTRUMENTATION LEVEL ONE

12111
TUBING

12112
PIPING –
2 INCHES AND UNDER

12113
HOSES

YOU ARE HERE

12108
GASKETS AND
PACKING

12109
LUBRICANTS, SEALANTS,
AND CLEANERS

12110
FLOW, PRESSURE, LEVEL,
AND TEMPERATURE

12107
INSTRUMENT DRAWINGS
AND DOCUMENTS,
PART ONE

12106
FASTENERS

12105
METALLURGY FOR
INSTRUMENTATION

12103
POWER TOOLS FOR
INSTRUMENTATION

12104
ELECTRICAL SYSTEMS
FOR INSTRUMENTATION

12101
HAND TOOLS FOR
INSTRUMENTATION

12102
ELECTRICAL
SAFETY

CORE CURRICULUM

CMAP110.EPS

Figures

Tables

Flow, Pressure, Level, and Temperature

Objectives

When you have completed this module, you will be able to do the following:

1. Identify and describe characteristics of flow measurement.
2. Identify and describe characteristics of pressure measurement.
3. Identify and describe characteristics of temperature measurement.
4. Identify and describe characteristics of level measurement.

Prerequisites

Before you begin this module, it is recommended that you successfully complete the following modules: Core Curriculum; Instrumentation Level One, Modules 12101 through 12109.

Required Trainee Materials

1. Pencil and paper
2. Appropriate personal protective equipment

1.0.0 ◆ INTRODUCTION

The accurate and precise measurement of process variables is essential to the proper operation and control of any process system. An understanding of process variables and the instruments used to measure and control processes is necessary to perform quality instrument work. Installation, maintenance, calibration, and repair of measuring devices is a primary responsibility in the instrumentation craft.

This module introduces four of the process variables most frequently measured in instrument and control systems: **flow**, pressure, **level**, and **temperature**. Each of these four process variables is defined. The different measurement units used to express flow, pressure, level, and temperature are described and explained. In addition, several types of instruments used to measure each of the four variables are introduced, along with a description of the principles of operation of the devices.

Later modules in the Instrumentation curriculum cover measuring instruments in greater detail, including installation techniques, maintenance, calibration, and repair procedures.

2.0.0 ◆ PRESSURE

Pressure is the amount of force exerted by a substance over a given unit of area. This is expressed mathematically as:

$$\text{Pressure} = \frac{\text{force}}{\text{area}}$$

A common measure of force is weight, expressed in pounds. Area is usually expressed in square inches. Pressure can be determined by dividing the weight of an object by the area of its base, as shown in *Figure 1*.

2.1.0 Units of Pressure Measurement

Pressure is generally expressed in pounds per square inch (psi). It is important to know if a pressure measurement is referenced to atmospheric pressure or absolute pressure.

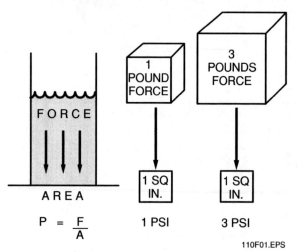

P = $\frac{F}{A}$ 1 PSI   3 PSI

110F01.EPS

Figure 1 ◆ Relationship of area, pressure, and force.

Absolute pressure is measured and expressed as pounds per square inch absolute (psia) and references the absence of atmospheric pressure. Gauge pressure is measured and expressed as pounds per square inch gauge (psig) and references the presence of atmospheric pressure.

The atmosphere at sea level exerts a pressure of about 14.7 psia. This means that 0 psig is equal to 14.7 psia. To convert from gauge pressure to absolute pressure, add atmospheric pressure to the gauge reading. Expressed mathematically:

psia = psig + atmospheric pressure

To convert from absolute pressure to gauge pressure, subtract atmospheric pressure from the absolute pressure reading. Expressed mathematically:

psig = psia − atmospheric pressure

NOTE

Substitute the local barometric pressure in the above formulas for atmospheric pressure.

Pressure can also be indicated and expressed by the height of a liquid in a column. For example, pressure may be described in inches of water (in. H_2O) or inches of mercury (in. Hg). One inch of water produces a pressure of .0360 psi. This means that .0360 psi will support a column of water that is 1 inch high.

Because mercury is heavier than water, it takes more pressure to support a column of mercury than it takes for a column of water of the same height. Because of this difference, inches of mercury units are generally used to measure higher pressures. Inches of water units are generally used to measure low pressures.

Table 1 shows some common pressure conversion factors used to convert between psi, inches of water, and inches of mercury.

Table 1 Common Pressure Conversions

Pounds per Square Inch (psi)	Inches of Water (in. H_2O)	Inches of Mercury (in. Hg)
.0360	1.0000	.0737
.4320	12.0000	.8844
.4892	13.5712	1.0000
1.0000	27.7417	2.0441

2.1.1 Pressure Calculations

The following are practice examples for working with pressure measurement units.

Example 1:

A pressure gauge that measures psig indicates a reading of 50. The local atmospheric pressure is 14.7 psi. What is the absolute pressure (psia) that corresponds to the psig reading?

Answer: 64.7 psia

Example 2:

A psia pressure-measuring instrument indicates a reading of 42.5 psia. The local atmospheric pressure is 14.6 psi. What is the corresponding gauge pressure (psig)?

Answer: 27.9 psig

Example 3:

What is the pressure (psi) exerted by a solid block weighing 24 pounds with a bottom surface area of 8 square inches?

Answer: 3 psi

2.1.2 Differential Pressure

In some cases, it is necessary to measure the difference between pressures at two related points. This is called **differential pressure**. Differential pressure is expressed as D/P or ∆P (pronounced delta P). To find differential pressure, subtract the lower pressure reading from the higher pressure reading. *Figure 2* illustrates differential pressure by showing the difference between the levels of liquid in the legs of the pressure measuring device (U-tube manometer).

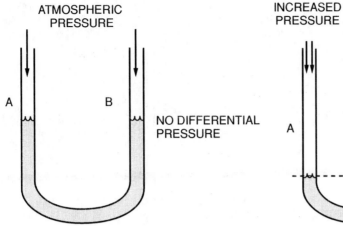

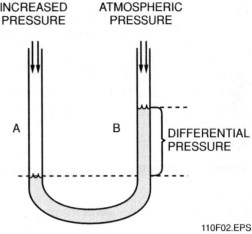

110F02.EPS

Figure 2 ◆ Differential pressure.

> **NOTE**
> When performing the differential pressure calculation, the two pressure readings used must be in the same pressure measuring units.

2.2.0 Pressure Measurement Devices

There are several types of instruments used to measure pressure and differential pressure. Some of the common types of pressure measuring devices include manometers, bellows-type pressure sensors, Bourdon tubes, and diaphragms.

2.2.1 Manometers

The basic principle of operation of a manometer is that a column of liquid of a certain height exerts a specific amount of pressure. Liquids commonly used in manometers include mercury, water, and certain types of oil. There are three basic types of manometers: U-tube, well, and inclined-well. Manometers are commonly used to measure pressures up to about 30 psi.

In a U-tube manometer (*Figure 3*), the input pressure is applied to the top of one side (leg) of the manometer, and the other side (leg) is vented to the atmosphere.

The amount that the liquid rises in the column indicates the applied pressure. A U-tube manometer can also be used to measure differential pressure. This is done by connecting the high-pressure input to the top of one side of the tube and the low-pressure input to the top of the other side. The differential pressure measurement is the difference between the levels of the liquid in the legs of the manometer.

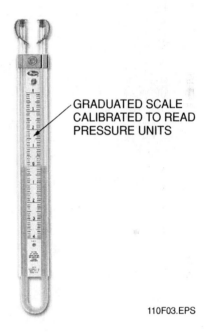

GRADUATED SCALE CALIBRATED TO READ PRESSURE UNITS

110F03.EPS

Figure 3 ◆ U-tube manometer.

In a well-type manometer (*Figure 4*), the pressure is applied to the well. The height that the **fluid** rises in the tube indicates the amount of applied pressure.

A variation of the well-type manometer is the inclined-well manometer (*Figure 5*). The inclined-well manometer has a slanted tube which gives a more accurate reading because the liquid rises more for a given pressure.

Manometers are simple to use and provide direct measurements, but their applications are limited to low-pressure measurement, and they do not handle overpressures.

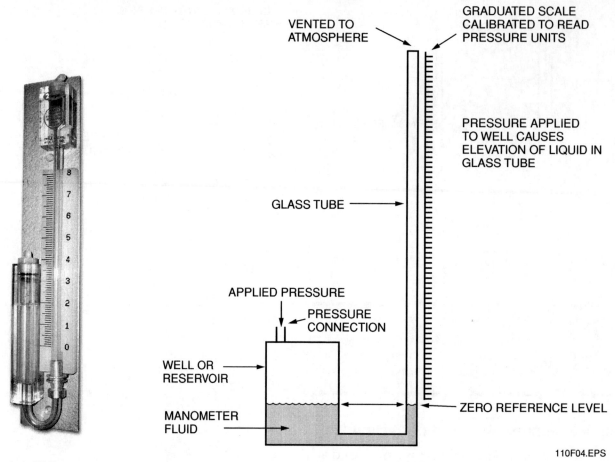

Figure 4 ◆ Well manometer.

110F04.EPS

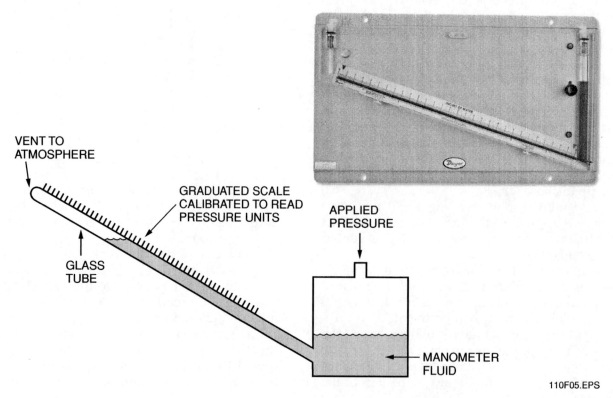

Figure 5 ◆ Inclined-well manometer.

110F05.EPS

2.2.2 Bellows-Type Pressure Sensors

A common type of pressure sensing device is a bellows-type pressure sensor, shown in *Figure 6*.

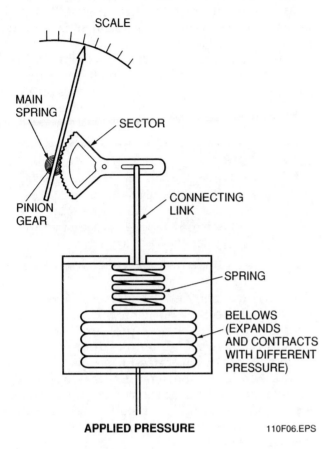

APPLIED PRESSURE

110F06.EPS

Figure 6 ◆ Bellows.

Bellows are made of a flexible metal formed in the shape of thin-wall tubes. The sides of the tube are folded like an accordion, allowing the bellows to expand and contract when pressure is applied. The bellows are sealed on one end and open on the other. Pressure applied to the open end acts on the inner surface of the bellows. This causes it to expand and contract, producing a movement at the other end. The movement, typically transmitted by a spring and related mechanism, can be used to indicate pressure on an attached indicator and scale. Because of the large surface area of a bellows compared to its physical size, the movement-to-pressure ratio is relatively high. Bellows are sensitive, very accurate, and fairly inexpensive. They are used primarily in lower-pressure applications.

2.2.3 Bourdon Tubes

Bourdon tubes are often used in pressure gauges and transmitters. There are three common types of Bourdon tubes: the C-type, spiral, and helical. (*Figure 7*).

In the C-type Bourdon tube, pressure is applied to the open end of a tube. This applied pressure causes the tube to straighten out. When the pressure is removed, the elasticity of the metal returns the tube to its original shape. The distance the tip of the tube travels during the straightening is proportional to the amount of pressure applied to the tube.

In a typical pressure gauge, a pointer is attached to the end of a C-type Bourdon tube through a mechanical linkage, as shown in *Figure 7(D)*. This linkage converts the tip travel to a larger amount of pointer travel, which is easier to read on an indicator scale.

The spiral and helical Bourdon tubes work on the same principle as the C-type. However, both of these pressure-sensing elements produce more tip travel and higher torque capacity at the free end than the C-type, and they are more capable of being used as direct readout devices. Instruments that use these types of sensing elements can respond to lower pressures since they are more sensitive. Spiral and helical Bourdon tubes are used primarily in pressure transmitters and receiver instruments.

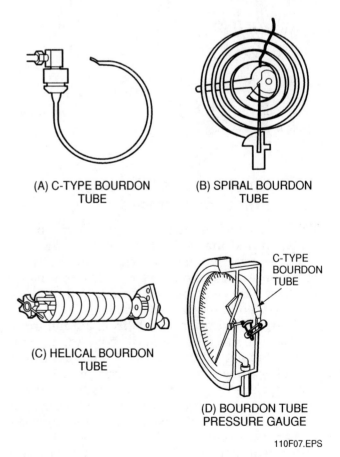

(A) C-TYPE BOURDON TUBE

(B) SPIRAL BOURDON TUBE

(C) HELICAL BOURDON TUBE

(D) BOURDON TUBE PRESSURE GAUGE

110F07.EPS

Figure 7 ◆ Bourdon tube types.

2.2.4 Diaphragms

A diaphragm (*Figure 8*) is a flexible disk. Pressure is applied to the surface of one side of the diaphragm. This applied pressure causes the other side of the diaphragm to move. The movement of the diaphragm surface is proportional to the change in pressure. Diaphragms are usually made of soft, pliable material such as metal, plastic, or vinyl. Diaphragms are sensitive to very small pressures. They can be used to measure pressures as low as 5 inches to 10 inches of water.

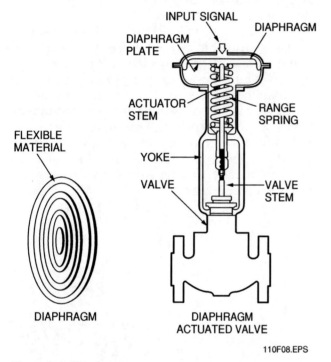

Figure 8 ◆ Diaphragm.

2.3.0 Conditions That Damage Pressure Elements

Pressure-sensing elements must be properly installed and maintained in order for them to operate properly and to prevent damage. Three common causes of damage to pressure-sensing elements are overpressurization, temperature extremes, and excessive vibration.

Overpressurization results from an abnormal increase or surge in pressure above the normal operating range of the element. Common signs of overpressurization are a ruptured or deformed sensing element or a bent pointer on the indicator. A common practice to prevent overpressurization is to first determine the maximum pressure conditions for the process. Then, select and install an instrument that has a range approximately twice as high as the maximum process pressure. The

normal pressure reading for the process typically falls at approximately mid-scale on the face of the indicating gauge of the instrument, and should never exceed 75 percent of the scale value.

Most pressure instruments are installed with isolation valves. When the instrument is returned to service, the isolation valve must be opened slowly so that the instrument gradually receives the pressure input. If the isolation valve is opened too quickly, the sudden surge of pressure can result in overpressurization of the instrument.

> **CAUTION**
>
> When isolating a differential pressure transmitter, always follow the manufacturer's procedure for opening and closing the valves. Failure to follow the proper procedure could damage the transmitter or other instruments in the system.

Pressure elements can be damaged by exposure to extremely cold or hot temperatures. Freezing temperatures can cause a pressure element to burst. Excessively high temperatures can cause soldered joints in some pressure elements to break or leak. For this reason, it is important to check the manufacturer's specifications for a pressure element to make sure it is compatible with the temperature ranges involved in the application where it is to be used.

Excessive vibration generated by equipment and transmitted by piping systems can cause pressure-sensing mechanisms to wear abnormally. Excessive vibration can also adversely affect the tolerance of the internal linkages of many pressure-sensing devices. When installing pressure elements, they should be installed in system locations free of vibration, if possible, or isolated from the vibrations by the use of a suitable vibration isolator.

2.4.0 Pressure Element Protection Devices

There are protection devices that can be used to help prevent damage to pressure-sensing elements. Two of the most common devices are isolation diaphragms and snubbers.

An isolation diaphragm is used to separate the pressure element from corrosive process fluids. It is made from a material suitable for use with the corrosive fluid involved. A properly installed isolation diaphragm does not interfere with the ability of the element to sense changes in pressure. The isolation diaphragm is filled with a non-corrosive fluid, such as glycerine. The pressure of the process fluid presses against the bottom of the isolation diaphragm. This causes the diaphragm to bulge or flex. When the diaphragm bulges, the process pressure is transmitted through the noncorrosive fluid to the pressure element.

A snubber (*Figure 9*) is installed at the input side of a pressure element to alleviate multiple rapid pressure changes at the input to the element. A snubber effectively reduces the size of a pressure inlet. The pressure element is still exposed to the same amount of pressure; however, it takes longer for the element to receive the full impact of the pressure. The pressure element responds to changes more slowly with the snubber installed, but the pressure readings are just as accurate.

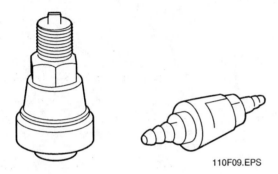

110F09.EPS

Figure 9 ◆ Snubbers.

3.0.0 ◆ FLOW

Flow is the actual volume of fluid that passes a given point per unit of time. Basically, there are three types of fluid flow: laminar flow, turbulent flow, and transitional flow.

Laminar flow occurs when the fluid flows in layers and is very smooth with little turbulence. Laminar flow is shown in *Figure 10(A)*.

Turbulent flow is erratic instead of smooth or streamlined. Turbulent flow is shown in *Figure 10(B)*.

Transitional flow, as shown in *Figure 10(C)*, is between turbulent flow and laminar flow. Its behavior is hard to predict because it tends to oscillate or transition between turbulent flow and laminar flow.

3.1.0 Flow Measurement Units

There are three basic ways that flow can be described: velocity, volume, or mass. Velocity refers to the time that it takes for a fluid to move a given distance. When velocity of the fluid is measured, the flow rate is usually expressed in *feet per second (fps)*.

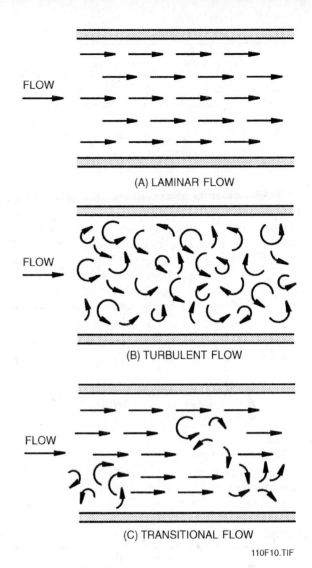

(A) LAMINAR FLOW

(B) TURBULENT FLOW

(C) TRANSITIONAL FLOW

110F10.TIF

Figure 10 ◆ Fluid flow.

When volume is used to describe flow, it is called the *volumetric flow rate*. The volumetric flow rate considers both the velocity of the fluid and the cross-sectional area of the pipe or other container. Volumetric flow is usually expressed in *gallons per minute (gpm)*.

The mass of the material can also be used to describe flow. The *mass flow rate* considers both the density of the fluid and the volumetric flow rate. Mass flow is usually expressed in *pounds per hour (pph)*.

3.2.0 Differential Pressure and Flow Relationship

Fluid flowing in a pipe exerts a pressure in two different directions, as shown in *Figure 11*. Pressure is exerted in the direction of flow and against the walls of the pipe. These pressure measurements can be used to determine flow rate.

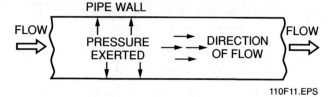

Figure 11 ◆ Pressure exerted by fluid flowing through a pipe.

If a restriction is placed in the pipe, narrowing the flow path, the velocity of the fluid increases after the restriction. As the velocity of flow increases, the pressure that the fluid exerts on the walls of the pipe decreases. The difference in the pressures before and after the restriction (differential pressure) is calculated and used to determine the flow rate through the pipe.

The mathematical relationship between differential pressure (D/P) and flow is shown by the formula:

$$Flow = \frac{\sqrt{\Delta measured D/P}}{\sqrt{\Delta maximum D/P}} \times maximum\ flow$$

As the formula shows, flow rate is proportional to the square root of the differential pressure. The following examples illustrate how flow is calculated using this formula.

Example 1:

Find the flow through a pipe if the maximum D/P is 100 inches of water, the measured D/P is 25 inches of water, and the maximum flow rate is 100 gpm.

Answer: 50 gpm

Example 2:

Find the flow through a pipe if the maximum D/P is 36 inches of water, the measured D/P is 16 inches of water, and the maximum flow rate is 10 gpm.

Answer: 6.67 gpm

3.3.0 Differential Pressure Flow Devices

Many types of flow devices are used to create a differential pressure in a system so that the flow rate can be determined. The most common types of these devices are orifice plates, flow nozzles, venturi tubes, and pitot tubes.

3.3.1 Orifice Plates

An orifice plate is a restriction that is usually placed in a flow line between two flanges. *Figure 12* shows three different types of orifice plates.

An orifice plate effectively decreases the inside diameter of a pipe, causing a restriction to flow. As fluid passes through the orifice plate, the velocity of the fluid increases. This causes the pressure in the pipe to decrease. By measuring the difference in the pressures upstream and downstream of the orifice plate (differential pressure), the flow rate can be determined.

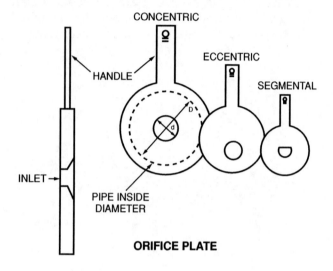

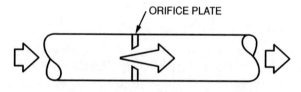

Figure 12 ◆ Orifice plates.

> **NOTE**
>
> Any change in the orifice plate will change the way the flow rate is read by the transmitter.

When replacing orifice plates, the replacement plate must be identical to the plate being replaced. The new plate must also be oriented in the pipe in the same way as the orifice plate being replaced. Orifice plates are inexpensive, but they are not considered to be extremely accurate. The inaccuracy in flow measuring systems using orifice plates results from the excessive turbulence caused by the orifice plate installed in the line.

In orifice plates, the ratio of the inner hole diameter (d) to the inside pipe diameter (D) is important. This ratio is called the *beta ratio* (beta = d/D). Ideally, this ratio should not be less than 0.3 and not more than 0.7, with the greatest accuracy occurring on an orifice plate having a beta ratio around 0.5. The beta ratio is normally stamped on the handle of the orifice plate.

3.3.2 Flow Nozzles

Like an orifice plate, a flow nozzle creates a restriction in a pipe run that produces a differential pressure. However, the flow nozzle provides a smooth transition from the pipe to the restriction at the input of the device. This smooth transition causes less turbulence in the input flow to the flow device. The downstream flow past the flow nozzle is turbulent, like that of an orifice plate. Flow nozzles are more accurate and more expensive than orifice plates. *Figure 13* shows a flow nozzle installed in a process line. Flow nozzles are commonly found on steam lines and are generally limited to pipe sizes of 2 inches or larger.

Taps used for differential pressure measurements are located on flow nozzles at a distance equal to one pipe diameter upstream and at one-half pipe diameter downstream from the inlet face of the nozzle (see *Figure 13*).

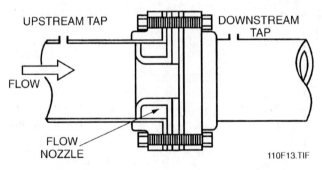

Figure 13 ◆ Flow nozzle.

3.3.3 Venturi Tubes

Venturi tubes (*Figure 14*) provide a smooth transition at both the input and output ends of the device.

The smooth transitions eliminate excessive turbulence from developing at the input or output sides of the device, thereby providing more consistent and accurate pressure readings as measured at the upstream and downstream taps. Venturi tubes are the most accurate of the restriction-type flow devices.

The venturi tube is generally installed in low-pressure applications such as in very large water

pipes and large gas or air ducts. It is more expensive, heavier, and larger than the other types of DP meters and has a tendency to plug up when used with slurries or other mixed processes.

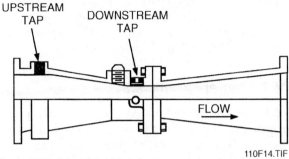

Figure 14 ◆ Venturi tube.

3.3.4 Pitot Tubes

A pitot tube can be used in conjunction with manometers and differential pressure gauges to determine the differential pressure of fluids flowing in a pipe or duct. It can also be used to measure flowing liquids not confined in a pipe or duct, such as with the flow of water in a river.

Pitot tubes are not standardized and each tube must be calibrated for its specific application. The simplest form of a pitot tube consists of a tube with a small opening, called the *impact opening,* at the measuring end (*Figure 15*). This impact opening is positioned such that it faces directly into the path of the flowing liquid. When the fluid contacts the pitot tube, the fluid velocity is zero and the pressure is at a maximum. The pitot tube impact opening and related tube tap provide the higher-pressure measurement point needed to determine a differential pressure. The lower pressure input needed to determine a differential pressure is typically obtained via an ordinary pressure tap located in the wall of the pipe or duct.

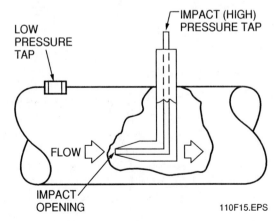

Figure 15 ◆ Basic pitot tube being used to provide a differential pressure measurement.

3.4.0 Other Types of Flow Measurement Devices

In addition to differential pressure, other types of measurements can be used to determine flow rate. There are a variety of flowmeters that use various measurement principles including target meters, electromagnetic flowmeters, turbine meters, vortex meters, and variable area meters.

3.4.1 Target Flowmeters

In a target (or impact) flowmeter system, a plate is supported directly in the fluid flow, as shown in *Figure 16*. The electronic or pneumatic output produced by the target flowmeter is proportional to the amount of plate deflection. The target flowmeter is well suited for use with fluids that have suspended solids, or sticky types of liquids that might interfere with a restriction device such as an orifice plate. It can be described as the reverse of an orifice plate, with the target plate having a beta ratio.

3.4.2 Electromagnetic Flowmeters

Electromagnetic flowmeters (*Figure 17*) produce a magnetic field across the metering tube. As the fluid passes through the magnetic field, a voltage is produced that is proportional to the velocity of the fluid passing through the pipe. The velocity of the fluid flow is used to calculate the volumetric flow through the pipe.

The electromagnetic flowmeter offers several advantages over other types of flow-measuring devices in certain applications. It has no moving parts and a completely unobstructed bore. There is no pressure loss across a restriction and no parts to become damaged. Because of this, the electromagnetic flowmeter is often used in systems with corrosive liquids or in slurries. One major limitation of electromagnetic flowmeters is that the fluid must be electrically conductive, which excludes all gases.

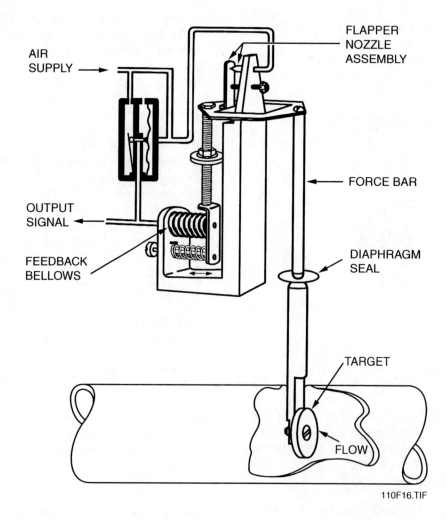

110F16.TIF

Figure 16 ◆ Target flowmeter.

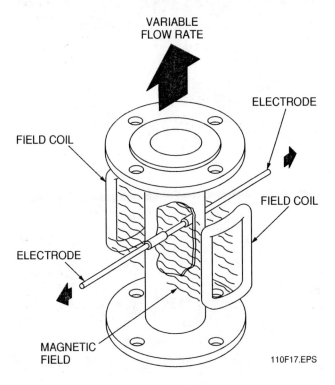

Figure 17 ◆ Electromagnetic flowmeter.

3.4.3 Turbine Flowmeter

In a turbine flowmeter (*Figure 18*), the moving fluid turns the blades of a rotor in the device. The speed of rotation of the turbine rotor is proportional to the flow rate. A magnetic pickup coil in the turbine meter counts the passing of each vane of the rotor to determine the flow rate.

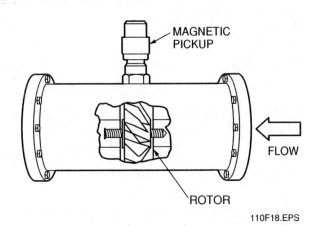

Figure 18 ◆ Turbine flowmeter.

A digital output provided by the turbine flowmeter is extremely accurate for low to medium viscosity fluids. Turbine flowmeters are suitable for use at any pressure and at extremely high and low temperatures. They are easy to install and relatively small and light. The major limitations of turbine meters are their incompati-

bility with high viscosity fluids, possible damage due to overspeeding, and the need for secondary readout equipment. Also, they are generally not recommended for steam applications since condensate does not have lubricating characteristics.

3.4.4 Vortex Flowmeters

There are several types of vortex flowmeters. Vortex flowmeters create fluid oscillations, which are used to determine flow measurements. For example, in the vortex flowmeter shown in *Figure 19*, an obstruction is placed in the line which creates a swirling action.

As the velocity of the fluid increases, whirls of fluid called *vortices* spin off from the obstruction. The greater the flow rate, the more vortices are produced. The vortices create areas of lower pressure which can be measured. A pressure sensor is attached to the flowmeter to count the frequency of vortex formation. Vortex flowmeters are suitable for gas or liquids. Generally, they have a wide flow range, require minimal maintenance, are very accurate, and have long-term reliability.

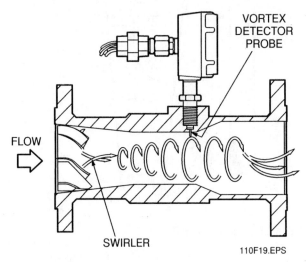

Figure 19 ◆ Vortex flowmeter.

3.4.5 Variable Area Flowmeters

Variable area flowmeters, also called rotameters, use a vertical tapered glass tube containing a float. A rotameter is shown in *Figure 20*.

The float rises in the tapered tube as the flow rate increases until the weight of the float is balanced by the lifting of the gas or liquid to a point of equilibrium, as shown in *Figure 20*. At the point of equilibrium, the position of the float indicates the rate of flow of the gas or liquid on the scale that is attached to or etched on the glass of the tube. Rotameters are inexpensive and used extensively in instrumentation applications.

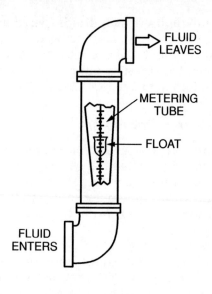

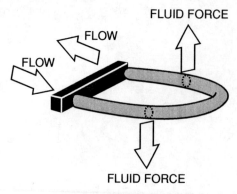

FLUID FORCES REACTING TO VIBRATION OF FLOW TUBE

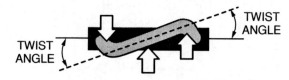

END VIEW OF FLOW TUBE SHOWING TWIST

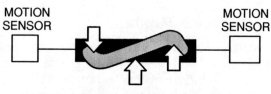

MOTION SENSORS DETECT NUMBER OF PASSES, PROVING FLUID FLOW

110F21.EPS

Figure 21 ◆ Coriolis meter.

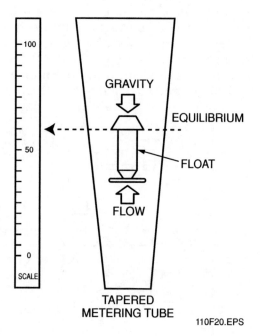

110F20.EPS

Figure 20 ◆ Rotameter.

3.4.6 Coriolis Meters

The Coriolis meter method for measuring flow uses one or two U-shaped tubes to sense flow, as illustrated in *Figure 21*. These sensors are located within a housing and are caused to vibrate, much like to a tuning fork. The U-shaped sensor tube (or tubes) are powered by an electromagnetic coil positioned at the center of the bend of the U. Not only does the tube vibrate when fluid flows through the tube, it also twists. Sensors located on each side of the U-tube detect this twisting motion, based on the number of times the tube passes in front of a motion sensor, and converts this motion into an output. These meters are only good for liquid processes.

3.5.0 Flow Device Installation Considerations

Flow devices are normally mounted horizontally to ensure that the effect of gravity is constant on the device. If the flow device is mounted vertically, the effects of gravity must be compensated for during the system calibration.

NOTE

Rotameters are designed to be vertically mounted.

There are additional components that may be used with a flow device in order to protect the element from conditions in the process. For example, straightening vanes are devices which are placed in a pipe upstream of a flow device. They reduce turbulence in the fluid flow prior to the fluid entering the flow device. There are two types of straightening vanes: the tube bundle arrangement and the grid arrangement.

A condensate chamber can be used to isolate the measurement device from the extreme **heat** of the process being measured. The condensate also acts as a medium so that pressure changes in the process being measured are felt at the measurement device.

Sediment traps prevent sediment from entering the flow device and causing inaccurate measurements.

4.0.0 ◆ TEMPERATURE

When two objects make thermal contact, the object with the higher temperature cools while the cooler object becomes warmer, until a point is finally reached where no more changes occur. At this point, the two objects are said to be in thermal equilibrium with each other. When a thermometer is placed in contact with any object or substance, including air, the material in the thermometer changes until thermal equilibrium is achieved with the object being measured.

In 1724, Gabriel Fahrenheit developed the system typically applied today that uses mercury as a thermometric liquid to measure temperature. He calibrated a scale by placing a thermometer in contact with a mixture of sea salt, ice, and water. He determined that the boiling point of water was 212 marks on the scale and the freezing point was 32 marks on the scale. This became known as the *Fahrenheit scale*. Other scales were soon developed, such as Celsius or Centigrade, Rankine, and Kelvin, that provide more applicable ranges (extreme highs or lows) suited to specific environments; however, they all use the concept developed by Fahrenheit.

4.1.0 Temperature Scales

Today, temperature is measured in four different scales: Fahrenheit, Celsius, Kelvin, and Rankine.

The Fahrenheit scale is commonly used in industrial measurement. As mentioned, in the Fahrenheit scale, the boiling point of water at sea level is 212°, and the freezing point of water is 32°.

The Celsius scale is the temperature scale used in the metric system. In the past, it was called the Centigrade scale. The Celsius scale is also commonly used in industrial temperature measurement. In the Celsius scale, the boiling point of water at sea level is 100°, and the freezing point of water is 0°.

The Kelvin scale is used in many scientific and engineering applications. In the Kelvin scale, the boiling point of water at sea level is 373°, and the freezing point of water is 273°.

The Rankine scale is also used for some scientific applications. In this scale, the boiling point of water at sea level is 672°, and the freezing point of water is 492°.

Figure 22 provides a comparison between the four temperature scales.

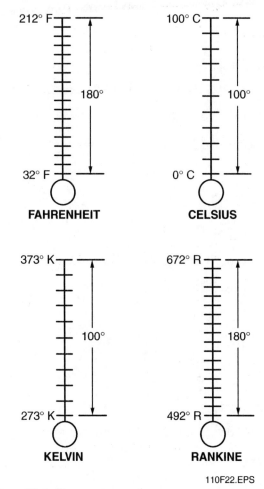

Figure 22 ◆ Temperature scales.

4.1.1 Temperature Conversions

It is sometimes necessary to convert from one temperature scale to another. Conversions between Fahrenheit and Celsius scales are the most common. Use the following formula to convert from Celsius (°C) to Fahrenheit (°F).

$$°F = (1.8 \times °C) + 32$$

Use the following formula to convert from Fahrenheit (°F) to Celsius (°C).

$$°C = \frac{°F - 32}{1.8}$$

The following examples illustrate how temperature conversion formulas are used.

Example 1:

Convert 20° Centigrade to Fahrenheit.

°F = (1.8 × °C) + 32

°F = (1.8 × 20) + 32

°F = 36 + 32

= 68°F

Example 2:

Convert 392° Fahrenheit to Centigrade.

°C = (°F − 32) ÷ 1.8

°C = (392 − 32) ÷ 1.8

°C = 360 ÷ 1.8

= 200°C

Example 3:

Convert 85° Centigrade to Fahrenheit.

°F = (1.8 × °C) + 32

°F = (1.8 × 85) + 32

°F = 153 + 32

= 185°F

Example 4:

Convert 86° Fahrenheit to Centigrade.

°C = (°F − 32) ÷ 1.8

°C = (86 − 32) ÷ 1.8

°C = 54 ÷ 1.8

= 30°C

4.2.0 Temperature Measurement Devices

A variety of temperature measurement devices are available. Some of the most commonly used temperature measurement devices in industrial applications are thermometers, thermocouples, resistance temperature detectors (RTDs), and infrared (non-contact) devices.

4.2.1 Fluid Thermometers

Fluid thermometers are composed of five principal parts: a bulb, a fluid, a capillary tube, an overload chamber, and a scale. A fluid thermometer is shown in *Figure 23*.

The bulb is a storage area that contains the fluid. The fluid responds to changes in temperature by expanding and contracting. This causes the fluid to move up and down inside the capillary tube. The capillary tube is a narrow cylinder through which the fluid travels. The tube is often equipped with a cavity for storing excess fluid, called an overload chamber. Without the overload chamber, it is possible that the fluid could exert enough pressure to rupture the tube if the temperature increased beyond the capacity of the thermometer. The scale is simply the part of the thermometer from which the temperature indications are read. The scale is calibrated in degrees and can either be permanently etched onto the capillary tube, or it can be a separate, movable part. A movable scale permits scale adjustment.

4.2.2 Bimetallic Thermometers

A bimetallic thermometer (*Figure 24*) uses a bimetallic element of some type. A bimetallic element is made of two different metals that have different thermal expansion coefficients. The two metals expand and contract at different rates in response to a change in temperature. Generally, the bimetallic element is shaped in a spiral. It is designed to uncurl when heated. A pointer is connected to the end of the element and mounted

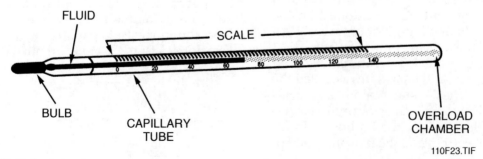

Figure 23 ◆ Fluid thermometer.

over a scale. When the element is exposed to a temperature change, the pointer will move either upscale or downscale to indicate the temperature. To calibrate a bimetallic thermometer, it must be immersed in a bath with a known temperature, adjusting the pointer on the thermometer to that temperature once thermal equilibrium is reached.

Bimetallic thermometers are a practical choice for use in industrial environments. They are quite rugged, can withstand a significant degree of overranging without damage, and are fairly inexpensive. The main disadvantage associated with bimetallic thermometers is that the metal hardens if exposed to extremely high temperatures over a prolonged period of time. Hardening of the element reduces the thermometer's sensitivity to temperature changes and renders its readings inaccurate.

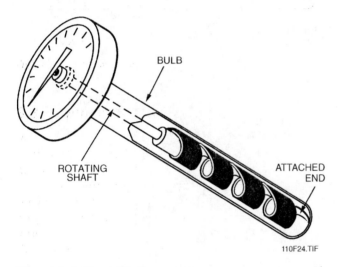

Figure 24 ◆ Bimetallic thermometer.

4.2.3 Thermocouples

Thermocouples work on the principle that when two dissimilar metals are in contact with one another, they produce a measurable potential or voltage. As the temperature changes, the potential or voltage also changes. If a thermocouple is connected to an electrical circuit, the voltage can be measured using a voltmeter. A thermocouple wired to a reference junction is shown in *Figure 25*.

There are several different types of thermocouples. Each type has a range of temperatures that it can measure. The temperature corresponding to the voltage reading in a thermocouple circuit can be found on a conversion chart for the particular type of thermocouple being used.

Thermocouples are usually identified by the color of the individual conductors in the pair that makes up the thermocouple. *Table 2* lists the three

most common types of thermocouples used in instrumentation along with their conductor colors and temperature ranges. It also shows the polarity of the conductors associated with each type of thermocouple.

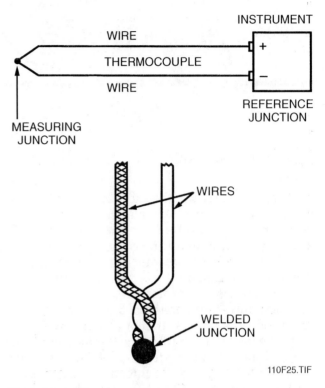

Figure 25 ◆ Thermocouple.

Table 2 Thermocouple Table

Type of Thermocouple	Metals Joined	Color of Conductors	Temperature Range
J	Iron Constantan	White + Red -	32°F to 1382° F
K	Chromel Alumel	Yellow + Red -	-328° F to 2282°F
T	Copper Constantan	Blue + Red -	-382°F to 662°F

Thermocouples are generally inserted directly into the process system by use of a thermowell. A thermowell is a tube-like structure that goes into a pipe or other area where the temperature is to be measured. It allows the thermocouple to be removed for maintenance without securing the system or losing any process fluid. A typical thermocouple inserted into a thermowell is shown in *Figure 26*.

A thermowell has a tendency to decrease heat transfer from the process to the thermocouple if

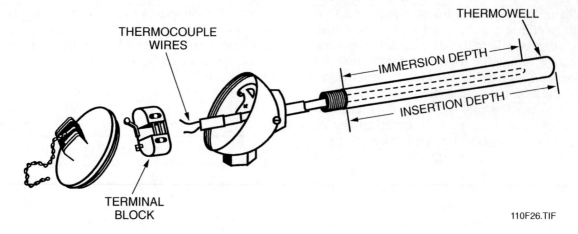

Figure 26 ◆ Thermowell.

the gap between the thermocouple and thermowell is substantial. Often, a filler material is used to improve the heat transfer, but this filler is subject to deterioration due to aging or shifting. Most manufacturers of thermocouples provide the installation instructions for installing their thermocouples in thermowells.

The depth of immersion of the thermocouple in the process is critical. It should not be confused with the insertion length of the thermowell, which is the distance from the free end of the thermowell to the inner edge of the threads on the thermowell, as indicated in *Figure 26*. Normally, an immersion depth of eight to ten times the thermowell diameter is recommended for an accurate measurement. However, if the thermocouple is installed in a liquid having high velocity, it may not need to be immersed as far.

4.2.4 Resistance Temperature Detectors

Resistance temperature detectors (RTDs) are devices which change their resistance in response to variations in temperature. RTDs can be used to measure temperature because there is a proportional relationship between changes in temperature and changes in resistance in the materials used to construct RTDs. As temperature increases, resistance increases proportionally, and vice versa. Any change in resistance can be recorded and converted to the representative temperature by using the appropriate graph or chart. The temperature can also be read directly on the scale of an indicating instrument attached to the RTD.

Generally, if the process temperature is less than 250°F and requires extreme accuracy, an RTD should be used because it has the ability to measure a temperature change as small as 0.00002°F.

RTDs are generally inserted directly into the process system by use of a protective well. *Figure 27* shows a three-wire RTD, as well as an RTD protective well.

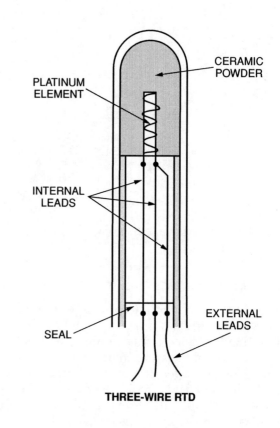

THREE-WIRE RTD

RTD PROTECTIVE WELL

Figure 27 ◆ Resistance Temperature Detector (RTD).

4.2.5 Thermistors

A thermistor is a semiconductor device whose resistance varies with variations in temperature, unlike thermocouples that produce an output proportional to the temperature change. Thermistors can have either a positive temperature coefficient, meaning the resistance increases with a rise in temperature; or a negative temperature coefficient, where the resistance decreases with a rise in temperature. Thermistors with negative temperature coefficients are normally used to measure temperature. *Figure 28* shows the schematic symbol for a thermistor and a resistance versus temperature chart for a negative temperature coefficient thermistor.

The resistance of thermistors is much greater than that of RTDs; in fact, it can be ten times or greater, with a very non-linear relationship between the temperature and the thermistor's resistance. Because of this non-linearity, thermistors are typically used over small ranges of temperature changes.

4.2.6 Non-Contact Pyrometers

Non-contact thermometers, also called *pyrometers*, are used to make temperature measurements of objects or materials without making direct physical contact with the item. They are commonly used to measure the temperature of moving objects, the temperature of an object or substance located in a hard-to-reach area, or when contact with an object or material can be hazardous.

Non-contact thermometers detect the thermal **radiations** emitted by all objects and materials. This radiated energy is emitted in the form of electromagnetic waves that encompass the IR spectrum portion (having wavelengths ranging from 0.75 to 1,000 microns) of the electromagnetic spectrum. The IR spectrum portion of the electromagnetic radiation spectrum is above that of radio frequency (RF) electromagnetic waves and below that of visible light waves. Using IR technology, non-contact thermometers convert the detected IR radiations from an object or material into a corresponding temperature readout shown on the instrument's display.

Non-contact thermometers are made in several styles and to measure different temperature ranges. *Figure 29* shows a handheld gun-type IR thermometer and a probe-type IR thermometer. The gun is operated by aiming it at the area on the object or material where the temperature is to be measured, pulling the trigger, then reading the temperature on the display. Most gun-type instruments have the capability to generate a laser beam

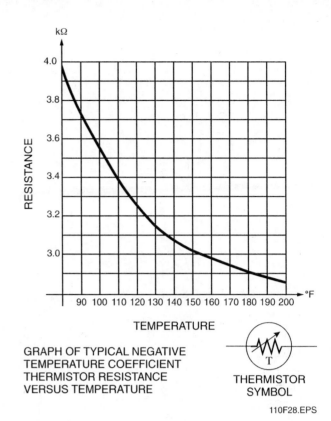

GRAPH OF TYPICAL NEGATIVE
TEMPERATURE COEFFICIENT
THERMISTOR RESISTANCE
VERSUS TEMPERATURE

THERMISTOR
SYMBOL

110F28.EPS

Figure 28 ◆ Thermistor resistance versus temperature chart.

used to pinpoint the center of the measurement target area. The area over which the temperature is measured depends on how far away the gun is held from the object being measured. The closer the gun is held toward the target area, the smaller the area over which the temperature is measured; the farther away, the larger the area over which the temperature is measured. The distance versus target area size being measured varies with different instruments. For this reason, operation of a non-contact thermometer should always be done in accordance with the manufacturer's instructions for the specific gun being used. Some IR temperature guns have the capability to generate two laser beams instead of one. This provides an indication for the exact diameter of the target area being measured. As shown in *Figure 29*, non-contact gun thermometers are commonly used to locate cracks or leaks in piping runs, as indicated by a heat loss that occurs adjacent to any crack or leak.

Non-contact IR thermometer probes are made that can be used with a compatible digital multimeter, or with a compatible J or K thermocouple-type digital thermometer. The probe is operated in the same way as a gun. However, a probe does not have the capability of generating a laser beam to help pinpoint the temperature measurement target area.

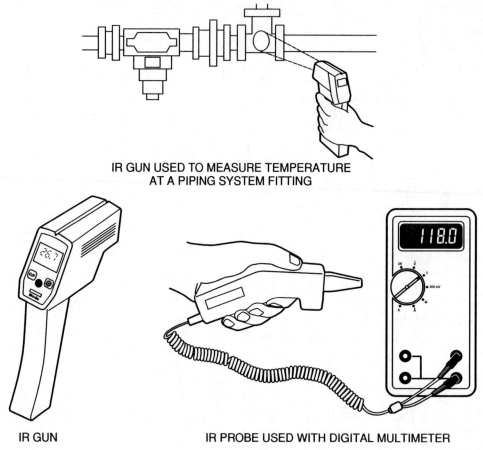

IR GUN USED TO MEASURE TEMPERATURE
AT A PIPING SYSTEM FITTING

IR GUN

IR PROBE USED WITH DIGITAL MULTIMETER

110F29.EPS

Figure 29 ◆ Handheld gun and probe-type non-contact thermometers.

5.0.0 ◆ LEVEL

Level is a measure of the height of a substance in a vessel, usually measured in feet or inches. Level is also often converted to a volumetric measurement.

5.1.0 Level Measurement and Pressure

In many industrial applications, pressure measurements are used to determine level.

5.1.1 Head Pressure

Head pressure is the pressure caused by a liquid on a given area at the base of a container. It is directly proportional to the height of the liquid in the container. For example, water exerts a pressure of 0.0360 psi per inch of height or 0.433 psi per foot of height.

5.1.2 Level Measurement and Specific Gravity

The relationship between pressure and level for substances other than water requires consideration of the **specific gravity** of the substance. The specific gravity of a solid or liquid substance is the ratio of the weight of that substance to the weight of an equal volume of water. Water has been assigned a specific gravity of 1 since it is the standard to which all other substances are compared.

One cubic inch of water weighs 0.0360 pounds, and 1 cubic inch of mercury weighs 0.4892 pounds. The ratio of the weight of 1 cubic inch of mercury to the weight of 1 cubic inch of water is 0.4892 divided by 0.0360. This equals 13.6 to 1. In other words, mercury is 13.6 times heavier than water. Therefore, mercury has a specific gravity of 13.6. In general, if a substance has a specific gravity of greater than 1, it is heavier than water. If a substance has a specific gravity of less than 1, it is lighter than water.

5.1.3 Level Calculations

The following formulas can be used to calculate the height of a volume of water:

$$H = \frac{P}{0.0360}$$

Where:

    H = height (in inches)
    P = indicated pressure (in psi)

or

$$H = \frac{P}{0.433}$$

Where:

    H = height (in feet)
    P = indicated pressure (in psi)

The following formulas can be used to calculate the height of a volume of liquid other than water:

$$H = \frac{P}{(0.0360 \times SG)}$$

Where:

    H = height (in inches)
    P = indicated pressure (in psi)
    SG = specific gravity

or

$$H = \frac{P}{(0.433 \times SG)}$$

Where:

    H = height (in feet)
    P = indicated pressure (in psi)
    SG = specific gravity

When using an inches-of-water scale to measure level, if the specific gravity of a substance is less than 1, the indicated level will be less than the actual level. If the specific gravity of a substance is greater than 1, the indicated level will be greater than the actual level. In many level-measuring systems, the transmitter calibration is compensated to account for the different specific gravity of the liquid being measured.

The following examples illustrate how level is calculated using head pressure measurements.

Example 1:

A gauge mounted at the bottom of an open tank of water indicates 10.8 psi. What is the level of water in the tank, expressed in inches and in feet?

Using the formulas:

$$H = \frac{P}{0.0360}$$

$$H = \frac{10.8}{0.0360}$$

$$H = 300 \text{ inches (of water)}$$

or

$$H = \frac{P}{0.433}$$

$$H = \frac{10.8}{0.433}$$

$$H = 24.942 \text{ feet (of water)}$$
$$\text{or } 25 \text{ feet rounded off}$$

If the liquid being measured is not water, the liquid's specific gravity must be incorporated in the calculation. If the liquid in the last example had been an oil with a specific gravity of 0.91, then the calculation would have been performed using the formulas:

$$H = \frac{P}{(0.0360 \times SG)}$$

$$H = \frac{10.8}{(0.0360 \times 0.91)}$$

$$H = 329.67 \text{ inches (of oil)}$$

or

$$H = \frac{P}{(0.433 \times SG)}$$

$$H = \frac{10.8}{(0.433 \times 0.91)}$$

$$H = 27.409 \text{ feet (of oil)}$$

The pressure reading is the same in both cases. However, since the oil is lighter than water, it takes a higher level of it to produce the same pressure reading.

Example 2:

A gauge mounted at the bottom of an open tank indicates a pressure of 22.4 psi. The tank contains a liquid with a specific gravity of 6.2. What is the level of the liquid in the tank?

Using the formula:

$$H = \frac{P}{(0.0360 \times SG)}$$

$$H = \frac{22.4}{(0.0360 \times 6.2)}$$

H = 100.36 inches (of the liquid)

Example 3:

A gauge mounted 2 feet from the bottom of an open tank indicates a pressure of 18.6 psi. The tank contains a liquid with a specific gravity of 4.3. What is the total level of the liquid in the tank?

Using the formula:

$$H = \frac{P}{(0.0360 \times SG)}$$

$$H = \frac{18.6}{0.1548}$$

$$H = \frac{120.16}{24 \text{ inches}}$$

H = 144.16 inches (of the liquid)

5.2.0 Direct Level Measurement Devices

Direct measurements of level are made using several different types of devices including dipsticks and lead lines, sight glasses, float-cable arrangements, and displacers. These devices often provide a direct visual indication of level.

5.2.1 Dipsticks and Lead Lines

The earliest and simplest form of level measurement used a rod or some type of stick with a calibrated scale to measure the depths of liquids. This method is still in use today. For example, a dipstick is used to check the oil level on a car. A dipstick level measurement system is shown in *Figure 30*.

Fuel quantities in underground gasoline storage tanks are often measured by using long poles with calibrated scales. Flexible lines fitted with end weights, called *chains* or *lead lines*, and steel tapes with special weights are also used for measuring the level and fuel quantities of large petroleum

storage tanks. Although this method of level measurement seems crude, it is accurate to about 0.1 percent with ranges up to about 20 feet. This is a higher accuracy than can be achieved with almost any other method of level measurement.

Even though these methods are accurate in some applications, there are some disadvantages associated with them. There cannot be a continuous representation of the process measurement using a dipstick or lead line. Another limitation is the inability to accurately and easily measure level in pressurized vessels.

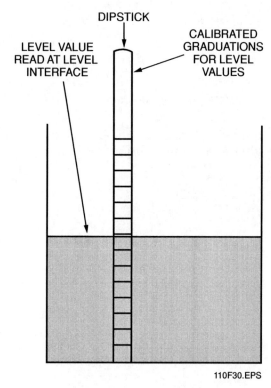

Figure 30 ◆ Dipstick level measurement.

5.2.2 Sight Glasses

Another direct method of determining level uses a sight glass, also called a gauge glass, as shown in *Figure 31*. A sight glass is simply a transparent tube mounted with a common connection to the vessel. As the liquid level in the vessel goes up or down, the level in the sight glass changes accordingly. This gives a true representation of the level.

5.2.3 Float and Cable Arrangements

Float devices are used to measure level directly. In a float-cable device, the float is connected to a pulley by a chain or a flexible cable. The rotating portion of the pulley is connected to an indicator. A float and cable level arrangement is shown in *Figure 32*.

As the float moves upward, the counterweight keeps the cable tight and positions the indicator along a circular scale. When chains are used to connect the float to the pulley, a sprocket on the pulley mates with the chain links. If flat metallic tape is used, metal studs on a rotation drum mate with holes in the tape.

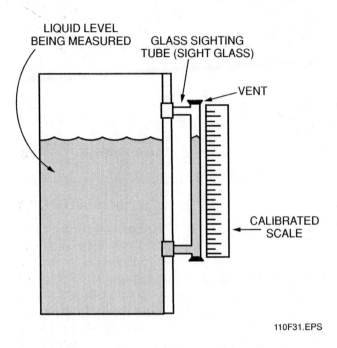

110F31.EPS

Figure 31 ◆ Sight glass level measurement.

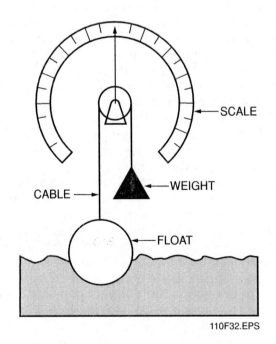

110F32.EPS

Figure 32 ◆ Float and cable level arrangement.

5.2.4 *Displacers*

An increasing level of liquid will exert a pressure upon an object held stationary with respect to the rising liquid level. Similarly, a decreasing liquid level will decrease the pressure being applied to the object. This is the principle of operation for a displacer type of level measurement instrument. A displacer and torque tube measurement device is shown in *Figure 33*.

A torque tube displacer is commonly used in industrial applications. The operation involves the raising and lowering of the liquid inside a standpipe where the displacer is suspended. As the level of the liquid inside the standpipe increases, the displacer will have an upward pressure applied to it and will rise very slightly. The amount of movement of the displacer is extremely small (invisible to the human eye). There is a torque tube attached to the displacer via a torque tube lever. The upward force on the displacer creates a torque via the attached lever which causes the torque tube to twist. The motion of the torque tube causes the rod attached to it to rotate. The rod is, in turn, attached to an indicator which represents the movement of the displacer and torque tube as a change in level.

5.3.0 Indirect Level Measurement Devices

In addition to direct level measurement devices, there are a variety of devices which measure level indirectly by measuring related variables.

5.3.1 *Hydrostatic Head Devices*

Level can be accurately measured by determining the hydrostatic head pressure produced by the fluid and converting the pressure measurement into its corresponding level. Measuring level in this manner is really measuring pressure and then converting that pressure to a level. These level calculations were performed earlier in this training module.

When a pressure transmitter or gauge is mounted at the bottom of a tank, then the pressure applied to the transmitter is proportional to level of the liquid inside the tank. In many cases, the output of the transmitter is connected to a device which automatically calculates the level for the measured pressure. In other cases, a pressure gauge with an indicator that is calibrated in level units instead of pressure units is used.

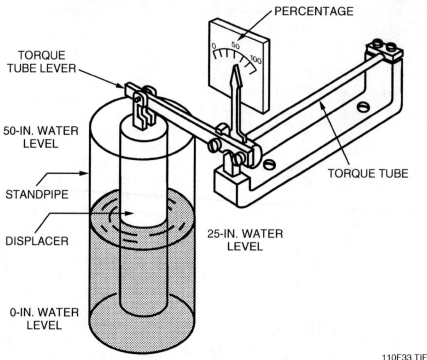

PERCENTAGE

TORQUE
TUBE LEVER

50-IN. WATER
LEVEL

STANDPIPE

DISPLACER

25-IN. WATER
LEVEL

0-IN. WATER
LEVEL

TORQUE TUBE

110F33.TIF

Figure 33 ◆ Displacer and torque tube for open-tank level measurement.

5.3.2 Bubbler System

A bubbler system uses hydrostatic head pressure to measure level. A bubbler system can be used with open or closed tanks. In an open tank, the low-pressure connection on the differential pressure transmitter measures the atmospheric pressure against pressure exerted by the liquid in the tank. The high-pressure connection measures the air pressure required to overcome the pressure of the liquid in the tank.

In a closed tank (*Figure 34*), the low-pressure connection on the differential pressure transmitter measures the pressure exerted on the liquid by the air in the top of the tank. The high-pressure connection measures the air pressure required to overcome the pressure of the liquid in the tank or the backpressure on the system.

In a closed tank installation, as shown in *Figure 34*, the low-pressure connection line is empty and is called a *dry leg* when the process vapors inside the tank are non-corrosive, non-plugging, with very low condensation factors. In these installations, the transmitter must be located above the highest level of the tank to prevent process liquid in the tank from entering the low-pressure line. It is important to keep the dry leg dry because any accumulation of liquid or condensate would cause error in the reading.

When the process vapors are corrosive or unstable, or the transmitter must be mounted at a lower level, this low-pressure connection line should be filled with an inert liquid prior to cali-brating, or *zeroing*, the transmitter's output. The low-pressure line is then referred to as a *wet leg*. Any change in the volume of liquid in the wet leg will cause error in the transmitter and the transmitter must then be re-calibrated to compensate for this change. It is often desirable to install a sight glass indicator at the top of the wet leg to permit visual inspection of the liquid.

One common problem faced by instrumentation technicians and maintenance personnel regarding bubbler systems is that pinholes often develop in the bubbler tubes caused by corrosive vapors or liquids (refer to *Figure 34*). Notice that any air that escapes from the bubbler tube from accidental holes located higher than the end of the tube will result in erroneous readings because the back pressure on the high-pressure side of the transformer will decrease. The height of the accidental hole on the bubbler tube is inversely proportional to the output of the level transmitter. In other words, the higher the hole on the tube, the lower the level indication. If the hole should occur above the liquid level, the transmitter would indicate a level of zero because both the high- and low-pressure connections will be in the same airspace or gap above the liquid.

In both systems, the differential pressure transmitter measures the difference between the two pressures. This difference in pressure is proportional to the level of the liquid in the tank and can be shown on a level indicator.

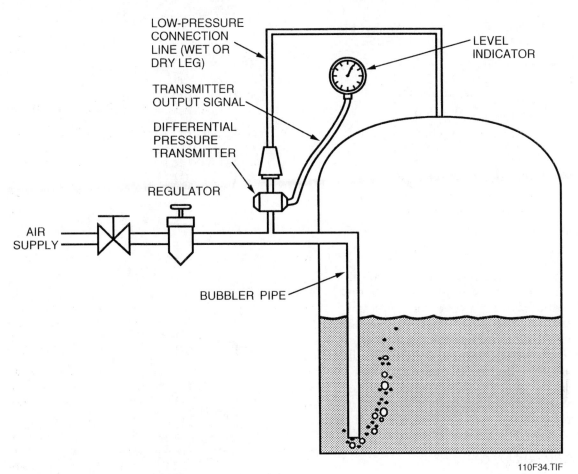

LOW-PRESSURE CONNECTION LINE (WET OR DRY LEG)

LEVEL INDICATOR

TRANSMITTER OUTPUT SIGNAL

DIFFERENTIAL PRESSURE TRANSMITTER

REGULATOR

AIR SUPPLY

BUBBLER PIPE

110F34.TIF

Figure 34 ◆ Bubbler system for level measurement.

5.3.3 Magnetic Float Devices

Measuring the levels of caustic liquids and acids is often difficult. A system using highly corrosion-resistant materials could cost too much to be practical. To overcome this, a magnetic float system is often used. In a magnetic float system, only the float itself comes into contact with the corrosive liquid. The float is a magnetic material coated with a protective, corrosion-resistant material. The float and a movable indicator are indirectly coupled by the magnetic field produced by the magnet in the float.

This type of magnetic float arrangement can also be used to operate position-sensitive switches connected to the float. In this configuration, the system can be used for measurement and control. *Figure 35* shows a magnetic float system.

5.3.4 Conductance Devices

Conductance is a measure of the ability of a material to conduct electricity. This electrical property can be used to measure level in a conductance probe level measurement system. The basic components of this system are a high-level probe, a

low-level probe, a ground lead, a control unit which houses relays, and control circuit wiring. A conductance level measurement device is shown in *Figure 36*.

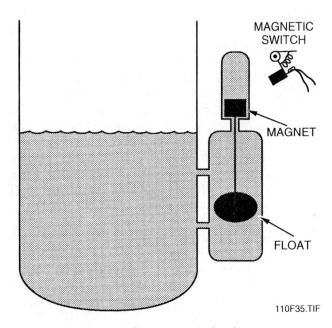

MAGNETIC SWITCH

MAGNET

FLOAT

110F35.TIF

Figure 35 ◆ Magnetic float system for level measurement.

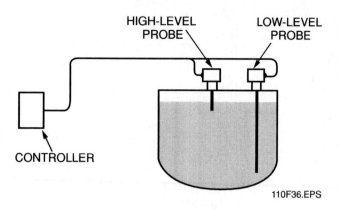

Figure 36 ◆ Conductance probe level measurement.

This type of system is basically either an on/off control circuit or an alarm circuit. As the level increases above the low-level probe, the low-level alarm will clear. The signal from the low-level probe can also be used to change the position of a control valve. If the level continues to rise, it will eventually contact the high-level probe and energize the high-level contacts. This contact closure can be used to activate a high-level alarm or to actuate a control valve.

5.3.5 Capacitance Devices

Capacitance is the ability to store electrical energy in the form of an electrostatic field. This electrical property can be used to measure level in a capacitance probe level measurement system. Capacitance level probes are on/off or go/no-go devices. The basic components of this type of system are probes, dielectric, and a power source.

Figure 37 illustrates two types of capacitance installations: one in a conductive liquid and the other in a non-conductive liquid. Notice that the probe is insulated from the process in the conductive liquid, while in the non-conductive liquid the only insulator required is between the probe and the top of the tank. The outside wires or leads are connected to the probe and the tank, respectively. Capacitance probes are susceptible to corrosive environments and must be kept relatively clean of scale and other types of build-ups on their surface. Increases in probe or tank-wall buildup result in increased resistance between the probe and the tank.

The liquid in the system acts as the dielectric between the probes. The probes act as the plates of a capacitor. As the level increases, the resistance between the probes will decrease. This decrease in resistance results in an increased current flow to the indicating device.

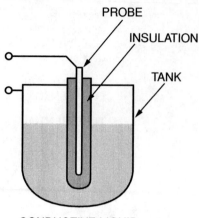

CONDUCTIVE LIQUID

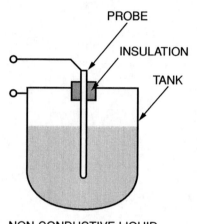

NON-CONDUCTIVE LIQUID

110F37.EPS

Figure 37 ◆ Capacitance probe level measurement.

5.4.0 Special Level Measurement Instruments

Several types of special level measurement instruments are used in applications where it is not appropriate for the sensor to contact the process material. Some special level measurement instruments include ultrasonic level-sensing devices and electrical load cells.

5.4.1 Ultrasonic Level Measurement

A typical ultrasonic level measurement system (*Figure 38*) consists of an ultrasonic transmitter/receiver, an electronic unit, and a level indicator installed on a vessel. The transmitter emits ultrasonic waves into the tank to the surface of the material where the level is being measured. The length of the time interval between the transmission of the ultrasonic wave and its return to the receiver is directly proportional to the distance between the transmitter/receiver and the material. As the level rises, the time interval decreases. The ultrasonic signal is converted into an electrical signal which represents the level in the vessel. The signal is sent to a level indicator and also may be used to operate recorders, controllers, alarms, or other level control equipment.

Solids consisting of large hard particles are good reflectors and are frequently measured using ultrasonic devices. It is common to use ultrasonic devices to measure the thickness or thinness of solid objects or levels of solid materials in tanks or silos, such as grain or other agricultural products. Materials such as foam, loose dirt, or dust or mist in a vapor space are poor reflectors because they have a tendency to absorb the ultrasonic pulse signal.

Normal operation for use of sonic or ultrasonic devices for measurement is to pulsate the signal from the transmitter in on/off cycles to achieve the ideal reflection back to the receiver.

5.4.2 Electric Load Cells

Electric load cells are normally made up of a number of resistance strain gauges. Strain gauges provide a measurable electrical output. This measurable electrical output is proportional to the stress applied by the weight of the load on the load cells. As the pressure (weight) on the load cells changes,

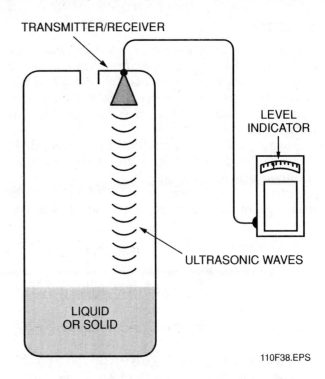

110F38.EPS

Figure 38 ◆ Ultrasonic level measurement.

the electrical resistances of the strain gauges change. The output signal can be calibrated to indicate units of weight.

Summary

The precise measurement of process variables is essential to the proper operation and control of most types of process systems. This module introduced four of the process variables most frequently measured: flow, pressure, level, and temperature.

Several types of devices used to measure flow, pressure, level, and temperature were described and their principles of operation explained. These measuring instruments are covered in detail in later modules in the Instrumentation curriculum.

The knowledge and skills covered in this module provide basic and fundamental competencies required to understand flow, pressure, level, and temperature systems. In your day-to-day work activities, take the time to practice the skills learned in this module. It takes a lot of practice, study, and on-the-job experience to develop the skills needed to be expert in working with process variables, measurement devices, and other control equipment.

Review Questions

1. An absolute pressure gauge reads 56.5 psia. If atmospheric pressure is 14.7 psi, the gauge pressure (psig) reading is _____.
   a. 41.8 psig
   b. 71.2 psig
   c. 41.8 psia
   d. 71.2 psia

2. A(n) _____ is used to measure pressure.
   a. orifice plate
   b. thermocouple
   c. bellows
   d. target meter

3. The _____ flow profile is hard to predict because it oscillates.
   a. transitional
   b. laminar
   c. turbulent
   d. ultrasonic

4. The _____ is commonly used to measure flow.
   a. manometer
   b. Bourdon tube
   c. venturi tube
   d. sight glass

5. The _____ uses a float in a tapered tube to indicate flow.
   a. venturi tube
   b. rotameter
   c. DP meter
   d. orifice plate

6. On the _____ temperature scale, the boiling point of water is 100° and the freezing point of water is 0°.
   a. Fahrenheit
   b. Celsius
   c. Rankine
   d. Kelvin

7. A temperature reading of 125°C equals _____ °F.
   a. 52
   b. 78
   c. 156
   d. 257

8. The colors of the conductors of a Type J thermocouple are _____.
   a. yellow and red
   b. blue and red
   c. white and blue
   d. white and red

9. The _____ uses a change in voltage to measure temperature.
   a. RTD
   b. bimetallic thermometer
   c. fluid thermometer
   d. thermocouple

10. A pressure gauge mounted at the bottom of an open tank of water indicates 17 psig. The level of water in the tank is _____.
    a. 472.222 inches
    b. 0.612 inches
    c. 356.120 inches
    d. 74.210 inches

Trade Terms Introduced in This Module

Differential pressure: The difference between two related pressures.

Flow: The actual volume of fluid that passes a given point per unit of time.

Fluid: A substance (as a liquid or gas) tending to flow or conform to the outline of its container.

Head pressure: The pressure of a liquid or gas on a given area at the base of a container. It is directly proportional to the height of the liquid in the container.

Heat: The addition of energy to a substance which causes it to rise in temperature.

Level: A measure of the height of a substance. A level measurement is often and easily converted to a volumetric measurement.

Radiation: A method of heat transfer in which heat is transferred across open space.

Specific gravity: The ratio of the weight of that substance to the weight of an equal volume of water at 60°F.

Temperature: The degree of hotness or coldness of a substance, measured on a definite scale.

Additional Resources

This module is intended to present thorough resources for task training. The following reference works are suggested for further study. These are optional materials for continued education rather than for task training.

Industrial Pressure, Level & Density Measurement, 1995. Donald R. Gillum. Research Triangle Park, NC: Instrument Society of America.

Instrument Engineers' Handbook, Volume 1: Process Measurement, 1995. Bela G. Liptak. Boca Raton, FL: CRC Press.

Instrument Engineers' Handbook, Volume 2: Process Control, 1995. Bela G. Liptak. Boca Raton, FL: CRC Press.

Process Control Systems, 1996. F. Greg Shinskey. New York, NY: McGraw-Hill Professional Publishing.

Purdy's Instrument Handbook. 1996. Ralph G. Dewey. Deer Park, TX: Good News Balloons.

Figure Credits

Dwyer Instruments, Inc.   110F03, 110F04, 110F05

NCCER CRAFT TRAINING USER UPDATES

The NCCER makes every effort to keep these textbooks up-to-date and free of technical errors. We appreciate your help in this process. If you have an idea for improving this textbook, or if you find an error, a typographical mistake, or an inaccuracy in the NCCER's Craft Training textbooks, please write us, using this form or a photocopy. Be sure to include the exact module number, page number, a detailed description, and the correction, if applicable. Your input will be brought to the attention of the Technical Review Committee. Thank you for your assistance.

Instructors – If you found that additional materials were necessary in order to teach this module effectively, please let us know so that we may include them in the Equipment and Materials list in the Instructor's Guide.

Write: Curriculum Revision and Development Department
National Center for Construction Education and Research
P.O. Box 141104, Gainesville, FL 32614-1104

Fax: 352-334-0932

E-mail: curriculum@nccer.org

Craft _____ Module Name _____

Copyright Date _____ Module Number _____ Page Number(s) _____

Description _____

_____

_____

_____

(Optional) Correction _____

_____

_____

(Optional) Your Name and Address _____

_____

_____

Tubing

COURSE MAP

This course map shows all of the modules in the first level of the Instrumentation curriculum. The suggested training order begins at the bottom and proceeds up. Skill levels increase as you advance on the course map. The local Training Program Sponsor may adjust the training order.

INSTRUMENTATION LEVEL ONE

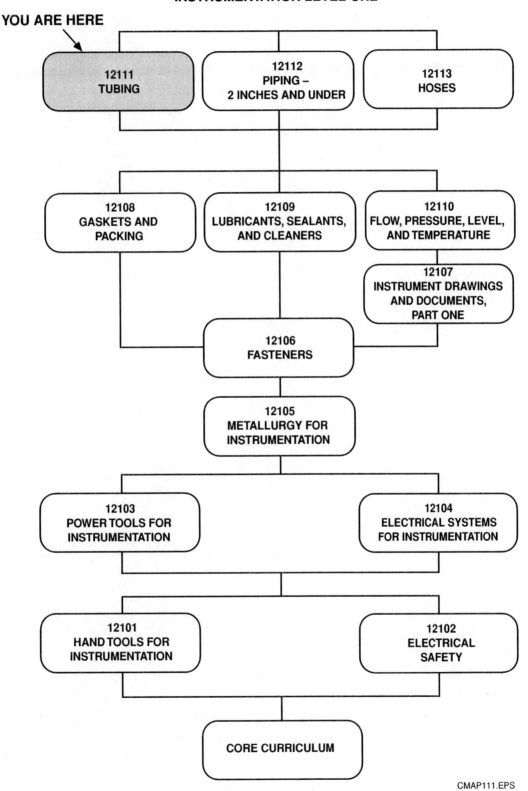

YOU ARE HERE

12111 TUBING

12112 PIPING – 2 INCHES AND UNDER

12113 HOSES

12108 GASKETS AND PACKING

12109 LUBRICANTS, SEALANTS, AND CLEANERS

12110 FLOW, PRESSURE, LEVEL, AND TEMPERATURE

12107 INSTRUMENT DRAWINGS AND DOCUMENTS, PART ONE

12106 FASTENERS

12105 METALLURGY FOR INSTRUMENTATION

12103 POWER TOOLS FOR INSTRUMENTATION

12104 ELECTRICAL SYSTEMS FOR INSTRUMENTATION

12101 HAND TOOLS FOR INSTRUMENTATION

12102 ELECTRICAL SAFETY

CORE CURRICULUM

CMAP111.EPS

Figures

Tables

Tubing

OBJECTIVES

When you have completed this module, you will be able to do the following:

1. Identify the different kinds of tubing and describe the properties and common uses for each kind.

2. Explain the purpose for tubing standards and specifications.

3. Properly handle and store tubing.

4. Cut tubing using the proper tools, cutting methods, and safety procedures.

5. Bend tubing using the proper tools, bending methods, and safety procedures.

6. Identify and select proper tubing fittings for selected instrumentation applications.

7. Flare tubing using the proper tools, flaring methods, and safety procedures.

Prerequisites

Before you begin this module, it is recommended that you successfully complete the following modules: Core Curriculum; Instrumentation Level One, Modules 12101 through 12110.

Required Trainee Materials

1. Paper and pencil
2. Appropriate personal protective equipment

1.0.0 ◆ INTRODUCTION

Piping and tubing systems are used in plants and other facilities to perform a number of functions, such as:

- Carrying process fluids, steam, water, and hydraulic fluids
- Carrying pneumatic control signals, lubricating oil, and compressed air
- Connecting instruments to process piping

The terms *piping* and *tubing* are sometimes used to mean the same thing. However, tubing is normally considered to be more flexible than piping and has thinner walls. Since tubing is not as hard as piping, it is easier to bend. Tubing installations usually require fewer **fittings** than a comparable pipe installation because bends can be made. *Figure 1* shows how bends in a typical tubing run can eliminate several fittings that would be necessary if piping were used for the same installation.

While there are some similarities in working with piping and tubing, there are special skills and different tools required for each. This module covers basic information and work practices for tubing systems. Other modules in your training program will focus on more advanced tubing skills and competencies related to piping systems.

Depending on the type of system, tubing may be used to carry process fluids. However, in instrument work, tubing is primarily used to connect instruments to process piping, to carry pneumatic signals between instruments, and to supply air to power pneumatic instruments.

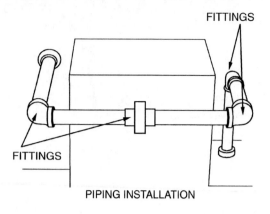

FITTINGS

FITTINGS

PIPING INSTALLATION

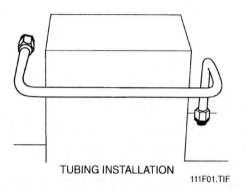

TUBING INSTALLATION

111F01.TIF

Figure 1 ◆ Tubing versus piping installation.

Figure 2 shows tubing installed in a typical instrument system. In several types of applications, tubing has advantages over piping:

- Its flexibility allows tubing to be bent to fit into tight spaces.
- Because tubing has considerable give, it can absorb shock and vibration that occur in some systems, which can damage components or cause leaks.

- Since tubing may be bent, fewer fittings are needed. Using tubing reduces installation time, decreases the number of potential places for leaks, and generally results in a more efficient installation.
- The types of materials used in tubing may be more compatible to certain process or environmental conditions and less likely to corrode.
- Since hard tubing connections are usually not threaded like pipe, wall thickness is not reduced and installation time is often decreased.
- Soft tubing can be joined using **flare** or **compression** fittings which are strong, yet easy and quick to install.
- Since the inside of tubing is usually smoother than the inside of piping, flow through the tubing may be more even, with less turbulence.

> **NOTE**
>
> The information given in this module is general in nature. When selecting tubing, it is important to make sure that your selection is compatible with the process or application where it is to be used. When in doubt, always consult the manufacturer.

Normally, the type of tubing selected depends on one or more of the following:

- System operating temperatures
- System operating pressures
- The type of fluid or other media the system or equipment handles
- The environment where it is to be installed

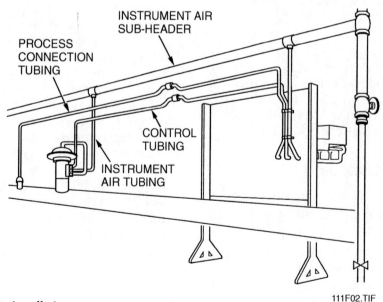

INSTRUMENT AIR SUB-HEADER

PROCESS CONNECTION TUBING

CONTROL TUBING

INSTRUMENT AIR TUBING

111F02.TIF

Figure 2 ◆ A typical tubing installation.

2.0.0 ◆ SIZES AND TYPES OF TUBING

It is important to use the proper size and type of tubing for specific applications. The engineering specifications, piping specifications, installation detail drawings, and other information for a project usually tell you what size and type of tubing to use. However, you must be able to identify and verify the size and type of the tubing once you know the requirements. Tubing is selected for specific applications according to a number of different factors, such as pressure and temperature conditions, corrosiveness of the environment, vibration in the system, system flow requirements, compatibility with the process fluids, and cost.

2.1.0 General Sizing Measurements for Tubing

Tubing is generally sized according to its outside diameter (O.D.) and wall thickness. The O.D. is normally expressed in fractions of an inch, such as ¼ inch, ⅜ inch, or ½ inch. The O.D. of most types of tubing ranges from ¹⁄₁₆ inch to 2 inches. The wall thickness of tubing is usually expressed in decimal units to the thousandth of an inch, such as .035 inch or .068 inch. The normal range of wall thickness for tubing is .010 inch to .188 inch. *Figure 3* shows the O.D., wall thickness, and inside diameter (I.D.) dimensions for tubing.

Normally, the manufacturer will print or stamp the O.D. and wall thickness on the tubing. However, if you need to measure the O.D. of tubing, you can use a rule, outside caliper, or vernier caliper as shown in *Figure 4*.

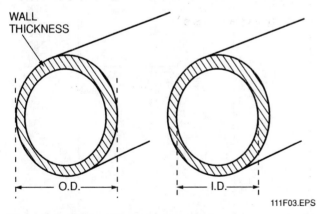

Figure 3 ◆ Tubing size measurements.

NOTE

When using a rule to measure the O.D. of tubing, remember to measure the diameter across the center of the tubing.

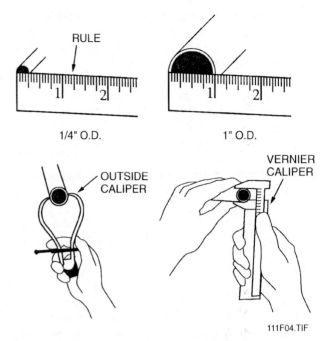

Figure 4 ◆ Measuring outside diameter of tubing.

While most instrument tubing in the United States is measured in inches and fractions of an inch, sometimes tubing sizes will be marked in metric units, measured as millimeters. If you are working with metric-sized tubing, remember to use a metric rule or other metric measuring tools to get your measurements.

Another common measurement for instrument tubing is the inside diameter (I.D.) of the tubing. As shown in *Figure 3*, this is the distance across the middle of the hole in the tubing from an inside wall to the opposite inside wall. The inside diameter of any tube is equal to the outside diameter minus twice the wall thickness. For example, tubing with a ½ inch O.D. and a wall thickness of .049 inch would have an I.D. of .402 inches, as calculated here.

Tubing I.D. = O.D. − (2 × wall thickness)

.402 = .500 − (2 × .049)

For any given O.D. of tubing, the I.D. decreases as the wall thickness increases. In other words, as the wall of the tube gets thicker, the hole in the middle gets smaller. *Table 1* shows typical O.D. sizes of tubing and their wall thicknesses and corresponding I.D.s.

2.2.0 Tubing Materials

Tubing is made from a wide variety of materials including different types of metals and poly or plastics. Each material has certain characteristics that make it desirable for particular applications.

Poly (plastic tubing) is generally considered to be less expensive than metal tubing, easier to install, and easier to bend and reshape. However, it has limitations regarding its strength, compatibility to certain process fluids, and ability to withstand certain temperatures and pressures.

Metal tubing comes in two general types, welded and seamless. Welded tubing is made by rolling flat strips of metal and then forming the metal into a tube. The seam is then welded. While the welded seam may not be visible on the outside of the tubing, it can usually be seen on the inside surface of the tubing.

Seamless metal tubing is made by passing a cylinder of metal through a die which cuts out the inside of the tube. This process is called *extruding*. Usually seamless tubing is **drawn** through additional die sets to get the proper wall thickness and to meet other specifications for the tubing.

Metal tubing may also be annealed. Annealing is a process in which the metal is reheated, then slowly allowed to cool. Annealing makes the metal softer and less brittle, allowing for easier bending and flaring.

Metal tubing comes in straight lengths (normally 20 feet). Random lengths can be obtained from 12 feet to 40 feet. Some types of tubing also come in rolls or coils, usually ranging from 50 feet to 100 feet.

The following describes materials used for tubing and some of the characteristics of the materials.

2.2.1 Copper Tubing

Copper is one of the most widely used metals for making tubing. Copper tubing is identified by its color when new. The color of untarnished copper is reddish-brown, similar to the color of a new penny. As it ages, copper tarnishes and becomes dull and dark in color. When you are not sure if the tubing material is copper, polish a small area to bring back the original color.

Copper tubing is often used in instrumentation pneumatic systems because it resists rust that could contaminate the air running through the tubing. It is lighter and easier to use than stainless steel, and it can be easily bent to form bends and angles. It holds up well in most environments, and it is strong enough to handle loads that would rupture plastic tubing. Copper tubing is usually used in systems where the temperature and pressure conditions are not extreme.

A disadvantage of copper tubing is that it is more costly than some other types of tubing. It also expands more than some other types, which can be a disadvantage in certain applications.

Table 1 Tubing Sizes

TUBE (IN.)	O.D. (IN.)	WALL THICKNESS (IN.)	TUBE I.D. (IN.)
1/16	.062	.010	.042
		.015	.032
		.020	.022
1/8	.125	.028	.069
		.035	.055
3/16	.187	.028	.131
		.035	.117
		.049	.089
1/4	.250	.028	.194
		.035	.180
		.049	.152
		.065	.120
5/16	.312	.035	.242
		.049	.214
		.065	.182
3/8	.375	.035	.305
		.049	.277
		.065	.245
1/2	.500	.035	.430
		.049	.402
		.065	.370
		.083	.334
5/8	.625	.049	.527
		.065	.495
		.083	.459
		.095	.435
3/4	.750	.049	.652
		.065	.620
		.083	.584
		.095	.560
		.109	.532
7/8	.875	.049	.777
		.065	.745
		.083	.709
		.095	.685
		.109	.657
1	1.000	.065	.870
		.083	.834
		.095	.810
		.109	.782
		.120	.760
1 1/4	1.250	.083	1.084
		.095	1.060
		.109	1.032
		.120	1.010
		.134	.982
		.056	.938
1 1/2	1.500	.095	1.310
		.109	1.282
		.120	1.260
		.134	1.232
		.156	1.188
		.188	1.124
2	2.000	.109	1.782
		.120	1.760
		.134	1.732
		.156	1.688
		.188	1.624

111T01.EPS

Copper tubing also may not be suitable for systems that are exposed to extremely corrosive substances.

Copper tubing is sometimes covered with PVC to resist attack by chemicals. PVC-covered copper tubing has all of the advantages of regular copper tubing with the added feature of being resistant to chemicals.

One way to identify copper tubing is by standard wall thicknesses designated by the American Society for Testing of Materials (ASTM). Grades of copper tubing are given in letters. Each grade represents a series of sizes with different wall thicknesses. The inside diameters depend on tubing size and wall thickness. A color code is also used for instant recognition on the job. The standard grades are:

- K – Heavy grade, usually hard-drawn tubing (*green*)

- L – Medium grade (*blue*)

- M – Light grade (*red*)

- DWV – Used for drains, waste lines, and vents (*yellow*)

Straight lengths of hard copper tubing are marked by a color-coded band printed along the tubing. Soft copper tubing that comes in rolls is not color coded on the tubing. The color codes of soft copper tubing are usually marked on the cartons and shipping tags.

Copper tubing used in air conditioning and refrigeration systems is called ACR tubing. It is designated by its actual outside diameter. ACR copper tubing is used with special fittings for connections, repairs, and alterations in air conditioning and refrigeration installations.

Copper tubing is also identified by its degree of hardness. Hard (drawn) copper tubing is more difficult to bend and cannot be flared without cracking. Hard copper tubing comes in straight sections only, not in rolls. Soft (annealed) copper tubing can be easily bent and flared. Soft copper tubing comes in both straight sections and rolls. Copper tubing types K, L, and M are available as either hard or soft. Type DWV is available only as hard tubing.

2.2.2 Steel Tubing

Steel is an alloy that contains iron plus a small amount of carbon. While other metals and non-metals are also added to make steel, the presence of iron and carbon defines the metal as steel. The higher the carbon content, the harder and stronger the steel. A black coating of iron oxide forms on the hot-rolled steel after it is rolled. This black color helps identify steel tubing. Some steel tub-

ing is dipped into a solution of molten zinc to give it better corrosion-resisting qualities. This type of steel tubing is called *galvanized steel tubing*. Galvanized steel tubing has a shiny silver color.

Steel tubing can be cold or hot rolled to its finished size. Where precise tubing I.D. wall thickness dimensions are required, cold-rolled tubing is used rather than the less precise hot-rolled steel tubing. Steel tubing is used in noncorrosive areas. It is very strong and is often used in high-pressure hydraulic systems. It also works well in other high-pressure and high-temperature applications.

Steel tubing is less brittle than stainless steel tubing. Therefore, it is often used in systems that have a lot of vibration, since it will give and absorb the vibration. Steel tubing has great strength, yet it can be bent, flared, flattened, welded, and threaded to make turns and joints.

2.2.3 Stainless Steel Tubing

Stainless steel is a steel alloy that contains at least 12 percent chromium by weight. Stainless steel tubing is stiffer and stronger than copper tubing. It is used to handle many types of corrosive fluids. It performs well in high-pressure and high-temperature applications.

Stainless steel tubing is designated by a number that refers to the alloy content of the metal. Two common types of stainless steel tubing used in instrument work are identified by the numbers 304 and 316. They each contain chromium and nickel but not manganese. The stainless steel tubing size, wall thickness, and compositional alloys determine the temperature and pressure ranges the tubing can withstand.

Even though stainless steel tubing is more expensive than some other tubing materials, it has several important qualities that make it practical for specific applications. Stainless steel is corrosion resistant and can easily be kept sterile to prevent contamination. For this reason, it is often used in pharmaceutical plants, food processing plants, and dairy plants.

Stainless steel tubing used in instrument work normally ranges in size from ⅛ inch to 2 inches. It is available in different wall thicknesses.

2.2.4 Aluminum Tubing

Aluminum is made from bauxite ore that contains aluminum oxide, iron, and silicon. Aluminum tubing has several advantages over other types of metal tubing for specific applications. It is softer, lighter in weight, and more flexible than most other metal tubing. It has a dull silver color and can be cut easily with a tubing shear or tube cutter.

Aluminum tubing resists corrosion and is easy to cut and shape. Aluminum tubing breaks easily and tends to oxidize at the fittings, which may cause them to leak.

Aluminum tubing is often used where sanitary conditions are required, since it is easy to clean and sterilize. It is also used in many low-temperature applications to carry liquefied gases, since its strength increases as temperature decreases.

2.2.5 Monel® Tubing

Monel® is the trade name that International Nickel Corporation uses for its various nickel-copper alloys. Monel® tubing is highly resistant to corrosion from the atmosphere. It also has good resistance to salt water, lye, sulfuric acid, most foods, and many chemicals. Monel® tubing is similar to stainless steel in appearance, brittleness, and other properties. It is often used where high strength and **ductility** are required.

2.2.6 Inconel® Tubing

Inconel® is a trade name that International Nickel Corporation uses for its various nickel-iron-chromium alloys. Inconel® tubing is often used in high-temperature applications since it remains strong at very high temperatures in normal atmosphere.

Inconel® shows good resistance to acidic foods, such as fruit juices, and is often used in food processing plants. Inconel® is also used in pharmaceutical applications because it does not contaminate the contents of the tubing system. Additionally, Inconel® tubing is frequently used to convey dry chlorine gas, which is highly corrosive.

2.2.7 Hastelloy® Tubing

Hastelloy® is a trade name that Union Carbide Corporation uses for its various nickel-based alloys. Hastelloy® tubing contains nickel plus molybdenum or silicon. It is highly resistant to corrosion, especially corrosion by hot concentrated acids or **liquors**. Hastelloy® tubing is often used in the chemical processing industry to convey highly corrosive materials, such as boiling sulfuric acid.

2.2.8 Poly Tubing

Poly (plastic) tubing is a broad category of tubing that covers a variety of materials, each with its own specific properties. Most instrument tubing is made from plastic resins called thermoplastics.

Tubing made from thermoplastics can be easily bent and reshaped. Poly tubing is used primarily in pneumatic control and junction boxes or in pneumatic control panels. Color-coded poly tubing is often used in pneumatic systems to show the difference between individual circuits. Black tubing is recommended when the tubing is exposed to sunlight or fluorescent light since it is less likely to deteriorate from the effects of the light.

> **NOTE**
> Black tubing can be color-coded with colored stripes.

Poly tubing is generally considered easier to install than metal tubing since it does not require bending, flaring, or deburring. It is lightweight, pliable, and resistant to most chemicals and moisture. It is used in processes that would corrode metal tubing, such as those involving chlorine and hydrochloric acid. Poly tubing does have limitations, including its inability to withstand high pressures and temperatures.

> **NOTE**
> Never use poly tubing unless it is specifically called for in the project specifications.

A commonly used type of poly tubing is polyvinyl chloride (PVC) tubing. Like most other types of poly tubing, PVC tubing is flexible. It can be bent without using a bending tool. It is easily cut with snips, **tubing cutters**, or a pocketknife. It is often used inside pneumatic control panels where there is little chance of it being cut or broken. PVC tubing comes in a variety of colors, sizes, and wall thicknesses, including:

- *Polyethylene (PE) tubing* – Polyethylene tubing is an inexpensive, flexible tubing that is widely used in laboratories, instrument air lines, and other applications where resistance to corrosion is important.
- *Polypropylene tubing* – Polypropylene tubing is a flexible tubing that is much stronger than polyethylene and has good corrosion resistance. It can withstand higher pressures and temperatures than most other types of poly tubing.
- *Teflon® tubing* – Teflon® (a trademark of the DuPont Company) tubing is made of a material that is much like the coating used on kitchen pots and pans to keep food from sticking.

Teflon® creates little resistance to fluid flow, is highly resistant to most chemical attacks, and can be used in moderately high temperature applications. Teflon® tubing is flexible, white, and soft.

- *Tygon® tubing* – Tygon® tubing is very soft, plasticized PVC tubing, often referred to as *surgical tubing*. It is extremely flexible, corrosion resistant, and clear or milky white in color. It is used in many laboratory, medical, food, and pharmaceutical applications. Tygon® tubing is often used when flexibility or transparency is an important consideration. Tygon® tubing is used in moderate temperature and pressure conditions.

- *Nylon tubing* – Nylon tubing is more rigid than other types of poly tubing. Nylon tubing can be used in higher temperature applications than most other types of plastic tubing. Nylon tubing doesn't require the use of special inserts for fittings.

> **NOTE**
> Poly tubing can use the same type of compression fittings as used with copper tubing. However, an insert should be used in the end of the poly tubing that is going to receive the fitting in order to prevent collapsing or crimping of the tubing. This is covered in detail later in this module. Be careful not to overtighten fittings used on poly tubing.

2.3.0 Tubing Standards and Specifications

Several organizations and professional societies, including the American Society of Testing Materials (ASTM), the American National Standards Institute (ANSI), and the American Society of Mechanical Engineers (ASME), have published standards and specifications for tubing. These standards describe the various characteristics, applications, and capabilities of different types and sizes of tubing. Engineers and designers use these standards in selecting and identifying the type and size of tubing for particular applications.

ASTM has a series of standards commonly used to identify and specify tubing. Some of the standards provide general requirements about certain types of tubing. Others contain specific requirements for finish, hardness, alloy, working pressures and temperatures, method of manufacture, etc., for particular types of tubing. In the ASTM system, each standard has an identification number consisting of a letter and a series of numbers.

If the metal contains iron (ferrous metal), the identification number begins with the letter A. If the metal does not contain iron (nonferrous metals), the identification number begins with the letter B. For example, A213 is a specification for seamless stainless steel tubing, and B68 is a specification for high-quality, soft, annealed copper tubing.

An example of a general ASTM standard is *ASTM A450*, which covers general requirements such as O.D. tolerances for steel and stainless steel, welded or seamless, tubing. *ASTM B165* is an example of a standard that refers to requirements for Monel® tubing. The ASTM identification number is often printed or stamped on the tubing.

When the project specifications list the required ASTM, ASME, or ANSI tubing identification number, you must use that type of tubing. You should review some of these specifications so that you know the type of information included in the specific tubing specifications. *Table 2* shows typical ASTM identification codes used to specify particular types of tubing.

Table 2 ASTM Identification Codes for Tubing

MATERIAL	MATERIAL CODE
Aluminum	A-
Brass	B-
Carbon steel	S-
Monel®	M-
Nylon	NY-
316 stainless steel	SS-
347 stainless steel	347-
TFE	T-
Hastelloy® B2	HB-
Hastelloy® C276	HC-
Inconel® 600	INC-
Copper-nickel 70-30	CN70-
Copper-nickel 90-10	CN90-

The ANSI *Code for Pressure Piping* B31.3 is often used to determine the required wall thickness of tubing needed for different system working pressures. *Table 3* shows a typical allowable pressure chart used to determine the size of aluminum tubing for various working pressures. *Table 4* is used for determining tubing pressure ratings at elevated temperatures.

When the working temperature of the process increases, the allowable working pressure of the tubing decreases. Different pressure charts are used for different types of tubing, such as aluminum, copper, stainless steel, and Monel®.

Table 3 Aluminum Tubing Working Pressure Chart

ALUMINUM TUBING					
Based on ultimate tensile strength 42,000 psi (289,400 kPa). For metal temperatures from -20° to 100°F (-29° to 37°C). Allowable working pressure loads calculated from S values (14,000 psi-96,500 kPa) as specified by ANSI B31.3. code.					
TUBE O.D. (IN.)	TUBE WALL THICKNESS (INCHES)				
	.035	.049	.065	.083	.095
⅛	8600	WORKING PRESSURE (PSIG)			
³⁄₁₆	5600	8000			
¼	4000	5900			
⁵⁄₁₆	3100	4600			
⅜	2600	3700			
½	1900	2700	3700		
⅝	1100	1600	2200		
¾		1300	1800	2300	
⅞		1100	1500		
1		900	1300	1700	2000

111T03.EPS

Table 4 Working Pressure and Temperature Factors for Elevated Temperatures

To determine the allowable pressure for aluminum at elevated temperatures, multiply the allowable working pressure from the **Aluminum Tubing Pressure Chart** by the appropriate factor from the chart below.

Example: The allowable working pressure for ½" O.D. × .035 wall tubing is 760 psi at 400°F.

FACTORS						
°F	°C	Aluminum	Copper	Steel	304SS	316SS	Monel®
200	93	1.00	.80	.95	1.00	1.00	.88
400	204	.40	.50	.86	.93	.96	.79
600	316	–	–	.77	.83	.85	.79
800	427	–	–	.58	.76	.79	.76
1000	538	–	–	–	.69	.76	–
1200	649	–	–	–	.30	.37	–

111T04.EPS

3.0.0 ◆ PROPER AND SAFE METHODS FOR STORING TUBING

Proper and safe storage of tubing may sound simple, but the amount of damage done to tubing, the number of personal injuries, and the time wasted because of improper storage techniques is surprising. There are correct ways to store tubing. Proper storage helps avoid costly damage, saves time in identifying stored tubing, and reduces the chance of personal injury to you and other workers.

Tubing racks like the one shown in *Figure 5* are commonly used for storing hard-drawn tubing. The racks provide support to prevent bending, sagging, distortion, scratching, or marring of tubing surfaces. Most racks have separate levels or compartments where different types and sizes of tubing can be stored for ease of identification and

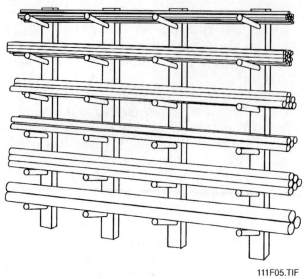

111F05.TIF

Figure 5 ◆ Typical tubing rack.

selection. Tubing racks are usually elevated to help avoid damage that might occur at floor level. Tubing that is stored at floor level is easily damaged or contaminated by people, materials, moisture, or equipment in the area.

Always inspect tubing before storing it to be sure it is clean inside and out and not damaged. The ends of stored tubing should be sealed to prevent damage. Tubing ends can be temporarily capped, taped, or plugged using any method that prevents unwanted entry. In the case of soft copper tubing rolls, the ends are sometimes sealed by crimping during storage.

To prevent contamination and corrosion, tubing should be covered while in storage. Covering stored tubing also helps prevent damage from sunlight and other environmental factors that affect some types of poly tubing.

 WARNING!
Be sure stored tubing is securely held in place to prevent it from falling or rolling in any way that could cause injury.

4.0.0 ◆ PROPER AND SAFE METHODS FOR HANDLING TUBING

Tubing is made to rigid specifications, but it can be degraded by careless handling. From the time tubing is delivered on a job site until its installation is complete, proper and safe handling methods must be used to ensure quality tubing installations. Some basic guidelines for handling tubing are given here:

- Never drag tubing off a delivery truck, storage rack, or on the ground. Dragging tubing across any rough surface can scratch or dent the outside surface, damage the ends, or contaminate the tubing. Scratches or nicks on tubing are potential paths for leaks.
- Keep tubing away from any material that might contaminate it during handling.
- Keep the end **caps** on during handling or transporting of tubing to avoid damage to ends and contamination from entering the tubing.
- Wear gloves when handling tubing to avoid injuring yourself on rough or sharp edges of the tubing.
- Don't use a vise to hold tubing unless it is equipped with special jaws for holding and protecting the tubing.
- Put flags on the ends of long lengths of tubing during handling and transporting so that you and others can easily see the tubing ends and avoid damage and/or accidents.
- Be aware of people, materials, and equipment around you when handling or transporting tubing so that you can avoid hitting anyone or anything with the tubing.
- Place straight lengths of tubing inside PVC piping or an aluminum tray while transporting them to prevent bending or damage.
- Handle soft copper and aluminum tubing with care to avoid damage. It's very easy to dent or scratch soft tubing or cause it to become out-of-round. This weakens the tubing and also makes it difficult to make good connections.
- Soft tubing that comes in rolls or coils must be carefully unrolled to prevent kinks from forming (*Figure 6*). The best way to unroll soft tubing is to first place the roll vertically on a flat surface like a table top, bench, flat board, or the floor. If the flat surface is rough, put down some type of padding to protect the tubing from scratches, dents, or other damage. Hold the loose end of the tubing on the flat surface with one hand while holding the coil in your other hand. Unwind the tubing by rolling the coil about 2 feet at a time. Carefully slide your hand along the tubing as it unwinds onto the flat surface, straightening each section as you go.

Remember to unroll the coil, not pull it, to avoid twisting. Twisting may weaken the tubing or cause it to get out-of-round. Do not unroll more tubing than you need, since repeated uncoiling can distort, harden, or stiffen the tubing. A tape measure or folding rule lying next to the coil will help determine when you have unrolled enough tubing.

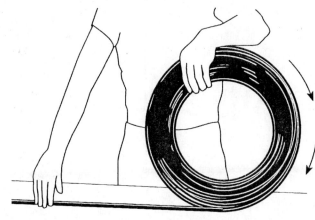

111F06.TIF

Figure 6 ◆ Unwinding rolled tubing.

Sometimes tubing is stretched, or drawn, after it is unrolled to ensure that it is straight and prepared for bending. Care must be taken, however, not to stretch the tubing so much that its O.D. is reduced. Tubing that is overstretched will not mate to fittings properly. This can cause leaks. Tubing can be stretched with a fabricated tube stretcher like the one shown in *Figure 7*.

The tubing stretcher is made of a length of channel notched on the end to accept a lever. The lever is made of a length of pipe (approximately 3 feet long and 1 inch in diameter) welded into a T shape. To operate the tubing stretcher, one end of the tubing is tied to the stretcher and the other end to the lever. When the lever is pulled back about 4 inches (measured at the top of the lever), the tube is stretched enough.

Instrumentation fitters who install soft copper tubing commonly carry a 50-foot roll of tubing with them and field stretch one piece at a time as needed, using the manual method. This is typically accomplished by cutting a length of tubing from the roll, tying one end to a stationary object, wrapping the other end to a short piece of pipe or lineman's pliers, then pulling the soft tubing until the correct tautness is achieved. Expertise in not over-stretching the tubing to a degree where its O.D. is decreased to an unacceptable dimension is gained only through practice and experience.

NOTE

Care should be taken not to create an excess of scrap tubing when twisting the ends of the tubing. Always save the scrap for recycling purposes. Be sure to support the tubing once it has been stretched to avoid sag that can impair the straightness of the stretched section of tubing.

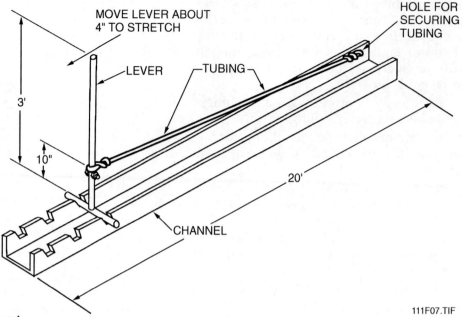

Figure 7 ◆ Typical tubing stretcher.

111F07.TIF

5.0.0 ◆ CUTTING TUBING

Before tubing can be installed, it must be properly cut to the correct length. Tubing is often cut with a tool called a *tubing cutter*. In cases of larger, hard-drawn tubing, a hacksaw or bandsaw may also be used to cut tubing. Some types of soft plastic tubing are cut with snips, a pocketknife, or a special V-shaped cutting tool made especially for cutting plastic tubing.

5.1.0 Types and Sizes of Tubing Cutters

Tubing cutters are available in several different types and sizes. Generally, a tubing cutter consists of a cutting wheel, a handle, and one or more rollers. On some types, the rollers are tightened to move the outside of the tubing against the cutting wheel, as shown in *Figure 8A*. Others have a sliding cutting wheel that is moved against the outside of the tubing, as shown in *Figure 8B*.

Some tubing cutters cut the tubing from the inside, as shown in *Figure 8C*. These internal tubing cutters are used where there is not enough room to use outside cutters. Tubing cutters are commonly used for cutting plastic, copper, aluminum, steel, and stainless steel tubing. Check the manufacturer's manual to make sure that the cutting wheel is designed to cut the type of tubing material that you are cutting.

5.2.0 Cutting Tubing With a Tube Cutter

It is a good practice to check the manufacturer's instructions before using any tubing cutter to make sure that you know the proper and safe way to use the cutter. The manufacturer's instructions may also specify the type and size of cutter and wheel needed for the specific cutting job.

Before using a tubing cutter, the tubing should be marked at the exact place where the cut is to be made. A sharp pencil, colored felt tip pen, or silver marking pencil are good tools for marking tubing. They make a nice thin line without scratching. It's best to make the mark all the way around the tubing so that it is always visible while you are cutting. A sleeve or **ferrule** can be used as a guide for making the mark around the tubing, as shown in *Figure 9*. A tubing cutter is then rotated around the tubing to cut it, as shown in *Figure 10*.

NOTE

Do not use grease pencils or crayons to mark metal tubing because the mark will be too wide. Wide marks may affect the accuracy of the cut. You should also not use sharp items like pens or scribes to mark metal tubing, since the scratch marks are points where corrosion or stress can dangerously weaken the tubing.

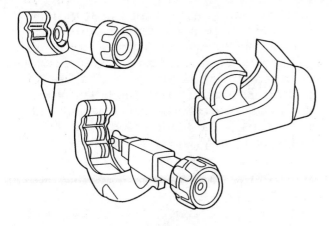

(A)
SLIDING CUTTING WHEEL

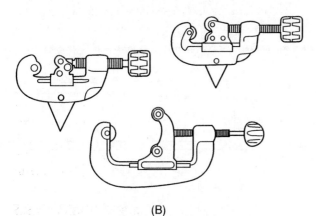

(B)
SLIDING ROLLER TYPES

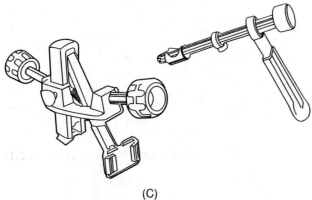

(C)
INTERNAL TUBING CUTTERS

111F08.EPS

Figure 8 ◆ Tubing cutters.

 WARNING!

Tubing cutters and ends of cut tubing have exposed sharp edges. Take care to avoid cuts to your hands and fingers. To protect the eyes when cutting tubing, always wear approved eye protection.

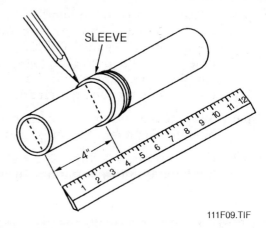

SLEEVE

111F09.TIF

Figure 9 ◆ Marking tubing.

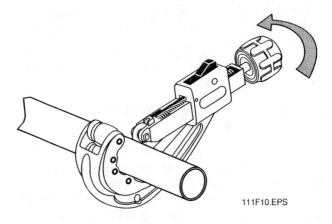

111F10.EPS

Figure 10 ◆ Using a tubing cutter.

The following steps are generally used when cutting tubing with an outside-type tubing cutter.

Step 1 Open the jaws of the cutter and place the tubing on the rollers of the cutter.

Step 2 Align the blade with the mark on the tubing.

Step 3 Turn the handle to tighten the blade (or rollers) until the blade is snug against the tubing.

 CAUTION

Squeezing the tubing too tightly against the blade can dig into or flatten the tubing.

Step 4 Rotate the cutter around the tubing, using a smooth motion and slightly pushing the cutting wheel farther into the groove being cut.

Step 5 Gradually tighten the handle of the cutter every few turns, making sure the blade remains against the tubing at all times. It is a good practice to tighten the handle of the cutting wheel at different positions on the tubing each time.

Step 6 Support the end of the tubing so it will not fall when the cut is completed.

Step 7 Keep turning the cutter and tightening the handle until the tubing cut is completed.

NOTE

Don't try to rush the cutting procedure. Applying too much pressure on the tubing could result in a poor cut, excessive wear on the cutting wheel, or flat spots on the tubing.

5.3.0 Cutting Tubing With a Hacksaw

Metal tubing is sometimes cut with a hacksaw. A hacksaw cut is preferred over a cut made with a tubing cutter for some types of tubing materials, for larger sizes of tubing, and when flare fittings are to be used. The hacksaw method is often used for cutting tubing made of hard metals. The heat and pressure that result when a tubing cutter is used can cause hard metals to become brittle near the cut, weakening the tubing. A tubing cutter can also bend the edge of the tubing inward, slightly reducing the O.D. This may make it difficult to get a good seal with some fittings.

WARNING!

Always wear approved eye protection when cutting tubing with a hacksaw to prevent metal chips from getting in your eyes.

When using a hacksaw to cut tubing, be sure to select the correct blade. Use a high-speed stainless (HSS) blade for stainless steel tubing. A general guideline is to choose a blade that allows two teeth of the blade to be in contact with the tubing. The distance between each tooth on a hacksaw blade is called the pitch. A pitch of 18 represents 18 teeth per inch (tpi). A hacksaw blade with at least 32 tpi is normally used to cut tubing.

Be sure to mark the tubing all the way around when cutting with a hacksaw. Keep the blade as square as possible to the tubing in order to pro-

duce an even, squared-off cut. Cut on the forward motion of the hacksaw. Keep light, even pressure on the tubing to avoid flattening.

Guideblocks are often used to ensure a square cut when cutting tubing with a hacksaw. The guideblocks also help keep the tubing from flattening out. If the cut is not square when you have finished, use a flat file to square it off. *Figure 11* shows tubing being cut with a hacksaw.

CAUTION

Hacksaw blades are designed to cut while being pushed forward, not when being pulled backward toward the user. For this reason, it is important to install the blade properly, with the teeth angled toward the end opposite the handle or grip of the hacksaw, as shown in the inset of *Figure 11*.

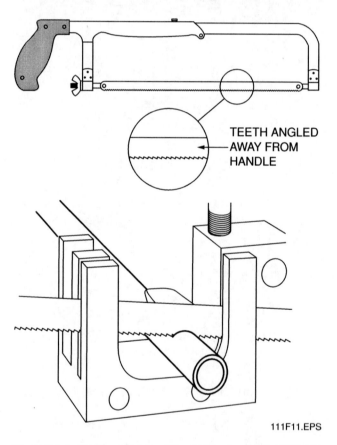

TEETH ANGLED AWAY FROM HANDLE

111F11.EPS

Figure 11 ◆ Cutting tubing with a hacksaw and guideblocks.

5.4.0 Cutting Tubing With a Bandsaw

Bandsaws are sometimes used to cut tubing when numerous cuts need to be made. A bandsaw cuts much faster than a hacksaw or tubing cutter and makes good, clean cuts. When cutting tubing with a portable bandsaw, be sure to place the brace

---

11.12

(back stop), located below the saw blade, firmly against the tubing to be cut, as shown in *Figure 12*. The weight of the saw alone is enough to provide the leverage needed for cutting. Very little pressure is needed to make a good clean cut with a bandsaw.

Check the operating manual for the bandsaw you are using. The manual will help determine the correct saw speed and blade to use for the type of tubing being cut. As a rule of thumb in selecting the right blade for cutting tubing with a bandsaw, the softer the material, the finer the tooth blade. For thin materials like tubing, at least two or three teeth should be in the cut. Where a smoother finish is important, select one of the finer tooth blades.

> **WARNING!**
> Always wear approved eye protection when cutting tubing with a bandsaw. Be aware of the moving blade and its proximity to your fingers and hands. Always connect electrical power tools to properly grounded circuits, preferably with GFCI protection.

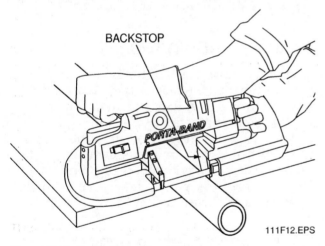

Figure 12 ◆ Bandsaw cutting tubing.

5.5.0 Cutting Poly Tubing With Snips

Soft, flexible poly (plastic) tubing and PVC tubing are easy to cut using specially designed snips (*Figure 13*). Before using snips to cut plastic tubing, mark the tubing at the exact place where the cut is to be made. A sharp pencil is a good tool for marking tubing since it makes a nice thin line. It's best to make the mark all the way around the tubing so that the mark is always visible. Grease pencils, which make thicker lines than regular lead pencils, are sometimes used to mark poly tubing since

precise measurements are not as critical on poly tubing runs. Grease pencil markings also show up well on the poly tubing.

When cutting tubing with snips, make a clean straight cut so the tubing will fit properly on the connector or fitting.

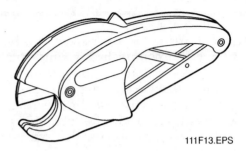

Figure 13 ◆ Tubing snips.

5.6.0 Deburring Tubing

When tubing is cut with a tubing cutter, hacksaw, or bandsaw, there may be burrs on the I.D., O.D., or both (*Figure 14*). Hacksaws normally leave burrs since the cutting action is not as smooth as that of other cutting tools. If not removed, burrs on the I.D. of tubing can break loose, causing chips and slivers to enter the tubing system. Chips and slivers can plug small pilot holes or vents, scratch valve seats and stem tips, or damage soft seals such as O-rings. The tubing I.D. can also be reduced because of the burrs. A smaller I.D. may affect flow through the tubing. Burrs on the O.D. of tubing make it difficult or impossible to properly install fittings to achieve a clean, leak-free tubing system.

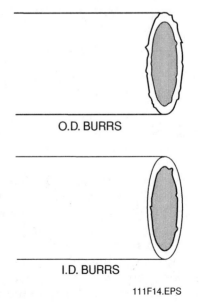

Figure 14 ◆ Tubing burrs.

Inside deburring of larger-sized, hard-drawn metal tubing is accomplished in much the same manner as when deburring pipe, using a spiral **reamer** similar to the one shown in *Figure 15*. Poly or PVC tubing may also need deburring, especially when cut with a saw. Deburring of poly or PVC tubing is usually done with a sharp-bladed tool, such as a knife.

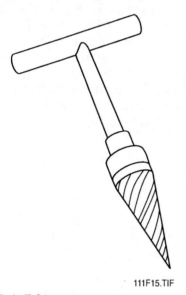

111F15.TIF

Figure 15 ◆ Tubing reamer.

Outside deburring of larger, hard-drawn tubing can be done using several methods including a flat file or sandpaper designed for use on metals. The file is normally held at a 45-degree angle while applying forward strokes with the file, making a uniform pattern completely around the end of the tubing. Sandpaper wrapped around the end of the tubing while manually turning the tubing will also remove the burrs.

Smaller tubing often used in instrumentation is usually reamed (deburred) using specially designed reaming tools, like the one shown in *Figure 16*, that have the capabilities of reaming both the inside and the outside of the tubing.

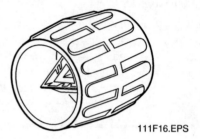

111F16.EPS

Figure 16 ◆ Tube inner-outer reamer tool.

6.0.0 ◆ BENDING TUBING

One of the advantages of tubing is that it can be bent and shaped for various types of installations. Layout, cutting, bending, and attaching fittings to tubing requires practice and a number of skills to become expert. This section describes common types of bends that are made in tubing installations and common types of **tubing benders**. Later in your training, you will receive additional instruction on measuring and bending tubing.

6.1.0 Standard Tubing Bends

Tubing installations require a number of different types of bends (*Figure 17*). The following standard bends are used for specific purposes in tubing installations:

- *Angle bend* – Used to change the direction of the tubing run.
- *Offset bend* – Used to move the tubing run to one side to avoid an interference.
- *Crossover bend* – Used to allow room for other tubes to cross (saddle).
- *U-bend* – Used to turn the tubing run around.
- *Expansion bend* – Used to allow room for the tubing line to expand or absorb vibration.

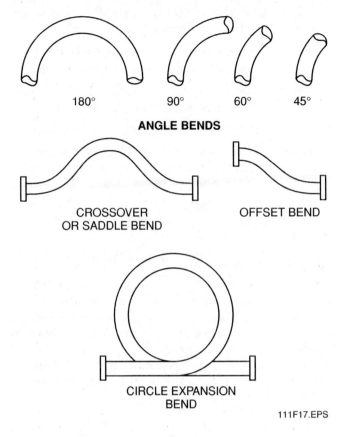

ANGLE BENDS

CROSSOVER
OR SADDLE BEND

OFFSET BEND

CIRCLE EXPANSION
BEND

111F17.EPS

Figure 17 ◆ Standard tubing bends.

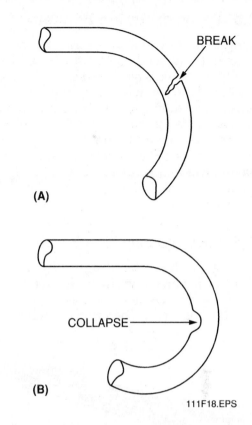

BREAK

(A)

COLLAPSE

(B)

111F18.EPS

Figure 18 ◆ Damaging effects of (A) overstretching and (B) compressing in tubing.

6.2.0 Tubing Bending Methods

Tubing must be bent carefully and correctly. A good tubing bend is smooth all the way around the bend, providing even flow through the tubing. Good tubing bends are made by using the right equipment and proper methods. Whenever tubing is bent, the metal at the back of the bend is stretched and the metal in the throat is compressed. A properly made bend will be smooth, stay in plane, and lie flat on a smooth surface. If the bend is too sharp, one of two things will happen:

- The metal at the back of the bend will be stretched too far and will break, as shown in *Figure 18A*
- The metal in the throat will collapse and close off the tubing, as shown in *Figure 18B*

A poor tubing bend can weaken the tubing or restrict the flow through the tubing. A good tubing bend has no flattening of the tubing through the bend. *Figure 19* shows some results of the incorrect use of tubing benders or improper methods of bending tubing. If you make a poor bend, you must not install the tubing. Obtain new tubing, then remake the bend.

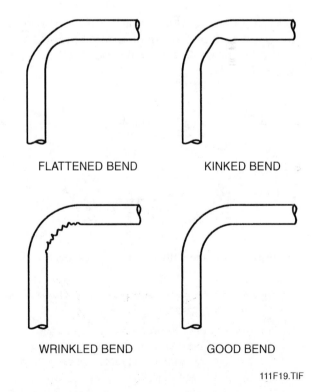

FLATTENED BEND

KINKED BEND

WRINKLED BEND

GOOD BEND

111F19.TIF

Figure 19 ◆ Improper and proper tubing bends.

6.3.0 Types of Tubing Benders

Tubing benders come in several different types and sizes. Hand benders are used to bend copper, aluminum, stainless steel, and special alloy types of tubing. Hand benders are typically used to bend stainless steel tubing up to ½ inch and copper and other soft tubing up to ¾ inch. Most machine benders are powered by hydraulic pumps or hand-operated gear actions. Machine benders are used to bend steel and stainless steel tubing or other hard tubing with larger O.D.s and heavier wall thicknesses.

6.3.1 Using a Spring Tube Bender

The simplest hand bending tool is a bending spring, such as the one shown in *Figure 20*. Note that spring tube benders are used in applications where the angle of the bend need not be exact.

111F20.TIF

Figure 20 ◆ Spring tube bender.

Spring tube benders come in different sizes and are used to bend small-diameter metal tubing. *Figure 21* shows tubing being bent with this type of bender.

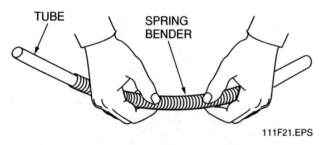

TUBE

SPRING BENDER

111F21.EPS

Figure 21 ◆ Bending with a spring tube bender.

WARNING!

Always wear approved eye protection when bending tubing to protect your eyes from the tubing ends when in the bending sweep. On spring benders, place your fingers so as to prevent pinching them between the bender spring coils.

The following steps are normally used when bending tubing with a spring tube bender.

Step 1 Fit the spring bender tightly over the center of the area of the tubing to be bent.

Step 2 Bend the spring and tubing by hand until the proper angle and radius are formed.

Step 3 Slip the spring bender off the tubing.

Step 4 Check to see if you achieved the correct angle for the bend by using a protractor, angle finder, or try square.

Step 5 Examine the tubing for kinks, cracks, flattened areas, or wrinkles.

6.3.2 Using a Compression-Type Hand Bender

A type of hand bender commonly used for bending tubing of 34 inches or less is shown in *Figure 22*. It is the most common type of bender used in the instrumentation trade. A typical set for field use includes a ¼-inch, ⅜-inch, and ½-inch lever bender. Other sizes are available, but their use is less common.

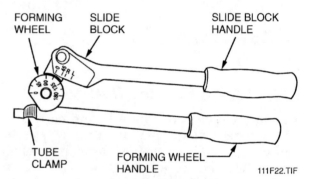

FORMING WHEEL   SLIDE BLOCK   SLIDE BLOCK HANDLE

TUBE CLAMP   FORMING WHEEL HANDLE

111F22.TIF

Figure 22 ◆ Compression-type hand bender.

The compression-type hand bender (also called a *lever bender*) consists of a slide block, slide block handle, forming wheel, forming wheel handle, and tube clamp. Before using a tubing bender, it is important to check the manufacturer's manual to make sure you have a bender of the correct size for the tubing being bent. Using a lever bender of a different size than the tubing will generally result in a flattened or kinked bend.

WARNING!

Always wear approved eye protection when bending tubing to protect eyes from tubing ends when in the bending sweep. On compression-type hand benders, place your fingers so as to prevent pinching them between slide block, forming wheel, and forming wheel handle.

The tubing to be bent is positioned in the groove in the forming wheel. It is held in place by the tube clamp. The numbers around the forming wheel refer to the angle of the bend that will be formed. The markings on the slide block are used for properly aligning the tubing in the bender. A groove along the outside of the forming wheel supports the tubing as it is bent. The bend is formed by the slide block moving around the outside of the tubing in the groove. As the slide block moves, it applies compression to bend the tubing. To form a 90-degree bend with this type of bender, follow these steps.

Step 1 Measure and mark the tubing exactly to get the desired bend.

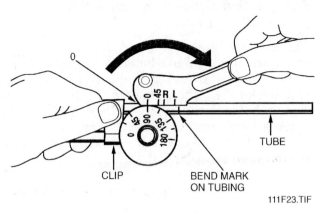

Figure 23 ◆ Starting position for bending tubing.

 NOTE

As shown in *Figures 22* and *23*, the tubing bender is marked *0*, *45*, *L*, and *R*. Align the mark made on the tubing with the mark on the slide block, based on the direction from which you measured the tubing. If the measurement was made from the left, place the tubing mark on the *L*. If the measurement was made from the right, place the tubing mark on the *R*.

Also, to make a 45-degree bend (or any bend ranging between 45 degrees and 33 degrees), align the mark on the tubing with the 45. For bends less than 33 degrees, you should move the mark on the tubing closer to the *0* on the slide block. If you place the tubing mark on the wrong letter, the mark will not be on the center of the bend, where it must be in order to make a correct bend.

Step 2 Insert the tubing in the bender, aligning the mark you made on the tubing with the *L* or *R* on the slide block.

Step 3 Clamp the tubing securely to the bender by dropping the clamp over the tubing to hold it in place.

Step 4 Align the *0* on the slide block with the *0* on the forming wheel as shown in *Figure 23*.

Step 5 Move the slide block handle around the tubing, forcing it to conform to the shape of the forming wheel until the *0* on the slide block aligns with the proper degree mark on the forming block as shown in *Figure 24*.

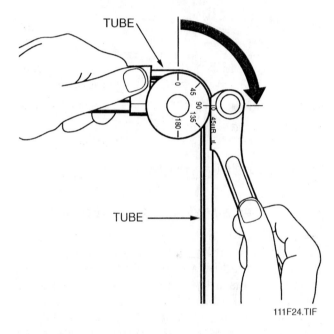

Figure 24 ◆ Making a 90-degree tubing bend.

 NOTE

Only bend the tubing in one direction so you don't overstretch or kink it. Also, when bending harder metal tubing, bend it slightly past the mark to allow for springback.

Step 6 Lift the handle, raise the clamp, and remove the tubing.

Step 7 Check the tubing to be sure you achieved the correct angle for the bend. Also check that the length from the end of the tubing to the center of the bend is correct. The mark should be at the center of the bend.

6.3.3 Using Table- or Bench-Mounted Tubing Benders

There are several types and sizes of table- or bench-mounted tubing benders (*Figure 25*) that are used to bend tubing of medium and heavy wall thicknesses. These benders are often used for tubing that is ¾ inch or larger. They are also used when a large number of bends are being made. Most table/bench benders work similarly to a hand bender except that there is some type of gear assembly used to power the bender.

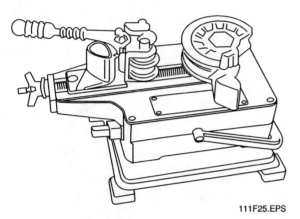

111F25.EPS

Figure 25 ◆ Typical benchtop tube bender.

6.3.4 Using a Hydraulic Tubing Bender

Most hydraulic tubing benders have a cylinder and ram assembly that bends the tubing with power supplied by a hydraulic pump. Hydraulic tubing benders are used to bend harder metals and larger types of tubing. Hydraulic benders are usually used for ¾ inch to 2 inch hard tubing, such as steel or stainless steel with heavy wall thicknesses.

NOTE

Hydraulic tubing bending is not covered extensively in this module because most tubing bending is accomplished using the methods covered in detail earlier in this module. However, should you need to use hydraulic methods, you must operate the particular type of hydraulic bender in accordance with the manufacturer's instructions, since most models operate somewhat differently.

7.0.0 ◆ TUBING FITTINGS

Tubing is connected to other components with tubing fittings to make a tubing run. For example, a tubing fitting might be used to make the connection between tubing and tubing, tubing and

piping, tubing and a valve, or tubing and a bulkhead. The sizes and types of fittings to be used for a specific job are usually specified in the engineering specifications, or on the instrument installation drawings for a project. Most tubing fittings are sized by the outside diameter of the tubing to which they are to be connected. For example, ½-inch tubing would take a ½-inch tubing fitting.

Fittings are specified to match the tubing material being used and the application. Such factors as pressure, temperature, and process characteristics are taken into consideration when selecting tubing fittings. You should never connect tubing of one material to a fitting of a different material, except in the case of poly tubing.

Fitting manufacturers use codes to identify the fitting material. The codes are sometimes stamped on the fitting. These codes may also indicate the heat (batch) number of the traceable lots. Some of these identification codes and other specifications have been developed by ASTM, ASME, and ANSI, like the codes for tubing materials. Other codes are manufacturer-specific.

If you have any questions, you will need to check the fitting manufacturer's catalog to determine the material codes. *Table 5* shows a partial list of material designator codes for one manufacturer.

The four most common types of tubing fittings used in instrument work are:

- Flare fittings
- Compression fittings
- Socket-welded fittings
- Butt-welded fittings

7.1.0 Flare Fittings

A flare fitting (*Figure 26*) is so-called because the end of the tubing is enlarged, or flared, slightly to create a rim against which the sleeve and body of the fitting can seal. Flaring will be covered later in this module. Flare fittings can be assembled and disassembled repeatedly, and provide a strong connection. They come in a variety of types, sizes, and materials for specific applications.

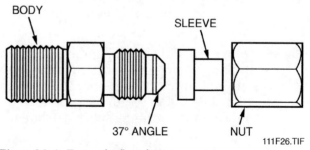

Figure 26 ◆ Parts of a flare fitting.

Table 5 Partial List of One Manufacturer's Material Designator Codes for Fittings

Stainless Steel	Carbon Steel	Copper Tubing	Aluminum Tubing	Monel® Tubing	Inconel®	Hastelloy®
ASTM – A213	ASTM – A161	ASTM – B68	ASTM – B210	ASTM – B165	ASTM – B167	ASTM – B622
ASTM – A249	ASTM – A179	ASTM – B75				
ASTM – A269		ASTM – B88				
ASTM – A450		ASTM – B251				
ASTM – A632						

Most flare fittings consist of three main parts: a body, a flare nut, and a flare sleeve. However, not all flare fittings include a sleeve. Sleeves are used primarily in flare fittings used for high-pressure applications. The fitting body of the flare fitting shown in *Figure 26* is part of a piping-to-tubing connector. The tip of the fitting body has a tapered angle of 37 degrees. Another commonly used fitting has a 45-degree angle taper. The tubing used with a particular flare fitting must be flared at the same angle as the tip of the fitting body. The 37-degree flare fittings are typically used for high-pressure applications such as hydraulic oil systems. The 45-degree flare fittings are usually used for low-pressure water and air systems.

CAUTION

To avoid possible rupture, always make sure that the flare angle matches the angle of the sleeve.

The sleeve in a flare fitting acts as a buffer between the nut and the flared end of the tubing. The nut holds the tubing flare against the fitting body. When the nut is tightened, it applies pressure against the sleeve. The sleeve, in turn, applies pressure against the tubing, securing and sealing the tubing against the body. *Figure 27* shows a cutaway view of an assembled flare fitting.

7.2.0 Compression Fittings

Compression fittings are considered very reliable and relatively easy to install. They can usually be disconnected and reconnected without damaging the tubing or the fitting. They come in a variety of designs, sizes, and materials to fit different tubing applications. When using compression fittings, the end of the tubing is not flared. The tubing is fitted with a compression ring, or ferrule, that pinches the tubing as the nut is tightened on the body of the fitting. Compression fittings have either one or two ferrules for each joint. The fer-

rule of the fitting must be harder than the tubing to allow the **swaging effect** to take place. *Figure 28* shows the parts of a one-ferrule compression fitting before and after making a tubing connection.

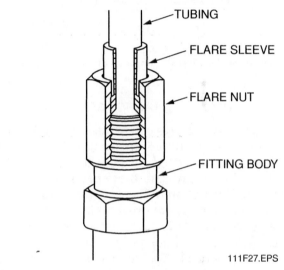

111F27.EPS

Figure 27 ◆ Assembled flare fitting.

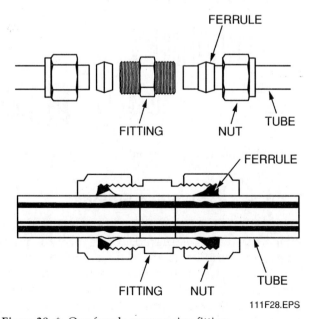

111F28.EPS

Figure 28 ◆ One-ferrule compression fitting.

Two-ferrule compression fittings have a back ferrule and a front ferrule for each joint. *Figure 29* shows the parts of a two-ferrule compression fitting before and after making a tubing connection.

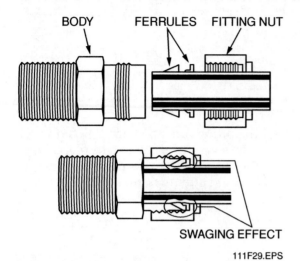

Figure 29 ◆ Two-ferrule compression fitting.

7.2.1 Poly Tubing Compression Fittings

Compression fittings can be used for connections on poly (plastic) tubing such as PVC, Tygon®, and Teflon®. Fittings used for poly tubing may differ slightly in design from those used on metal tubing. The fittings may have nylon ferrules rather than metal ferrules to prevent damage to the tubing as the ferrule is compressed. Most compression fittings used for poly tubing have a tube-support insert. The insert provides a rigid surface against which the tubing can be compressed so that it does not collapse. A compression fitting with an insert is shown in *Figure 30*.

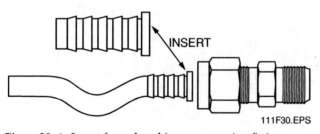

Figure 30 ◆ Insert for poly tubing compression fitting.

7.3.0 Socket-Welded Fittings

A socket-welded fitting has a hole, or socket, into which the tubing is placed. A fillet weld is made where the outside of the tubing wall protrudes from the end of the fitting. Socket-welded fittings can either be socket-to-socket or may connect the socket to some other form of tubing connector, as shown in *Figure 31*.

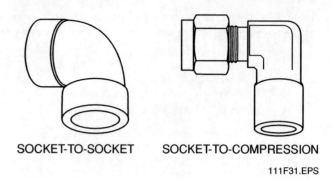

Figure 31 ◆ Socket-welded fittings.

Socket-welded fittings are usually used with high-grade, heavy-walled tubing that may be difficult to flare or use with a compression-type fitting. They are often used when there is concern that vibration in the system might loosen the connection. Socket-welded fittings ensure there will be no leaks in the system. When welding a socket-welded fitting, it is important that the other end of the tubing be protected, since it can be damaged by the hot spatter from the welding process, particularly if the fitting is a socket-to-flare or socket-to-compression type.

NOTE

When inserting tubing into a socket-weld tubing fitting, do not let it bottom out. Allow $\frac{1}{16}$ inch to $\frac{1}{8}$ inch for expansion space.

7.4.0 Butt-Weld Fittings

Butt-joint or butt-weld fittings can be used for making tubing-to-tubing connections or to change a run from butt-welded piping to tubing. When butt-welding tubing or piping, the ends to be joined are beveled, lined up, and welded around the outside of the joint. A bevel is an angle cut on the end of the tubing, as shown in *Figure 32*.

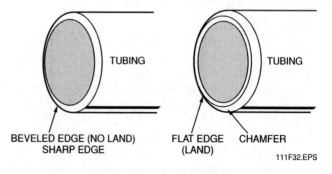

Figure 32 ◆ Beveled and chamfered ends of tubing.

Sometimes the terms *bevel* and *chamfer* are improperly used interchangeably. They are not the same. A chamfer is an angle cut only on the edge of the tubing, as shown in *Figure 32*. The flat edge of the tubing left after a chamfer is cut is called the *land*.

In the piping-to-tubing type of connection, the butt-joint is often welded on the piping side of the fitting. The tubing side is fitted with some other type of fitting, such as a flared or compression fitting.

7.5.0 Types of Tubing Fittings

There are numerous types of fittings used to change direction of tubing runs, provide branch connections, close ends of tubing, and connect tubing to tubing, tubing to piping, and tubing to instruments. The following sections describe several of the most commonly used types of tubing fittings.

7.5.1 Male and Female Connectors and Adapters

The term *male fitting* refers to fittings that have outside threads which connect tubing to a component with a female, or internal, thread. The term *female fitting* refers to fittings that have internal threads which connect tubing to a component with male, or outside, threads. While many types of fittings are referred to as male or female type fittings, two of the most common are male and female connectors and adapters (*Figure 33*). A male connector fitting has a male end, which connects to a female threaded component. A female connector fitting has a female end which connects to a male threaded component. A male adapter fitting connects tubing to female piping. A female adapter connects tubing to male piping.

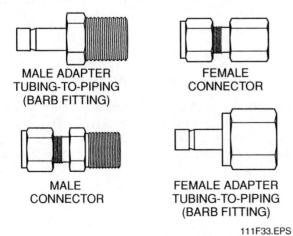

Figure 33 ◆ Male and female connectors and adapters.

7.5.2 Tee Fittings

Tee fittings (*Figure 34*) are a commonly used type of branch fitting. They are available in a variety of designs and sizes. All tee fittings are designed to branch tubing at a 90-degree angle. When all of the outlets of the tee are the same size, the tee is specified by the nominal size (for example, 1-inch tee). When the main outlets and the branch outlets are different sizes, the tee is referred to by giving the main tubing run size first, and then the branch run size (for example, 1 × ¼-inch tee).

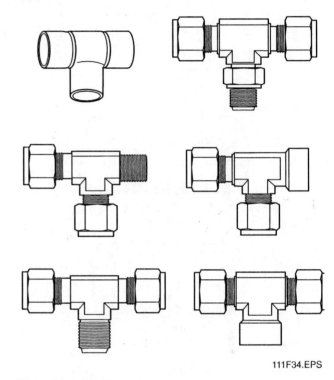

Figure 34 ◆ Tee fittings.

7.5.3 Elbow Fittings

Elbow fittings (*Figure 35*) are curved fittings that connect tubing to tubing or piping to tubing at various angles. An elbow fitting is commonly referred to as an *ell*. The standard angles are 45 degrees and 90 degrees, although other angle sizes are available.

7.5.4 Coupling Fittings

Coupling fittings (*Figure 36*) connect two pieces of tubing, or tubing and piping, without branching or stopping the flow through the run. Unlike union fittings, coupling fittings cannot be removed without disturbing the position of the tubing or piping. Coupling fittings may be connected by butt- or socket-welding or threaded ends.

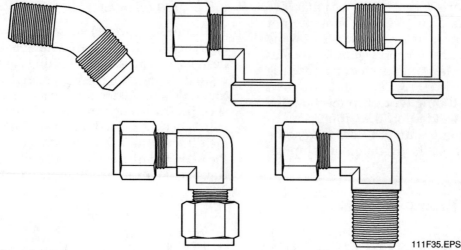

Figure 35 ◆ Elbow fittings.

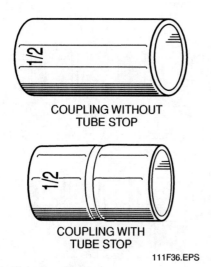

COUPLING WITHOUT
TUBE STOP

COUPLING WITH
TUBE STOP

111F36.EPS

Figure 36 ◆ Coupling fittings.

7.5.5 Union Fittings

Union fittings (*Figure 37*) connect two pieces of tubing, or tubing and piping, without branching or stopping the flow through the run. Union fittings can be connected and disconnected without disturbing the position of the tubing or piping.

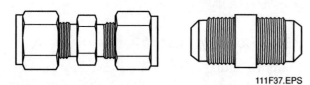

111F37.EPS

Figure 37 ◆ Union fittings.

7.5.6 Cross Fittings

Cross fittings (*Figure 38*) have two branch outlets that form the shape of a cross, providing four outlets spaced 90 degrees from each other. Cross fittings come in a variety of sizes and designs. All four outlets in a straight cross fitting are equal in dimension. In a reducing cross fitting, the two branch outlets are smaller than the run outlets. This type of cross fitting is used to obtain the desired flow and pressure through the system.

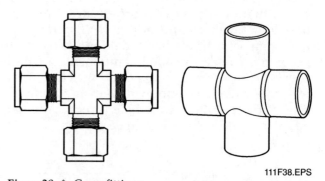

111F38.EPS

Figure 38 ◆ Cross fittings.

7.5.7 Tubing Caps and Plugs

Caps are used to close off the end of tubing. **Plugs** are used to close off an unused port of a tubing fitting. Caps and plugs come in various sizes and shapes. *Figure 39* shows one type of tubing cap and plug.

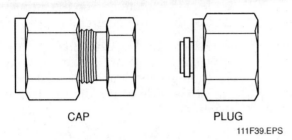

CAP   PLUG

111F39.EPS

Figure 39 ◆ Cap and plug fittings.

7.5.8 Reducer Fittings

Reducer fittings (*Figure 40*) are designed to change the run or branch from a larger size to a smaller size of tubing. This is usually done to increase flow pressure, or to reduce the volume of flow in a tubing system. One face of the reducer matches the larger size of tubing, and the other matches the smaller size of tubing. A reducer may be a separate fitting or may be a built-in part of another fitting like a tee, cross, adapter, or connector.

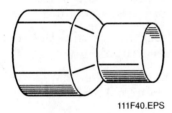

111F40.EPS

Figure 40 ◆ Reducer fitting.

7.5.9 Bulkhead Fittings

Bulkhead fittings are used to connect two pieces of tubing through a plate, junction box, or control panel by use of a locknut. Bulkhead fittings come in several types, sizes, and materials. *Figure 41* shows some typical bulkhead fittings.

7.5.10 Thermocouple Fittings

Thermocouples are widely used devices for measuring temperature in industrial processes. Most industrial thermocouples have a female connector at the end of the metal sheath that surrounds the thermocouple wires. To run the wires to a junction box or another instrument, the male connector of the thermocouple fitting (*Figure 42*) is connected to the female connector of the thermocouple. The fitting then connects to tubing or a conduit that houses the wires until they terminate.

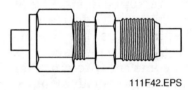

111F42.EPS

Figure 42 ◆ Thermocouple male connector fitting.

8.0.0 ◆ FLARING TUBING

Flaring is a method used to connect flare fittings and tubing. The end of the tubing is spread, or flared, using a flaring tool (*Figure 43*). Flaring tools are available in several types, including manually and hydraulically operated. Manual flaring tools are used for smaller, softer tubing. Hydraulic flaring tools are usually used with larger, harder tubing. All flaring tools consist of three basic parts: the die block, the cone, and the yoke.

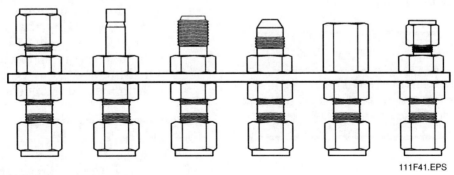

111F41.EPS

Figure 41 ◆ Bulkhead fittings.

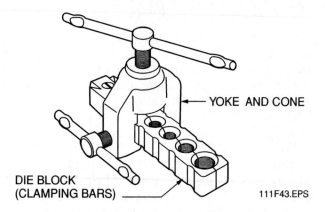

Figure 43 ◆ Manual flaring tool.

The holes in the die block correspond to the different sizes of tubing that the block can accommodate. Each hole has a flared side to create a flare at the desired angle. Flared connections used in high-pressure applications, like hydraulic systems, usually use a 37-degree flare angle. Low-pressure applications, like pneumatic systems, use a 45-degree angle for flared connections. Flaring cones come in different angles, with the degree of the angle usually stamped on the cone. If the wrong cone is used, the flare will have the wrong angle, and the tubing will not fit properly over the fitting body. Always follow the manufacturer's instructions when using flaring tools.

Tubing that is to be flared must be seamless tubing and should be cut with a hacksaw. Tubing made with seams tends to split along the seam during the flaring process. For a proper seal, the end of the tubing should be cut squarely. A square cut allows the tube to fit flush against the nose of the fitting body. The tubing must be free of burrs and ridges before starting to flare. The following steps describe how to flare tubing with a manual flaring tool.

Step 1   Cut the tubing to the desired length.

Step 2   Remove all burrs. This is very important to ensure metal-to-metal contact.

WARNING!
Wear approved eye protection when flaring to protect eyes from the free end of the tubing. When using a flaring tool, be careful not to pinch or cut your fingers on the sharp edges of the tubing.

Step 3   Slide the fitting nut (and sleeve, if included with the fitting) over the tubing. This is important because the nut and the sleeve will not fit over the end of the tubing after it has been flared unless the other end of the tubing is free. The nut and the sleeve can be slipped out of the way while the tubing is being flared.

Step 4   Select a flaring tool that produces a flare of the correct angle for the fitting. Verify the angle of the tapered tip on the fitting body against the manufacturer's part number.

Step 5   Insert the end of the tubing into the appropriate hole in the die block so that the tubing extends about 1/32 inch to 1/16 inch out of the side of the die block that has the taper.

Step 6   Tighten the wing nut on the die block to clamp it around the tubing.

Step 7   Slide the yoke over the die block so that the cone is aligned with the center of the tubing.

Step 8   Tighten the handle of the yoke, screwing the cone into the end of the tubing to form the flare. Turn the handle until the cone is snug inside the tubing and the handle becomes hard to turn.

Step 9   Loosen the yoke handle and remove the flaring tool and the tubing.

Step 10   Inspect the completed flare for cracks, debris, and smoothness.

Step 11   Check to see that the fitting nut and sleeve fit properly on the flare.

Step 12   Test the finished flare against the fitting body to make sure it fits properly.

Step 13   To complete the connection, place the tapered end of the fitting body into the flared end of the tubing. Slide the fitting nut and the sleeve down the tube. Screw the fitting nut into the fitting body by hand, ensuring that the pieces thread together properly. Use two wrenches to tighten the assembly. With one wrench holding the fitting body, tighten the nut with the other wrench.

NOTE
It is important for the fitting to be tightened snugly, but do not overtighten, since this may damage the fitting or split the tubing at the flare.

Summary

In this training module, you learned about the various types and applications of tubing and tubing fittings, how to properly handle and store tubing, and procedures for cutting, deburring, bending, and flaring tubing.

Tubing installation is an important part of instrument work. The knowledge and skills covered in this module provide basic and fundamental competencies required to effectively work with tubing installations. In your day-to-day work activities, take the time to practice the skills learned in this module. It takes a lot of practice, study, and on-the-job experience to develop the skills to be expert in working with tubing.

Review Questions

1. In instrument work, _____ is a primary function of tubing.

   a. carrying milliampere signals between instruments
   b. carrying pneumatic control signals between instruments
   c. supporting instruments on stands
   d. supporting tubing trays

2. If tubing has an O.D. of 0.125 and a wall thickness of 0.028, what is its I.D.?

   a. 0.069
   b. 0.097
   c. 0.153
   d. 0.181

3. One of the disadvantages of using copper tubing in some applications is that it _____ more than some other types of tubing.

   a. expands
   b. shrinks
   c. discolors
   d. becomes brittle

4. Stainless steel is a steel alloy that contains at least 12 percent _____ by weight.

   a. chromium
   b. iron
   c. zinc
   d. lead

5. The type of poly tubing often referred to as *surgical tubing* is _____.

   a. nylon
   b. Teflon®
   c. polypropylene
   d. Tygon®

6. When the working temperature of the process increases, the allowable working pressure of tubing _____.

   a. increases
   b. decreases
   c. stays the same
   d. is not a factor

7. A possible result of improperly stored tubing is _____.

   a. less costly damage
   b. time saved in identifying tubing
   c. kinked or cracked tubing
   d. reduction in personal injuries

8. To prevent soft tubing that comes in rolls from kinking, place the roll _____ on a flat surface and _____ the tubing from the roll about 2 feet at a time.

   a. vertically; pull
   b. horizontally; unroll
   c. horizontally; pull
   d. vertically; unroll

9. After tubing has been stretched in a tubing stretcher, it is referred to as _____ tubing.

   a. drawn
   b. annealed
   c. alloyed
   d. thin

10. A V-shaped cutting tool is made especially for cutting _____ tubing.

    a. copper
    b. plastic
    c. steel
    d. Monel®

11. The manufacturer's instructions supplied with a tubing cutter specify the type and size of _____ needed for the specific cutting job.

   a. fittings
   b. handle
   c. tubing stretcher
   d. cutter and wheel

12. A hacksaw blade with at least _____ teeth per inch is normally preferred when cutting tubing.

   a. 6
   b. 12
   c. 18
   d. 32

13. Tubing should be reamed only until _____ , leaving the wall thickness as close to normal wall thickness as possible.

   a. the burrs are removed
   b. the metal is shiny
   c. cracks begin to appear
   d. a sharp edge is achieved

14. A saddle bend is another name for _____ bend.

   a. an angle
   b. a crossover
   c. a 45-degree
   d. an expansion

15. Whenever tubing is bent, the metal at the back of the bend is _____.

   a. compressed
   b. annealed
   c. flattened
   d. stretched

16. The simplest tool used to bend tubing is a _____.

   a. hickey
   b. machine bender
   c. bending spring
   d. compression bender

17. The most common type of bender used in the instrumentation industry is a _____.

   a. bending spring
   b. hydraulic bender
   c. compression-type or lever bender
   d. table or bench bender

18. Using a compression or lever bender of a different size than the tubing will generally result in a _____ bend.

   a. flattened
   b. over-radius
   c. under-radius
   d. crooked

19. The only type of tubing that may be connected to fittings fabricated from a different material than the tubing is _____ tubing.

   a. aluminum
   b. copper
   c. poly or plastic
   d. stainless steel

20. Common types of tubing fittings used in instrument work include all *except* _____.

   a. compression
   b. butt-welded
   c. flared
   d. slip-fit

21. _____ are used primarily in flare fittings for high-pressure applications.

   a. Sleeves
   b. Nuts
   c. 45-degree angle tapers
   d. Seamed tubing

22. The _____ of the fitting must be harder than the tubing to allow the swaging effect to take place.

   a. nut
   b. housing
   c. body
   d. ferrule

23. Fittings used for poly or plastic tubing may have _____ ferrules, rather than metal ferrules.

   a. nylon
   b. fibrous
   c. silicone
   d. ferrous

24. The following are parts of a flaring tool *except* a _____.

   a. die block
   b. cutting die
   c. yoke
   d. cone

25. Low-pressure applications, like pneumatic systems, usually use a _____-degree angle for flared connections.

   a. 22½
   b. 37
   c. 45
   d. 90

Trade Terms Introduced in This Module

Cap: A tubing fitting used to close off the end of tubing.

Compression: The process of mechanically connecting a length of tubing by compressing or squeezing a ferrule between a fitting and nut by tightening the nut.

Drawn: Soft tubing which is pulled or stretched by hand, or by mechanically feeding it through a die to reduce diameter and wall thickness. In the case of instrumentation copper tubing, drawing allows for uniformity and straightness in installation.

Ductility: The characteristic of a metal that allows it to be stretched, drawn, or hammered thin without breaking.

Ferrule: A sleeve- or ring-type component of a tubing fitting, often referred to as a *barrel*, that forms an intricate part of the tubing connection and sealing process.

Fitting: A device, such as an elbow, tee, or union, used with tubing to connect tubing to tubing, tubing to instruments, or tubing to piping. Fittings are also used to close off tubing and/or to branch tubing.

Flare: The angle made at the enlarged end of a piece of tubing to match a fitting and create a leak-free connection.

Liquors: Spent water-like solutions resulting from any process that usually contains nonvolatile residue substances that can either be added back to the process, disposed of, or stored using approved methods.

Plug: A tubing fitting used to close off a port of another fitting.

Reamer: A device used to remove burrs and ridges from the inside of tubing.

Swaging effect: Mechanically enlarging the diameter of tubing on one end with a swaging tool to allow one piece of tubing to fit over the joining piece. This same effect occurs with tube fittings, where the tubing in front of the ferrule is expanded by tightening the fitting nut, thus preventing the removal of the nut and ferrule.

Tubing bender: A device used to bend tubing without kinking or crimping. Tubing benders may be hand-operated, bench- or table-mounted, or hydraulically powered.

Tubing cutter: A device that has a cutting wheel(s) and rollers and that is rotated around tubing to cut it.

Additional Resources

This modules is intended to present thorough resources for task training. The following reference works are suggested for further study. These are optional materials for continued education rather than for task training.

Standards and Specifications for Tubing. Washington, DC: American National Standards Institute (ANSI).

Standards and Specifications for Tubing. New York, NY: American Society of Mechanical Engineers (ASME).

NCCER CRAFT TRAINING USER UPDATES

The NCCER makes every effort to keep these textbooks up-to-date and free of technical errors. We appreciate your help in this process. If you have an idea for improving this textbook, or if you find an error, a typographical mistake, or an inaccuracy in the NCCER's Craft Training textbooks, please write us, using this form or a photocopy. Be sure to include the exact module number, page number, a detailed description, and the correction, if applicable. Your input will be brought to the attention of the Technical Review Committee. Thank you for your assistance.

Instructors – If you found that additional materials were necessary in order to teach this module effectively, please let us know so that we may include them in the Equipment and Materials list in the Instructor's Guide.

Write: Curriculum Revision and Development Department
National Center for Construction Education and Research
P.O. Box 141104, Gainesville, FL 32614-1104

Fax: 352-334-0932

E-mail: curriculum@nccer.org

Craft _____   Module Name _____

Copyright Date _____   Module Number _____   Page Number(s) _____

Description _____

_____

_____

_____

(Optional) Correction _____

_____

_____

(Optional) Your Name and Address _____

_____

_____

Piping –
2 Inches and Under

COURSE MAP

This course map shows all of the modules in the first level of the Instrumentation curriculum. The suggested training order begins at the bottom and proceeds up. Skill levels increase as you advance on the course map. The local Training Program Sponsor may adjust the training order.

INSTRUMENTATION LEVEL ONE

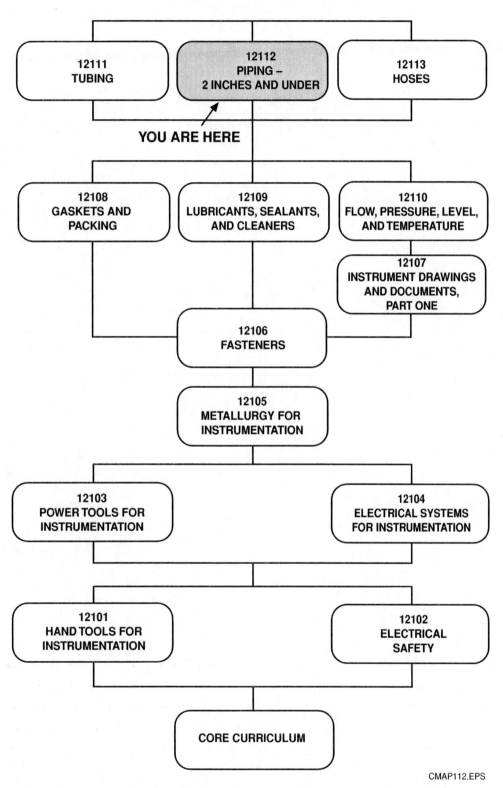

CMAP112.EPS

Figures

Tables

Piping –
2 Inches and Under

OBJECTIVES

When you have completed this module, you will be able to do the following:

1. Identify the different kinds of welded and seamless piping and give their process applications.
2. Discuss national tubing standards
3. Store and handle pipe properly to prevent damage and/or contamination to the pipe or personal injury.
4. Use proper procedures for cutting piping.
5. Use proper procedures for threading piping.
6. Identify and select appropriate fittings for selected piping applications.

Prerequisites

Before you begin this module, it is recommended that you successfully complete the following modules: Core Curriculum; Instrumentation Level One, Modules 12101 through 12111.

Required Trainee Materials

1. Pencil and paper
2. Appropriate personal protective equipment

1.0.0 ◆ INTRODUCTION

Piping and tubing systems are used in plants and other facilities to carry process fluids, steam, water, hydraulic fluids, pneumatic control signals, instrument air supply, seal water, lubricating oil, and compressed air. Piping is also used to connect instruments to process piping. The terms *piping* and *tubing* are sometimes used to mean the same thing. However, pipe is considered to be more rigid than tubing and has thicker walls. Since tubing is not as hard as piping, it is easier to bend. Pipe installations usually require more pipe fittings than a comparable tubing installation because bends cannot be made as easily.

While there are some similarities in working with pipe and tubing, there are special skills required for each. This module covers piping systems. Tubing systems are covered in the Instrumentation Level One Module, *Tubing*.

> **NOTE**
>
> The information given in this module is general in nature. When selecting piping, it is important to make sure that your selection is compatible with the process or application where it is to be used. When in doubt, always consult the manufacturer.

Normally, the type of piping selected depends on one or more of the following (as applicable):

- System operating temperatures
- System operating pressures
- The type of fluid or other media the system or equipment handles
- The composition of the system components
- The environment where it is to be installed

2.0.0 ◆ TYPES AND SIZES OF PIPE

There are two major factors that must be considered when pipe is to be installed:

- The type of pipe material
- The size of the pipe

The type and size of pipe used in a system depend on the physical and chemical properties of the process. The physical properties include pressure, flow, and the temperature requirements of the process. The corrosiveness of the environment to which piping is exposed is another consideration.

Specific piping requirements and applications vary depending on the job. When installing pipe, always consult the project piping specifications. Verify the size and type of materials specified on the piping and instrument drawings (P&IDs), specifications, and piping plans. Use only the type and size of pipe specified for the job.

2.1.0 Types of Pipe

Pipe is made from a variety of materials. Piping used in plant systems is commonly made of carbon steel, copper, stainless steel, Monel®, Hastelloy®, Inconel®, chromium molybdenum (chrome-moly), and polyvinyl chloride (PVC). Aluminum pipe is also sometimes used. Pipe is sometimes lined with glass, in which case it is known as *glass-lined pipe*.

You will recognize that many of the materials used to make pipe are the same as those used to make tubing. For pipes made from these materials, this section focuses on their uses and other details relevant to piping installations. For more information about the materials themselves, you may want to review the information given about them in the Level One Module, *Tubing*. This section also covers in detail some new types of pipes not covered in the tubing module.

2.1.1 Carbon Steel

Carbon steel pipe is often used in aboveground gas, air, and water systems, and other noncorrosive areas. It is very strong, allowing it to be used in high-pressure and high-temperature applications, such as in high-pressure hydraulic systems. Carbon steel is less brittle than stainless steel piping. This allows it to be used in systems subjected to vibration because it can absorb the vibration.

2.1.2 Copper

Copper pipe is often used in pneumatic systems because it resists rust that could contaminate the air. Typically, it is used in systems where the tem-

perature and pressure conditions are not extreme. Copper pipe expands more than some other types of pipe, making it unsuitable for certain applications. Copper pipe also may not be suitable for systems that are exposed to extremely corrosive substances. Some copper pipe is made with a PVC covering that helps it resist attack by chemicals.

2.1.3 Stainless Steel

Stainless steel pipe is stiffer and stronger than copper pipe. It is used to handle many types of corrosive fluids and performs well in high-pressure and high-temperature applications. Stainless steel pipe is expensive in comparison to some other types of pipe, but it has several important qualities that make its use practical in specific applications. Stainless steel pipe is often used in pharmaceutical, food processing, and dairy plants because it is corrosion resistant and can easily be kept sterile to prevent contamination. Stainless steel pipe is available in different wall thickness designated as Schedule 40, 80, 160, and double extra heavy.

2.1.4 Monel®

Monel® pipe is highly resistant to corrosion from the atmosphere and to salt water, lye, sulfuric acid, most foods, and many chemicals. It is often used where high strength and ductility are required.

2.1.5 Hastelloy®

Hastelloy® pipe is highly resistant to corrosion, especially corrosion by hot concentrated acids or liquors. It is often used in the chemical processing industry to convey highly corrosive materials, such as boiling sulfuric acid.

2.1.6 Inconel®

Inconel® pipe is often used in high-temperature applications because it remains strong at very high temperatures. It has high resistance to acids in foods, making its use common in food processing plants. It also is used in the pharmaceutical industry because it does not contaminate the contents of the piping system. In addition, Inconel® pipe is widely used to convey highly corrosive dry chlorine gas.

2.1.7 Chromium Molybdenum

Chromium molybdenum (chrome-moly) pipe is made of a low carbon steel alloy that contains chromium and molybdenum. The chromium and molybdenum additives increase the strength and hardness of the pipe, and enhance its corrosion resistance. Chrome-moly pipe is often used in high-pressure, high-temperature applications, such as in steam systems.

2.1.8 Polyvinyl Chloride

Polyvinyl chloride (PVC) pipe is used extensively throughout the chemical industry. Different chemical compounds may be added to PVC during the manufacturing process to make different forms of PVC that have a greater ability to resist attack by heat, light, or oxygen. PVC can be used to carry fluids with a maximum operating temperature of about 140°F without causing distortion of the piping.

Another type of PVC pipe is CPVC (chlorinated polyvinyl chloride) pipe. CPVC pipe looks like PVC pipe except that it is usually lighter in color. CPVC pipe can handle higher temperatures than PVC pipe, usually ranging up to 200°F.

Most PVC pipe connections are made using a special cement. The PVC pipe and fittings are prepared for connection by first applying a primer that removes any contaminants on the pipe and fitting surfaces, then applying a solvent-based cement that acts to soften the surfaces so that a fusing action occurs between the mating surfaces. Some types of PVC pipe have extra thick walls, allowing them to be joined using standard pipe-threading techniques.

2.1.9 Glass-Lined Steel

Steel pipe may be lined or coated with glass. Glass-lined pipe combines both ferrous and nonferrous materials. It has the strength of steel and the corrosion-resistance properties of glass. The advantage of glass-lined pipe is its resistance to contamination, heat, and corrosion. The glass lining breaks easily, so it requires special handling, installation, and maintenance. Glass-lined pipe is widely used in wastewater and sewage treatment applications.

2.1.10 Aluminum

Aluminum pipe has several advantages over other types of metal pipe for specific applications. It is softer, lighter in weight, and more flexible than most other metal pipe. Aluminum pipe resists corrosion and is often used where sanitary conditions are required because it is easy to clean and sterilize. The strength of aluminum pipe increases as temperature decreases. Because of this characteristic, it is sometimes used in low-temperature applications to carry liquefied gases. Aluminum pipe can break easily and it also tends to oxidize at the fittings, resulting in possible leaks.

3.0.0 ◆ PIPE AND PIPE FITTING IDENTIFICATION SYSTEMS

Pipe and pipe fittings are made from many different metal alloys. They come in a variety of types, sizes, and strengths. The American Society for Testing and Materials (ASTM) has developed a system to identify the characteristics of metals. The ASTM method is used to designate types of metal pipe and pipe fittings.

3.1.0 Identification of Types of Metal Pipe and Fittings

In the ASTM system, each metal is identified by a series of letters and numbers, called an identification number. This identification number is stamped or printed on the pipe and fittings. When designers and engineers prepare the project drawings and piping specifications, they usually specify the type of pipe by its ASTM identification number.

NOTE

You must use the type of pipe specified on the drawings and specifications for a particular job.

If the metal contains iron (ferrous metal), the ASTM identification number begins with an A. If the metal does not contain iron (nonferrous metal), the number begins with a B.

After the first letter, there is a number, usually three digits. This number identifies the specific properties of the metal within the ferrous/nonferrous group. For example: ASTM B622 identifies the nonferrous, nickel alloy metal Hastelloy® and the properties of seamless, nickel alloy pipe.

The ASTM identification system is only one of several systems used. Other systems include those of the American National Standard Institute (ANSI) and the American Society of Mechanical Engineers (ASME). Each of these organizations has its own identification numbering system.

3.2.0 Identification of Sizes of Pipe and Fittings

Pipe and fittings are sized according to two factors: inside diameter (I.D.) and wall thickness (*Figure 1*).

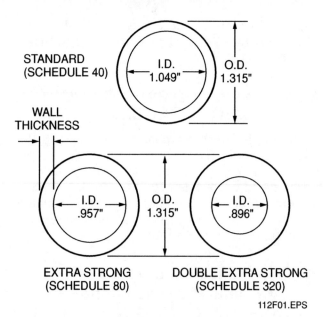

STANDARD
(SCHEDULE 40)

I.D.
1.049"

O.D.
1.315"

WALL
THICKNESS

I.D.
.957"

O.D.
1.315"

I.D.
.896"

EXTRA STRONG
(SCHEDULE 80)

DOUBLE EXTRA STRONG
(SCHEDULE 320)

112F01.EPS

Figure 1 ◆ Inside diameter and wall thickness.

Pipe sizes are generally given in terms of the approximate inside diameter of the pipe rather than the actual I.D. This method is used because the actual I.D. varies as a pipe's wall thickness varies. The approximate inside diameter is called the **nominal pipe size (NPS)**. NPS is usually expressed in inches and fractions of an inch, such as ¼-inch NPS, ½-inch NPS, or 2-inch NPS.

For each NPS, there is one corresponding outside diameter size, but more than one inside diameter. The **schedule number** of a pipe designates its wall thickness. The higher the schedule number, the thicker the pipe wall. For each NPS, there is more than one schedule number. *Table 1* shows the wall thickness and inside diameter for various NPS sizes of pipe.

In addition to schedule numbers, there are other methods used by manufacturers to express pipe wall thickness. One common way is by weight, using three common classifications. In ascending order of wall thickness, they are:

• STD – Standard
• XS – Extra strong
• XXS – Double extra strong

Standard weight pipe is not the same size as Schedule 40 pipe. For sizes of carbon steel pipe 10 inches and under, Schedule 40 is the industry standard. For pipe sizes 12 inches and over, STD-standard weight is the industry standard.

To help select the proper pipe and fitting for a specific application, ANSI has developed allowable working pressure ratings (ANSI B31.3 code) for different types and sizes of pipe. For example, Schedule 80 steel pipe has a higher pressure rating than Schedule 40 steel pipe. These pressure rat-

ings are listed in pounds per square inch (psi) or just pounds. A pipe fitting rating of 150 pounds means that the pipe fitting can be safely used in systems that are exposed to no more than 150 psi.

 WARNING!
Never use a fitting with a lower pressure rating than the specified pipe or the stated system requirements.

When joining pipe and fittings, be sure that both the pipe and the fittings have acceptable pressure ratings for the application. Generally, the pipe and fittings for a job are made of the same material and should meet or exceed the design limitations for pressure and temperature as expressed in the pipe specifications.

3.3.0 Identification of Copper Pipe and Fittings

Copper pipe has its own special identification and sizing method. Different types of copper pipe are identified by standard wall thicknesses designated by ASTM. Each type, K, L, M, and DWV, represents a series of sizes with different wall thicknesses. The inside diameters depend on piping size and wall thickness. The standard grades are:

• K – Heavy grade (*green*)
• L – Medium grade (*blue*)
• M – Light grade (*red*)
• DWV – Used for drains, waste lines, and vents (*yellow*)

Straight lengths of hard copper pipe are marked by a color-coded band printed along the piping. The color codes just indicated are for each specific grade of copper pipe. Soft copper pipe that comes in rolls is not colored coded on the piping. The color codes of soft copper piping are usually marked on the cartons and shipping tags.

4.0.0 ◆ TYPES OF PIPE JOINTS

Industrial piping is connected (joined) to other pipes, pipe fittings, valves, and equipment in various ways. Each method of joining pipe has its advantages and disadvantages. The four most common methods of joining pipe are:

• Threaded joints
• Socket-weld joints
• Flanged joints
• Butt-weld joints

Table 1 Pipe Size Chart

Nominal Pipe Size (Inches)	Schedule Number	Wall Thickness (Inches)	Inside Diameter (Inches)	Outside Diameter (Inches)
⅛	10	0.049	0.269	0.405
	40	0.068	0.215	
	80	0.095	0.307	
¼	10	0.065	0.410	0.540
	40	0.088	0.364	
	80	0.119	0.302	
⅜	10	0.065	0.545	0.675
	40	0.091	0.493	
	80	0.126	0.302	
½	5	0.065	0.710	0.840
	10	0.083	0.674	
	40	0.109	0.622	
	80	0.147	0.546	
	160	0.187	0.466	
	320	0.294	0.252	
¾	5	0.065	0.920	1.050
	10	0.083	0.884	
	40	0.113	0.824	
	80	0.154	0.742	
	160	0.218	0.614	
	320	0.308	0.434	
1	5	0.065	1.185	1.315
	10	0.109	1.097	
	40	0.133	1.049	
	80	0.179	0.957	
	160	0.250	0.815	
	320	0.358	0.599	
1¼	5	0.065	1.530	1.660
	10	0.109	1.442	
	40	0.140	1.380	
	80	0.191	1.278	
	160	0.250	1.160	
	320	0.382	0.896	
1½	5	0.065	1.770	1.900
	10	0.109	1.682	
	40	0.145	1.610	
	80	0.200	1.500	
	160	0.281	1.338	
	320	0.400	1.100	
2	5	0.065	2.245	2.375
	10	0.109	2.157	
	40	0.154	2.067	
	80	0.218	1.939	
	160	0.343	1.689	
	320	0.436	1.503	

4.1.0 Threaded Joints

Threaded joints (screwed joints) are usually used for smaller pipe sizes. A threaded joint is relatively easy to make up and offers the advantage of not requiring welding. This is important in areas where fire hazards might exist. A disadvantage of threaded joints is that they tend to weaken the pipe wall. They are also subject to leaks.

Many different types of threads are used for piping. The most common is the American Standard Pipe Thread, National Pipe Tapered (NPT), that is made to specifications outlined in ANSI Standard B1.2.

Threaded joints are made by screwing the **male threaded end** of a piece of pipe into the **female threaded end** of a fitting or fixture. In a properly threaded joint, the male threads must engage the female threads a certain amount (distance). As the pipe size increases, the **engagement depth** requirement increases. An engagement depth chart for different sizes of iron pipe is shown in *Table 2*.

Table 2 Engagement Depth Chart

Distance Iron Pipe is Turned into Standard Fittings			
Pipe Size (inches)	Engagement (inches)	Pipe Size (inches)	Engagement (inches)
⅛	¼	1¼	11⁄16
¼	⅜	1½	11⁄16
⅜	⅜	2	¾
½	½	2½	15⁄16
¾	9⁄16	3	1
1	11⁄16	3½	1 1⁄16

4.2.0 Socket-Weld Joints

In socket-weld joints, the pipe is inserted into a fitting that has a slightly larger opening than the outside diameter of the pipe. The components are welded around the outside (circumference) of the joint as shown in *Figure 2*.

Socket-weld joints are usually used on smaller pipe sizes. They are easier to align than butt-welded joints, and they are leakproof. The shape of a socket-weld fitting prevents any weld material from entering the bore of the pipe. When using socket-weld fittings, do not allow the pipe to bottom out in the fitting. Since the pipe slips into and is supported by the socket, the socket-weld joint is almost self-aligning.

Socket-welded joints should not be used if there is a potential for corrosion unless stainless steel pipe and fittings are used and welded with the proper welding rod and procedures.

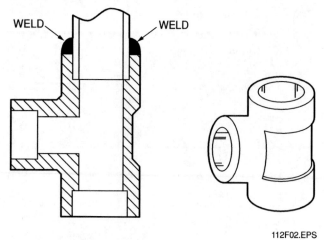

Figure 2 ◆ Socket-weld joint.

4.3.0 Flanged Joints

Flanged joints allow one section of pipe to be bolted to another section of pipe or to instruments, vessels, or valves. Flanges provide a leakproof joint that can easily be taken apart for inspection or repair. A gasket installed between the flange parts aids in eliminating leaks. A flanged joint is shown in *Figure 3*.

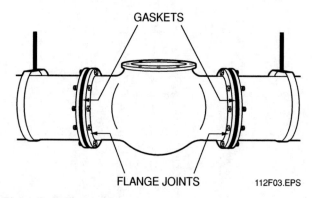

Figure 3 ◆ Flanged joint.

Flanges are identified by size (NPS), pressure rating (psi), type of face, type of mounting (how it is mounted to the pipe), and type of material. A flange size (in inches) refers to the NPS nominal I.D. of the pipe with which the flange is being used.

ANSI has developed a set of standards that are used to determine the pressure ratings for various types and sizes of flanges. The safe pressure limit for any given flange depends on a number of factors including the type of material and temperature range for the system.

Normally, designers or engineers specify that the flange for a particular application conform to the pressure, temperature, and flow requirements of the system. Conditions, such as the corrosiveness of the process fluid, are also considered in the selection of flanges. Generally, flanges are made of the same material as the piping used in the system.

There are several methods of mounting flanges to pipe. There are flanges for butt-welded, socket-welded, and threaded-joint piping systems.

4.4.0 Butt-Weld Joints

Large diameter pipe is sometimes butt-welded. Butt-welded joints are normally used in pressure systems to join pipes and fittings. When butt-welding joints, the edges are prepared by either chamfering or beveling, as shown in *Figure 4*.

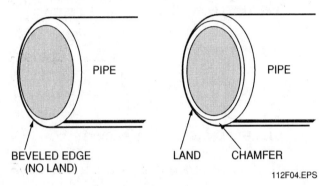

Figure 4 ◆ Bevel and chamfer.

A bevel is an angle cut on the end of the pipe. A chamfer is an angle cut only on the edge of the pipe. The flat edge of pipe left after a chamfer is cut is called the *land* or *root face*. A chamfer is sometimes improperly called a bevel. After the ends of the pipes have been beveled or chamfered, the two pipes are lined up and welded around the outside of the joint.

When using butt-welded fittings, the pipe ends must be chamfered. Chamfering helps the welder get good **penetration** at the joint and produces a strong weld. The chamfer should extend to about ¹⁄₁₆ inch from the inside wall. The land that is left makes a wall that helps to fit up the joint.

5.0.0 ◆ FITTINGS

Pipe fittings are devices used to join pipe and **pipe run** components. Fittings should be the same size (NPS) and made of the same material as the pipe to which they are connected. Pipe fittings are made to perform one of five functions:

- Connect pipes and components of different sizes
- Extend the length of a straight pipe run
- Change the direction of a pipe run
- Provide branch connections
- Close off the end of a pipe run

5.1.0 Nipples

Nipples are pieces of pipe less than 12 inches long, with outside threads on both ends as shown in *Figure 5*. Pipe over 12 inches long is classified as cut pipe.

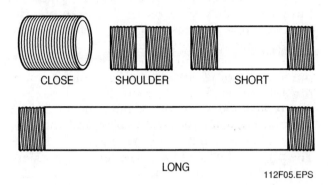

Figure 5 ◆ Nipples.

Nipples have a variety of uses. They are used to extend the length of a pipe run so that a piece of pipe can be joined with another component. They are also used with fittings to change the direction of a pipe run. Nipples are used to mount instruments to a process and gauges to an instrument or pipe. Since a nipple has outside (male) threads, a fitting with inside (female) threads, such as a coupling or a **union**, must be used to join the nipple to the pipe. Nipples come in different lengths and are classified as *close nipples, shoulder nipples, short and long nipples*, and by their NPS length in inches.

5.2.0 Couplings

Couplings are used to connect two components in a piping system, such as two pieces of pipe or a pipe and a nipple. Couplings do not change direction, branch, or stop the flow through the run. Sometimes, reducers and **bushings** are classified as couplings. Couplings can be threaded or welded, as shown in *Figure 6*.

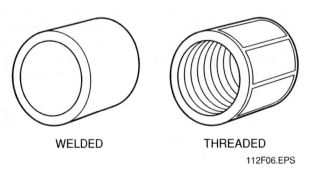

Figure 6 ◆ Couplings.

5.3.0 Unions

A union is used to join two components such as two pieces of pipe. Unions do not change the direction, branch, or stop the flow through the run. A union differs from a coupling in that a union can connect two components that cannot be turned and screwed together. For example, two pieces of pipe that have been bracketed to a wall can be connected with a union. The union can make the connection even though the brackets prevent the pipes from turning. Unions can be threaded or welded.

A typical union consists of three pieces: a union nut and two end pieces. On a typical threaded union (*Figure 7*), both ends have internal threads. The pipes to be joined are screwed into each end of the union. Then, the union nut is tightened to draw the two pipes together. On a socket-weld union, the pipe is welded into each end of the union. Then, the union nut is tightened to draw the two pipes together.

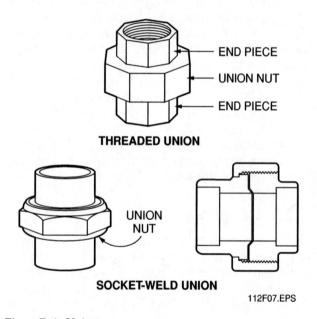

Figure 7 ◆ Unions.

It is important that the union be compatible with the piping material it is mounted with (steel to steel, brass to brass, etc.). Also, the two ends of the union that the union nut ties together are a female and male end. Be certain that the male end is installed on the upstream section of pipe to help prevent leakage.

5.4.0 Elbows

An elbow is a fitting that changes the direction of a piping run. It is commonly referred to as an *ell* (or L). The standard angles of elbows are 45 degrees and 90 degrees, although they are also available in other angles, as shown in *Figure 8*.

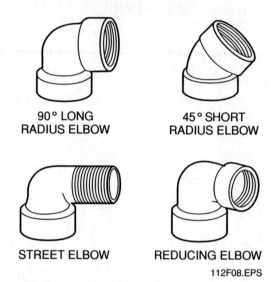

Figure 8 ◆ Threaded elbows.

There are two main types of elbows: long radius and short radius. Other types include reducing ells and street ells. Reducing elbows change the size of a pipe run. Street elbows have male threads on one end and female threads on the other end.

Elbows can be threaded or welded. Normally, threaded elbows have inside threads on both ends. They are used to connect two components that have outside threads. A threaded elbow is installed by screwing it, by hand, to a component until the elbow is finger tight. Then, the elbow is tightened with pipe wrenches until its open end faces in the desired direction for connection to the other component. The other component is then screwed into the open end of the elbow until it is tight. If the fitting is tightened past the desired direction, do not turn the fitting back because this could cause leaks. Take the fitting off and start again.

5.5.0 Tees

Tees are the most commonly used type of branching fitting. They are available in a variety of sizes and designs. Tees are used to join a main pipe run to a branch pipe at a 90-degree angle, as shown in *Figure 9*.

When all the outlets of the tee are the same size (regular tee), the tee is specified by that size, such as a 2-inch tee. If the outlet sizes vary, the tee is

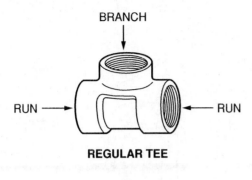

REGULAR TEE

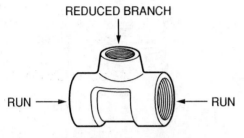

**REDUCING TEE STRAIGHT RUN,
REDUCED BRANCH**

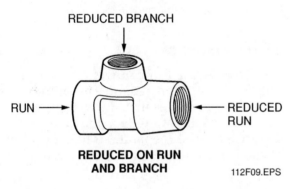

**REDUCED ON RUN
AND BRANCH**

112F09.EPS

Figure 9 ◆ Tees.

called a *reducing tee*. When the sizes of the run and the branch are different, the tee is referred to by giving the main run size first and then the branch size, such as a 2-inch × 2-inch × 1-inch tee. In a reducing tee, the branch outlet is smaller than the run outlets, thus reducing the flow of material through that section of the system. Some reducing tees have both smaller branch and run outlets. For example, a tee with one run outlet of 2 inches, a second run outlet of 1 inch, and a branch outlet of ¾ inch is referred to as a 2-inch × 1-inch × ¾-inch tee. Tees can be threaded or welded.

5.6.0 Crosses

Cross fittings, or crosses, are similar to tees, except that crosses have two branch outlets instead of one, as shown in *Figure 10*. The outlets form the shape of a cross. Crosses, like tees, are made in a

variety of sizes and designs. Crosses can be threaded or welded. All four outlets in a straight cross are equal in size. In a reducing cross, the two branch outlets are smaller than the run outlets in order to obtain the desired material flow and pressure through the system.

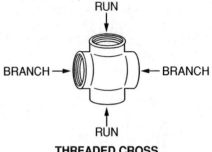

THREADED CROSS

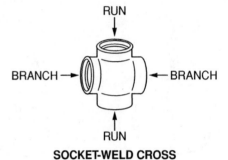

SOCKET-WELD CROSS

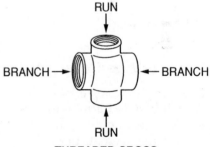

**THREADED CROSS
WITH REDUCED RUNS**

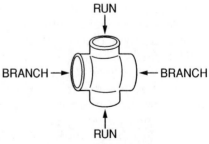

**BUTT-WELD CROSS
WITH REDUCED RUNS**

112F10.EPS

Figure 10 ◆ Crosses.

5.7.0 Caps and Plugs

Caps and plugs (*Figure 11*) are used to close openings in other fittings. They can be threaded or welded and are available in many sizes and shapes. Threaded caps have inside threads. They are screwed onto the end of components with outside threads, such as pipes, to close off the end. Threaded plugs are similar to caps, except that plugs have outside threads. They are screwed into components with inside threads, to close off their ends.

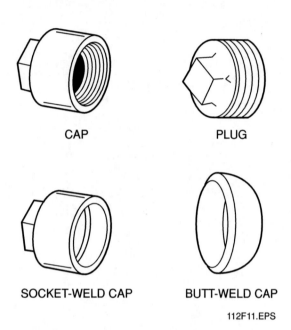

CAP   PLUG

SOCKET-WELD CAP   BUTT-WELD CAP

112F11.EPS

Figure 11 ◆ Caps and plug.

5.8.0 Tube-to-Pipe Connector

Many pneumatic systems contain both pipe and tubing. A fitting called a tube-to-pipe connector, or adapter, is used to make connections between pipe and tubing. Two types of tube-to-pipe adapters are shown in *Figure 12*.

On a male adapter, one end of the adapter has male NPT threads that can be screwed into a pipe fitting or component. The other end of the adapter is designed to take a piece of tubing.

On a female adapter, one end of the adapter has female NPT threads. The adapter is screwed onto the end of pipe with outside threads. The other end of the adapter is designed to take a piece of tubing.

When specifying tube-to-pipe adapters, the size of the tubing is given first. For example, a tube-to-pipe adapter for joining ½ inch outside diameter tubing to a ¼ inch NPT screwed connection is called a *½ inch × ¼ inch male adapter*.

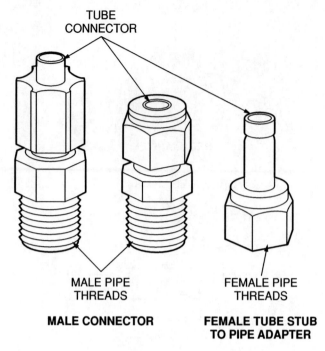

TUBE CONNECTOR

MALE PIPE THREADS   FEMALE PIPE THREADS

MALE CONNECTOR   **FEMALE TUBE STUB TO PIPE ADAPTER**

112F12.EPS

Figure 12 ◆ Tube-to-pipe adapters.

5.9.0 Reducers

A reducer is used to connect a larger pipe to a smaller pipe. One reason for doing so is to increase flow pressure in a piping system. Another reason is to reduce the volume of fluid. Reducers may be a separate straight fitting or may be shaped like a reducing elbow tee, as shown in *Figure 13*.

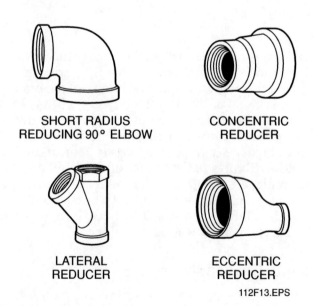

SHORT RADIUS REDUCING 90° ELBOW   CONCENTRIC REDUCER

LATERAL REDUCER   ECCENTRIC REDUCER

112F13.EPS

Figure 13 ◆ Reducers.

Most fittings that cause a change of direction or have branch connections are available with reduced outputs. Reducers can be **concentric** or **eccentric**. Both of the outlets on a concentric reducer are on the same plane; the outlets of an eccentric reducer are on different planes. Reducers can be threaded or welded.

5.10.0 Bushings

A bushing (*Figure 14*) is a fitting that can be used to connect pipes or components of different sizes. Bushings are commonly used to reduce the size of the pipe run by being inserted into another fitting in the pipe run. Bushings can be threaded or welded. Most threaded bushings have male threads on one end and female threads of a different size on the other end. This allows the bushing to connect a smaller component to a larger component. A socket-weld bushing is called an *insert*.

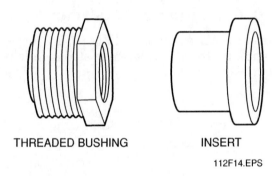

THREADED BUSHING   INSERT

112F14.EPS

Figure 14 ◆ Bushings.

5.11.0 Return Bends

A return bend is a U-shaped fitting that carries the fluid in the pipe through a 180-degree turn. Return fittings, as shown in *Figure 15*, are often used for piping in heater coils and heat exchangers.

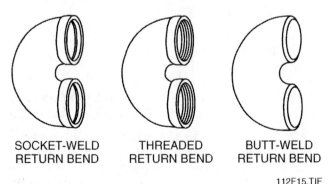

SOCKET-WELD   THREADED   BUTT-WELD
RETURN BEND   RETURN BEND   RETURN BEND

112F15.TIF

Figure 15 ◆ Return bends.

5.12.0 Branch Connections

Branch connections are fittings that divide the flow of a piping run into two or more lines (branches), as shown in *Figure 16*. Any addition to the main pipe run in a piping system is made using a branch connection. Tees and crosses (described earlier) are specific types of branch connections. Branch connections can be threaded or welded.

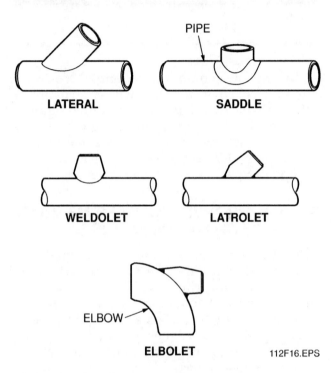

LATERAL   SADDLE

WELDOLET   LATROLET

ELBOW

ELBOLET   112F16.EPS

Figure 16 ◆ Branch connections.

6.0.0 ◆ PROPER AND SAFE METHODS FOR STORING PIPE

Proper and safe storage of pipe may seem like a simple task. However, a surprising amount of pipe is damaged, a great deal of time is wasted, and many personal injuries occur from improper pipe storage.

Pipe racks are commonly used for storing pipe. The racks provide support to prevent bending, sagging, distortion, scratching, or marring of pipe surfaces. Most racks have compartments where different types and sizes of pipe can be separated for ease of identification and selection. The storage compartments in racks are usually elevated to help avoid damage that might occur at floor level. Pipe stored at floor level is easily damaged or contaminated by people, other materials, moisture, or equipment in the area.

The ends of stored pipe should be sealed to help prevent damage. Pipe ends can be capped, taped, or plugged to seal them. Always inspect pipe before storing it to make sure it's clean inside and outside and not damaged.

> **WARNING!**
> Be sure stored pipe is securely held in place to prevent it from rolling in any way that can cause injury.

To prevent contamination and corrosion of stored pipe, cover the pipe with a tarpaulin or other suitable covering. Covering stored pipe also helps prevent damage from sunlight and other environmental factors that affect some types of plastic pipe. Different types of pipe should also be separated from noncompatible materials.

7.0.0 ◆ PROPER AND SAFE METHODS FOR HANDLING PIPE

Pipe can be damaged or otherwise degraded by careless handling. From the time pipe is delivered on a job site until its installation is complete, proper and safe handling methods must be used to assure quality work. Some basic guidelines for handling pipe that will help you avoid damaging or contaminating the pipe or injuring yourself or others are given here:

- Never drag pipe off a delivery truck or storage rack, or drag it on the ground or floor. Dragging pipe across any rough surface can scratch or dent the outside surface, damage the ends, or contaminate the piping. Scratches on piping are paths for leaks.
- Keep pipe away from any material that might contaminate it during handling.
- Put flags on the ends of long lengths of pipe during handling and transporting so that you and others can easily see the pipe ends and avoid damage or accidents.
- Be aware of people, materials, and equipment around you when handling or transporting pipe so that you can avoid hitting anyone or anything with the pipe.
- Keep the end caps on during handling or transporting of pipe to avoid damage to ends and/or dirt or other contamination from entering the pipe.
- Wear gloves when handling pipe to avoid injuring yourself on rough or sharp edges of the pipe or pipe threads.

- Don't use a vise to hold pipe unless the vise is equipped with special jaws for holding and protecting pipe.
- When two people are carrying pipe, each person should grasp the pipe at about one quarter of the length of pipe from the end. Walk in step while carrying the pipe. Lift and set down the pipe together.
- When carrying pipe, make sure the load is balanced.

8.0.0 ◆ PIPE LENGTH CALCULATION METHODS

There are three basic ways to find the correct length of pipe needed between two fittings:

- The center-to-center method
- The face-to-face method
- The shoulder-to-shoulder method

8.1.0 Center-to-Center Method

To find the correct length of pipe using the center to center method, follow these steps while referring to *Figure 17*.

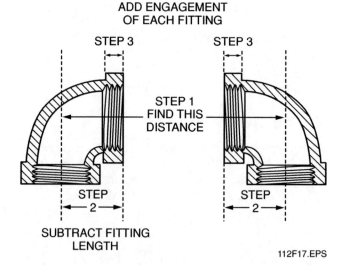

Figure 17 ◆ Center-to-center.

Step 1 Measure the distance from the center of one fitting to the center of the other fitting.

Step 2 Subtract the distances from the center of each fitting to the face of each fitting from the center-to-center measurement in Step 1.

Step 3 Add the engagement depth of each fitting to the result of the calculation in Step 2. This is the length of pipe that needs to be cut.

8.2.0 Face-to-Face Method

To find the correct length of pipe using the face-to-face method, follow these steps while referring to *Figure 18*.

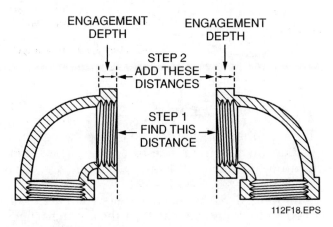

Figure 18 ◆ Face-to-face.

Step 1   Measure the distance from the face of one fitting to the face of the other fitting.

Step 2   Add the engagement depth of each fitting to the distance from face-to-face measured in Step 1. This is the length of pipe that needs to be cut.

8.3.0 Shoulder-to-Shoulder Method

To find the correct length of pipe using the shoulder-to-shoulder method (*Figure 19*), measure the distance from the shoulder of one fitting to the shoulder of the other fitting. This is the length of pipe that needs to be cut.

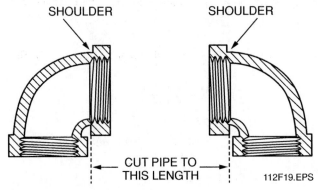

Figure 19 ◆ Shoulder-to-shoulder.

9.0.0 ◆ PIPE CUTTING TOOLS

Pipe is generally cut with a pipe cutter or with saws such as a hacksaw, band saw, or backsaw. It can also be cut with a tubing cutter or a cutting torch.

The type of cutting tool used depends on the size and type of pipe to be cut. It is recommended that you check the manufacturer's manual to make sure you are using the correct cutting tool.

9.1.0 Pipe Cutters

Pipe cutters have cutting wheels that are rotated around a pipe to cut it, making quick and accurate cuts. The advantage of using a pipe cutter over a saw is the accuracy and smoothness of the cut. There are several different types of pipe cutters that can be used to cut pipe:

- Single-wheel cutter
- Two-wheel cutter
- Four-wheel cutter
- Plastic pipe cutter
- Tubing cutter
- Chain pipe cutters

9.1.1 Single-Wheel Pipe Cutter

A single-wheel cutter, shown in *Figure 20*, is rotated entirely around the pipe during cutting.

Single-wheel cutters can only be used when there is enough space available to rotate the cutter all the way around the pipe. The pipe cutter is placed over the pipe until its cutting wheel is aligned with the mark where the pipe is to be cut. The handle is then turned to tighten the cutting wheel. Next, the pipe cutter is rotated around the pipe as the handle is gradually tightened, causing the cutting wheel to cut into the pipe. The cutter rotation and tightening of the handle continue until the pipe is cut completely through. It is good practice to tighten the handle when the cutting wheel is at a different position on the pipe each time.

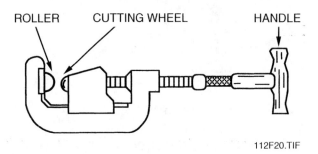

Figure 20 ◆ Single-wheel pipe cutter.

9.1.2 Two-Wheel Pipe Cutter

A two-wheel cutter (*Figure 21*) is used like the single-wheel cutter, except that you need to rotate the cutter around the pipe only in half-turns instead of complete turns when cutting pipe.

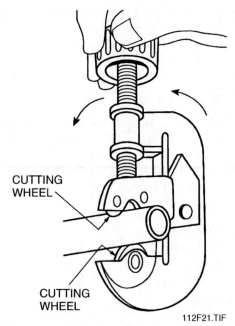

Figure 21 ◆ Two-wheel pipe cutter.

9.1.3 Four-Wheel Pipe Cutter

The four-wheel cutter (*Figure 22*) can be used when there is not enough space to rotate the cutter around the pipe more than one-third of a turn. The four-wheel cutter is operated like a single- or two-wheel cutter, except that the pipe cutter is not rotated around the pipe. The four-wheel cutter is rotated back and forth as the handle is tightened.

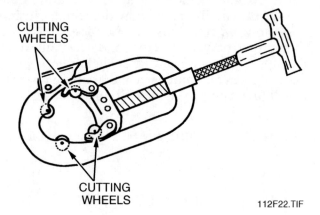

Figure 22 ◆ Four-wheel pipe cutter.

9.1.4 Plastic Pipe Cutter

A plastic pipe cutter like the one shown in *Figure 23* has a spring-loaded compound leverage ratchet mechanism and a hardened steel blade. This type of cutter is typically used to cut ⅛-inch to 1½-inch O.D. plastic pipe. Other plastic pipe cutters are made that are similar in construction to the metal pipe cutters described earlier, except they use a chisel-like blade instead of a cutting wheel.

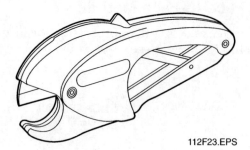

Figure 23 ◆ Plastic pipe cutter.

9.1.5 Tubing Cutters

Tubing cutters (*Figure 24*) can be used to cut thin-walled metal pipe made of copper, brass, aluminum, or steel. Tube cutters come in several types and sizes. Small, single-wheel cutters are commonly used. Some have rollers that are tightened to force the pipe against the cutting wheel. Others have a sliding cutting wheel that is forced against the pipe.

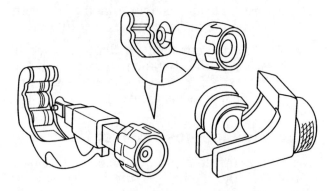

SLIDING CUTTING WHEEL

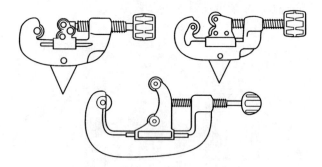

SINGLE ROLLER TYPES

Figure 24 ◆ Tubing cutters.

9.1.6 Chain Pipe Cutter

Several types of chain pipe cutters are used to cut cast-iron soil pipe. A typical chain pipe cutter is shown in *Figure 25*. The different types of chain pipe cutters work in basically the same way. Each link of the chain contains a cutting wheel.

The chain is slipped over the pipe and tightened. Pressure is then applied to tighten the chain around the pipe while the cutter is rocked until the pipe is cut.

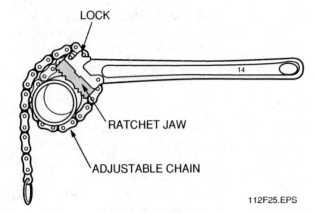

Figure 25 ◆ Chain pipe cutter.

9.2.0 Saws

Hacksaws and band saws can be used to cut metal and plastic pipe. When using a saw to cut pipe, make sure to choose the correct blade for the job. Two teeth of the blade should always be in contact with the pipe. For thin-walled pipe, use a blade with smaller teeth.

9.2.1 Hacksaw

Hacksaws (*Figure 26*) can be used to cut metal and plastic pipe. Blades used with a hacksaw are made of steel that has been hardened and tempered. The distance between each tooth on the blade is called the *pitch*. A pitch of 1/18 represents 18 teeth per inch. The most common blades used for instrumentation work have 14, 18, 24, or 32 teeth per inch.

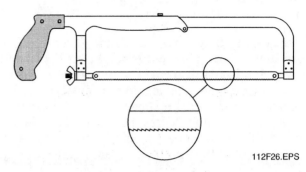

Figure 26 ◆ Hacksaw.

When using a hacksaw to cut metal pipe, guide-blocks (*Figure 27*) are often used to hold the pipe steady. This ensures a square cut. Cutting with a hacksaw is done on the forward motion of the blade. Two teeth of the blade should always be in contact with the pipe. For thin-walled pipe, use a blade with smaller teeth. When cutting stainless steel pipe, use a high-speed stainless steel blade.

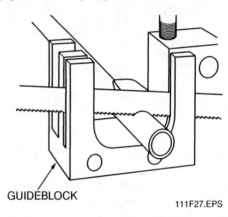

GUIDEBLOCK

Figure 27 ◆ Cutting pipe with a hacksaw and guideblocks.

Figure 28 shows the recommended blade pitches for cutting different types of metal.

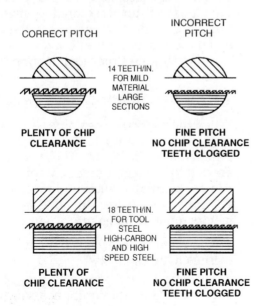

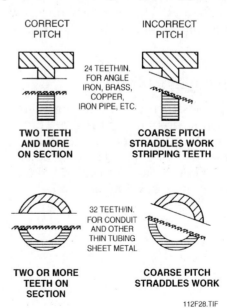

CORRECT PITCH		INCORRECT PITCH
PLENTY OF CHIP CLEARANCE	14 TEETH/IN. FOR MILD MATERIAL LARGE SECTIONS	FINE PITCH NO CHIP CLEARANCE TEETH CLOGGED
PLENTY OF CHIP CLEARANCE	18 TEETH/IN. FOR TOOL STEEL HIGH-CARBON AND HIGH SPEED STEEL	FINE PITCH NO CHIP CLEARANCE TEETH CLOGGED

CORRECT PITCH		INCORRECT PITCH
TWO TEETH AND MORE ON SECTION	24 TEETH/IN. FOR ANGLE IRON, BRASS, COPPER, IRON PIPE, ETC.	COARSE PITCH STRADDLES WORK STRIPPING TEETH
TWO OR MORE TEETH ON SECTION	32 TEETH/IN. FOR CONDUIT AND OTHER THIN TUBING SHEET METAL	COARSE PITCH STRADDLES WORK

Figure 28 ◆ Recommended pitches.

9.2.2 Portable Band Saw

Heavy-duty band saws are ideal for continuous production use. They cut much faster than hacksaws. Band saws also cut cleaner than pipe cutters or oxyacetylene torches. When cutting with a portable band saw, be sure to place the brace or stop plate located below the saw blade firmly against the pipe to be cut, as shown in *Figure 29*. The weight of the saw alone is enough to provide the leverage needed for cutting. Very little pressure is needed to make a good, clean cut with a band saw.

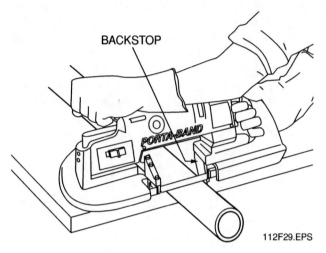

BACKSTOP

112F29.EPS

Figure 29 ◆ Cutting pipe with a portable band saw.

To select the correct blade for a band saw, the size and shape of the work and type of material to be cut must be taken into consideration. As a rule of thumb, soft materials require fine-tooth blades. For thick materials, coarse-tooth blades work best because the large gullets allow room for the long chips. For thin materials, at least two teeth should be in the cut. Fine-tooth blades are usually used to cut tubing and pipe when a smoother finish is important.

9.3.0 Beveling Machine

On most large construction sites, a pipe beveling machine is used to prepare pipe edges. The pipe beveling machine is fitted over the end of the pipe and then tightened to the pipe. It is then adjusted to cut the correct bevel. There are several different types and sizes of pipe beveling machines.

9.4.0 Cutting Torch

 WARNING!
Follow all manufacturer's instructions and safety precautions when working with cutting torches. Only trained and authorized persons are permitted to use oxyfuel equipment and cutting torches.

If you are properly trained and authorized to use oxyfuel equipment, you may use a cutting torch to cut bevels to form pipe joints for welding. When using a torch to cut a piece of pipe, keep the torch pointed toward the centerline of the pipe. Start the cut at the top and cut down one side. Then begin at the top again and cut down the other side, finishing at the bottom of the pipe.

Cutting pipe with a torch requires a steady hand to get a good bevel cut (one that is smooth and true). Do not try to cut and bevel a heavy pipe in one operation until you have developed considerable skill. Cut the pipe off square first, removing all slag from inside the pipe. Then proceed to bevel the pipe.

10.0.0 ◆ PIPE RUN PREPARATION

One of the first steps in preparing to install a pipe run is to determine what tools and materials are needed. In many cases, you will receive a work order (a written description of the job to be done). The work order may include diagrams showing the route that the pipe is to follow and a list of required parts and materials referred to in the piping specifications. If diagrams are not provided, it is helpful to make a sketch of the pipe run. Note the lengths, sizes, and types of pipe needed and the types of fittings required to make the connections. If possible, all tools and materials should be assembled at one time to avoid making several trips back to the storeroom or shop.

10.1.0 Calculating Pipe Length

When the materials for a pipe run have been gathered, it is necessary to determine the lengths of pipe required in the run. The exact lengths of pipe needed to connect components or fittings in a pipe run are normally cut from longer pieces of pipe. For pipe runs using threaded connections, two factors must be taken into account:

- The distance between the components or fittings to be connected
- The length (engagement depth) of pipe needed to thread into the components or fittings

To calculate pipe length using the face-to-face method described earlier, follow these steps.

Step 1 Measure the distance from the face of one fitting to the face of the other fitting.

Step 2 Add the engagement depth of each fitting to the distance from face to face measured in Step 1. This is the length of pipe that needs to be cut.

For example, using the face-to-face method to determine the exact length of pipe needed to connect the fittings (A and B) shown in *Figure 30*, the first step is to measure the face-to-face distance between the fittings.

Let's assume that the face-to-face measurement indicates that the distance between fittings A and B is 5 feet and that we are using 2-inch NPS iron pipe. The next step is to determine the length of pipe needed to thread into the fittings (engagement depth). These measurements are added to the face-to-face measurement. Use of an engagement depth chart shows that the engagement depth for 2-inch iron pipe is ¾ inch for each fitting (measurements C-D and E-F). The result of this calculation (5 feet + ¾ inch + ¾ inch = 5 feet, 1½ inches) is the exact length of pipe needed to connect the fittings.

> **NOTE**
> The engagement depth varies with the size of the pipe.

10.2.0 Cutting Pipe

Once the required length of pipe has been calculated, it can be measured with a rule and then cut.

Pipe is generally marked with a pencil at the spot where it is to be cut. If using a hacksaw, use a wrap around to mark the pipe all the way around. The pipe should be held securely in a pipe vise and the vise tightened only enough to prevent the pipe from slipping, but not enough to damage the pipe walls.

Metal pipe is generally cut with a pipe cutter or a hacksaw. Plastic pipe is generally cut with snips, or with a hacksaw and miter box. As discussed earlier, a pipe cutter is a tool with cutting wheels that is rotated around a pipe to cut it (*Figure 31*).

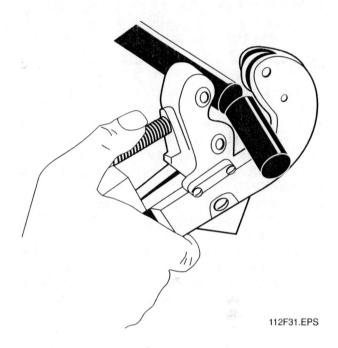

112F31.EPS

Figure 31 ◆ Cutting pipe.

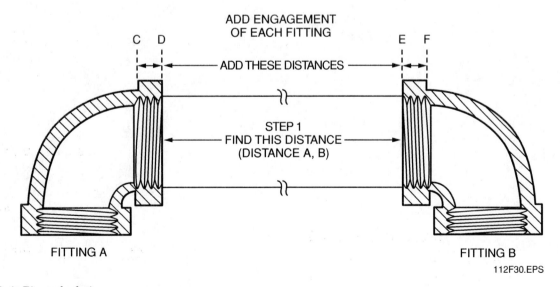

112F30.EPS

Figure 30 ◆ Pipe calculation.

The pipe cutter is placed over the pipe until its cutting wheels are aligned with the mark where the pipe is to be cut. Next, the handle is gradually turned to tighten the cutting wheels as the pipe cutter is rotated around the pipe. This causes the cutting wheels to cut into the pipe. The rotation continues until the pipe is cut all the way through. Make sure to support the free end of the pipe so that when the cut is made, the free end of the pipe does not fall on your foot, the ground, or the floor.

CAUTION

Be careful not to apply too much pressure to the cutter since this could cause the pipe to collapse or flatten. Tighten the handle with the cutting wheel at different positions on the pipe each time.

A hacksaw can also be used to cut pipe. When using a hacksaw to cut pipe, the blade should be kept as perpendicular as possible (at a right angle) to the pipe. When the blade is not perpendicular to the pipe, the hacksaw may cut the pipe unevenly. An uneven pipe cut must be squared off with a file.

Cutting pipe may leave burrs and ridges on the inside or outside of the pipe. Burrs are jagged bits of pipe. A ridge is a lip, or shoulder, left on the pipe's end. Burrs and ridges can restrict flow through the pipe and can prevent the pipe from being properly connected to other components. Internal burrs and ridges can be removed with a pipe reamer (*Figure 32*).

WARNING!

Spiral pipe reamers have a tendency to grab or bite the inner wall of the pipe and rapidly screw into the pipe. Use extreme caution when using this type of reamer, as injuries can result in attempting to correct this tendency.

The flute of the reamer is inserted into the pipe and pushed enough to exert a slight pressure without damaging the pipe wall. The reamer is then rotated to remove the internal burrs and ridges. The inside of the pipe should be reamed until it is smooth.

NOTE

Do not ream beyond the inside diameter of the pipe.

A half-round file or a round (rattail) file, as shown in *Figure 33*, can also be used to remove internal burrs and ridges from pipe. A round file should only be used when the pipe I.D. is too small to use a half-round file. A round file can leave indentations on the inside walls. This makes the pipe wall thin in places and may lead to early failure.

External burrs and ridges can be removed with a flat file. The pipe should be filed with an arc-like motion, moving around the circumference of the pipe. Filing with a flat motion can leave flat spots on the pipe.

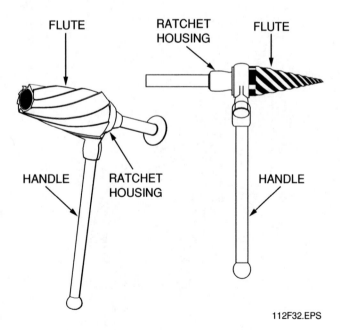

Figure 32 ◆ Spiral ratchet pipe reamers.

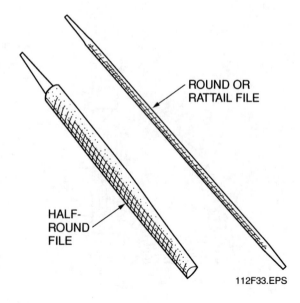

Figure 33 ◆ Files for deburring.

Another method of removing minor external burrs and ridges is to rub the end of the pipe with emery cloth. After all burrs and ridges have been removed, the pipe should be wiped clean inside and out with a rag. Shavings left inside the pipe can contaminate the piping system.

When one or more pipe sections in a pipe run have been measured, cut, and reamed, the pipe is ready to be threaded.

10.3.0 Threading Pipe

Male threads on pipe are made with a **pipe die** (*Figure 34*). The teeth of the pipe die cut into the outside walls of the pipe to form threads. The size of the die used must match the size of the pipe to be threaded. For example, a ½-inch – ¾-inch pipe die can thread ½-inch and ¾-inch NPS pipe. The size of a pipe die is usually indicated on the die.

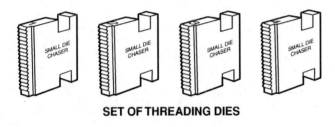

SET OF THREADING DIES

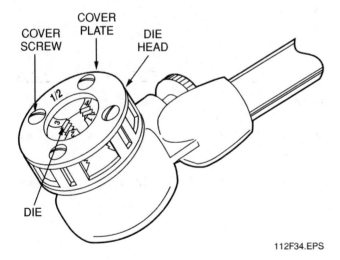

112F34.EPS

Figure 34 ◆ Pipe die.

You must also choose a die that will cut the correct number of threads per inch. If you use the wrong die, the pipe threads will not match the fitting threads. **Thread gauges**, such as the one shown in *Figure 35*, can be used to check the threads of existing threaded pipe.

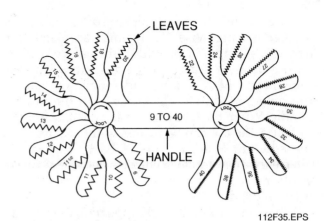

112F35.EPS

Figure 35 ◆ Thread gauge.

When cutting threads on a pipe, you must also cut the proper length of threads. If the thread length is too short, the joint will be weak and may leak. If the thread length is too long, the pipe joint may be hard to put together and may leak.

The sample chart in *Table 3* shows the correct die to use, the correct length of threads to cut, and the number of threads to cut for each size of pipe up to 12 inches in diameter.

 CAUTION

Only Schedule 40 or higher metal pipe can be threaded. Schedule 120 PVC pipe may also be threaded.

Table 3 Die Chart

Pipe I.D. Size (inches)	Die Threads (per inch)	Thread Length (inches)	Number of Threads
⅛	27	⅜	10
¼	18	⅝	11
⅜	18	⅝	11
½	14	¾	10
¾	14	¾	10
1	11½	⅞	10
1⅛	11½	1	11
1½	11½	1	11
2	11½	1	11
2½	8	1½	12
3	8	1½	12
3½	8	1⅝	13
4	8	1⅝	13
5	8	1¾	14
6	8	1¾	14
8	8	1⅞	15
10	8	2	16
12	8	2⅛	17

When hand threading pipe, it must be firmly secured in a pipe vise. Cutting oil is applied to the end of the pipe to provide lubrication and to reduce the heat caused by the die cutting into the pipe. Next, the die is pressed against the end of the pipe and turned clockwise with the ratchet handle. When the teeth of the pipe die take hold of the pipe, the die can be turned without having to press the die against the pipe. Back off the head after each turn to clear chips. After a few turns, apply more cutting oil to the pipe through the holes in the die.

When one or two threads appear on the outside of the die, as shown in *Figure 36*, the pipe is fully threaded. Reverse the knob on the ratchet to back the die head off of the threads. Remove the cut shavings and chips from the pipe to preserve the threads.

> **WARNING!**
> Be careful when cleaning and handling pipe threads. The threads are sharp and can cut you.

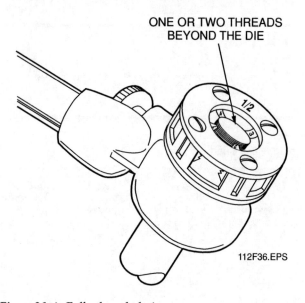

ONE OR TWO THREADS BEYOND THE DIE

112F36.EPS

Figure 36 ◆ Fully threaded pipe.

After the pipe has been threaded, clean it with a wire brush to remove any shavings. Next, apply **joint compound** or some other kind of thread lubricant to the pipe to prepare it for connection to a fitting.

Summary

Piping installation is an important part of instrument work. Take the time to practice the skills learned in this module. It takes a lot of practice, study, and on-the-job experience to develop the skills needed to be expert in working with piping systems.

An important element in proper piping installation is the ability to identify types of piping and fittings. An installer must be familiar with the standards that pertain to piping and fittings. Proper procedures for storing and handling piping as well as those for cutting and threading pipe must be followed.

Review Questions

1. Which of the following statements about pipe or piping systems is *not* true?
   a. Pipe is more rigid than tubing.
   b. Pipe has thicker walls than tubing.
   c. Pipe is harder to bend than tubing.
   d. Pipe runs normally require fewer fittings than tubing runs.

2. _____ pipe is corrosion-resistant and can easily be kept sterile to prevent contamination.
   a. Copper
   b. Inconel®
   c. PVC
   d. Stainless steel

3. _____ pipe is used for highly corrosive applications such as boiling sulfuric acid.
   a. Carbon steel
   b. Copper
   c. Hastelloy®
   d. PVC

4. The purpose of applying a primer solution when connecting PVC piping is to _____.
   a. soften the pipe
   b. initiate fusing
   c. remove contaminants
   d. harden the pipe

5. Ordinary PVC piping can safely be used to transport fluids with a maximum operating temperature of approximately _____ without distortion occurring in the piping.
   a. 140°F
   b. 200°F
   c. 300°F
   d. 450°F

6. An ASTM pipe identification number beginning with a B indicates that the pipe is made of _____ metal.
   a. ferrous
   b. nonferrous
   c. annealed
   d. hardened

7. Pipe is normally sized according to its _____.
   a. inside diameter and wall thickness
   b. nominal size and schedule
   c. wall thickness and length
   d. material and outside diameter

8. _____ pipe comes in standard grades K, L, M, and DWV.
   a. Carbon steel
   b. Stainless steel
   c. Copper
   d. Monel®

9. In _____ connections the pipe is inserted into a fitting that has a slightly larger opening than the O.D. of the pipe.
   a. butt-weld
   b. flanged
   c. socket weld
   d. threaded

10. _____ connections allow two sections of pipe to be bolted together.
    a. Flanged
    b. Butt-weld
    c. Socket-weld
    d. Threaded

11. When storing pipe it is good work practice to _____.
    a. lay the pipe on the floor
    b. store different sizes and types of pipe together
    c. remove the end caps to let the pipe breathe
    d. cover the pipe with protective covering

12. The pipe length calculation method that requires only one measurement is called the _____ method.
    a. face-to-face
    b. shoulder-to-shoulder
    c. center-to-center
    d. fitting-to-fitting

13. When using a single-wheel pipe cutter, you should _____.
    a. tighten the cutter at different positions on the pipe as you rotate it around the pipe
    b. tighten the cutting wheel as hard as possible against the pipe before starting to cut
    c. turn the pipe rapidly while holding the cutter steady
    d. mark the pipe about ½-inch from where the actual cut is to be made to allow for cutting wheel angle

14. When using a portable band saw to cut piping, the brace or stop plate on the saw should be positioned _____.
    a. firmly against the material to be cut
    b. so that it is not touching the pipe
    c. lightly pressed against the pipe
    d. loosely and at an angle to the material being cut

15. A _____ file is preferred for removing burrs from the inside of newly cut piping.
    a. flat
    b. half-round
    c. rattail
    d. round

Trade Terms Introduced in This Module

Bushing: A pipe fitting with male and female threads used to connect pipes or components of different sizes.

Concentric: A term meaning *to have a common center*. The term is used in piping to describe a reducer fitting (concentric reducer) where the centers of the outlets are on the same plane.

Eccentric: A term meaning *not having the same center*. The term is used in piping to describe a type of reducer fitting (eccentric reducer) where the centers of the outlets are on different planes.

Engagement depth: A measure of the length of pipe that is screwed into a component.

Female threaded end: An end or fitting with threads on the inside.

Joint compound: A type of thread lubricant that is applied to the outside threads of a pipe.

Male threaded end: An end or fitting with threads on the outside.

Nipple: A short piece of pipe, 12 inches or less, with male threads on both ends used to connect two female components.

Nominal pipe size (NPS): The approximate size of a pipe's inside diameter. NPS is usually used to designate the size of pipe.

Penetration: In welding, the depth of the molten weld pool into the workpiece.

Pipe die: A device used for making outside threads on pipe.

Pipe run: The network of pipe for a given process or control system.

Schedule number: A means of referring to a pipe's wall thickness. The higher the schedule number, the thicker the pipe wall.

Thread gauge: A tool used to determine how many threads per inch are cut in a tap, die, bolt, nut, or pipe.

Union: A fitting used to join two sections of pipe without changing the direction, branching, or stopping the flow through the run. A union has a union nut for assembly or disassembly.

Additional Resources

This module is intended to present thorough resources for task training. The following reference works are suggested for further study. These are optional materials for continued education rather than for task training.

Standards and Specifications for Piping. 1819 L Street NW, Washington, DC: American National Standards Institute (ANSI).

Standards and Specifications for Piping. Three Park Avenue, New York, NY: American Society for Mechanical Engineers (ASME).

NCCER CRAFT TRAINING USER UPDATES

The NCCER makes every effort to keep these textbooks up-to-date and free of technical errors. We appreciate your help in this process. If you have an idea for improving this textbook, or if you find an error, a typographical mistake, or an inaccuracy in the NCCER's Craft Training textbooks, please write us, using this form or a photocopy. Be sure to include the exact module number, page number, a detailed description, and the correction, if applicable. Your input will be brought to the attention of the Technical Review Committee. Thank you for your assistance.

Instructors – If you found that additional materials were necessary in order to teach this module effectively, please let us know so that we may include them in the Equipment and Materials list in the Instructor's Guide.

Write: Curriculum Revision and Development Department
National Center for Construction Education and Research
P.O. Box 141104, Gainesville, FL 32614-1104

Fax: 352-334-0932

E-mail: curriculum@nccer.org

Craft _____ Module Name _____

Copyright Date _____ Module Number _____ Page Number(s) _____

Description _____

_____

_____

_____

(Optional) Correction _____

_____

_____

(Optional) Your Name and Address _____

_____

_____

Hoses

COURSE MAP

This course map shows all of the modules in the first level of the Instrumentation curriculum. The suggested training order begins at the bottom and proceeds up. Skill levels increase as you advance on the course map. The local Training Program Sponsor may adjust the training order.

INSTRUMENTATION LEVEL ONE

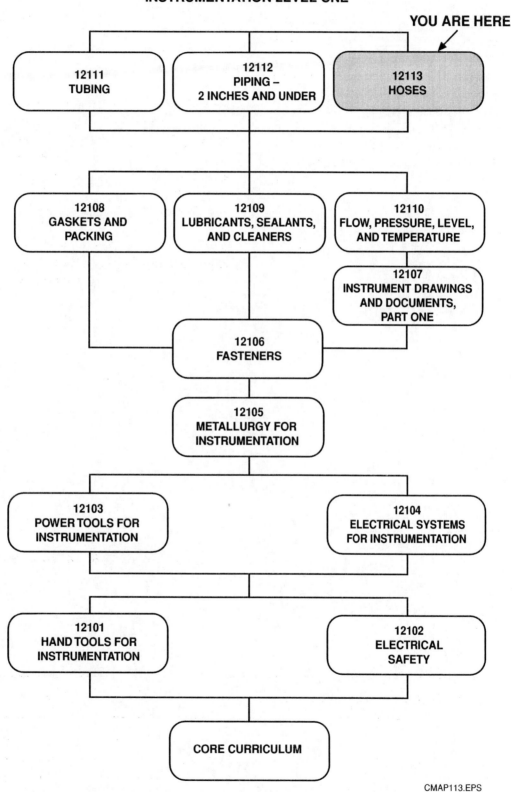

YOU ARE HERE

12111
TUBING

12112
PIPING –
2 INCHES AND UNDER

12113
HOSES

12108
GASKETS AND
PACKING

12109
LUBRICANTS, SEALANTS,
AND CLEANERS

12110
FLOW, PRESSURE, LEVEL,
AND TEMPERATURE

12107
INSTRUMENT DRAWINGS
AND DOCUMENTS,
PART ONE

12106
FASTENERS

12105
METALLURGY FOR
INSTRUMENTATION

12103
POWER TOOLS FOR
INSTRUMENTATION

12104
ELECTRICAL SYSTEMS
FOR INSTRUMENTATION

12101
HAND TOOLS FOR
INSTRUMENTATION

12102
ELECTRICAL
SAFETY

CORE CURRICULUM

CMAP113.EPS

MODULE 12113 CONTENTS

Figures

Hoses

Objectives

When you have completed this module, you will be able to do the following:

1. Identify various types of hoses and fittings.
2. Select appropriate types and sizes of hoses and fittings for selected applications.
3. Recognize standards and codes used to identify hoses and fittings.
4. Store and handle hose properly to prevent damage and/or contamination to the hose or personal injury.
5. Install a reusable fitting on a hose.

Prerequisites

Before you begin this module, it is recommended that you successfully complete the following modules: Core Curriculum; Instrumentation Level One, Modules 12101 through 12112.

Required Trainee Materials

1. Pencil and paper
2. Appropriate personal protective equipment

1.0.0 ◆ INTRODUCTION

Hose is used in similar applications as pipe and tubing in instrumentation work. Hose, pipe, and tubing are all used to transport a variety of fluids under various conditions. The main difference between hose and pipe or tubing is the material from which hoses are made. Hoses are made of flexible materials such as rubber, Teflon®, poly, nylon, and specially constructed metals. The flexibility of hose has advantages over rigid pipe and tubing in certain applications. These advantages include:

- Routes easily
- Absorbs vibration well
- Reduces sound
- Accommodates movement of connected components

While the flexibility of hose offers some advantages over pipe and tubing, there are limitations to the use of hose. Hose lines must be used with caution in order to provide long service and to guard against potentially dangerous failure. Several factors must be considered when hose and hose fittings are being selected for a particular application. Designers and engineers must carefully consider many properties of the system, including:

- The process temperature and ambient temperature must not exceed the ratings of the hose and fittings. Special care must also be taken when routing hoses near hot equipment or high-temperature areas.
- Hose and fittings must have a recommended maximum operating pressure rating that is equal to, or greater than, the system pressure. Surge pressures higher than the maximum operating pressure must be taken into account. Also, hoses and fittings that are used for suction applications must be able to withstand the negative pressure of the system in order to prevent collapsing.

- Hose and fittings must be compatible with the material being transported. Care must be taken to ensure that the hose and fittings are either compatible with, or protected from, the environment to which they are exposed. Environmental conditions such as ultraviolet light, ozone, salt water, chemicals, and air pollutants can cause degradation and premature failure of hose.

Hoses of different types and sizes are made for use in a variety of applications. Lightweight hose is commonly used in low-pressure (usually below 250 psi) air systems for ventilation and air supplies. Medium-grade hose is used in moderate pressure systems (approximate range is from 250 to 3,000 psi) to carry water and other fluids that normally are not subject to high pressure. Heavy-grade hoses made for use in industrial plants are made to withstand high pressures (approximate range is from 3,000 to over 6,000 psi), high temperatures, adverse process fluids, and extreme environmental conditions. Heavy-grade hoses are used to carry fluids in industrial hydraulic, chemical, and steam systems.

2.0.0 ◆ HOSE STANDARDS AND SPECIFICATIONS

Several organizations and professional societies publish standards and codes for hoses. These standards are used in selecting and identifying the type and size of hose for a particular application. The Society of Automotive Engineers (SAE); Department of Defense, U.S. Military Specification (MIL); and the **Food and Drug Administration (FDA)** are three organizations that publish standards, codes, and specifications for hoses.

When the project specifications list the required SAE, MIL, or FDA hose identification number, you must use that type of hose. You should review some of these standards, codes, and specifications so that you are familiar with the type of information included in them.

The recommendations for selection, installation, and maintenance of hose and assemblies established by SAE J1273 are intended as a guide to assist system designers and users in the selection, installation, and maintenance of hose. Designers and users make a systematic review of each application and then select, install, and maintain the hose to fulfill the requirements of the application.

All SAE hoses are branded (marked) with a line parallel to the longitudinal axis as a visual aid to prevent installing hose in a twisted position. As part of this line, the hose is marked with the applicable SAE specification number and the size (*Figure 1*).

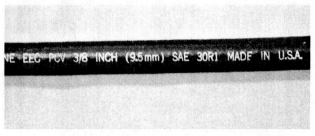

113F01.EPS

Figure 1 ◆ Hose SAE specification and size.

2.1.0 Sizing Measurements for Hoses

It is important to use the proper size and type of hose for specific applications. Hose size is normally identified by the inside diameter (I.D.) of the hose. The I.D. size of hose is usually expressed in inches and fractions of an inch, such as ½-inch hose, 1-inch hose, or 1½-inch hose.

A dash numbering system is used by most hose and fitting manufacturers to identify sizes of hose and hose fittings. To determine a dash size, the hose I.D. size is simply converted into sixteenths of an inch. The numerator (top number) of the fraction is the dash size. For example, a ¼-inch hose size is converted into the fraction $\frac{4}{16}$. Since the numerator is 4, this hose size is expressed as -4 (dash 4). A 1¼-inch hose is converted to $\frac{20}{16}$ and is expressed as -20 (dash 20).

A hose can be connected to a pipe or **tube** by matching the I.D. of the hose with the I.D. of the pipe or tubing to which it is to be connected. By using the same I.D. of hose as the tubing or pipe in a run, the fluid flow through the system will be smooth and uninterrupted.

2.2.0 Pressure Ratings for Hoses

A safety margin is designed into hoses to help prevent ruptures, which could cause injury to personnel or damage to equipment. This safety margin is called the *minimum burst pressure*. Generally, the minimum burst pressure of a hose should be four times the rated working pressure of the hose. For example, if a hose has a maximum rated working pressure of 400 psi, it should not burst until at least 1,600 psi has been reached.

3.0.0 ◆ TYPES OF HOSES

Hoses are made from a wide variety of materials including different types of metal, rubber, Teflon®, and poly. Each hose material has certain characteristics that make it desirable for particular applications. Hoses can be classified by material, by type of service (such as hydraulic or acid resistant), by pressure rating, and by type of construction.

Elastomers mixed with various chemicals provide a wide range of hose materials with physical properties required for specific service needs. For example, hose materials like Teflon®, polyethylene, nylon, neoprene, and vinyl nitrile are used to carry different types of process fluids at different pressure and temperature conditions.

The following sections describe several common types of hoses and some of the characteristics of the materials from which they are made.

3.1.0 Metallic Hoses

Flexible metal hoses are used as general all-purpose hose for conveying liquids and gases. Metallic hose is considered pressure-tight. It is often used for applications involving vibration or other types of movement. Other common uses for metallic hose include saturated and superheated steam lines, gas and oil lines, and lubricating lines.

Metallic hoses are generally made of stainless steel, carbon steel, bronze, aluminum, Monel®, and other corrosion-resistant metals. Some metal hoses have a liner of flexible, corrosion-resistant material, such as Teflon®.

As the working temperature of metal hose increases, the pressure rating of the hose decreases. Always consult the manufacturer's manual for the hose specifications, temperature conversion factors, and maximum service temperatures of different metal hoses.

Figure 2 shows the construction of a **braided**, flexible metal hose. Flexible metal hoses are typically constructed with annular corrugations from stainless steel, carbon steel, or seamless tin bronze tubing. The tube is usually covered with a woven **wire braid** for protection against abrasion and to provide increased resistance to pressure.

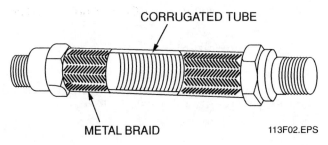

CORRUGATED TUBE

METAL BRAID   113F02.EPS

Figure 2 ◆ Metal hose.

Series SS (standard gauge) hoses are constructed of close pitch, annular corrugations in different types, such as hose only, hose with single braid, and hose with double braid. Standard sizes range from 1 inch to 12 inches.

Series B hoses are constructed with annular corrugations from seamless tin bronze tube usually covered with a bronze wire braid. Standard sizes range from ¼ inch to 3 inches.

Two general categories of metal hose are commonly used:

- Hose made entirely of metal is used when no plastics or synthetics are permitted in the system. A corrugated metal bellows-type hose is covered with a metal braid. They are welded to each other at each end at a weld ring. The tube fittings, pipe fittings, weld fittings, or tube adapter ends are then welded to the hose ends. This type of metal hose is ideally suited to applications where vibration, thermal expansion, misalignment, or intermittent flexing are present. Single-braided and double-braided stainless steel hoses are available for use at pressures up to approximately 3,825 psi and temperatures to +1200°F.
- Metal braided hose lined with Teflon® is used where an extremely smooth, corrosion-resistant interior is required. Instead of annular corrugations, the metal hose is lined with Teflon® tubing. An outer braid of metal encloses the Teflon® tube. If made out of 304 stainless steel, this type of metal hose has a temperature range of approximately −100°F to +450°F and a pressure rating to 4,000 psi.

3.2.0 Nonmetallic Hoses

Many hoses are constructed from nonmetallic materials and covered with metal braiding, such as the Teflon®-lined braided hoses discussed previously. However, many nonmetallic hoses are not covered with metal braiding and are typically applied in less critical or lower pressure applications. These hoses may be made from materials such as nylon, rubber, neoprene, vinyl nitrile, or vinyl.

3.2.1 Nylon Hoses

Nylon hose has good mechanical strength, is light in weight, and has good chemical and vibration resistance. It is not normally covered with any braiding. Black nylon hose, which is common in industrial locations, has an operating temperature range of approximately −80°F to +150°F, a typical working pressure of 200 psi at 72°F, and a bursting pressure of 700 psi at 72°F. As with any hose, pipe, or tubing, the bursting pressure is inversely proportional to the size of the hose, pipe, or tubing. As the size increases, the bursting pressure decreases. Nylon hoses are suitable for transporting pneumatics, oils, chemicals, liquids, and alkalis. They have many uses in the engineering and pharmaceutical industries for pneumatic equipment, fuel pipes, and lubrication. Flexible or semi-rigid grades are available. An FDA-approved version is available for use in the food, beverage, and medical industries.

3.2.2 Natural Rubber Hoses

Natural rubber hoses are abrasive resistant and weather resistant. Natural rubber hoses must not be used for any petroleum products because of the incompatibility of the natural rubber with any petroleum-based product. White natural rubber hoses are often used in the dry bulk food industry. They are typically covered with a **reinforcement** of braided yarn and can contain two or more stainless steel wires that act as both reinforcement for the hose and as static charge drain wires. Static charge drain wires are used in applications where the dust created by the transfer of dry bulk foods, such as grains, can cause a potential explosion hazard. Natural rubber hoses in this industry have an operating temperature range of –40°F to +180°F, and a maximum working pressure of 250 psi.

Many other types of natural rubber hoses may be found in other industries such as the automotive industry, utilities, and others. These applications may call for natural rubber hoses with various reinforcement methods and wall thicknesses that allow for lesser or greater temperature ranges and working pressures.

3.2.3 Silicone Rubber Hoses

Silicone rubber hoses are used in applications that require a higher operating temperature than that of natural rubber hoses. The hose is normally constructed of an inner natural translucent silicone rubber, with outer braided, polyester, multifilament yarn reinforcement. As with any type of hose, special hoses are available for specific industries and hose properties may vary from one hose manufacturer to another A typical operating temperature range is in the area of –80°F to 300°F. Bursting pressures are dependent on the size of the hose and may range from 200 psi for 1-inch hose to 800 psi for $\frac{1}{16}$-inch hose. Silicone rubber hose is suitable for use with most chemicals, acids, and alkalis. Typical applications include coolant hose for industrial machinery and equipment, connecting hoses for food, beverage, medical processing, chemical, and adhesive filling systems.

3.2.4 Neoprene Hoses

Neoprene is a synthetic rubber-like material developed by DuPont Chemical Company in the early 1930s. It is made in a process of dissolving acetylene under pressure in acetone. Neoprene hoses are often used in processes that contain oil and other petroleum products since acetylene, its base material, is a hydrocarbon product. Some high-temperature rated neoprene hoses are constructed of a double **ply** of neoprene and reinforced with an inner coil of flexible wire. These are commonly used to transport hot or cold air, fumes, and light abrasive dust at relatively low pressures (less than 200 psi). A typical operating temperature range for this type of neoprene hose is –60°F to 300°F. They may also be used as suction hoses in utilities and fire protection industries. These hoses are generally constructed with inner reinforcement including fibers and wires, but do not have an outer cover due to neoprene's ability to tolerate exposure to most products and environments, including ultraviolet (UV) rays.

3.2.5 Vinyl Nitrile Hoses

Vinyl nitrile hoses are constructed using a composite of vinyl and nitrile synthetics. Both are synthetic rubber-like products. Vinyl nitrile hoses are resistant to abrasion, animal fat, oil, and the elements of weather. These hoses are typically used to transport nondairy products and bulk liquids such as liquid sugar, syrups, and vegetable oils. They often have an inner spiral wire reinforcement, a working temperature range of –40°F to 180°F, and a working pressure of 150 psi. These hoses are installed on various food product tanker trucks that transport nondairy and bulk liquid products. Vinyl nitrile meets most FDA requirements, allowing it to be used with processes involving food products. Wire-reinforced vinyl nitrile hoses may also be used in vacuum applications.

3.2.6 Vinyl Hoses

A common type of vinyl hose is reinforced with an open weave polyester inner braid for increased working pressures up to 250 psi. The smooth bore, full flow I.D. dimensions of small vinyl hoses are sized to fit standard commercial barbed fittings. The FDA grade of vinyl hose is suitable for food and beverage dispensing. Other applications include air lines, chemical transfer coolant lines, offset powder transfer, and water lines. A typical working temperature range is –30°F to +120°F. Vacuum rating is to 18 in. Hg. (inches of mercury).

4.0.0 ◆ HOSE CONSTRUCTION

Most hoses are made from more than one material. The hose materials are constructed in layers (plies) which reinforce the hose to increase its strength and pressure capabilities. The type of reinforcement and the number of layers is the main difference between low-pressure, medium-pressure, and high-pressure hoses.

Low-pressure hose is typically reinforced with a fabric braid. Medium- and high-pressure hoses have single- or multiple-wire reinforcing braids. There are also special wire-wrap hoses that are used for extra high-pressure applications.

The inner tube or lining of hoses is usually made from some type of rubber, synthetic rubber, or plastic. The tube or lining is surrounded by a braided material (**carcass**) which is covered by rubber or cotton. The type of braiding used is determined by the application of the hose.

4.1.0 Vertical Braiding

Hoses reinforced with vertical braiding are strengthened against pressure applied at right angles to the tube or lining. Vertical-braided hose, shown in *Figure 3*, is constructed of a seamless rubber tube with one or more layers of braided yarn wrapped around the tube. Vertical-braided hoses are typically used in low-pressure systems. Depending upon the type of tube and braiding, vertical-braided hoses can be used to carry water, air, fuel, lubricating oils, antifreeze solutions, and diesel fuels.

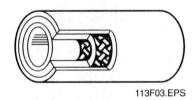

113F03.EPS

Figure 3 ◆ Vertical-braided hose.

4.2.0 Horizontal Braiding

Hoses reinforced with horizontal braiding are strengthened to resist expansion and contraction. Horizontal-braided hoses are used for high-pressure or high-suction (vacuum) systems.

Horizontal-braided hoses are made by wrapping a seamless tube with one or more layers of braided fibers or wire. Depending upon the type of tube and braiding, horizontal-braided hose can be used in higher pressure systems for hydraulic, gasoline, fuel oil, lubricating oil, air, and water applications.

Hoses with horizontally braided reinforcement may include one or more layers of wire braid between two or more layers of fiber braid. This type of construction makes the hose mechanically strong for use in high-pressure or high-vacuum systems. Depending upon the type of tube and braiding, wire-reinforced hoses can be used for the transfer of water-based liquid fertilizers and pesticides; pumping, suction, and discharge of water and slurries; and petroleum applications.

4.3.0 Wrapped Hose

Wrapped hose (*Figure 4*) is made by wrapping the tube with several plies of fabric. The tube may be made from Teflon® or synthetic rubbers. The type of tube selected is dependent on the application.

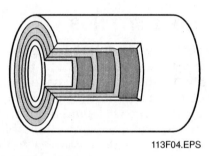

113F04.EPS

Figure 4 ◆ Wrapped hose.

4.4.0 Wire-Reinforced Hose

Wire-reinforced hose (*Figure 5*) is made by winding braided wire around the tube. Wire-reinforced hose may include layers of fabric. When fabric is used, the wire braid reinforcement layers are inserted between the fabric layers. Wire-reinforced hose is typically used in high-pressure systems because of its strength.

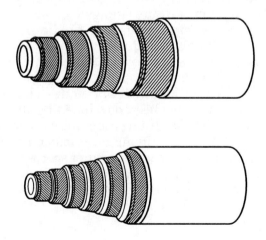

113F05.EPS

Figure 5 ◆ Wire-reinforced hose.

Wire-woven hose (*Figure 6*) is made by wrapping the tube with woven wire in a spiral. Layers of fabric may be inserted between the layers of woven-wire reinforcement. Woven-wire hose stands up well under severe operating conditions, including high-pressure hydraulic systems and high-vacuum applications.

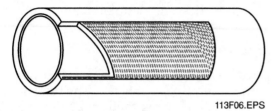

Figure 6 ◆ Wire-woven hose.

5.0.0 ◆ HOSE FITTINGS

There are several types of hose fittings. Each type is designed to perform a specific job. For example, a hose fitting might be used to make the connection between hose and hose, hose and pipe, hose and tubing, or between hose and a valve. Hose fittings can be either permanent or reusable. Some types of fittings are made to connect and disconnect quickly, an advantage and requirement in many applications.

Hose fittings are matched with the hose material being used and the application. As with hoses, factors such as pressure, temperature, and process characteristics are taken into consideration when selecting hose fittings.

Fitting manufacturers use codes that are usually stamped on the fitting to identify the fitting material and size. High-pressure fittings are similar to medium-pressure fittings. Both have a socket with a size designation to fit the hose. Most manufacturers identify high-pressure fittings from medium-pressure fittings by stamping *HP* on high-pressure fittings and *MP* on medium-pressure fittings. In addition, the sockets of high-pressure fittings are notched. Medium-pressure fitting sockets are not notched.

Some fitting identification codes and other specifications have been developed by the SAE, MIL, and FDA. The fitting codes are similar to the codes used for identifying hose materials; other codes for fittings are manufacturer specific. Check the manufacturer's catalog if you have any question about the material, properties, or proper use of a particular fitting.

5.1.0 Permanently Crimped (Skived) Fittings

Permanent **crimped (skived)** fittings (*Figure 7*) are one-piece fittings consisting of a crimp nipple and crimp socket that are fastened together. This type of fitting is used for high-pressure applications such as hydraulic fluid; crude, fuel, and lubricating oils; and water. Permanently crimped (skived) fittings are generally considered good for pressures up to 5,500 psi, depending on the dash size.

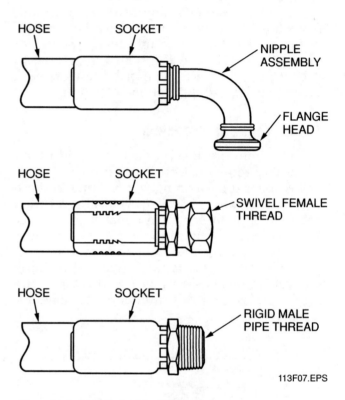

Figure 7 ◆ Crimped (skived) fittings.

5.2.0 Reusable (No-Skived) Fittings

Reusable (no-skived) fittings (*Figure 8*) are two-piece fittings that consist of a nipple and socket. The nipple can be reused if the fitting needs to be replaced. This type of fitting is often used for high-pressure hydraulics, fuel and lubricating oil, gasoline, and water-glycol base fluids. These fittings are generally considered good for pressures up to 5,500 psi, depending on the dash size. Some manufacturers do not recommend reusing this type of socket.

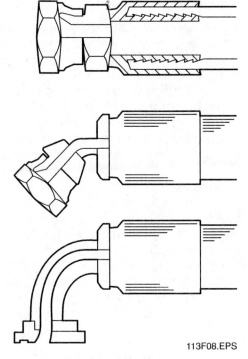

113F08.EPS

Figure 8 ◆ Reusable (no-skived) fittings.

5.3.0 Push-On Fittings

WARNING!

Push-on fittings or *barbed* fittings are not designed to be used, and never should be used, for high-pressure applications or in chemical process applications. They are designed for use on low-pressure pneumatic or water applications. These fittings only provide minimal mechanical resistance to leaks or disconnects.

Push-on fittings (*Figure 9*) are primarily used for general, low-pressure, low-temperature air and water service. In the fittings shown, the hose grips the barb through distortion of the braid.

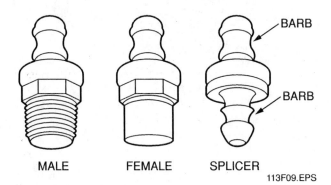

BARB

BARB

MALE   FEMALE   SPLICER

113F09.EPS

Figure 9 ◆ Push-on fittings.

5.4.0 Swivel Joint Fittings

Swivel joint fittings (*Figure 10*) are not rigid. Therefore, they are capable of absorbing some shock incurred when a system pulses. The swivel action of the joint prevents the hose from twisting and **kinking** when used on moving equipment. Swivel joints are typically made of brass/steel, steel, or stainless steel. Depending upon the process and the size of the fitting, swivel joint fittings are generally capable of handling a range of 25 inches/Hg (inches of mercury) vacuum to 10,000 psi operating pressure.

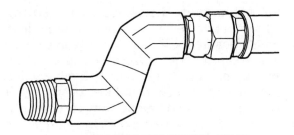

MULTI-PLANE SWIVEL JOINT

BALL SWIVEL   113F10.EPS

Figure 10 ◆ Swivel joint fittings.

CAUTION

Swivel joints can fail spontaneously if not correctly selected. Always check the manufacturer's selection chart before using any swivel joint to make sure the joint is compatible for use in your application.

5.5.0 Quick-Disconnect Fittings

Quick-disconnect fittings (couplings) permit easy, immediate connection and separation of fluid lines. When installed in a fluid system, quick-disconnect couplings save time by eliminating the necessity to close valves, bleed the system, recharge with fluid, and purge entrapped air whenever an accessory is being replaced. Dependability is assured because the coupling valves of a quick-disconnect fitting automatically open and close when connected or disconnected.

The automatic valve actions also minimize the possibility of air, dirt, and moisture being trapped in the system.

Quick-disconnect couplings may be used in systems to help align components. The swivel feature of quick-disconnect fittings helps prevent twisting of hose assemblies. However, quick-disconnects are not intended to be used as swivel joints in applications subjected to constant rotation.

There are two basic types of quick-disconnect fittings: valve-type and nonvalve-type.

5.5.1 Double Valve Quick-Disconnects

Double valve quick-disconnects have spring-loaded poppet valves in each half to provide an immediate positive seal. The double valve design prevents escape of liquids and gases upon disconnection. A small cavity between the valve halves permits some air inclusion and loss of some fluid upon connection and disconnection. Double valve couplings, such as the one shown in *Figure 11*, are generally used for fuel, oil, pneumatic, and hydraulic systems, or where the fluid provides little or no lubrication.

5.5.2 Single Valve Quick-Disconnects

Single valve quick-disconnects provide positive shutoff in only one half of the fitting. Either the male half or the female half of the quick-disconnect can be the valved half. A poppet valve is a machined, self-aligning, spring-loaded internal valve in one half of the quick-disconnect. It closes when the disconnect halves are separated, preventing the fluid from escaping. The nonvalved half is open, allowing for fluid drainage upon disconnection.

In a spring-loaded valve, there is no cavity ahead of the valve to cause air inclusion or fluid spillage. A single valve coupling, such as the one shown in *Figure 12*, incorporates a spring-operated sleeve to close the ports of the valve.

Typical applications of single valve quick-disconnects include fluid transfer, hydraulic, fuel, oil, or any application where the agent provides lubrication.

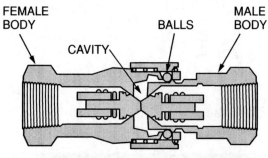

PARTIALLY CONNECTED – NO FLOW

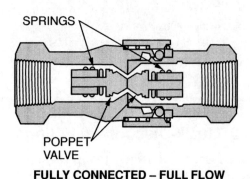

FULLY CONNECTED – FULL FLOW

113F11.EPS

Figure 11 ◆ Double valve coupling.

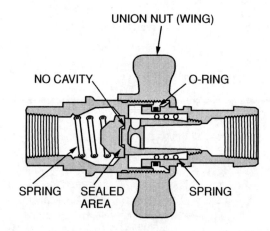

PARTIALLY CONNECTED – NO FLOW

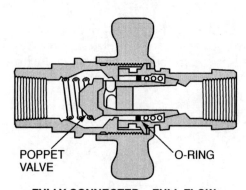

FULLY CONNECTED – FULL FLOW

113F12.EPS

Figure 12 ◆ Single valve coupling.

5.5.3 Nonvalve-Type Disconnects

Straight-through quick-disconnect couplings, cam lever couplings, quick-acting couplings, and interlocking clamp couplings do not incorporate valves. Straight-through quick-disconnect couplings can be used for alignment of components to prevent twisting of hose assemblies. Also, the large inside diameters through the coupling allow maximum flow with minimum pressure drop.

Straight-through quick-disconnect cam lever couplings (*Figure 13*) provide for fast, simple connections. Cam lever couplings can be used in a number of different applications, such as transporting and blending raw materials used in processing, on trucks used in vacuum cleaning, to transport flour from a railroad car to a processing plant, and for delivering gasoline from a tank truck to a service station. Cam lever couplings are also often used in low- and medium-pressure water, petroleum, and chemical transfer applications.

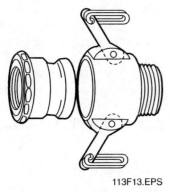

113F13.EPS

Figure 13 ◆ Cam lever coupling.

 WARNING!
Both halves of a cam lever coupling are open to fluid drainage when disconnected.

Quick-acting couplings, often referred to as *Chicago-type* couplers, such as those shown in *Figure 14*, are often used for low- to medium-pressure air, water, or oil service. Large air compressors are commonly connected to hoses using these types of couplings. Air supplies in industrial facilities, such as petrochemical installations, also use these types of fittings for service or maintenance-type air needs. The fittings are universal in that two of the same type can be connected to one another.

Each coupling is fitted with a facing seal that fits within a groove on the face of the coupling. The sealing effect takes place seal-to-seal as the couplings are interlocked by turning and interlocking the claws that extend out from the coupling body. Once the couplings are connected, a safety wire like the one shown in *Figure 14* may be secured through eyes provided on each coupling to prevent the couplings from disengaging.

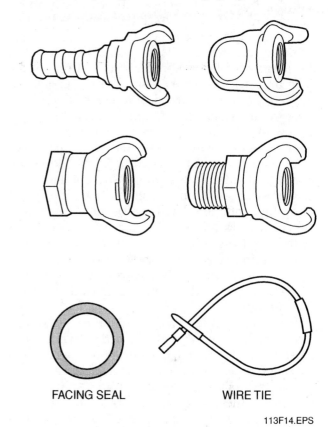

FACING SEAL   WIRE TIE

113F14.EPS

Figure 14 ◆ Quick-acting couplings.

Interlocking clamp couplings (*Figure 15*) are used for heavy-duty high-pressure applications, such as air, steam, water, spray, LPG, and anhydrous ammonia.

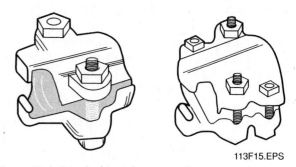

113F15.EPS

Figure 15 ◆ Interlocking clamp couplings.

6.0.0 ◆ PROPER AND SAFE METHODS FOR STORING HOSES

Proper and safe storage methods for hoses may sound like a simple task, but you may be surprised at the amount of damage done to hoses, personal injuries received, and time wasted due to improper storage methods. The appropriate method for storing hose depends on the hose size (diameter and length), hose construction, the quantity to be stored, and the way in which it is packaged.

Hose should not be piled or stacked to an extent that the weight of the stack creates distortions on the lengths of hose stored at the bottom. Since hose products vary considerably in size, weight, and length, it is not practical to establish definite recommendations for storage. Hose with a very light wall will not support as much weight as hose with a heavier wall or hose with wire reinforcement. Hose shipped in coils or bales should be stored so that the coils are in a horizontal plane.

Rubber hoses should be stored in their original shipping containers. This is especially true when the containers are wooden crates or cardboard cartons that provide some protection against the deteriorating effects of oils, solvents, and corrosive liquids. Shipping containers also afford some protection against deterioration caused by ozone and sunlight.

To prevent contamination and damage of stored hoses, the hose should be wrapped with burlap or other suitable material. Covering hoses also helps prevent damage from sunlight and other environmental factors which are known to be harmful to rubber products. Certain rodents and insects will also damage rubber hose if the hose is not adequately protected.

The ideal temperature for the storage of rubber hose ranges from 50°F to 70°F, and a maximum limit of 100°F. If stored below 32°F, some hose becomes stiff and requires warming before being placed in service. Rubber hose should not be stored near sources of heat, such as radiators or base heaters, or under conditions of high or low humidity.

To avoid the adverse effects of high ozone concentration, rubber hose should not be stored near electrical equipment that may generate ozone. They also should not be stored for any lengthy period in geographical areas of known high ozone concentration. Exposure to direct or reflected sunlight, even through windows, should be avoided. In addition, uncovered hose should not be stored under fluorescent or mercury lamps, which generate light waves harmful to rubber.

Cotton-jacketed hose should be protected against fungal growths if the hose is to be stored for prolonged periods under conditions in which the relative humidity exceeds 70 percent.

Storage areas should be relatively cool and dark, and free of dampness and mildew. Hose should be stored and used on a first-in, first-out basis. Under the best of conditions, an unusually long shelf life can deteriorate certain rubber products.

Hose racks provide support to prevent bending, sagging, distortion, scratching, or marring of hose surfaces. Most racks have separate levels or compartments where different types and sizes of hose can be stored for ease of identification and selection. Hose racks are usually elevated to help avoid damage that might occur at floor level. Hose stored at floor level is easily damaged or contaminated by people, other materials, moisture, or equipment in the area.

Before placing a previously used hose that has been subjected to chemicals or other harmful media in storage, the hose must be completely drained and any potentially explosive vapors or corrosive residues flushed out.

WARNING!

Wear approved eye, glove, and other protection when flushing out a chemical hose with water. Some chemicals, such as concentrated acids, may react with the water and cause spattering. When flushing a hose, disposal of the waste fluid must be done in accordance with the prevailing environmental laws and regulations.

Chemical hose should be stored so that air can circulate through it. It should be laid straight on a solid support. The hose should be stored in a cool, dark, dry place at a temperature less than 100°F.

7.0.0 ◆ PROPER AND SAFE METHODS FOR HANDLING HOSES

Hoses made to rigid specifications can be degraded by careless handling. From the time the hose is delivered to a job site until its installation is complete, proper and safe handling methods will help greatly in ensuring a quality hose installation. Some basic guidelines for handling hose that will help you avoid damaging or contaminating the hose or injuring yourself or others are given here:

- Do not subject the hose to any form of abuse. Never drag the hose over sharp or abrasive surfaces unless the hose was specifically designed for such service.
- Do not subject the hose and coupling assembly to pulling forces for which they are not designed.
- Do not kink the hose or run over it with equipment.

- Never drag the hose on the ground or floor. Dragging hose can cause damage to the ends or contaminate the hose.
- Keep the hose away from any material that might contaminate it during handling.
- Keep the end caps on the hose during handling or transporting to avoid damage to the ends and/or contamination.
- Wear gloves when handling the hose to avoid scrapes and cuts from hose assemblies.
- If possible, coil long lengths of hose and place the coils on a pallet for transport.
- Be aware of people, materials, and equipment around you when handling or transporting hose so that you avoid hitting anyone or anything with the hose. Hitting someone or an object with the hose may cause injury to another person or yourself or damage to the hose, fittings, other material, or equipment.
- Dollies or fork trucks should be used whenever possible when moving large quantities of bulk hose or hose assemblies from place to place. Slings or handling rigs should be used to support heavy hose or hose assemblies.

8.0.0 ◆ REUSABLE FITTING INSTALLATION

There are several different types of reusable fittings. Each is installed in a particular way. In the following section, the procedure for installing a standard reusable fitting is described.

8.1.0 Standard Reusable Fitting Installation

The following procedure describes the general steps for installing a standard reusable hose fitting.

Step 1 Select the proper hose and fitting for the application.

 WARNING!
Always wear approved eye protection when cutting hose. Be aware of sharp edges and wear appropriate hand protection to avoid cuts. If cutting hose that has been in service, know what product the hose has been exposed to and take necessary precautions in cleaning and flushing out the hose prior to cutting it.

Step 2 Secure the hose in a vise, then cut the hose off square with a fine-tooth blade hacksaw as shown in *Figure 16*.

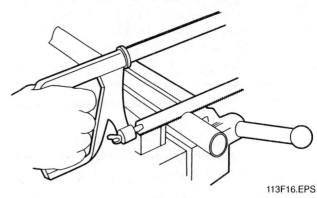
113F16.EPS

Figure 16 ◆ Cutting hose with hacksaw.

 WARNING!
Wear approved eye protection and point the hose down toward the floor when cleaning it out with compressed air.

Step 3 Clean out the inside of the hose using compressed air.

Step 4 Put the socket in a vise.

Step 5 Liberally lubricate the hose cover with an approved hose lubricant or heavyweight oil. Read the hose manufacturer's manual to determine the proper lubricant to use. Heavy-weight oil cannot be used on some types of hose.

Step 6 Screw the hose into the socket counterclockwise until the it bottoms on the shoulder of the socket as shown in *Figure 17*.

SOCKET

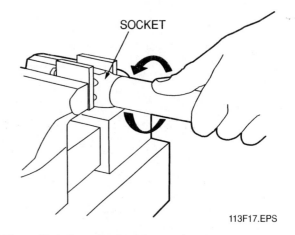
113F17.EPS

Figure 17 ◆ Inserting hose into socket.

NOTE

When assembling long lengths of hose, it may be preferable to put the hose in a vise just tight enough to prevent it from turning. The socket is then screwed onto the hose counterclockwise until the shoulder of the socket bottoms out on the hose.

Step 7   Liberally lubricate the nipple threads and the inside of the hose with a heavy-weight oil or hose-assembly lubricant, as shown in *Figure 18*.

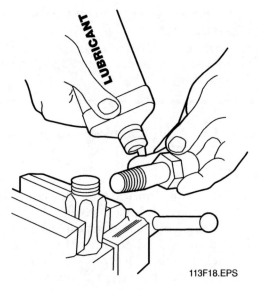

Figure 18 ◆ Lubricating nipple threads.

Step 8   Screw the nipple clockwise into socket and hose, as shown in *Figure 19*. Leave about a $\frac{1}{32}$-inch to $\frac{1}{16}$-inch clearance between the nipple hex and the socket.

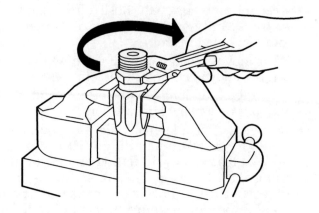

113F19.EPS

Figure 19 ◆ Inserting nipple into socket and hose.

WARNING!

Wear approved eye protection and point the hose down toward the floor when cleaning it out with compressed air.

Step 9   Clean the hose assembly by blowing it out with clean, low-pressure compressed air. Some assemblies may be rinsed out with R66 mineral spirits if the tube stock (Teflon®, nitrile, neoprene) is compatible with oil. If not, use hot water at a maximum temperature of +180°F.

Summary

In this module, you learned about the different types and applications of hose and hose fittings, how to properly handle and store hose, and the procedures for cutting hose and installing a reusable hose fitting.

Installation of hose is an important part of instrument work. Always make sure the type of hose you use is compatible for your application. Practicing the skills learned in this module, further study, and on-the-job experience will help you develop the skills needed to be expert in working with hose.

Review Questions

1. Hoses and fittings that are used for _____ applications must be able to withstand the negative pressure of the system to prevent collapsing.
   a. NASA
   b. high-pressure
   c. acidic
   d. suction

2. SAE hoses are marked with a line _____ to the longitudinal axis.
   a. parallel
   b. vertical
   c. perpendicular
   d. in a spiral plane

3. The inside diameter (I.D.) of a -24 (dash 24) hose is _____ inches.
   a. 1¼
   b. 1½
   c. 2.4
   d. 24

4. The minimum burst pressure of a hose should be _____ the rated working pressure of the hose.
   a. half
   b. equal to
   c. four times
   d. less than

5. Flexible metal hoses are typically constructed with _____ from stainless steel, carbon steel, or seamless tin bronze tubing.
   a. fibers
   b. annular corrugations
   c. alloys
   d. castings

6. The tubing fittings, pipe fittings, weld fittings, or tube adapter ends are connected to a corrugated metal bellows-type hose _____.
   a. using screw connectors
   b. by pressing onto the hose
   c. by welding to the hose ends
   d. by attaching clamps

7. Low-pressure hose is typically reinforced with a _____.
   a. metallic braid
   b. fabric braid
   c. layer of Teflon®
   d. spiral stainless wire

8. In addition to stamping HP on high-pressure fittings, they are also _____.
   a. color-coded
   b. tapered
   c. hex-shaped
   d. notched

9. Quick-acting couplings are also known as _____ couplings.
   a. Chicago
   b. cam lever
   c. Baltimore
   d. shank arm

10. Hoses that are shipped in coils or bales should be stored so that the coils are in a _____.
    a. vertical plane
    b. heated vault
    c. tilted plane
    d. horizontal plane

Trade Terms Introduced in This Module

Braid: The reinforcement material put over the hose.

Carcass: The fabric, cord, and/or metal reinforcing section of hose, as distinguished from the tube or cover.

Crimping: Crimping is a method used for attaching fittings to a hose. It is done by pressing a set of dies against the outside of the fitting and compressing the shell around the hose.

Food and Drug Administration (FDA): A department of the federal government that regulates the materials used in foods and drugs, or in the manufacture or processing of foods or drugs. It issues standards and codes pertaining to the use of hoses in the drug and food industries.

Kinking: A temporary or permanent distortion of a hose, induced by winding or doubling upon itself.

MIL: An abbreviation used to indicate a standard developed by the military. The military issues standards relating to the use of hoses.

Ply: One concentric layer of material.

Reinforcement: The material put over the tube of a hose to provide resistance to pressure, either from the inside or outside.

Skive: To cut off the hose cover from wire reinforced hose in preparation for installing permanently attached fittings.

Tube: The inner section or core of a hose through which the fluid flows.

Wire braid: A ply of braided wire reinforcement.

Additional Resources

This module is intended to present thorough resources for task training. The following reference works are suggested for further study. These are optional materials for continued education rather than for task training.

Standards and Specifications for Hose. 5600 Fishers Lane, Rockville, MD: Food and Drug Administration.

MIL Standards and Specifications for Hose. 732 North Capitol Street NW, Washington, DC: Government Printing Office.

Standards and Specifications for Hose. 400 Commonwealth Drive, Warrendale, PA: Society of Automotive Engineers.

Figure Credits

Gerald Shannon   113F01

The NCCER makes every effort to keep these textbooks up-to-date and free of technical errors. We appreciate your help in this process. If you have an idea for improving this textbook, or if you find an error, a typographical mistake, or an inaccuracy in the NCCER's Craft Training textbooks, please write us, using this form or a photocopy. Be sure to include the exact module number, page number, a detailed description, and the correction, if applicable. Your input will be brought to the attention of the Technical Review Committee. Thank you for your assistance.

Instructors – If you found that additional materials were necessary in order to teach this module effectively, please let us know so that we may include them in the Equipment and Materials list in the Instructor's Guide.

Write: Curriculum Revision and Development Department
National Center for Construction Education and Research
P.O. Box 141104, Gainesville, FL 32614-1104

Fax: 352-334-0932

E-mail: curriculum@nccer.org

Craft _____ Module Name _____

Copyright Date _____ Module Number _____ Page Number(s) _____

Description _____

_____

_____

_____

_____

(Optional) Correction _____

_____

_____

(Optional) Your Name and Address _____

_____

_____

_____

Index

Index
